Befriending the Other

Christian Embrace of Other Religions

AF729630

JV Philosophy Series - 15

Befriending the Other

Christian Embrace of Other Religions

Editor

Kuruvilla Pandikattu SJ

Jnana Deepa

&

Christian World Imprints

© Jnana Deepa, Pune

First Published in 2021 by

Jnana Deepa
Ramwadi, Nagar Road, **Pune-411014**
jdvoffice@jdv.edu.in
www.jdv.edu.in
Phone: +91 20 41036111

&

Christian World Imprints
Christian Publishing & Books from India
C-3, Shop No. 14, Ground Floor
Wazirpur Industrial Area, **Delhi-110052**
cwidelhi2017@gmail.com
www.ChristianWorldImprints.com
Phone: +91 11 41526079

ISBN: 978-93-5148-563-6

"Published with the help of the Institute of Missiology – Germany"

All rights are reserved. No part of this publication can be reproduced, distributed, performed, publicly displayed, stored in a retrieval system, made into a derivative work, transmitted or utilized in any form or by any means; electronic, mechanical, photocopying, recording or any information storage system, without the prior written permission of the copyright holder(s), as indicated, and the publishers.

Jurisdiction: Any conflict or dispute in relation to this publication shall be adjudged in accordance with the laws of India and the matter shall be subject to the jurisdiction of the Courts, Tribunals or any other Forums of New Delhi, India, only.

Disclaimer: The views, facts, contents, any copyright material used and analysis arrived at in the Articles included/published in this work are solely of the Contributors who assert the right to be identified as Authors; the Publishers - JD, Pune and CWI, New Delhi - do not take any responsibility for the same in any manner whatsoever.

Printed in India.

CONTENTS

JD PHILOSOPHY SERIES - 15

Since 1893 Jnana has been pioneering philosophy discussion and debate inspired by prominent personalities like Richard De Smet, Jean de Marneffe, Salvino Azzopardi, Cyril Desbruslais, Noel Sheth, John Vattanky, etc. It has been in the forefront of promoting Indian philosophy and making philosophical thinking relevant for contemporary times. In its effort to reach out to like-minded scholars, JD Philosophy Series has been visualized as a catalyst for interdisciplinary thinking and contemporary exploration on social issues fostering holistic liberation, integral development and creative engagement.

General Editor
Kuruvilla Pandikattu SJ

Editorial Board Members
George Karuvelil SJ, Nishant Irudayadason, Henry D'Almeida SJ, Stephen Jayard, Isaac Parackal OIC, Shiju Joseph CSC, Sebastian V SJ,
Clement Jesudoss SJ, Dinesh Braganza SJ and Dollychan Kollarath SJ.

Special Advisory Board Members

Carlos Augusto Casanova Guerra, Universidad de Santo Tomas, Santiago Chile
Carlos Miguel Gomez Rincon, El Rosario University, Bogota Colombia
Chae-Yong Kim, President (2014-16), Korean Association for Religious Studies, South Korea
Chris Baglow, Notre Dame Seminary, New Orleans LA USA
Donald Frohlich, University of St. Thomas, Houston TX, USA
Felix Raj, Vice-Chancellor, St Xavier's University, Kolkatta
George Pattery, Former Vice-Chancellor, Jnana Deepa, Pune, India
Jerome Stanislaus D'Souza, Vice-Chancellor, Jnana Deepa, Pune, India
Kamal Misra, Vice-Chancellor, Utkal University of Culture
Louis Caruana, Former Dean of Faculty of Philosophy, Gregorian University, Rome, Italy
Maribel Nonato, University of St. Thomas, Manila, Philippines

Paul Fernandes, Former Vice-Chancellor, XUB, Bhubaneshwar
Philippe Quentin, University of Bordeaux, France
Raul Melendez, Nacional Universidad, Bogota, Colombia
Renu Jain, Vice-Chancellor, Devi Ahilya Vishwavidyalaya, Indore
Rubén Herce, University of Navarra, Spain
Savarimuthu Ignaci, Former Vice-Chancellor, University of Madras, Chennai
Stephen Mavely, Vice-Chancellor, Assam Don Bosco University, Guwahati
V. N. Magare, Pro VC, Mumbai University

JD Philosophy Series

1. Salvino Azzopardi: ***Epistemology and Phenomenology of Religions*** (2018)
2. Kuruvilla Pandikattu & Thomas Karimundackal (eds): ***Melodies from the Flute***: For Prof Noel Sheth SJ (2018)
3. Kurien Kunnumpuram: ***Freedom and Joy*** (2018)
4. Cyril Desbruslais SJ: ***Postmodernity: An Indian Christian Philosophical Appraisal*** (2019)
5. Cyril Desbruslais SJ: ***Metaphysics: Philosophy of Be-ing for Today*** (2019)
6. John Peter Vallabadoss: ***Indian Thinkers: Modern and Contemporary Period*** (2019)
7. Thomas Karimundackal & Kuruvilla Pandikattu (eds): ***Logic and Love***: For Prof John Vattanky SJ (2019)
8. Fabian Jose UMI: ***Relevance of Thomas Merton's Spirituality for the Consecrated Life in India*** (2019)
9. Kuruvilla Pandikattu & PT Mathew (eds): ***Committed to the Church and the Country***: For Prof Kurien Kunnumpuam SJ (2019)
10. Cyril Desbruslais SJ: ***The Philosophy of God*** (2019)
11. Thomas Karimundackal & Kuruvilla Pandikattu: ***Fully Spiritual, Fully Human:*** For Dr Stephen Chundanthadam SJ (2020)
12. Kuruvilla Pandikattu: ***Fully Human and Fully Alive:*** For Dr Cyril Desbruslais SJ (2020)
13. Thomas Karimundackal SJ & Dolichan Kollareth SJ (eds) ***Reason: Faithful and True: For Dr. George Karuvelil SJ*** (2020)
14. Kuruvilla Pandikattu SJ, Sebastian Vazhapilly SJ & Prasad Lankapilly SJ (eds) ***Serving the Church and the Nation: Gratefully and Faithfully***
15. Kuruvilla Pandikattu (ed) ***Befriending the Other: Other Religions***

EDITORIAL:
Befriending the Other

Who is the other? How does the other relate to me? Is the other only a rival or adversary? How does relating to the other makes me a better and more genuine person? How does befriending the other make all of us survive better? What can we do to befriend the other? These were some of issues raised in an International Conference, held at Pune, India.

Jnana Deepa: Pontifical Institute of Philosophy and Theology (JD) has celebrated the Diamond Jubilee of its transfer from Kandy, Ceylon to Pune, India in 1955. At the time of transfer JD was known as the Papal Athenaeum, the academic wing of Papal Seminary. In 1994 the Vatican declared Jnana-Deepa and Papal Seminary to be thenceforth two institutions but still related to each other in friendly cooperation. On this auspicious occasion, Jnana-Deepa commemorated this event through various academic and cultural activities including this International Conference on the theme "Befriending the Other" on 24-28 November 2015. The papers in this volume are selections from this International Conference.

Since the conference takes into account the religious and cultural pluralism of India, Asia and Africa, we want to focus on the living together in harmony. So from diverse theological, philosophical sociological, psychological and anthropological perspectives, we attempt at various means and modes of befriending the others, while preserving the identities ("other") of the other. Thus the main theme of the Conference and of this volume is recognizing and affirming the other as different from us and reaching out and befriending the other in their otherness. Only when we respectfully recognize the other as other can we really embrace them. Then we can cherish diversity and celebrate differences, since the other is not a threat to my identity. The other becomes part of my identity. The other constitutes me, challenges me, enables me and empowers me.

Given the prevalence of terrorist violence,[1] cultural conflicts ("clash of civilizations"), religious rivalries and national struggle in our contemporary world (particularly in the Asian and African context), we are challenged to present a world-view that engages people and bring them together. It is our Christian responsibility to bring different communities together, so that the diversity of the other as the other is reaffirmed. Such genuine encounter with the other fosters creativity and affirms one's own identity.

In this context the conference aims to encounter the actual situation of conflict and struggle and the consequent suffering that affects thousands of people. Based on these actual experiences of woundedness and pain, the conference explores the larger issues of identity, community and otherness, which are central to our understanding of differences and possible confrontation. This is followed by specific examples of actual living together, with a view to enlarge our horizon of understanding so that we can acknowledge, affirm and accept the other as individual and communities, who are different from (even sometimes opposed to) us.

So the conference is an invitation to genuine encounter between different cultures, communities and groups that fosters creative interaction and harmonious progress.

Some of the topics the Organising Committee proposed for deeper study and reflection are as follows:

Theological Perspectives

- Trinity and Perichoresis: Discovering the Fundamental Human Interrelatedness
- Christ and the Other: The Woman at the Well
- God as the *Ganz Andere* (Totally Other)
- Table Fellowship with the Other: Jesus Approach to the Marginalized
- The Trace of God and the Human Face
- Universalism and Inclusiveness in the Bible
- Boundary Making and Breaking in the Bible
- Is Not Christ the Only Saviour?
- Towards an All-Inclusive and Dialogical Church
- Encountering the Other Religions in Vatican Ii Documents
- "My Father Was a Wandering Aramaen" (Deut 26:5): Old Testament Perspectives on the Stranger
- Christian Fundamentalism Today: A Theological Perspective
- Fear of the Other and the Genesis of Original Sin
- Christ: The Otherness of God/Son as the Otherness of the Father

Religious Dimensions

- The other in Islam
- Judaism: Wanderer
- Hindu Understanding of Other

- The Other in the Jain Tradition
- The Other in the Sikh Tradition
- Washing the Feet of the Guests: Tribal Hospitality Towards the Other
- The Pagans and the Gentiles: St Paul and The Early Christian Approach to the Other
- The Church's Approach to the Other Religions: A Historical Evolution
- Quakers and the Treatment of the Other
- One in Many or Many in One? Ecumenical Efforts at Rediscovering Our Fractured Identity and Tradition
- Christian Fundamentalism and Challenge of 'The Other Faiths'
- Significance of the Other in Church's Understanding of Other Religions
- Starting with The Family: Befriending in The Domestic Churches

Philosophical Basis

- Oneself as the Other: The Other as Distinct from and Related to Me
- The Other as Constitutive of Me
- The Other as a Phenomenological Thou
- I-Thou Relationship Leading to the Acceptance of the Other
- Identity, Difference and Crisscrossing
- Dancing to Diversity: The Other as The Possibility of Me
- Ricoeur: History, Memory, Forgetting and Befriending
- Derrida: Unconditional Hospitality to The Other
- Levinas: Responsibility to the Other
- Jürgen Habermas and Pope Benedict: Communication and Consensus
- Every Insider as an Outsider Here or There
- Trace of God in the Face of the Other: Levinas

Moral Issues

- The Other: A Moral Dilemma or Opportunity
- Moral Dilemmas in Bioethics
- The Relational-Ethics to the Other
- Feminist Viewpoints
- The Widow and the Orphans: The Women as the Other
- The Valuable and Vulnerable Other: Women Perspectives on Diversity and Differences
- The Unsayable Atrocity on The Female Bodies: Objectifying the Other
- Sociobiological/Psychological Outlook

- Evolution of Altruism in the Animal Species
- Mirror Neuron: Neurological Appraisal of the Other as Other
- In-Group and Out-Group as Binaries in Identity Formation
- The Other: Psychological Perspectives
- Reconciliation as Recognizing the Other
- Desire: Meeting with and Parting from the Other
- Wounded Healers: Transformation through Self-Transformation
- Nomads (Gypsies) as Strangers of Today
- Socio-Economic and Political Angles
- The Poor Does Not Exist: The Economics of the Other as Disregarding Those Without the Buying Power
- The Poor and the Marginalized as the Other
- The Caste and the Exclusion of the Other

Identity Formation and Nationalism

- Identity Politics: Need and Danger
- War and Violence: The Wounded Self and the Wounded Other
- Manufacturing Violence: Economic and Political Straggles
- Boundaries and Thresholds: Erasing or Crossing
- The Subaltern Other: Voices from Below
- The Otherness: Addressing Issues of Racial, Class and Caste Divisions
- Refugees and The Migrants Today: The Other in Their Otherness
- The African Approach to the Other
- The Japanese Understanding of the Other
- Construction of the Other and The Politics of Identity

Ecological Vision

- Essential Interconnectedness of Cosmos
- The Leaf that Smiles: Befriending Nature
- Human Uniqueness: Human vs Animals

Indian Perspectives

- Ambedkar and Gandhi: Befriending the Other Respectfully
- Sanskristisation: Appropriating the Symbolic Significance tf the Other
- Advaita and the Relation to the Other
- Befriending the Other
- "An Eye for an Eye Makes the Whole World Blind." Gandhian Way of Befriending by Forgiving
- Forgiveness as Being the Essence of Relationship: A Study of the Christian Vision of Reconciliation

- Loving Your Enemies: A Christian Vision of Dealing with Violence
- Communal Conflicts: A Case Study at Befriending Two Communities
- Inter-Religious Dialogue Leading to Communal Harmony
- Dealing with The Opponents and Rivals: Psychological Approach to Inclusive Growth
- "Live Together as Brothers or Perish Together as Fools." Martin Luther King's Approach to Befriending the Other
- Pope Francis and the Other: A Pastoral Approach

Case Studies

- The Stockholm Syndrome: Real or Illusory?
- Sri-Lankan Tragedy: Need for Community Befriending
- Thomas Chakalakal: Converting the Kidnappers
- Graham Staines: Conversation and Conversion
- Peace and Reconciliation: The Irish Story
- Truth and Reconciliation Commission: South African Experiment
- Naxal Movement in India: Need for Ecological and Economic Befriending

JD Specific Topics

- 60/123 Some Contributions of JD to the Local Church: A Historical Overview
- Some Stalwarts of JD: George Soares-Prabhu, George Lobo, Richard De Smet, Salvino Azzopardi, Etc.
- Inculturation and Indigenization: JD's Contribution to the Indian Church?
- JD: The Future Vision

Given these different themes, we have been able to take up some of them. It is hoped that the insights drawn out of our modest living encounters will enhance our lives, making a significant contribution to the Church and Nation.[2]

In this connection it may be remembered that the JD Family – Administration, Staff, Students, Co-workers and many volunteers – has made the diamond jubilee celebration a truly memorable one for all of us! So I am grateful to the whole JD family for making this Conference possible, widening our horizons to include everyone, including those who think and live differently from us. Thus the challenge to Christian leaders, thinkers and practitioners is to be committed to the Christian roots and befriend the Other, who may or may not be radically different from us. That is the only way for the survival of Christianity as well as the whole world!

Thus, these collection of articles is a modest step to foster "the culture of encounter" and promote life in its diversity and richness! May we work together to foster love, compassion and friendship among ourselves!

It is hoped that these articles on "Befriending the Other" will make our world a more inclusive and compassionate one! May we learn to embrace the other with all the differences and uniqueness. May we learn to celebrate diversity and learn from dissimilarities. May we befriend everyone, including our enemies, so that we may heed the warning of Martin Luther King, Jr: "We must learn to live together as brothers [and sisters] or perish as fools!"

Kuruvilla Pandikattu, SJ

Editor June 2020

Notes

1. For example, the coordinated assault on Paris on the evening of November 13, 2015 that killed 129 people. It may be recalled that along with the world leaders Pope Francis explicitly addressed the Paris carnage, expressing his "deep sorrow for the terrorist attacks that bloodied France late on Friday, causing many casualties." Along with offering his condolences to the victims and their families, Francis condemned the massacre as an "unspeakable affront to human dignity."
2. Adapted from *Abstracts and Proceedings of the International Conference on "Befriending the Other,"* JD, Pune, 2015

The Other

Before 900; Middle English; Old English ōther (pronoun, adj., and noun); cognate with German ander, Gothic anthar; akin to Sanskrit antara-, anya,

Of a different character or quality: "a strange, other dimension & ellipsis; where his powers seemed to fail" Often Other A person or thing considered to represent or epitomize difference or an outgroup.

"The eyes of others our prisons; their thoughts our cages" (Virginia Woolf).

"In your school you take part in various activities that habituate you not to shut yourselves in on yourselves or in your small world, but to be open to others, especially to the poorest and neediest, to work to improve the world in which we live. Be men and women with others and for others, real champions in the service of others. To be magnanimous with interior liberty and a spirit of service, spiritual formation is necessary. Dear children, dear youths, love Jesus Christ ever more!" (Pope Francis 6/7/13 Jesuit Schools)

1

Inaugural Address and Homily: Befriending the Other

His Grace Salvatore Pennacchio
Apostolic Nuncio to India and Nepal, New Delhi

His Excellency, Archbishop Salvatore Pennacchio, Apostolic Nuncio to India and Nepal, provides a clear understanding of the theme in the context of the present religious, social and cultural scenario of Asia, in order to better understand the theme "Befriending the Other." Following Pope Francis, he holds that Dialogue of life and heart is essential for love and communion. The followers of Christ are called to have the gentle and humble heart of their Master (Mt 11:29). "Interreligious relations are best developed in a context of openness to other believers, a willingness to listen and the desire to respect and understand others in their differences. For all this, love of others is indispensable. This should result in collaboration, harmony and mutual enrichment." Finally, he hopes that with the help of God's Spirit who is always ready with surprises, we will befriend the human race. The second part of the article is the homily delivered by His Grace at the Inaugural Mass.

Keywords: Befriending, Asian characteristics, Pope Francis, dialogue, inculturation.

I am happy to participate in the International Conference on "*Befriending the Other*" conducted on the occasion of the completion of sixty years of the transfer of the Pontifical Athenaeum from Kandy to Pune. At the outset, I take this opportunity to wish every success to this great endeavor. I also take this opportunity to thank Rev. Dr. Selva Rathinam SJ, the president of Jnana-Deepa, and Rev. Dr. Kuruvilla Pandikattu SJ, the Chief Organizer of the Jubilee Committee for inviting me to this Conference.

"*Befriending the Other*" is the theme of this International Conference. Befriending literally means to make friends or become friendly with, or act as a friend without keeping any barriers of what so ever. To befriend someone is to cause him or her, to be a friend. It may be harder to befriend people from the other side, or people having opposite ideologies. Mahatma Gandhi once said, "*It is easy enough to be friendly to one's friends. But to befriend the one who regards himself as your enemy is the essence of true religion.*" And Jesus exhorted his disciples and us today: "*Love your enemies, do good to those who hate you (...) If you love those who love you, what credit is that to you*?" "*Be merciful, just as your Father is merciful*" is the theme of the Extraordinary Jubilee Year of Mercy, announced by Pope Francis.

Before entering into a discussion, I think it is better to try to have a clear understanding of the theme in the context of the present religious, social and cultural scenario of Asia.

1. Religious, Social and Cultural Realities in Asia

As we all know, Asia is the earth's largest continent and is home to nearly two-thirds of the world's population. The most striking feature of the continent is the variety of its peoples, cultures, religions, beliefs, traditions and languages. It is also the cradle of the world's major religions—Judaism, Christianity, Islam and Hinduism. It is the birthplace of many other spiritual traditions such as Buddhism, Taoism, Confucianism, Zoroastrianism, Jainism, Sikhism and Shintoism. Millions of others embrace traditional or tribal religions. (*Ecclesia in Asia* no. 6).

At the same time the economic development in the Asian continent is really complex. Some Asian countries are highly developed, and others are developing. Some still find themselves in abject poverty. In the process of development, materialism and secularization are also gaining ground, especially in urban areas. Organized forms of crimes, terrorism, abuse, and the exploitation of the weaker sections of society are also widespread (*Ecclesia in Asia* no. 7). The political panorama is tremendously complex, displaying an array of ideologies ranging from democratic forms of government to theocratic ones. Undemocratic regimes and atheistic ideologies are very much present. In some places Christians are not allowed to practice their faith freely and proclaim Jesus Christ to others and minorities are denied of their rights (*Ecclesia in Asia* no. 8).

Consequently, in effect, the Church's approach of "*befriending the other*" has a specific relevance in Asian context where there are so many tensions, divisions and conflicts, caused by ethnic, social, cultural, linguistic, economic and religious differences. While keeping her teaching faithfully, the Church in Asia has to foster greater communion of mind and heart through close cooperation among different Countries. This is even vital to her evangelizing mission. She has to develop a healthy relationship with other Christian Churches and ecclesial communities, and with the followers of other religions.

Certainly, in a society where we live, there are cultural tensions, competing religious identities and diversities in the articulation of Christian faith. But in spite of all these there is a common ground on which the human society can build up its dreams and aspirations that is "love." We have all been created by God to his own image. God is our loving Father. This sensibly brings up the perception of universal brotherhood. Thus, befriending the other is not merely a philosophical dream but also a practical need of humankind desired by the Creator. It is the fulfillment of the fundamental commandment of Jesus Christ that "love one another" (Jn 15:17). Being all created by God we are called to love everyone, even our enemies.

Holy Father Pope Francis is a man of friendship, dialogue, committed to the culture of encounter, who looks for the best in people and is not judgmental. He is a peacemaker who contributed significantly to the rapprochement between peoples, countries, beliefs and cultures.

During his recent visit to USA on 23rd September last, the Holy Father Pope Francis stated that we want "a society which is truly tolerant and inclusive, one that safeguards individual rights and rejects every form of unjust discrimination," but also respects the deeply held religious beliefs of citizens and the moral and ethical obligations that flow from them."

Christians belonging to different Churches and ecclesial communities are no longer enemies or indifferent neighbors. Christian witness in a pluralistic world includes, befriending others, engaging in dialogue with people of different faith, religion and cultures (Acts 17:22-28). Christians are called to commit themselves to work with all people in mutual respect, promoting together justice, peace and common good. The purpose this International Conference is to help the Catholic Church in India to continue her dialogue with other Churches, religious faiths, various cultures, and individuals, while proclaiming the Word of God, and witnessing the joy of the Gospel.

As I have mentioned before, we are living in a period which is often characterized also by secularization, discrimination, religious fundamentalism and terrorism. In such an atmosphere it is not easy to realize befriend others. But, being Christians, it is our call to take positive steps to promote the pattern of befriending others. For this, I would like to suggest certain possible ways.

a. Dialogue is a way Forward Towards Befriending

Dialogue of life and heart is essential for love and communion. The followers of Christ are called to have the gentle and humble heart of their Master (Mt 11:29). "Interreligious relations are best developed in a context of openness to other believers, a willingness to listen and the desire to respect and understand others in their differences. For all this, love of others is indispensable. This should result in collaboration, harmony and mutual enrichment" (*Ecclesia in Asia* no. 31).

Saint Pope John Paul II in his ecumenical Encyclical *"Ut Unum Sint"* describes the fruits of the dialogues as "*brotherhood rediscovered.*" Today, the "universal brotherhood" of the Church has become a firm ecumenical conviction, bearing in mind the situations of the past, communities which were once rivals are now in many cases helping one another. Places of worship are sometimes lent out.

Scholarships are offered for the training of ministers in the Communities most lacking in resources. Approaches are made to civil authorities on behalf of other Christians who are unjustly persecuted (no.42).

The Pontifical Council for Interreligious Dialogue, the World Council of Churches, the World Evangelical Alliance and the ecumenical dialogues are fostering a friendly atmosphere in the world. But, still several social and cultural factors separate the human race. There are frustrations and oppositions.

Dialogue involves both listening and responding. It is a seeking both to understand and to be understood. It is a readiness to put questions and to be questioned. True and frank dialogue shall be guided by authentic love and truth. It allows members of different faiths to get to know one another, to identify matters of faith and practice which they share and points on which they differ and thus build up a communion. The easiest way to befriend someone, however, is just to smile and say "hello," and to look at people of different faiths without prejudice, keeping however our own identity.

b. Inculturation, a Pathway to Befriend

A culture is the result of the life and activity of a human group. The persons belonging to that group are shaped to a large extent by the culture in which they live. As persons and societies change, the culture changes with them. As a culture is transformed, so are persons and societies transformed. "From this perspective, it becomes clearer why evangelization and inculturation are naturally and intimately related to each other. The Gospel and evangelization are certainly not identical with culture; they are independent of it. Yet the Kingdom of God comes to people who are profoundly linked to a culture, and the building of the Kingdom cannot avoid borrowing elements from human cultures" (*Ecclesia in Asia* no. 21).

This engagement with cultures has always been part of the Church's pilgrimage through history. But it has a special urgency today in the multi-ethnic, multi-religious and multi-cultural situations of Asia, where Christianity is still too often seen as a foreign religion. "In the process of encountering the world's different cultures, the Church not only transmits her truths and values and renews cultures from within, but she also takes from the various cultures the positive elements already found in them" (*Ecclesia in Asia* no. 21).

"In every case inculturation must be guided by compatibility with the Gospel and communion with the faith of the universal Church, in full compliance with the Church's Tradition and with a view to strengthening people's faith" (*Ecclesia in Asia* no. 22). Unity does not mean uniformity. On the contrary what we can think of is a unity in diversity and diversity in unity. We have to uphold a balanced position in this respect, while witnessing the full truth of the Gospel.

c. Caring and Sharing

A "culture of care" will make the way to befriending much easier. Pope Francis has spoken repeatedly of the need for a Christian identity that reaches out in relationship. In his first interview as Pope, he urged: "*The thing the church needs most today is the ability to heal wounds and to warm the hearts of the faithful; it needs nearness, proximity...*" Simplicity of life, deep faith and genuine love for all, especially the poor and the outcast, are luminous signs of the Gospel in action. Therefore, the Church shall also accompany those who are undergoing severe suffering, and persecution. She has to lend moral, spiritual and material support to them (*Ecclesia in Asia* no. 28). She has to promote and witness the quality of befriending because it is her way of life.

Last but not least, from the very outset the concept of befriending the other will continue to be an impulse and a gift of the Holy Spirit. As we embark upon the new period of time we need new vision of communion and friendship. But this does not mean inventing unrealistic dreamlands of the future. Patience is the little sister of Christian hope. Instead of staring at the impossible, and chafing against it, we have to live the already given and possible communion, and do what is possible today. By advancing in this way, step by step, we may hope that, with the help of God's Spirit who is always ready with surprises, we will befriend the human race.

With these few words, in God's name, I formally inaugurate this International Conference on "Befriending the Other." May God bless us all!

Homily

Readings: Jam 1:27 -2:9 and Jn 15: 12-15

Dear Fr. Selva Rathinam, SJ, President of JD, Reverend Fathers, Reverend Brothers, and all my Brothers and Sisters,

It is a matter of great joy and happiness that I am able to celebrate this Holy Mass, with you, on this auspicious occasion of the Diamond Jubilee Celebrations of the *Jnana-Deepa*. At the outset, let me express my hearty congratulations to all of you. As the representative of His Holiness Pope Francis, I impart to you loving greetings from the Holy Father. I shall also confer on you His Apostolic Blessings, at the end of the Holy Mass. As we celebrate this Jubilee Thanksgiving Eucharistic Liturgy, let us express our indebted gratitude to God for the various Graces, He has bestowed on *Jnana-Deepa* - on all its staff, students and well-wishers. I pray that the Lord might shower up on you his choicest blessings in the days and years to come.

2. Biblical References to the Jubilee Year Celebrations

In Leviticus 25:8-12, 18, the Lord gave to the people of Israel the command to celebrate a *Jubilee Year*. Mentions to the Jubilee Year are also found in Num 36:4; Neh 5:1-13; and Ezek 46:17. "Jubilee" literally denoted to trumpets and joyful celebration. The Jubilee Year, with its main focus on emancipation and restoration, was to be proclaimed by the blast of trumpets throughout the land. Slaves were to be set free. Property rights of land were returned and everyone got to go back home. The Jubilee Year thus, had brought jubilation and celebration everywhere and to all the people, especially to the under privileged, the poor and the slaves. ***"The Jubilee Law"*** further taught a merciful form of civil justice (De 15:1-18): "no one could remain very poor for long, and the rich were not punished, but rather blessed!" The most prominent promise of the Jubilee was that the Lord will provide safety for all his people (De 15:10,18). The Lord protects family, individual, and their freedom. Jubilee also demanded that one shall not use God's Word for personal interest and to oppress people; instead righteousness and mercy towards others shall prevail always (Lev 25:14-17).

Yes, the Lord wants to show mercy to his people and asks them to be merciful among themselves. Dear Friends, The 'Extraordinary Jubilee of Mercy' starting from the Feast of the Immaculate Conception of Mary on 8 December 2015 to the Feast of Christ the King on 20 November 2016 is a happy coincidence with your Diamond jubilee Celebrations. The Holy Year of Mercy will also be conducted in tune with the commands of the Lord about the Jubilee Year celebrations in Leviticus. Pope Francis writes about the Year of Mercy: "the celebration of the Holy Year to be for all believers a true moment of encounter with the mercy of God. It is indeed my wish that the Jubilee be a living experience of the closeness of the Father, whose tenderness is almost tangible…" The Pope wants that, in this Holy Year of Mercy, everyone should "experience the love of God who consoles, pardons, and instils hope." Dear Fathers and Brothers, the Lord gives you a clear directive, how you shall celebrate your Diamond Jubilee:- it shall be for you a Jubilee year of remission of sins and pardon of failures focusing particularly on forgiveness and mercy. ***"It shall be holy to you."*** Again, in Lev 25:12, the Lord reminded the people that they shall keep the Jubilee Year holy, and in v. 18, He gave them directions, how they shall keep it holy: "*you shall do my statutes, and keep my ordinances and perform them; so you will dwell in the land securely.*" Dear Fathers and Brothers, the Lord gives you another command, how you shall celebrate this Jubilee: it shall be holy to you; you shall, all the more, do God's statutes, keep His ordinances and perform them.

3. The First Reading: James 1:27-2:9

The verse 1 reads: "My brethren, show no partiality as you hold the faith of our Lord Jesus Christ." He says: you shall not make "distinctions among yourselves, and become judges with evil thoughts" (v. 4). The intention of James here, is to teach the people not to show discrimination to the poor. He asks: "has not God chosen those who are poor in the world to be rich in faith and heirs of the kingdom which he has promised to those who love him?" (v. 5). He reminds them that "religion, that is pure and undefiled before God," is this: "to visit orphans and widows in their affliction" (1:27). The concluding verse of the reading is strongly worded: "if you show partiality, you commit sin, and are convicted by the law as transgressors" (v. 9). James aims in this passage to narrow the gulf between the rich and the poor. If we look deep at the command of the Lord about the Jubilee Year Celebrations, in Leviticus 25, we understand the Lord wants more mercy to the poor and to the slaves in the Jubilee Year. The Jubilee Year characteristics such as - "slaves were to be set free"; "everyone got to go back home"; "no one could remain very poor for long" – all these concentrate that, in the Jubilee Year, the difference between the rich and the poor need to be diminished. Therefore, both the Command of the Lord about the Jubilee Year Celebrations in Leviticus 25 and the reading from the Letter of James for this Diamond Jubilee Year Celebrations have something in common:- there shall be no partiality or discrimination among the people of God whether they are rich or poor. There shall be no barriers or distance among them.

There are innumerable teachings of the Church and pronouncements of the Popes on the role of the Church in helping the poor. You, as Professors and Seminarians are well aware of them. I shall refer here to the words of Pope Francis in *Evangelii Gaudium.* In paragraph 188 he writes: "In this context, we can understand Jesus' command to his disciples: 'You yourselves give them something to eat!' (Mk 6:37): it means working to eliminate the structural causes of poverty and to promote the integral development of the poor, as well as small daily acts of solidarity in meeting the real needs which we encounter." Again, in paragraph 191 he notes: "In all places and circumstances, Christians, with the help of their pastors, are called to hear the cry of the poor.... Seeing their poverty, hearing their cries and knowing their sufferings, we are scandalized because we know that there is enough food for everyone and that hunger is the result of a poor distribution of goods and income." Dear friends, you are going to be pastors. You make a promise to yourselves in this Jubilee Year that you shall not show any partiality or discrimination to any person because he or she is poor. Be on the side of the poor to diminish the gap between rich and the poor and to eliminate the distance between the members of the people of God. Pope Francis expects from you, as he writes in his *Letter* to the Consecrated Persons, dated 24 November 2014: "to come out of yourselves and go forth to the existential peripheries." He continues: "A whole world awaits you: men and women who have lost all hope, families in difficulty, abandoned children, young people without a future, the elderly, sick and abandoned, those who are rich in the world's goods but impoverished within, men and women looking for a purpose in life, thirsting for the divine... Don't be closed in on yourselves, don't be stifled by petty squabbles, don't remain a hostage to your own problems. These will be resolved if you go forth and help others to resolve their own problems, and proclaim the Good News." As the Apostolic Nuncio, I exhort you to translate these words of the Pope in the multifaceted Indian situations. You shall extend your service reaching out to the existential peripheries where the great majority of India: the poor, the downtrodden, the Dalit, the uneducated, the unemployed live. Proclaim to them the "Jubilee Year" as directed by the Lord in Leviticus; proclaim to them the "Jubilee Year of Mercy" as Pope Francis desires.

4. The Gospel Reading Today: John 15:12-15

Jesus tells his disciples: "This is my commandment, that you love one another as I have loved you" (v. 12). He continues: "You are my friends if you do what I command you. No longer do I call you servants...but I have called you friends..." (v. 14-15). Jesus reminds his disciples that their relationship is not of "master and slaves" but of friends. There should not be any gap or distance between them. They are friends. Moreover, there shall be no partiality, no discrimination and no differences between his disciples. He commands them: "love one another as I have loved you." They should be Friends of Jesus and friends among themselves.

Dear Fathers and brothers, the Gospel today, gives you a Jubilee Year Message: **You shall be Jesus's friends; you shall be friends among yourselves and love one another as Jesus loves you.** Learn and practice to develop an intimate and friendly relationship with Jesus in accordance with his commandments. I know that you are trained for this in this Institution. I make here only a few references. In the Book of Wisdom 7:7-14, we read about the Great King Solomon who is known for his wisdom. He prayed to God not for "scepters and thrones but for the Spirit of Wisdom" (v. 8) and "to obtain friendship with God" (v. 14). Yes, prayer leads to a friendship with God. We all know that St. Theresa of Avila, whose Fifth Birth Centenary we celebrate this year, had established a deep friendship with God. Pope Francis commends about it in his Letter to Fr. Saverio Cannistra: Her prayer consists simply in "a relation of friendship ... with Him whom we know loves us." Theresa of Avila herself says about prayer: "Prayer is nothing else than being on terms of friendship with God." Again, she adds: "Mental prayer in my opinion is nothing else than an intimate sharing between friends; it means taking time frequently to be alone with God." Dear Friends, there is no need to stress the importance of prayer in our life. You are well aware of it. The question to be asked intensively by all of you is: Does your payer lead you beyond the prayer formulas, to "a relation of friendship," a simple, warm and cordial "friendship with God"? If yes, let this Jubilee Celebrations intensify that friendship with God. If not, let this Jubilee Celebrations be a beginning for your deep "relation of friendship" with God.

Before I conclude, I thank the *Jnana Deepa* for the magnificent service you are doing to the Indian Church through the formation of future priests. Once more, my hearty congratulatory best wishes for the Diamond Jubilee Celebrations. May God bless you with his choicest blessings through the intercession of Mary, Mother of God. Thank you.

2

Guest of Honour Address: On "Befriending the Other"

His Excellency Oswald Cardinal Gracias
Mumbai

Abstract: Since the hallmark of Christianity is the movement towards the other, the church is also a servant of the kingdom of god, following the footsteps of Jesus Christ himself who came "not to be served but to serve, and to give his life as a ransom for many." The church serves the kingdom by establishing communities and founding new particular churches, and by guiding them to mature faith and charity in openness toward others, in service to individuals and society, and in understanding and esteem for human institution. The church serves the kingdom by separating throughout the world the 'gospel values' which are an expression of the kingdom and which help people to accept God's plan. Then the Cardinal wishes that we reach out to the poor and support them so they can feel the warmth of our presence, our friendship, and our fraternity!

Keywords: Social teachings, Human dignity, Pope Francis, Solidarity with the poor.

Introduction: The Meaning of the Other and Its Importance for Us Christians

The hallmark of Christianity is a movement from self-centeredness to other-centeredness. As Jesus was a man for others, the central challenge of Christianity is living for others. The church, in Christ, is a sacrament -- a sign and instrument, that is, of communion with God and of the unity of the entire human race (*Lumen Gentium*, no.1). The church is also a servant of the kingdom of god, following the footsteps of Jesus Christ himself who came "not to be served but to serve, and to give his life as a ransom for many" (Mark 10.45). The church serves the kingdom by establishing communities and founding new particular churches, and by guiding them to mature faith and charity in openness toward others, in service to individuals and society, and in understanding and esteem for human institution. The church serves the kingdom by spreading throughout the world the 'gospel values' which are an expression of the kingdom and which help people to accept God's plan.[1]

One of the key achievements of the Second Vatican council was to give importance to the image of the church as the people of god. The church serves the people of god in its struggle for the liberation of the oppressed and in search for justice and peace. Dietrich Bonhoeffer defined the church as the communion that exists for others, he emphasized that the church "must share in the secular problems of ordinary human life, not dominating but helping and serving."[2] As the *Catechism of the Catholic Church (CCC)* teaches us, collaboration among Christians in various areas of service to humankind is essential to the following of Christ.3 It affirms that "in economic matters, respect for human dignity requires the practice of the virtue of temperance, to moderate our attachment to the goods of this world: of the virtue of justice to preserve our neighbor's rights and to render what is his or her due and of solidarity following the golden Rule and in keeping with the generosity of the Lord who 'though He was rich yet for your sake ..... became poor, so that by his poverty you might become rich (2 Cor 8:9)."[4]

Redemptoris Missio succinctly states that "the Church's mission derives not only from the Lord's mandate but also from the profound demands of God's life within us. Those who are incorporated in the Catholic Church ought to sense their privilege and for that very reason their greater obligation of bearing witness to the faith and to the Christian life as a service to their brothers and sisters and as a fitting response to God. They should be ever mindful that "they owe their distinguished status not to their own merits but to Christ's special grace; and if they fail to respond to this grace in thought, word and deed, not only will they not be served, they will be judged severely.[5]

1. Scriptural Understanding of the Other

In 1987 at Xavier University in New Orleans, St. John Paul II stated that it is not enough to offer to the disadvantaged of the world crumbs of freedom, crumbs of oneself to reject introversion and to concentrate on the needs of others. For example, the parable of the rich man and the poor man is directed to the conscience of humanity (cf. Luke 16:19ff) and, today in particular, to the conscience of the developed nations and rich countries and rich people.[6] The rich man was consumed in self-centered living and only cared about himself.

He had no concern and compassion for the poor and hence he was condemned. Christ demands our concern and compassion on the poor and hence he was condemned. Christ demands our openness to the poor and the disadvantaged. Here, we recollect the words of St. John Paul II: "The human person lives in a community, in society. And with the community he shares hunger and thirst and sickness and malnutrition and misery and all the deficiencies that result there from. In his or her own person the human being is meant to experience the needs of others."[7] We need to inspire people to get involved in social concerns that will not only enlarge their horizons but will also challenge their lifestyles and encourage them to reach out to the marginalized and the weak of society.

St. John Paul II's Encyclical Letter, *Veritatis Splendour* clearly notes that "both the Old and the New Testaments explicitly affirm that without *love of neighbor,* made concrete in keeping the commandments, *genuine love of God* is not possible. St. John makes the point with extra ordinary forcefulness: "If anyone says, 'I love God', and hates his brother, he is a liar; for he who does not love his brother whom he has seen, cannot love God whom he has not seen" (1 Jn 4:20). The Evangelist echoes the moral preaching of Christ, expressed in a wonderful and unambiguous way in the parable of the Good Samaritan (cf. Lk 10:30-37) and in His words about the final judgment (cf. Mt 25:31-46).[8]

Jesus' Attitude to Others: The attitude of Jesus in the Gospels can be seen from his attitude, his behavior, his words and deeds. It clearly depicts a man totally for others.[9] He was in solidarity with the least and the outcasts. He showed concern for suffering people by reaching out to them. *Veritatis Splendor* explains that "Jesus brings God's commandments to fulfillment, particularly the commandment of love of neighbor, by *interiorizing their demands and by bringing out their fullest meaning.* Love of neighbor springs from a *loving heart* which, precisely because it loves, is ready to live out the loftiest challenges. Jesus shows that the commandments must not be understood as a minimum limit not to be gone beyond, but rather as a path involving a moral and spiritual journey towards perfection, at the heart of which is love (cf. Col 3:14)."[10]

To live is to love: And living the Gospel of life means to live in love. The parable of the Good Samaritan (Lk 10:25 -37) invites us to reflect upon two very important questions, viz. Who is my neighbor? And Am I my brother's keeper? It reveal to us that everyone is our neighbor, especially the ones who are living on the fringes of society and all those who are most in need (Mt 25:40). The Good Samaritan is anyone who has compassion, stops by and helps the suffering person, and truly gives himself, his very "I" to the "Other" person. Here we focus upon one of the key points of all Christian anthropology, viz, that man cannot find himself except through a sincere gift of himself.[11] In this regard, St. John Paul II remarked: "We must care for the other as person for whom God has made us responsible." He insisted that when human life is involved the service of charity must be profoundly consistent as human life is sacred and inviolable at every stage and in every situation; it is an indivisible good.[12] For St. John Paul II, the parable of the Good Samaritan is Christ's personal call for Christians to be in solidarity with all those who suffer. And the cross of Christ is the ultimate proof of his solidarity with human beings.[13]

In the New Testament passage on the healing of the Roman Centurion's servant (Mt 8:5-3; Lk 7:1-10), we observe that the centurion, even though he was a gentile, had tremendous faith that Jesus would heal his servant. The Centurion cared for his servant and strongly believed that Jesus could heal him with his Word. He crossed racial barriers and risked his reputation by going to a Jew for help. Jesus was amazed at his faith. Our faith must be reflected in the life we lead and the values we live by. Our life has to be transformed by what we believe. So, the principal quality that our faith should have is love. In *Lumen Fidei*, Pope Francis remarked: "Christian faith in as much as it proclaims the truth of God's total love and opens us to the power of that love, penetrates to the core of our human experience. Each of us comes to the light because of love, and each of us is called to love in order to remain in the light."[14] The Centurion cared so much for his servant that he humbled himself to ask the help of Jesus to heal him. Mother Teresa said that she saw the face of Jesus in the face of every sick and dying person she met. May our faith in God inspire us to reach out in love especially to our less fortunate brothers and sisters.

The incident of Jesus' conversation with a Samaritan woman at the well (Jn 4: 4-26) teaches us the lesson that God loves each of us in spite of our sinful lives. No one loved her, not even herself. But Jesus befriended her. The Samaritan woman was considered an outcast by her own people was invited by Jesus to drink the water that he gives, water that gives eternal life. Christ's loving way of acting, the Gospel of his words and deeds, transformed the woman and led her to become his disciple. She then went on to proclaim Christ to the inhabitants of Samaria, and they too received him with faith.15 May Christ's love for us inspire us to reach out to every single person in faith and love and doing so reveal to them the mercy of God.

2. The Church's Love and Concern for the Other Is Seen in Its Social Teachings

The Church's social teaching is a valid instrument of evangelization (Cf. *Centesimus Annus,* no. 54) since it places the human person and society in relationship with the light of the Gospel.[16] "By means of her social doctrine, the shows her concern for human life in society, aware that the quality of social life, that is, of the relationship of justice and love that form the fabric of society- depends in a decisive manner on the protection and promotion of the human person, for whom every community comes into existence."[17] *The Compendium of the Social Doctrine of the Church* boldly affirms that "no legislation, no system of rules or negotiation will ever succeed in persuading men and people to live in unity, brotherhood and peace; no line of reasoning will ever be able to surpass the appeal of love. Only love can animate and shape social interaction, moving it towards peace in the context of a world that is ever more complex. In this perspective, love takes on the characteristic style of social and political charity. Social charity makes us love the common good, it makes us effectively seek the good of all people, considered not only as individuals or private persons but also in the social dimension that unites them."[18]

a. The Church's Concern for Human Work and the Working Class

According to St. John Paul, human work is the essential key to the whole social question. The Pope is keenly interested in work because he is interested in the human person. In the initial pages of the book of Genesis the Church finds the source of her conviction, that work is a fundamental dimension of human existence on earth.[19] The Biblical words; "Be fruitful and multiply, and fill the earth and subdue it," even though they do not refer directly and explicitly to work, beyond any doubt they indirectly indicate it as an activity for man to carry out in the world. Indeed, they show its very deepest essence. Man is the image of God partly through the mandate, received from his Creator to subdue, to dominate, the earth.[20] In carrying out this mandate, every human being reflects the very action of the Creator.[21] Thus, we cannot understand work without understanding man, and since man was created by God, by seeing the original plan for man, we can get some insight into man's nature and purpose. In fact, human work has an ethical value of its own because of the fact that the one who is doing the work is a person. Hence, work is for the person and not the person for work.[22] From all this, St. John Paul II draws out an important principle of Catholic Social Doctrine, a principle that has always been taught by the Church, viz, the principle of the priority of labour over capital. Without man and without work, things would not serve their purposes and be means to fulfill the commandment to subdue the earth.[23] To show his concern for the workers and their rights, St. Pope John Paul II defends four traditional rights of labour, viz, suitable employment for those who are capable of it, just remuneration for work done, the organization of the labour process to respect the requirements of each person and his or her life and the right of workers to form unions.[24]

b. Solidarity with others and Interdependence: Two Important Principles of the Church's Social Teaching

Today, more than ever the world needs solidarity as a solution to the deep seated economic and social problems. We all need to realize that we cannot live in isolation but rather in a society. In this context, Joseph Cardinal Hoffner states that the principle of the solidarity "rests on the existential reciprocal relationship and mutual involvement between the individual and society. On the other hand it denotes the moral responsibility (mutual liability) emanating from this essential condition. Hence, solidarity is both an ontological and ethical principle."[25] According to Hoffner, the existence of world hunger is the greatest sign that solidarity is lacking in our world. He appeals to every nation to examine their economic and political policies in order to change those situations across frontiers so that all nations achieve economic and social progress and contribute to the welfare of all.[26]

The Congregation for the Doctrine of the Faith in its *Instruction on Christian Freedom and Liberation* describes solidarity as a necessary principle and also as an obligation. It affirmed that "Solidarity is a direct requirement of human and supernatural brotherhood. The serious socio-economic problems which occur today cannot be solved unless new fronts of solidarity are created: solidarity of the poor among themselves, solidarity with the poor to which the rich are called and solidarity among the workers. Institutions and social organizations at different levels, as well as the state, must share in a general movement of solidarity. When the Church appeals for such solidarity, she is aware that she herself is concerned in a quite special way."[27] It also stated that by virtue of the principle of solidarity, "man with his brothers is obliged to contribute to the common good of the society at all its levels. Further, international solidarity is necessary not only in cases of extreme urgency but also to aid true development, to find concrete technical solutions to problems and to create a new mentality among our contemporaries.[28] Hence the Church's doctrine is opposed to all the forms of social and political individualism."[29]

St John Paul II describes solidarity as "a firm and persevering determination to commit oneself to the common good; that is to say to the good of all and of each individual, because we are all really responsible for all."[30] The good of each person is bound up with the good of the community. Each person must fulfill his responsibility to achieve the common good in the light of his abilities. For the Pope, this is the essence of solidarity. For the Christian, this requires a deep Christian Maturity in which the answer to the question "Am I my brother's keeper?" is a spontaneous 'yes'.

c. The Fact of Interdependence

Requiring the Response of Solidarity: St. John Paul II sees interdependence as a challenge having a very positive potential. "The conviction is growing of a radical interdependence and consequently of the need for a solidarity which will take up interdependence and transfer it to the moral plane."[31] Donald Dorr states that "these words are the key to understand the word *solidarity* in the specific technical meaning the Pope is giving to it: solidarity is the correct moral response to the fact of interdependence.[32] The fact of interdependence is thus a necessary condition for solidarity: interdependence must be transformed in to solidarity, which is based on the principle that the goods of creation are meant for all, and that the other person is to be seen as our neighbor.[33] Solidarity should make the more powerful feel responsible for those who are weak and be ready to share with them what they have. When this moral dimension is ignored, there arises instead an attitude of an overriding desire for profit and thirst for power, which when established on an international level are expressed in different forms of imperialism and the division of the world in to blocs.[34] This mutual independence is an essential ingredient of justice.

d. The Church's Concern for Other Religions: Ongoing Dialogue Is Essential

Nostra Aetate, the declaration on the relationship of the church to Non-Christian religions is the shortest of the Second Vatican Council's documents. However, it was the first time a Council made a positive statement to Jews, Muslims and Hindus. The declaration is a *magna carta* for dialogue. It urged Christians to acknowledge, preserve and encourage, the spiritual values and moral truths of other religions together with their social life and culture.[35] It revolutionized the Catholic Church's relations not only with Judaism but also with Islam and Hinduism, the major world religions. It still continues to inspire us to be faithful to the spirit of dialogue in the church. What the church needs is effective dialogue with people of other religions, which is always possible on the basis of culture. A religion without dialogue has the potential danger of alienation. St. Pope John Paul II remarked, "Dialogue is a sign of the hope that religions of the world are becoming more aware of their shared responsibility for the well- being of the human family.[36] Since Vatican Council II, there have been important dialogue initiatives between Christians and Jews. St. John Paul II had emphasized that the Jews are our older brothers. We remember, a reflection on the Shoah, was the first universal document of the Catholic Church dedicated to remembering the particularity of Jewish suffering in the Holocaust and the evil of the *Shoah.* It was a milestone in the journey of reconciliation with the Jews. In India 80.5 % of the population is Hindu and 13.4 % is Muslim, efforts of inter-religious dialogue continue, however, not without challenges and difficulties.

In 1989, the CBCI Commission for Dialogue and Ecumenism brought out the *'Guidelines for Inter-religious Dialogue',* a unique document that explains dynamism of dialogue. The Commission elaborates also the attitudes for genuine dialogue. They are prayer, commitment to faith, willingness to change, truthfulness, honesty, humility, spirit of forgiveness, knowledge of the other and sense of justice.[37]

Such dialogue is not only limited to religions. St. John Paul II also stated that" science can purify religion from error and superstition; religion can purify science idolatry and false absolutes. Each draws the other into a wider world, a world in which both can flourish."[38] Today, the need for an effective and constructive dialogue between modern science and religion is all the more important. We need to constantly search for creative expressions of inter-religious and inter-cultural dialogue in our Church institutions such as peace meals, sports for peace and seminars on common social issues including food, water, environment and healthcare.[39]

e. The Church's Respect for the Freedom of the Other and Respect for Human Rights

Blessed Pope Paul VI called the "Declaration on Religious Freedom," *Dignitatis Humane,* as one of the major texts of the Council.[40] It soon emerged as one of the most influential documents created by the Council. It recognized the human right to religious liberty. It advocated for the principle of religious liberty to be treated as a civil right and obligated governments to protect this right. The fact is the right to religious freedom has already been accepted and affirmed by the common consciousness of human kind."[41] It is not only a civil and political right, but is "a cornerstone in the structure of human rights and the most profound expression of the freedom of conscience."[42]

St. John Paul II repeatedly stated that the dignity of the human person is the pivot on which the entirety of Catholic social doctrine turns. He said that "religious freedom is an essential requirement of the dignity of every person, a cornerstone of the structure of human rights, and for this reason an irreplaceable factor in the good of individuals and of the whole society. The freedom of individuals and communities to profess and practice their religion is an essential requirement for peaceful coexistence."[43] The teaching of the Second Vatican Council clearly states that religious freedom is inseparable from human rights. Hence, the Church's demand for religious freedom is to be seen in the wider context of the church being a champion of all human rights, since all human rights belong to all people. By the time the Council passed the Declaration on Religious Freedom in December 1965, over a hundred countries including India had made provisions for this right in their respective laws. The Church has the duty to demand for the religious freedom of every person in every country.[44] In light of the continuing attacks on the dignity of the human person through rampant abortion, euthanasia and religious persecution, it is becoming all the more necessary to return to the text of *Dignitatis Humanae.*

The United Nation's documents too indicate that this right to religious freedom is universal. The Universal Declaration of Human Rights recognizes the inherent dignity and equal and inalienable rights of all the members of the human family. Article 18 states the right to Religious Freedom clearly.

On 25 March 2011 the United Nations' Human Rights Council has adopted a resolution recognizing freedom of religious belief and abandoning a longstanding concept of religious "defamation." According to a recent survey by Pew Research Center, India is among the countries that have highest support for religious freedom, with eight out of ten Indians believing that it is very important to have the freedom to practice their faith compared to a global median of 74 %.[45] It is one thing to desire religious freedom; it is another to experience it in day to day life. The journey to freedom of religion is long and arduous, but we must not give up. A process of Conscientization and dialogue are the key to change and transformation.

f. Befriending the Environment

According to the new research performed by an international team of researchers, human beings are "eating away at our own life support systems" at a rate unseen in the past 10,000 years by degrading land and freshwater systems, emitting greenhouse gasses and releasing vast amounts of agricultural chemicals into the environment. Out of nine worldwide processes that support life on Earth, four have exceeded "safe" levels, viz., human-driven climate change, loss of biosphere integrity, land system change and the high level of phosphorus and nitrogen flowing into the oceans.[46] In the light of this environmental degradation, Pope Francis in his recent Encyclical, *Laudato Si,* is guiding the Church to watchfulness for an urgent, "sign of the times." He is reminding us of the beauty of Creation and our Dignity as its stewards entrusted by the Creator to nurture and protect that creation for the sake of our whole human family and for generations to come. As the human family strives to recalibrate its relationship to the environment, the Church has an important role to play.

The earlier Popes too showed their concern for nature and care for the environment. In 1971 in his apostolic letter marking the 80th anniversary of the publication of *Rerum novarum.* Bl. Paul VI prophetically remarked: "the Christians must turn to these new perceptions in order to take on responsibility, together with the rest of men, for a destiny which from now on is shared by all." The new perceptions indicated by the Pope are those of a "wide-ranging social problem that concerns the entire human family" and were addressed in the paragraph entitled *The Environment.*[47] St. John Paul II was the first Pope to talk about the consequences of industrial growth, massive urban concentrations and vastly increased energy needs in his Encyclical *Sollicitudo Rei Socialis,* stating that "one must take into account the nature of each being and of its mutual connection in an ordered system, which is precisely the cosmos."[48] At the end of the 1980s the Pope warned of using natural resources, some of which are not renewable, as if they were inexhaustible, and, furthermore in industrialization, he saw a risk of contaminating the environment and of the quality of life.[49]

Each and every one of us needs to respect and protect the environment, so that through nature people can "contemplate the mystery of the greatness and love of God." Also, according to the principle of justice, each of us has a moral responsibility to protect the natural order. The growing environmental crisis in the recent years is posing a great challenge to Asia. There is a greater awareness today that the goods of the earth cannot be used as it was unfortunately used in the past. Many countries, states and people are consuming the very earth on which our very livelihood depends. The growing phenomenon of climate change and natural disasters call into question our use of the earth's resources. One of the biggest challenges in reducing poverty and environmental degradation is neither scientific nor technological, "but rather within our minds and hearts."[50] Blessed Pope Paul VI in *Populorum Progressio* asserts that "the whole of creation is ordered in the first place towards its creator and the rationality of humans is directed not to using nature in a thoughtless way but to recognition of God's plan and thus to the 'prior God-given purpose' of nature."[51]

The ruthless exploitation of earth's resources may benefit a few people but has adverse effects on the masses in Asia. The absolute thirst for profits over the dignity of the human person and unbridled technological development divorced from integral human development are the root causes that are alienating us from our natural environment. In his 1900 World Day of Peace Message, Saint Pope John Paul II affirms that the ecological crisis is "a profound moral crisis of which the destruction of the environment is only one troubling aspect."[52] In this regard he urged that we must go to the heart of the ecological degradation. St John Paul II advocated an education in ecological responsibility because "we are all really responsible for all."[53]

g. Solidarity with the Poor

After stating that poor countries lack the economic means either to gain access to existing sources of non-renewable energy or to finance research into new alternatives, Pope Benedict XVI then urged the international community to find institutional means of regulating the exploitation of non-renewable resources of these poor countries. He also called for a worldwide redistribution of energy resources.[54] In his encyclical, *Caritas in Veritate,* he expressed the hope that the international community and individual governments will succeed in countering harmful ways of treating the environment. The covenant between human beings and the environment should mirror the creative love of God, from whom we come and towards whom we are journeying.55 Respect for nature and respect for human life are inextricably related. Pope Benedict XVI clearly stated that individuals in rich countries must change their life styles and their consumption with responsibility if the world's resources are to be protected. "The ecological crisis," St. John Paul II stated, "reveals the urgent moral need for a new solidarity, especially in relations between the developing nations and those that are highly industrialized" (EC, no. 10). Only with sustainable development (which includes sustainable food, water and basic sanitation)[56] the developing nations curb the continuing environmental degradation and avoid the destructive effects of the kind of development that has used natural resources irresponsibly. The ecological problem is closely connected to those who are poor and hence treated unjustly. According to St. Pope John Paul II, "the goods of the earth, which in the divine plan should be a common patrimony, often risk becoming the monopoly of a few who often spoil it and, sometimes destroy it, thereby creating a loss for all humanity."[57] The option for the poor is rooted in the Gospel and in the Church's social teaching. It awakens our conscience to the fact that the poor suffer most directly from environment decline and often have the least access to relief from their suffering. Justice is rooted in compassion for our own weakest members.[58]

Pope Francis in his Encyclical *Laudato Si'* asks a very pertinent question, viz. "what kind of world do we want to leave to those who come after us, to children who are now growing up?" (*Laudato Si',* No.160). At the general audience April 22 2015, the day on which *Earth Day* was celebrated, Pope Francis said: "I urge all to look at the world through the eyes of the creator: the Earth is an environment to protect and a garden to cultivate. May the relationship between man and nature not be driven by greed, to manipulate and exploit, but may the divine harmony between beings and creation be conserved in the logic of respect and care, so as to be placed at the service of brothers and sisters, of future generations as well."

3. The Challenge of Peace Today in the Light of Terrorism

During the last few days the newspapers and journals are flooded with analysis and comments of the terrorist attacks that took place on 13 November in Paris. 129 innocent people have lost their lives and hundreds of others were wounded. Earlier, on 31 October, the downing of a Russian airliner in Egypt's Sinai Peninsula killed all the 224 people on board. Unfortunately radical terrorism and increasing terrorist threats have been on the increase around the world. According to the Global Terrorism Index (edition of 2014) from the institute for Economics and Peace, the world has experienced 61 % increase in terrorist attacks in the last year.[59] About 17,958 people were killed in terrorist attacks last year, and of those deaths 82 % occurred in just 5 nations: Iraq, Afghanistan, Pakistan, Nigeria, and Syria.[60] The compendium of the Social Doctrine of the church boldly states that "terrorism is one of the most brutal forms of violence traumatizing the international community today: it sows hatred, death, and an urge for revenge and reprisal... The fight against terrorism presupposes the moral duty to help to create those conditions that will prevent it from arising in the future,"[61] years ago. The challenge we are confronted with today is how we promote the common good of all and in particular the good of the other when the other violently attacks us with terror, suicide bombing and the like. We face the Christian challenge of loving one's enemies and recognizing the humanity of all those who want to destroy us. Here we recollect the words of Bl Pope Paul VI who stated: "if you want peace work for justice." The road to peace is a very long and difficult journey. Let us work together with people of all religions and cultures and search for long-term political, economic and social strategies that will result in the creation of a peaceful society. "The promotion of peace in the world is an integral part of the Church's mission of continuing Christ's work of redemption on earth."[62]

Conclusion: The Teachings of Pope Francis on Befriending the Other

A few days after his election as Pope, Pope Francis set forth his vision in the clearest possible terms: "And how I would like a church that is poor and for the poor." (*E como Vorrei una chiesa povera e per i poveri*).[63] According to him focusing on poverty and sacrificing for the poor are at the heart of the Gospel.[64] In his homily at Lampedusa, he lamented what he called the anesthesia of the heart: "We are a society which has forgotten how to weep, how to experience compassion"- "suffering with" others; the globalization of indifference has taken from us the ability to weep![65] In explaining the need to reach out to the other, in *Evangelii Gaudium* he aptly remarked: "Each Christian and every community must discern the path that the Lord points out, but all of us are asked to obey his call to go forth from our own comfort zone in order to reach all the "peripheries" in need of the light of the Gospel."[66] In his speech to the United States Congress he clearly tells its members that "the fight against poverty and hunger must be fought constantly and on many fronts."[67]

Misericordiae Vultus, the Papal Bull of Pope Francis, is a beautiful invitation to each one of us to contemplate on the mystery of mercy and to rediscover the joy that comes from the encounter with the tenderness of God's mercy. It demonstrates to us how we are to relate to others. According to him, mercy is the bridge that connects God and man, opening our hearts to a hope of being loved forever despite our sinfulness. Especially in this Holy Year of Mercy, he invites each of us to open our hearts to others, in a spirit of mercy. He emphasized: "We look forward to the experience of opening our hearts to those living on the outermost fringes of society: fringes modern society itself creates. How many uncertain and painful situations there are in the World today! How many are the wounds borne by the flesh of those who have no voice because their cry is muffled and drowned out by the indifference of the rich."[68]

I would like to conclude my reflection today with the words of Pope Francis: "May the balm of mercy reach everyone, both believers and those far away, as a sign that the kingdom of God is already present in our midst." His response to the other, especially to those on the fringes of society is heartwarming. He wrote: "Let us open our eyes and see the misery of the world, the wounds of our brothers and sisters who are denied their dignity, and let us recognize that we are compelled to heed their cry for help! May we reach out to them and support them so they can feel the warmth of our presence, our friendship, and our fraternity! May their cry become our own, and together may we break down the barriers of indifference that too often reign supreme and mask our hypocrisy and egoism!"[69]

Notes

1. St. John Paul II, *Redemptoris Missio*. No. 20.
2. Bonhoeffer, *Letters and Papers from Prison* (New York, Macmillan, 1967), p.204.
3. *Catechism of the Catholic Church* (CCC) no.821 and *Unitatis Redintegratio*, no.12.
4. *Catechism of the Catholic Church* (CCC) no.2407.
5. St. John Paul II, *Redemtoris Missio*, No.11.
6. St. John Paul II, *Address at Xavier University in New Orleans at a meeting with Representatives of Catholic Universities on the occasion of Apostolic Visit to the USA and Canada,* 12 September 1987, no.8.9.
7. St. John Paul ll, *Homily in Edmonton*, Alberta, 17 September 1984.
8. St. John Paul ll, *Encyclical Letter, Veritatis Splendor*, no. 14.
9. St. John Paul ll,, *Redemptor Hominis*, no. 8 (and Gaudium et Spes, no. 22) "For, by his Incarnation, he, the son of God, in a certain way united himself with each man. He worked with human hands, he thought with a human mind. He acted with a human will, and with a human heart he loved. Born of the Virgin Mary, he has truly been made one of us, like to us in all things except sin."
10. St. John Paul ll, *Encyclical Letter, Veritatis Splendor*, no. 15.
11. St. John Paul ll, *Apostolic Letter, Salvific Doloris, On the Christian mystery of Human suffering*, no.28.
12. Alan Schreck, *The Legacy of Pope John Paul II: The central Teaching of his 14 Encyclical Letters*, Emmaus Road Publishing, Ohio, 2012,p.115.
13. Hung Pham, *St. John Paul II's Solidarity with the Poor as a Eucharistic Dimension of the Christian Moral Life: A Dissertation*. Faculty of the School of Theology and Religious Studies of the Catholic University of America, Washington DC, 2009
14. Pope Francis, *Encyclical Letter, Lumen Fidei*, no. 32.
15. St. John Paul II, Apostolic Letter, *Mulieris Dignatatem, On the Dignity and Vocation of Women,* no. 15.
16. Cardinal Angelo Sondano, *Letter to the Cardinal Renato Martino on Preface of Compendium of the Social Doctrine of the Church*, Vatican City, 2004.
17. Pontifical Council for Justice and Peace, *Compendium of the Social Doctrine of the Church* (henceforth called Compendium), no.81.
18. Pontifical Council for Justice and Peace, *Compendium*, no.207.

19. St. John Paul II, *Laborem Exercens*, no.4.
20. St. John Paul II, *Laborem Exercens*, no.4.
21. St. John Paul II, *Laborem Exercens*, no.4.
22. St. John Paul II, *Laborem Exercens*, no.6.
23. Thomas Stork, *Catholic Social Teaching: John Paul II, Laborem Exercens, and Catholic Education,* Research Centre, Canada.
24. David O'Brien and Thomas Shannon, Catholic Social Thought: The Documentary Heritage, OrbisBooks, Maryknoll, New York, 1992, p.350.
25. Hoffner, Joseph, "The World Economy in the light of Catholic Social Teaching" in *Church and Economy in Dialogue*. Roos, Lothar, ed. Association for the advancement of Christian Social Sciences: Germany, 1987, p.27.
26. Ibid.
27. Congregation for the Doctrine of the faith, *Instruction on Christian Freedom and Liberation*, 22 March 1986, no.89
28. Congregation for the Doctrine of the faith, *Instruction on Christian Freedom and Liberation*, 22 March 1986, no.91
29. Congregation for the Doctrine of the faith, *Instruction on Christian Freedom and Liberation*, no.73.
30. St. John Paul II, *Sollicitudo Rei Socialis*, no.38.
31. St. John Paul II , *Sollicitudo Re Socialis*,no.26
32. Donal Dorr "Solidarity and Integral Human Development" in *The Logic of Solidarity*, eds. Gregory Baum and Robert Ellsberg (Maryknoll, NY: Orbis Books, 1989),148.
33. St. John Paul II *Sollicitudo Rei Socialis*,no.39.
34. St. Jhon Paul II *Sollicitudo Rei Socialis*, no.36, 38.
35. The second Vatican council, *Nostra Aetate* no.2.
36. Pope John Paul II, "Dialogue with the World Religions," *Origins*, 29/24, Nov, 25, 1999, p.398.
37. CBCI Commission for Dialogue and Ecumenism, *Guidelines for Inter-religious Dialogue*, New Delhi: CBCI Centre, 1989, nos: 31, 40-55.
38. Pope John Paul II, Message to Rev. George Coyne, the Director of the Vatican Observatory, 1 June 1988.
39. Cardinal Oswald Gracious, Fifty Years of the Second Vatican Council and the New Evangelization.
40. John Courtney Murray, "Religious Freedom "in Abbott, *The Documents of Vatican Council and the New Evangelization.*
41. Pelotte, Donald E., John Courtney Murray: *Theologian in Conflict*. New York: Paulist Press, 1975, p.100.
42. Archbishop Renato Martin, Permanent Observer of the Holy See to the United Nation in his Intervention in the U.N. on 10 November 1999.
43. Pope John Paul II, *World Day Peace Message*, 1998.
44. Editorial, "Religious freedom and plural societies" In *Vidyajyothi Journal of Theology Reflection*, Vol.66 No.6 (June 2002),401-404: "Nobody may persecute a Muslim for being a Muslim or a Hindu for being a Hindu, however much their beliefs may contrast with those of the societies in which they live."

45. "83% Indians Bat for Religions Freedom," *Times News Network* (TNN), New Delhi, 20 November 2015.
46. *The Guardian*, 15 January 2015, UK.
47. St. John Paul II, *Octogesima Adveniens*, no.21.
48. St. John Paul II, *Sollicitudo Rei Socialis*, no.34.
49. St. John Paul II, *Sollicitudo Rei Socialis*, no.34.
50. Cardinal Peter Turkson, UN Conference on Climate Change, New York, 29 June 2015.
51. Archbishop Diarmuid Martin on Populorum Progressio; *Zenit News*, 22 October 2007. Cf Bl Pope Paul VI, *Populorum Progessio*, no.16.
52. St. John Paul II, *World Day of Peace*, 1990, no.5. Cfr. also no.15.
53. St. John Paul II, SRS no.38.
54. Pope Benedict XVI, *Caritas in Varitate,* no.49.
55. Pope Benedict XVI, *Caritas in Varitate,* no.50.
56. According to the Brundtland Commission of the UN in 1987: "Sustainable development is development that meets the needs of the present without compromising the ability of future generations to meet their own needs "
57. October 25, 1991 address at Conference Marking the presentation of the Second Edition of the St. Francis "Canticle of the Creatures" International Award for the Environment.
58. Renewing the Earth, p. 8.
59. This Global Terrorism Index Covers 99.6% of the world's population and ranks 162 countries based on the impact of terrorist activities along with analysis of economic and social factors
60. Amanda Macias, The State of Terrorism in the world Today in Business Insider India, 19 November 2014.
61. Pontifical Council for Justice and Peace, Compendium of the Social Doctrine of the Church, no. 513.
62. Pontifical Council for Justice and Peace, Compendium of the Social Doctrine of the Church, no. 516.
63. Address to members of the communication media.16, March 2013.
64. Pope Francis, Homily on 6th June 2015.
65. Pope Francis, Homily on 8th July 2013.
66. Pope Francis, *Evangelii Gaudium*, no.20.
67. Pope Francis, Address to the United States Congress, 24 September 2015.
68. Pope Francis, *Misericordiae Vultus, Bull of Indiction of the Extraordinary Jubilee of Mercy*, April 2015, n, 15.
69. Pope Francis, *Misericordiae Vultus, Bull of Indiction of the Extraordinary Jubilee of Mercy*, April 2015, n, 16.

3

Understanding Christ as the Only Saviour Today

Rt Rev Bishop Thomas Dabre
Bishop of Poona

Abstract: In this article, the author, Bishop of Poona, holds that the significant pronouncements of the Christian faith emphatically enunciated in *Dominus Iesus* are compatible with a courageously positive and constructive approach to other Christians and other religions. He asks the fundamental question: Is Jesus the only Saviour? This leads to committed dialogue with other religions and traditions. Then he presents some important task for the theologians

Keywords: *Dominus Iesus*, Jesus Christ, Theology, Inculutration.

1.We Hold Some Truths as Being Essentials of the Christian Faith

The fundamental affirmations of the Christian faith emphatically enunciated in *Dominus Iesus (DI)* are compatible with a courageously positive and constructive approach to other Christians and other religions. In this article I want to outline some of the salient challenges that *Dominus Iesus* poses to the Indian theologians.

The Catholic Church teaches that she alone is the unique Church of Christ, and that all other religions, whether Christian or non-Christian, are sects. Pope Pius XII teaches in his encyclical *Mystici Corporis*: "For in one spirit, says the Apostle, 'were we all baptized into one Body, whether Jews or Gentiles, whether bond or free.' As therefore in the true Christian community there is only one Body, one Spirit, one Lord, and one Baptism, so there can be only one faith."

Dominus Iesus states emphatically. "The definitive and complete character of the revelation of Jesus Christ, the nature of Christian faith as compared with that of belief in other religions, the inspired nature of the books of Sacred Scripture, the personal unity between the Eternal Word and Jesus of Nazareth, the unity of the economy of the Incarnate Word and the Holy Spirit, the unicity and salvific universality of the mystery of Jesus Christ, the universal salvific mediation of the Church, the inseparability - while recognizing the distinction - of the kingdom of God, the kingdom of Christ, and the Church, and the subsistence of the one Church of Christ in the Catholic Church." (DI 4). Knowing the definitive character of revelation we understand that, "Christ, is at the same time the mediator and the fullness of all revelation" (DI 5). Therefore any limited, incomplete, or imperfect character of the revelation of Jesus Christ is contrary to the Church's faith (DI 6).

The Church had taught that there was no salvation outside the Catholic Church. It is our faith that the divinity is in all its fullness in Jesus and this fullness is given to the Church, the Body of Christ. However, this does not mean that in our grasp of the faith and in living it out we cannot learn anything from these sources of the other religions. Certainly we can be enriched by them and particularly we Indians can be helped immensely in the process of the inculturation of the faith-life.

Vatican II admits, fundamentally, that non-Catholic Christians are members of the Mystical Body and not merely ordered to it. And so we need to understand that Christ does not fail to make himself present in many ways, not only to individuals, but also to entire peoples through their spiritual riches, of which their religions are the main and essential expression, "Therefore, the sacred books of other religions, which in actual fact direct and nourish the existence of their followers, receive from the mystery of Christ the elements of goodness and grace which they contain" (DI 8). It acknowledges the work of Jesus and the Holy Spirit in the work of salvation. "In contemporary theological reflection there often emerges an approach to Jesus of Nazareth that considers him a particular, finite, historical figure, who reveals the divine not in an exclusive way, but in a way complementary with other revelatory and salvific figures. The Infinite, the Absolute, the Ultimate Mystery of God would thus manifest itself to humanity in many ways and in many historical figures: Jesus of Nazareth would be one of these. More concretely, for some, Jesus would be one of the many faces which the Logos has assumed in the course of time to communicate with humanity in a salvific way." (DI 9).

According to the Christian faith the divinity and unicity of the mediatory role of Christ are non-negotiables. However, this does not mean that we cannot be enriched by the other religions and their founders. We should be the first to recognize all that is good in them. "...an economy of the eternal Word that is valid also outside the Church and is unrelated to her, in addition to an economy of the incarnate Word. The first would have a greater universal value than the second, which is limited to Christians..." (DI 9).

2. Tasks Before Indian Theologians

The theologians are called to listen to *Dominus Iesus*. In the practice of dialogue between the Christian faith and other religious traditions, as well as in seeking to understand its theoretical basis more deeply, new questions arise that need to be addressed through pursuing new paths of research, advancing proposals, and suggesting ways of acting that call for attentive discernment. Without exaggeration we can say that religious pluralism is a great challenge facing the Church today in our country. We cannot deny the fact that Christianity originated as minority movement and the early church is the classical example of it. Keeping this point in mind it is clear that the document, however, clearly admits that other religions can cooperate with the one universal mediation of Christ for salvation and thus they can participate in this one mediation of Christ (DI 14). In this sense *Gaudium et Spes* holds: "... theology today, in its reflection on the existence of other religious experiences and on their meaning in God's salvific plan, is invited to explore if and in what way the historical figures and positive elements of these religions may fall within the divine plan of salvation" (GS 22). The second important point in connection with religious pluralism is the operative presence of the Holy Spirit in cultures and religions and God's saving grace in view of his universal salvific will and participated mediation in the process of salvation.

This is the task for Indian theologians since we in India are surrounded by people of other religions and cultures. The Indian Theologians have carried on their thinking on interreligious dialogue, inculturation and the value of Indian religions and people.

1. A lived experience of the Christian community as a miniscule minority encountering religious fervour and the sincerity and genuine goodness of the people have a healthy influence on Indian theological pursuit. 2. The message from all these experiences, however, is that with regard to the religions of the others, we have to guard against an overtly negative description because people are too sensitive and defensive.

I think it is the task of Indian theologians to ensure a more acceptable and less provocative communication of the Christocentric ecclesial faith. Such a mode of communication is the greater burden and challenge laid upon us in the light of *Dominus Iesu*. As we keep the memory of Jesus alive, we keep his ongoing presence. Jesus always thought of the Father and his needy brothers and sisters. He is inviting us to go beyond us to give priority to the other.

4

Jesus as the Man for Others

Rt Rev Valerian D'Souza
Bishop (Emeritus), Diocese of Poona

Abstract: In this article, the Bishop (Emeritus) of Poona, traces Jesus as the man for others. Jesus exhorts us: "Whatever you do to the least of my brethren you do unto me " (Mt 25:40). Here my love for Jesus should be the measure of my love for others. Thus Jesus demands what seems impossible. "Love one another as I have loved you " (Jn 13:34). The yardstick now is the love Jesus has for us. Our love is too small in order for us to love as Jesus loved us. Jesus does not ask the impossible from us. We can fulfil this commandment only to the extent that we open ourselves to the love Jesus is waiting to pour into our hearts. Christianity means befriending the other, just as Jesus was a man for others.

Keywords: Other, Jesus, Christian love, Man for others, Embracing the unknown.

Jesus is called "A Man for Others". It is evident from his life. He is the Son of the Father and truly became man for the salvation of humankind. He loved, lived and he died for others. Before his death he gave us the commandment of love. The Bible gives us the commandment of love in three stages: love of self, love of others and love of God.

1. Love for the Other and Befriending the Other

So the Bible says clearly: "Love your neighbor as you love yourself' (Lev 19:18, Mt 19:19). The golden rule is, "Do to others as you would have them do to you (Lk 6:31). The love you have for yourself should be the criterion of the love you expect from others. As a man for others, Jesus raised the bar higher. "Whatever you do to the least of my brethren you do unto me" (Mt 25:40). Here my love for Jesus should be the measure of my love for others. Finally Jesus demanded what seems impossible. "Love one another as I have loved you" (Jn 13:34). The yardstick now is the love Jesus has for us. Our love is too small in order for us to love as Jesus loved us. Jesus does not ask the impossible from us. We can fulfil this commandment only to the extent that we open ourselves to the love Jesus is waiting to pour into our hearts. Thus Jesus is a man for others and Christianity means befriending the other.

An illustration may help here. Dr. E. Stanley Jones, an American missionary in India, who knew Mahatma Gandhi well once asked him, "How can we make Christianity naturalized in India, not a foreign thing, identified with a foreign government and a foreign people, but a part of the natural life in India and contributing its power to India' uplift ?" Gandhiji's response showed he was way ahead of his times. "First, I would suggest that all Christians, missionaries begin to live more like Jesus Christ. Second, practise it without adulterating it or toning it down. Third, emphasize love and make it your working force, for love in central in Christianity. Fourth, study the non-Christian religions more sympathetically to find the good that is within them, in order to have a more sympathetic approach to people." Thus Gandhi expected from Christians nothing but love of the other and befriending the other.

2. Dialoguing with Others

Befriending the other is based on Jesus' command to love. The opposite of love is not hate, but selfishness. Love is outward oriented. "What can I do for you? How can I make you happy? How can I serve you?" The opposite is selfishness. "What can you do for me? How can you make me happy? How can you serve me?" Jesus thought not of himself but only of others. It is salutary for those exercising authority to examine themselves whether they are befriending the other or being selfish. "The Son of man came not to be served but to serve and give his life as a ransom for many" (Mk 10:45).

Such a befriending implies reaching out and encountering the others. Jesus also commissioned his disciples to go out and make disciples of all nations. (Mt.28:19). "The Church was sent by Christ to reveal and communicate the love of God to all peoples and nations" (Vat II, ad gentes,10). It is not the Church as a whole but every disciple who has the duty to evangelize, to bring the Good News of The Father's love and forgiveness, and our redemption through Jesus, to others. It is a great joy to have Jesus but a still greater joy to give Jesus to others. The typical illustration is Mother Mary, who did not keep Jesus to herself but gave him to the whole world.

Such spreading of the Gospel to others presupposes genuine dialogue. The Good News has to be spread by good methods and not by arrogance, force or denigrating other religions . In his very first encyclical Bl Pope Paul VI spoke on how the Church must carry out its mission in the contemporary world and spoke of dialogue. (*Ecclesiam Suam*, 65). Dialogue does not mean one-way traffic, the donor model. "I have something you don't have. Listen to me". But it means being open to what the other has to say and being ready to be enriched by the other. "By dialogue we let God be present in our midst, for as we open ourselves to one another, we open ourselves to God" (St. John Paul II in Chennai, 5th February 1986). For true dialogue, love of the other, including befriending the other, is indispensable.

From all this we may hold that to be a true disciple of Jesus and to carry on his mission every individual in the Church must imitate him and live for others. This calls for an openness to the unknown.

3. Openness to the Unknown

Unfortunately today, instead of imitating Jesus, we tend to seek comfort and security. Security for the most people lies in the maintenance mode. The unknown can cause apprehension but can also be a challenge. The unknown is present all through the Bible. Abraham, Joseph and Moses are typical cases. Abraham dared to go to the unknown land and believed in the unknown promise of God. Joseph believed in God, even when he was sold and imprisoned. Moses could only gaze at the promised land, which remained elusive to him. Further, Mary's question to the angel and conversion of Paul are illustrations of such openness to the unknown.

Further, we may say that for the religious believers, faith is the solution to the unknown. It is a leap in the dark. We may not know the future, but we know who holds the future. God is with us and he is in full control of our lives. Precisely therein lies our openness to the unknown and to the other. In the same way Jesus as the man for others was open to the unknown.

Accordingly the challenge before us is to be men for others, following Jesus, even in the unknown contexts and cultures. There we need to encounter others warmly, dialogue with them genuinely and discern together properly.

Conclusion

Jesus was truly a man for others. He challenges us his followers to encounter others and befriend them. This may call for prophetic commitment that may cost us very much.

Thus, when we, following Jesus, become men and women for others, we need to be courageous enough to proclaim the message of life and to be ready to suffer, if needed!

5

Evangelization as Befriending and Building Relationships

Rt Rev George Palliparambil, SDB
Bishop of Miao, Arunachal Pradesh

Abstract: In today's world, relationships in every aspect is collapsing. It is being measured in terms of money and production. The bold words of Pope Francis "Ours is a battered church. It is a church in a battlefield" assumes great importance and throws a great challenge to the whole church and to the entire human society. It is in the battlefield and when we are wounded and battered that even the helpless enemy becomes a friend and people begin to care for each other. That is the beginning of true evangelisation, where we begin to reach out to others and build bridges.

Keywords: Relationship, Befriending the other, Pope Francis, Respect for poor, Dignity of labour.

The most often heard and said words today are "I have no time," "I am busy, I shall get back to you". This applies to most people in every part of the world, in every walk of life. The race for success, the zest for excellence, the rush to outshine others and the cut throat competition that envelopes life in general, place people on a nonstop run. Parents have no time for children; husbands and wives have no time for each other, children have no time for parents and for their siblings. Priests and religious, men and women chose to minister to others too have been affected by this. They have no time for prayer, for the Word of God, for the community activities but are affected by the standards set by the contemporary society. No one has the time to stop by and look at the wounded, the fallen, the defeated, the weak and the needy.

A father of three, recently was sharing with me his painful experience where the children look up at him only when they need money. In other words, to many children the parents have become a portable ATM machine. Unfortunately, they were not made to realize that ATM will give money only if it is deposited earlier in the account! Relationships in every aspect is collapsing, it is being measured in terms of money and production. The bold words of Pope Francis "Ours is a battered church. It is a church in a battlefield" assumes great importance and throws a great challenge to the whole church and to the entire human society. It is in the battlefield and when we are wounded and battered that even the helpless enemy becomes a friend and people begin to care for each other.

Despite all that Jesus taught about His mission and the mission He left to us of being witnesses in words and deeds, and the renewed calls from the church to reach out to the people. Sadly, there are some in the church who confuse others through their opinions. They teach that we need not proclaim the Good News, we should not disturb others and so on. Even if many share such opinions, the Lord's teachings cannot be altered. They are eternal. They are for all times and places, for all races and nations.

We call the Words of Jesus, the Good News. Every person has a right for the Good News. In this age where there is so much confusion, chaos, fear and exploitation, the need for the Good News is more than ever before. The daily reports that we get of the world matters convey to us more frightening, bad, shocking news than good news. Wars, communal clashes, missing planes, planes and trains blown up, rape, murder, robbery, bribery, unjust punishments, manipulated judicial judgements etc. haunt us making us wonder whether humanity itself has been replaced by animality! These are but symptoms of a sick society. The absence of love, care, concern and willingness to share is the sickness. The society does not need preachers who are mere poachers feeding on the poor people, it does not need apothecary who have a remedy for everything but men and women who like the good Samaritan in the gospel, like Veronica who broke lines and wiped the face of the condemned Jesus and Mother Theresa in our own times can get down to the wounded, the aged, the orphan, the leper and all the marginalised and tell them not in words, but through courageous actions "I love you". This language of relationship is understood by all even the most insensitive. In their teachings the three recent Popes tell us very clearly that "we cannot give what we do not have".

By Evangelization I mean something much broader than the *Mission ad gentes* and the new evangelization. I feel, in many cases we have stooped far below in our relationships than the pagans or barbarians of old. Something worse than paganism and barbarianism has gripped our communities. While strongly believing in both the *Mission ad gentes* and the new evangelization, I feel that we need to work on re-establishing the snapped ties.

1. In the Beginning

The Book of Genesis shows us an enviable life situation. Gen. 2: 15-25 presents a picture of perfect relationship. God, Man, woman and nature. God makes man in His own image, finds him happy with nature and everything in nature. But the loneliness he experiences impresses God and He provides man with the perfect companion, whom he welcomes saying "this at last is bone of my bone and flesh of my flesh"! the book adds, "for this reason man leaves his Father and mother and becomes one with his wife". The Lord walks in the garden in the cool of the evenings and man and woman who are such a part of nature and experiencing such unbroken relationship with each other that even nakedness does not embarrass them.

When we talk about the establishment of God's kingdom, evangelization etc., what else can we mean than to establish this unbroken relationship between human beings, human beings and the whole of nature and all these leading to God, who is able to freely mingle with them? Just as Eve wanted to be wiser than God and live better than Him, fell to the vileness of the evil one, the desire to excel, to outdo others, outshine others, to have more degrees and possessions and positions blind most of us we fall victims to fanciful theories and pernicious invitations which may appeal to us in moments of thoughtless and in the absence of serious reflection. Once this begins, we make every effort to hide from God, from each other and from the society itself. We withdraw, mental, spiritual and physical ailments begin to haunt us and we push ourselves down into the valley of death from where a return is possible only if we become humble enough to admit our mistake and to restore broken relationships. Like our ancestor, most of us like that courage and humility and we indulge in a blame game where every one around, everything in nature and God himself gets blamed.

It is true that with the advancement of psychology and sciences, a lot of people are helped and a lot of healing process has been initiated and accomplished. At the same time, it is frustrating to hear many people finding flawed shelter under these very instruments of help. Many people these days fail to admit their sins and failures and weaknesses. They always find excuse for gross blunders and violations of natural laws of life and relationships and blame it on parents, on the circumstances when they were conceived, when they were in their mother's womb, their childhood and so on. Lack of responsibility should not be tagged as 'force of circumstances'! Jesus, in a number of instances made it very clear to His listeners that we should not blame our ancestry but accept our own failures and reconnect ourselves with God and people.

Every page of the Old Testament presents us with instances of broken relationships and how they are restored. The history of Israel is one of a chain of such events. In other words, the breaking of relationships is not the issue but the refusal and failure to re-establish and reconnect. If every man and woman is humble and bold enough to say a bold "mea culpa" and do one's part, there will be no more broken families, fragmented societies, misguided youth who pose great threats to families, lives and property. If the right relationship is established in society through the power of the Lord not through human manipulations, girls and women will be safe on our streets, the deserving will find jobs and helps, as the Prophet Isiah said, "the lion and the kid will lie down together".

2. In His Days

Jesus in His public ministry taught and worked a lot of miracles. In all these, never for once did he try to promote himself or to go against the society or its system. He used the harshest words possible against the rich and the powerful but never a word against the sick, the sinner and those marginalised by the society. He was bold enough to dine at the house of Levi and Zaccheus and say out loud "It is the sick who need the doctor not those who are well" and "I have come to call sinners". He was bold enough to challenge those who brought the woman caught in adultery and to stand in her defence. He was not afraid to be seen alone with the Samaritan woman at the well and make the public declaration of the water of life. Much against all calculations, the Samaritan woman sees the new way and the entire village accept him not because she told them but they experienced his presence. A new bridge is built, a new community is won.

The marginalised had a special place in Jesus ministry. The woman who was healed of bleeding who was excluded from the society, Jesus making a hero out of the Samaritan who came to thank him from the ten lepers who were healed (Lk 17: 11-19), the transformation that came in the woman who was a sinner (Lk 7:36-50), the assurance to the woman who anointed his feet in the house Simon the Pharisee were all loud and clear points of the new manifesto he was presenting. "Go into the whole world ..." (Mk 16:15), Jesus still challenges us. But our lack of availability, our lack of preparedness, our fear, our shyness and above all our not wanting to be seen as disciples lead us to our hesitations, our new theories, our taking shelter behind the various explanations against proclamation and evangelization leave us lethargic, what the Book of Revelation calls "neither hot nor cold" (Rev 3:16).

3. The Disciples

We live in an age of elections, choices, selections, going for the best, setting goals and looking for the star. It is against this background, we find Jesus leaving his church to a bunch of fishermen, who today form one of the lowest strata of the human society especially in India. Economically and in many other aspects they are poor and unprepared for leadership. Jesus did not conduct a selection process or an election process. He just appointed Peter to lead the church. He called Saul of Tarsus the greatest enemy of the new way to be a greater missionary than even Peter. He inspired the doubting Thomas to travel the farthest all the way carrying his message.

Interestingly neither Peter nor Paul, neither Stephen nor any of the early apostles and church members were taught theology, philosophy, logic, psychology or any of the allied subjects. They had never heard of software and hardware, they had no classes in management, they had never been to forty days retreats and one year courses, but had just attended a few talks but accompanied and lived with Jesus on his mission. That prepared them for their task. They had no fear, no shyness, no hesitation. They were able to stand up and ask the highest authorities of their days; "can we stop telling what we have seen and heard?" "It is not through our power but by the power of His name that this blind man stands before you healed". They had seen and heard and the Lord and his message had become a part of their lives. No wonder Paul could say "woe to me if I do not preach the Gospel". In his eternal ode to love in Corinthians he makes it clear that love surpasses all (1 Cor 13).

Coming down to the days after the apostolic days, we find convinced men and women who dared to stand for Jesus and establish the new order. Francis of Assisi was called to rebuild the church from the level of spiritual decadence it had fallen into. His was an immediate yes and embracing a life against the expectations even of his family. Ignatius Loyola and a host of others heard the inner call and had the emphatic answer YES. Like Peter and Paul, they have changed the world. In a time not very different from ours, a world turned topsy-turvy by the industrial revolution and the moral degradation and poverty which resulted from it, the number of families and youth that it adversely affected, a young Priest from Turin, who could have been bitter all his life because of the hostile situation he grew in, boldly came onto the streets, literally swimming against the current and became the father of the youth on the streets. Don Bosco who wanted to be a missionary in some distant land gave more missionaries to the church than he could ever have dreamt of. I am sure that the even the lowliest follower of Francis, Ignatius or Don Bosco and all the great saints who made a mark on the church are more qualified than them today. Leaving the so-called Christian countries aside, in a multi religious country like India, the alumni organizations of these groups, consisting mainly of non-Christians have been so active and have contributed a lot to building a better society by being willing to reach out to the needy. This was possible only because, their educators built up a healthy rapport with them and inspired them. In spite of the mightier, better equipped and numerous institutions, the efficacy of these in transforming lives is obviously much less because of the lack of personal contact and inspiring presence among them by religiously motivated leaders among them. As I move around and meet some of the senior leaders in Arunachal Pradesh, who decades ago studied in Don Bosco School Dibrugarh, still speak about a certain Fr. Visentin. I have not known him. But they say, he never taught them in school, he was the Parish Priest always moving around in the villages but whenever he was back home, he spent a lot of time with the boys, playing with them, chatting with them and listening to them. The relationship he had established with them left indelible impressions on their minds.

To put all these into a nutshell, the Apostles never missed a chance to relate with people of all kinds so that their Lord would be known. Philip did not hesitate to go up to the Ethiopian's chariot and enter into a conversation. He could have left that stranger from a foreign land to himself. Paul never missed an opportunity to get in touch with new people, new groups, venturing even into the areopagus or public spaces.

4. In Our Own Days

Whatever be the conclusions drawn, the whole world is puzzled at the disappearance of the ill fated M 370, the Malaysian flight with full passengers, all because it had lost its connectivity. Hardly any one stops to think of the tragedies that take place daily on earth just because of the absence of proper connectivity. Connection to God, to nature, to family, and in other innumerable ways! In his Laudato Si and through his call for "the care for creation" Pope Francis places the need for the connection at the centre of modern social, economic and ecclesiastical life.

St. John Paul II reached out to every land and nation. His was not a campaign but missionary journeys. The world youth days, mission congresses, reaching out to the poor and children without being shy or afraid, endeared him to the world. The church began to have a less worn out face. The charm that Pope Francis has brought to the world and the acceptance he has gained in the world is a clear proof that our world of broken relationships and broken lives is eager for repairs. Only the love and active presence of the Lord can make this happen. Only a deep love springing from the heart and inspired by the Lord can make us reach out to the others.

Our societies which were deeply family oriented have sadly begun to loose that characteristic. Our tribal societies that were very much community based have unfortunately become fragmented. Exploitation of all kinds abound in all the settings of life. In societies where orphans and uncared for old people were unheard of, these abound today. In communities where suicide was not known, it has become a common event. Places where houses had no doors have to have iron gates today. It is not an enemy from outside who have brought these evils into our midst, but our growing selfishness, our forgetfulness of God leading to ignoring human beings and abandoning relationships preferring gain or profit over them leads to these tragedies. Instead of multiplying counselling centres, speciality facilities and superstructures, it is time that we all embark on a journey along with Pope Francis to evangelise the world. It is not to preach but to live. It is not to give but share. It is not about showing the way but walking the way. We are not expected to give explanations or excuses, we are not called upon to give scientific and psychological solutions but prayer from the heart, that can give meaning to every situation both tragic and joyful.

Like Jesus, we need to be inventive enough to make every interaction of ours catechetical. The interactions of Jesus never sounded jarring to his listeners to viewers but appealed to the core of their heart. At the tomb of Lazarus he communicated the most important teaching of all "I am the resurrection and the life........" Though he incurred the wrath of the Jewish authorities, all those who were present and many who heard of it became believers. The billions we spend on education, academic, technical, medical and to help the poor, the thousands of man hours that we spend on courses and events produce results that are no where in proportion to the effort and expense. Is it because the listeners are bad? Though not easy to admit, the only reason we can cite is that unlike Jesus who was on His father's mission, we are not on a mission but on duty.

5. Reaching Out

Reaching out to the people in their own setting has been the greatest success of mission. In the Acts of the Apostles we hear of the people being scattered by the persecution. It helped the spread of the faith. They shared not their sad story to evoke pity in the listeners but shared the story of Jesus. They did not go as defeated people but as people who were scattered with a mission and a people whom the Lord would never fail.

When the Lord said, "I must go to the other villages too" or "there are other sheep that do not yet belong to the fold," it was not just curiosity that he manifested but the zeal for his father and the urge to fulfil the mission he came to accomplish. His going to the houses of Peter's mother in law, Levi, Zaccheus and the Samaritan village. The numerous visits he made always ended up with the people coming to the Father. If we put all the miles that the church men and women fly today, if we count all the miles that they drive, if we calculate all the money that they spent on fuel and the precious hours that they spent in social gatherings and community building exercises, the figures will be staggering and ruthlessly scandalous when we look at the visits of Jesus, of the Apostles and of the missionaries of yester years. The standards we set in our institutions under the name of preparing people for life, all done in the name of the carpenter from Nazareth and the fisherman from Galilee whom the Lord entrusted with the "keys of the kingdom" and the power "to bind and loose on earth"...is often awe inspiring. It makes us wonder often if the boy Jesus were to seek admission in any of our Catholic schools today, he would get an admission. Joseph was the migrant worker, with no permanent address, phone number or email to give, Mary was a village girl and Jesus had never been to a play house or kindergarten. In the interview of the student and the parents both would be disqualified! How many Joseph's and Jesus's we must be turning away each year!

The first question asked by our forefathers was "am I my brother's keeper"? When the Lord chided and questioned Adam and Eve, they only had excuses but no questions. For Cain, who initiated envy and murder, there was no answer but a counter question. Is this enveloping our minds and lives today? Like Cain, is our brother, sister and neighbour a threat to us, an obstacle on our path of self aggrandizement and self-promotion?

I would like to conclude in the words of Archbishop Dom Helder Camara of Olinda and Recife in North East Brazil who through his talks and interventions created a slot for the church in the third world at Vatican II and let the idea of the church of the poor develop. "There is no need to talk, thinking is enough. During my vigil I try to recover unity with Christ. And with him I relive the meetings of the past day. I think for instance, about the mother who told me about the problems she has with her husband, with her children, and how hard she finds it to feed them. And, through this very real mother whom I know by name, I think about all the mothers throughout the world throughout the ages: the poor ones, the rich ones, the happy ones, the unhappy ones. Or I think about the man I saw working in the street, emptying dustbins. I had caught his eye. He didn't dare offer me his hand. I virtually had to force him: Work isn't what soils our hands, friend. No hand was ever soiled by work. Self-centeredness is what spoils them. This man, Francisco or Antonio as he may be, reminds me of working men throughout the world throughout the ages. Then I say to Christ our brother, 'Lord, two thousand years after your death injustices are growing worse and worse. Reviewing the day like this, I find time passes very quickly".

6

Challenge to Discover Christ *within* Cultures

Jacob Parappally, MSFS

Professor of Systematic Theology, Tejas Vidya Peetha, Bangalore

Abstract: We need to discover Jesus Christ in the heart of human cultures. Though distinct from the reality of culture, Christ is not separate from it. Our contention is that Jesus Christ is not exclusively *above, against* or *of* the cultures. He is not *a paradox* in relation to cultures or a *transformer of the cultures* in the strict sense. He is *within* the cultures. No one can separate authentic human culture from him. So the relationship of Christ and culture is neither dualistic nor paradoxical. It is non-dualistic in the sense that Christ cannot be separated from culture even though it cannot be identified with him. Everything authentic in culture is Christic. Whatever is negative and dehumanizing, whether systems or structures of injustice, oppression and dehumanization whether it is social, religious, or political, is not authentically cultural. With him culture is already transformed. Therefore, the mission of those who believe in him is to discover the transformation he brought about in the culture by his becoming a part of it and to actualize it so that both humans and their world will become what they are called to become and find their destiny.

Keywords: Jesus Christ, Culture, Plurality, Incarnation, Non-dualistic Relationship, Docetism, Transformation.

Introduction

What has Christ to do with cultures? This was a question raised in a seminar on inculturation by a participant. Though the question evoked a mixed reaction among the rest of the participants, the questioner was earnest in raising such a question. Obviously, some thought it was a naïve question. However, the questioner explained that whatever, he believed about Christ had nothing to do with culture. Jesus Christ was above all cultures. God chose to be born in history and so it had to be in one culture and among a particular group of people with their own traditions, social structures, ethnicity, religious belief-systems, attitudes, behaviour, life-style, food habits, and a way of social relationships and interactions. Of course, Jesus was born in a culture as all of us are. There is nothing more or nothing less to it. Each culture is unique and we need not bother about such trivial matters. If at all anything is needed, it is to liberate Jesus from the trapping of the Jewish culture so that he can remain universal as the Son of God. In fact, the dogmas and doctrines about him have done so. We need not inculturate him in any culture and relativise him. These were the main points of the explanation given by the one who thought that it is a futile exercise to discuss about Christ's relation to cultures. However, what the questioner himself failed to recognize was that even the term 'Christ' itself is a religio-cultural construct.

In this paper an attempt is made to 'see' Jesus Christ as a part of human culture whatever be its diversity of expressions, distinct from the reality of culture but not separate from it. Culture makes the inner world and world-view of a person in which s/he lives and finds her or his identity in the family, in the society with a language that helps the relationship with others through a system of symbols. Our contention is that Jesus Christ is not exclusively *above, against* or *of* the cultures. He is not *a paradox* in relation to cultures or a *transformer of the cultures* in the strict sense. He is *within* the cultures. No one can separate authentic human culture from him. With him culture is already transformed. Therefore, the mission of those who believe in him is to discover the transformation he brought about in the culture by his becoming a part of it and to actualize it so that both humans and their world will become what they are called to become and find their destiny.

1. Christ's Relation to Cultures

In his book, Christ *and Culture,* H. Richard Niebuhr attempted to explain the relationship with Christ and Culture from the perspective of a Lutheran Theologian. In his approach he sees Christ in a double relationship. In his vertical relationship, Christ is in relation with his Father and his whole life is oriented towards him. Christ is primarily theocentric. At the same time in his horizontal relationship he is also anthropocentric. It is in this horizontal dimension of his relationship that culture plays a crucial role. There is not much difference between culture and 'the world' mentioned in the New Testament. So, what would be his relationship with cultures? Niebuhr suggests five ways of looking at the relationship between Christ and culture that are found in history. They are not mutually exclusive. In a way they are complimentary.

a. Christ against Culture

In its radical form the followers of this understanding of relationship between Christ and culture would argue that Christians should make a choice between Christ or culture. According to them both are incompatible. The culture stands for everything that is anti-Christ and anti-Christian. Therefore, there should not be any compromise with the culture one lives in. Those who subscribe to this view would find a basis for their argument in some passages in the NT. In the First Letter of John, the followers of Christ are exhorted to shun this world of lies and lust, murder and theft and all kinds of evil (I Jh 2:8-9, 11, 15,17; 3:8-11; 5: 4-5, 19). This negative attitude to towards everything in culture denies the possibility of anything good in culture. It is possible that those who see Christ as against culture have a disincarnated Christ in their faith-system and they find that commitment to him means that it is necessary to disengage oneself from culture. Such an understanding in the final analysis is self-contradictory because culture is the way one is and thinks. One cannot dissociate even the most sublime faith in God from culture. What one can hold is to negate the values and attitudes that seem to be a part of the culture and would not be seen as compatible with one's belief in God revealed through Jesus Christ in a particular culture.

Christ *against* culture is the paradigm of radical following by desert fathers, ascetics and radical monastic orders. Even here an extreme denial of genuine culture is not envisaged. The allurements of the world and world as a principle opposed to God would be the world that is ungodly and not the world that manifests the presence of God. So too a culture that does not have any relation to the transcendence and has no relation to those values beyond the transitory and ephemeral would be the culture that is often seen as opposed to faith in Christ. Tertullian was the first one to develop a negative idea about culture in his books on *Apology* and on *Idolatry*. In Protestantism, there are sectarian groups like Mennonites and Quakers who developed a very negative attitude towards culture. They see that faith in Christ is incompatible with recognizing culture as a value.

The *countercultural movements* are often seen as falling into this paradigm of relationship between Christ and culture. But in fact, countercultural attitudes and movements do not fall into this category. It is not against culture as such but against a perversion of culture that creates oppressive structures and systems, dehumanizes humans and alienates humans from their authentic selves. Counter-culture is also culture albeit a culture opposed to the perversion of culture.

In the missionary enterprises of colonial time, the Asian religions and cultures were seen as opposed to Christian culture and values. Therefore, they were seen as opposed to Christ. Christ *against* culture model was the force behind the legendary missionary zeal of hundreds of missionaries from the West. Here again Christ was seen as one who is against particular cultures which were considered as steeped in idolatry, superstition, ungodliness and under the power of Satan and not culture per se. Therefore, Christ *against* culture is an ambivalent model of relationship between Christ and cultures. On the one hand it cannot be against culture as such while it uses everything positive in the culture to articulate its own position and on the other hand it cannot deny the fact that God has become human in a culture and transformed it to be something different from what it was. At best it can be the affirmation of the dominion of Christ over everything and a rejection of everything in culture that is not Christic.

b. The Christ of Culture

This model of relationship between Christ and culture is seen as the opposite of Christ-against- culture. Christ is understood as the fulfillment of culture and so there is no conflict between Christ and culture. Culture can be interpreted through Christ and Christ can be interpreted through culture. This approach is often seen as accomodationism as the attempt here is to reconcile Christianity with divergent cultures and best in all cultures. In the early Church the Judaizers, the Gnostics and the Hellenists attempted to interpret Christ from their particular cultures and religious and philosophical perspectives.[1] Neibuhr sees in this model of relationship between Christ and culture an error equal to and opposite of the first position. In this understanding of concentration on the world Christ's relationship with the world is emphasized at the cost of Christ's transcendental or vertical relationship. Without emphasis on grace or after-life religion degenerates into legalistic 'self-reliant humanism" and idolatrous worship of humans and denigration of God.[2] This is considered by Lutheran theology as an accommodation of the world by which both the horizontal relationship of humans with the world as well as the vertical relationship with God is distorted.

There are many who oppose this model of relationship between Christ and culture. They find that it would compromise with the Lordship of Christ when he is so much part of the culture. If Christ is of culture, then how would one explain the presence of sin, oppression, injustice, discrimination and all kinds of evil in all cultures? Therefore, this model would not be the right relation of Christ to culture. However, those who would hold the view "Christ of culture" find it the best way to express the right relationship of humans among themselves as well as the kingdom of God realized in the right relationship among humans as the children of God in this world. In the context of Asia the Christ of religions cannot be a relevant model of relationship between Christ and culture according to Aloysius Pieris.[3] Christ of the culture is based on the fact that God became human and entered into human culture and became very much a part of it.

c. Christ above Culture

This model of relationship between Christ and culture too is based on his incarnation. Jesus Christ is both human and divine. As a human he is *of* the culture but as God he is *above* culture. The fact that Christ was God overtakes the human dimension of Christ and both cannot be equated. The emphasis is on the divine dimension of Christ. Therefore, though Christ is very much a part of the culture he is infinitely above culture. Justin, the Martyr and Clement of Alexandria could be considered the patristic representatives of this model. In the middle ages Thomas Aquinas and the Catholic theological tradition in general held this view of Christ's relation to culture.[4] This approach seems to synthesize the various opposing approaches. It is based on the incarnation of God in a particular culture. However, if this culture is elevated to a position of Christian culture and if it is made universal it can lead to a cultural hegemony and it can stand against or even suppression of other cultures. In fact, there are many tragic instances of such approach to diverse cultures in history.

One of the other dangers of this approach is that it does not take the grace-filled world which was created and re-created by the incarnation of the Word seriously though it claims to do so. It is the consequence of a faith affirmation in Christ bordering on doceticism. Throughout the history of Christological development what the Church wanted to overcome was the heresy of docetics that Christ is not human but only appears to be so. As an offshoot of Gnosticism with its dualistic philosophy that matter is evil and spirit is good, true incarnation was thought to be impossible. So while Jesus Christ is truly divine he cannot be truly human. Ignatius of Antioch and Irenaeus fought such heresy and later in the council of Chalcedon (CE 451) affirmed the Church's faith that Jesus Christ is truly God and truly human. However, even today it is difficult for many Christians to believe that Jesus was truly human like anyone of them. It is easy to believe that he is God. In this context, Christ *above* culture would appear to many as Christ has nothing to do with any culture. Such an image of Christ, disengaged from any culture make him universal and people of any culture could relate with him as the transcendent God. So the fears expressed by those who are not in favour of this approach that the traditional synthesis achieved by this model does not take into consideration all that is evil and sinful in cultures, become unfounded. Christ can be thought of truly above all cultures. Though it seems to be a synthesis, in effect, in this model Christ has nothing to do with the cultures.

d. Christ and Culture

Beginning with Paul there is a certain dualistic understanding in the relationship between Christ and culture. In fact, in this model it is not a relationship between Christ and culture but how a believer relates herself or himself with Christ and culture. The relationship with Christ is permanent, everlasting and grace-filled while with the world it is temporal, transitory and filled with God's wrath and severity. This relationship is expressed by Paul as our relation to the "earthly tent" and "a building from God, a house not made with hands, eternally in heavens" (2 Cor 5:1-2). Augustine would develop this theme further contrasting the earthly city with the heavenly city or the city of God. In Luther's view there are two kingdoms, namely, the kingdom of God and the kingdom of the world. The first one is of grace and mercy and the second one is of God's wrath and severity. The Christian existence is between these two kingdoms till the end when there would be only one kingdom that is the kingdom of God.

The dualistic understanding of Christ and culture has its consequences for Christian commitment to transform this world. It recognizes the evils in the culture. Sin pervades culture, injustice, dehumanization, discrimination, oppression, exploitation, greed and violence rule cultures and societies. New cultures are created with all kinds of negative values that would further destroy the life of humans and the nature. Still a Christian can live a life without any commitment to this world and take a position of isolating oneself from this world and believe that s/he can remain uncontaminated by this world with the grace of God. Laws, regulations, duties etc., can be understood as necessary evils one has to bear with for a short time. As everything in this world is transitory one need not make any commitment to this world or its destiny.

The dualistic model of relationship between Christ and culture devalues the meaning of God's creation as something good enough that God freely chose it to be a part of God himself through incarnation or hominization. Dualistic attitude to Christ and culture makes Christ as the one who is above, separated and isolated from culture and negates the value of culture as something good and as an inalienable dimension of being human. Any dualism between absolute and relative, infinite and finite, God and world, Christ and culture negates the possibility of God becoming human and thus denies this basic Christian belief.

e. Christ Transforming Culture

This model of relationship between Christ and culture claims to be based on the participation of the Logos in creation as well as in the incarnation. God created everything through his Word and it is the same Word, the Son who became human and redeemed the world. Therefore, the Logos transformed the world (Jn 3:16-18). It is said that in the sacramental vision of John the ordinary things are transformed into symbols that would be instruments of God's presence in this world as in the case of the sacrament of the Eucharist and baptism.[5]

In this model it is admitted that the Word became a part of the world but his function to transform the world would be as if it were from outside of the world. He does not seem to enter into the reality of the world, its cultures and history. Certainly, in this model Christ transforms and re-orients cultures through his sanctifying and redeeming presence. According to Augustine, though originally everything that God created was good, it was vitiated, corrupted, lost and dead by sin. Therefore, Christ heals and renews what was perverted by sin. Since God is at work in creation and history, culture and institutions of culture have a positive value but it needs to be constantly converted to the Kingdom of God.

All these models of Christ's relation to culture emphasize onc or other aspects of this relationship. If they are seen as mutually exclusive it would not do justice to the biblical understanding of God's involvement in our history. Though culture is built on nature, if that nature is viewed completely in a negative light any culture that evolves from the nature of humans will also be something completely perverted and evil. Christ cannot relate with that culture. A very negative anthropology would give only a superficial recognition of even what is good and positive in any culture. But if we take the biblical witness seriously, we can see that culture is an extension of life of humans as humans in the givenness of a particular place with its accumulation of human experiences preserved, transmitted and lived in history. It is the 'world' of humans in which they live, move and have their being in their historical existence. It is through the cultural paradigms they relate with one another and even with the Ultimate Reality whom they call God or by any name, knowing fully well that this Ultimate is beyond name and form. So as humans cannot be separated from the culture in which they are born and have grown, the Word became human also cannot be separated from culture.

2. Christ *within* Cultures

If culture is the sum total of everything that gives meaning to a person's existence in history or if it is broadly described as *a way of life*[6] as Michael Amaladoss expresses it, human beings cannot be separated from it. It is through culture that one finds her/his fundamental identification in relation to a family, to a society, to a language, to an ethnic group, to a religion etc. Though one may be able to make abstractions about human nature, a human person can be thought of only in a net-work of relationships. It is in a conscious and free relationship with other human persons and with the reality of the world and the

Ultimate Source of everything that one finds one's identity as a human person. In a way it is culture that mediates relationship and qualifies relationships. Authentic culture is everything that gives meaning to one's existence as a human person. For a great majority of humans' religion provides a meaning system in which one can discover her/his beginning and end or origin and ultimate destiny. No wonder then, sociologists and anthropologists include religion in their definition of culture. If culture is such an all-encompassing dimension of humans to be human then it must be assumed by the Word that everything authentic and true in it must become Christic.

If what we mean by culture is everything that makes human life to unfold itself as humans intended by God, Christ can never be against, above and paradoxical to culture. Christ is then really *of* culture or *within* the reality of culture. What is authentic in the culture is Christic. It is Christ who is the beginning and end, the alpha and the omega of authentic culture. Humans are the ones who develop culture with the evolution of their self-understanding as humans or pervert it to a dehumanizing one depending on how they use or misuse their freedom. Humans transform culture either for better or for worse. Authentic culture continues to evolve in history at different places and different times according to the self-understanding of humans as humans. Multiculturalism, migration, shared knowledge etc. open up ways of new self-understanding and development of humans and consequently cultures will also develop progressively. Christ is *within* cultures because it is in and through him culture will progress not for its own sake but to make humans to evolve to the "full stature of Christ" as Paul puts it. Humans become "mature, attaining to the whole measure of the fullness of Christ" (Eph 4:13). From the perspective of Christian faith, to become human like Christ is the goal of human existence. It is in authentic culture humans can reach this destiny. So Christ is not only an exemplar for the development of culture but it is Christ's power working through his Spirit that gives dynamism to the evolution of culture as well as the standard to judge the authenticity of a culture.

In this sense, Christ is really of culture. But not in the way Niebuhr and others with a selective understanding of culture perceive it. Christ's presence in the culture should not be seen as related only to a specific culture. This selective application of Christ's presence in the culture of one's choice limiting Christ to that particular culture is to make an idol of Christ. This was the problem of Judaizers or Gnostics. It would also be a problem if Christ is reduced exclusively to be a Brahmin Christ or a Dalit Christ or a Tribal Christ. Christ *within* the culture means that it is Christ who is the inner dimension of everything that is humanizing in every culture but not of anything that is divisive, discriminatory, and exploitative and in fact, dehumanizing in any culture. The specificity and uniqueness of any culture is not to be seen in its opposition to the other cultures but in its capacity to promote the development of humans opening up new vistas for the enhancement of human capacity to become more and more human and its possibility to relate with other cultures.

a. Christ and Culture: Non-dualistic Relationship

If we take incarnation and resurrection of Christ seriously, we have to admit that by God's entering into history and by God's involvement in the movement of the world to its final destiny, Christ has assumed everything that is human except that which negates the unfolding of humans as humans. According to Origen whatever is to be redeemed must be assumed. God assumes human nature and culture. God's relation to human history and culture would be different from what it was before the incarnation. However, God was not far from everything human according to the Fathers of the Church. For Irenaeus God created everything with his two hands, namely, Logos and Pneuma, the Word and the Spirit. God has created everything for perfection and therefore there is an inner dynamism in all humans and the entire creation to reach its God-intended perfection. The Incarnation itself is for the purpose of leading creation to its perfection which will be finally 'recapitulated' by Christ and will be returned to the Father. Athanasius would develop the theology of Logos present in the creation as distinct from creation but not separated from it. "In one sense indeed, He was not far from it before; no part of creation had ever been without Him who, while ever abiding in union with the Father, yet fills all things that are. But now He entered the world in a new way, stooping to our level in His love and Self-revealing to us."[7] Further, he says, "You know how it is when some great king enters a large city and dwells in one of its houses; because of his dwelling in that single house, the whole city is honored, and enemies and robbers cease to molest it. Even so is it with the King of all; He has come into our country and dwelt in one body amidst the many, and in consequence the designs of the enemy against humankind have been foiled and the corruption of death, which formerly held them in its power, has simply ceased to be."8 By incarnation God's relation to the world is revealed as non-dualistic. The Word, though distinct from the world is not separate from the world. As human, the Word assumed everything that makes human as human. Therefore, it is also the assumption of culture which cannot be separated from the reality of being human. Certainly, the cultural dimension of his humanity was expressed in a definite and historical Jewish culture. Culture cannot be separated from its expression. By being a part of the Jewish culture Christ is related to every culture. Being in a "single house" as Athanasius would affirm, Christ affects every house. By being in one culture Christ is present in every culture. He is the heart of every culture that provides the 'world' for every human to relate with everyone and everything in such a way that s/he evolves into an authentic human being.

b. Negation of Culture and Christ

A question can be raised about the presence of evil and sin, ungodliness and inhuman values in every culture. What about the culture of greed, war and violence? How can Christ be related to these so-called cultures of inhumanity and cruelty? How can one justify the perverse presence of discrimination in the name of caste, class, gender, ethnicity etc.? Is it not the absence of Christ one finds in such human attitudes and behaviour? Is it not a naïve understanding of culture to see Christ within the cultures when we look at only what is true, good and beautiful in cultures and ignore the cruel aspects of culture?

It must be admitted that in all cultures there are systems and structures of injustice, oppression and inhumanity. There are humans in cultures who develop attitudes and create systems and structures in order to amass wealth, power and position at the cost of other humans. They would go to any extent of dehumanizing themselves to achieve their evil ends. No culture is free from such persons who become a law unto themselves by alienating themselves from God who is the ultimate source of everything, from their own true selves, from other humans and nature. Everybody and everything become a means for them to exploit to reach their goals. Blinded by their own greed and selfishness they would not be able to see the road to destruction they are treading on and the suffering they cause to God, other humans and the world. Therefore, perverse behaviour of humans by misusing their freedom cannot be considered as culture. In every culture we find such humans who misuse their freedom and negate culture and Christ. The term culture cannot be used for any expression of humans' inhumanity to humans through personal agenda, systems or structures that destroy humans or thwart the innate dynamism of humans to evolve to the fullness of humanity.

c. Discovering Christ within Cultures

The Logos theology of John and the theology of the Cosmic Christ in Paul affirm that the reality of Christ encompasses everything that is human and cosmic. If everything is created in him, through him and for him and everything is glorified through his resurrection, Christ's presence in all cultures through his Spirit needs to be constantly discovered by the believer. Therefore, it must be with reverence one must delve deep into one's own culture as well as enter into the depths of cultures other than one's own. If God has become human in order to reveal what humans are and what they can become according to God's plan for humans, then the humanizing forces of cultures must be discovered and promoted. This is possible only through genuine dialogue among people of different cultures sharing their riches so that the further evolving of humans are made possible through integration of them in their lives.

If anything, authentically human is Christic, discovering the humanizing elements in every culture is, in fact, discovering that dimension of Christ hidden from those who had no previous experience of that particular culture. Thus, authentic culture becomes a means of revelation not only of God's diverse presence but also the possibilities of humans to unfold themselves. The riches of every culture thus reveal the goodness of God that gifted such a variety of gifts through humans for humans to become what they are called to become. Christ has already transformed culture. It is the mission of the disciple to discover the transformation that Christ has brought about through his presence in the culture and proclaim it so that it becomes a challenge to humans to accept it for their transformation as better human beings.

It is only through a contemplative attitude towards cultures one will be able to discover the presence of Christ within the cultures. As humans and their culture are in a non-dualistic relationship, Christ too is in a non-dualistic relationship with cultures. What is authentic in all cultures is a manifestation of his person because there is nothing that is humanizing outside the reality of Christ. Precisely, because of his presence in the culture everything that is dehumanizing and everything that is a perversion of authentic culture must be prophetically denounced. Those structures and systems that dehumanize humans or individual attitudes, behaviour or misuse of power and positions that hinder authentic human relationship need to be opposed with the strength of human spirit for the sake of Christ and culture. In truth, authentic culture would express the presence of Christ and bring people to live in harmony, peace and communion. Thus culture becomes the temple of God. It needs true freedom, openness and an attitude of reverence to discover him in culture and a plurality of its expressions.

Conclusion

A narrow vision of Christ and culture would find both Christ and culture as opposed to each other or Christ above cultures. Culture is permeated by the presence of Christ as everything is created in him and through him and for him. So the relationship of Christ and culture is neither dualistic nor paradoxical. It is non-dualistic in the sense that Christ cannot be separated from culture even though it cannot be identified with him. Everything authentic in culture is Christic. Whatever is negative and dehumanizing, whether systems or structures of injustice, oppression and dehumanization whether it is social, religious, or political, is not authentically cultural. They cannot be considered as elements of culture but as a misuse of freedom by humans who alienate themselves from their ultimate source of life, themselves, others and their world. This has to be prophetically denounced. Christ is *within* the culture and through the dynamic power of his Spirit makes culture as means to cultivate human spirit to move to higher levels of being human and thus become the glory of God. God's plan for humans begun at creation through his Word and further deepened by incarnation and transformed through resurrection becomes expressed in varied ways through all authentic elements of culture. Therefore, authentic culture becomes a sacrament of Christic presence and means of communion among humans.

Notes

1. Benne, Robert. *The Paradoxical Vision: A Public Theology for the Twenty-first Century*. Minneapolis, MN: Fortress Press, 1995, pp. 26-44.
2. Niebuhr, H. Richard. *Christ and Culture*. New York, NY: Harper and Row, 1951. (First Harper Torch Book, 1956.), p.113.
3. Aloysius Pieris, "Towards an Asian Theology of Liberation: Some Religio-Cultural Guidelines," in *Asia's Struggle for Full Humanity,* Virginia Fabella (Ed), Maryknoll, N.Y., Orbis Books, 1980, p. 75.
4. R. P. McBrien, *Catholicism,* London: Geofrey Chapman, 1994, p. 409.
5. Ibid., p. 411.
6. Michael Amaladoss, *Making Harmony: Living in a Pluralist World*, Delhi:ISPCK, 2003, p. 63. See also Michael Amaladoss, *Beyond Inculturation. Can the Many be One?* Delhi, ISPCK, 1998.
7. Athanasius: *The Divine Dilemma and its Solution in the Incarnation,* No.8.
8. *Ibid.*, No.9.

7

Befriending the Other and Another: Trinities and Trilogue

Francis Gonsalves, SJ
Dean, Faculty of Theology, JD, Pune

Abstract: This paper carries the conversations between the 'I-Thou' or 'I-Other' a step further by introducing a 'Third' therein. We randomly use clichés like: "Two is company, three is a crowd." Begging to differ, the author hypothesizes that, "Two is comfort, three is either community or conflict." Beginning with examples of family life and cinema, and acknowledging contributions of thinkers like Homi Bhabha and Martin Buber who've reflected upon 'threeness' or 'thirdness' as hybridity or some Absolute Being, respectively, the paper is more specifically theological. Noting that many of the world's religions have Trinitarian conceptions of the Divine, the paper reflects upon the Christian Trinity—Father, Son, Spirit—as a model of communion and community. With insights from eminent theologians, and also from Pope Francis's insights on "The Trinity and the Relationship between Creatures," in his encyclical entitled '*Laudato Si*'', it strives to show how the Christian Trinity inspires us to comprehend and commune with 'threeness' not only among human beings, but with God-Others-Nature, which 'is' the heart of reality. Finally, it proposes that all peoples of goodwill embark upon a path of 'trilogue'—transcending dialogue, which could be the meeting ground of all those cooperatively working for a better world.

Keywords: I-Thou; Thirdness; Dialogue; Trilogue; God; Trinity; Community.

Introduction: Befriending 'An-other'

Human beings are relational beings. At birth, a baby is the most helpless of creatures who gradually grows into 'being human' in and through its relationships with other human beings. Being-in-relationship shapes our humanity; for, the 'other' is indispensable in building a stable and mature sense of the 'self'.[1] In technical terms, such relationships have been studied as an 'I-Thou' category.[2] Indeed, the study of the dynamics of 'otherness' or 'alterity' in the fields of philosophy, theology, sociology and psychology has led to much theorizing on the complexities of relationship. Moreover, the JD Diamond Jubilee seminar's theme 'Befriending the Other' is yet another instance of delving deeper into the subject.

While accepting that the 'I-Thou' primordial relationship is of great significance, this paper argues for a tridimensional view of reality and discusses its possibilities in the field of theology. In other words, I attempt to take our conversations a step further by introducing a 'third' in the dynamics between the 'I-Thou' or 'I-Other'. The 'third', I hold, engenders situations of cooperation and communion, on the one hand, as well as conflict and crises, on the other. This is best seen in the Christian paradigm of the Triune God, which holds together one-ness and three-ness in perfect harmony. I begin with mundane, everyday ideas of two-ness and three-ness, and then transport the discussion to the transcendental terrain.

1. Negotiating the 'Third' in Everyday Encounters, in the Arts, and Academy

"Two is company, three is a crowd" is a cliché which most people hold to be true. Simply stated, most people think that a relationship of two people—for example, between husband and wife, or two friends or two parties in a contract—ensures smooth functioning. Bring in a third party and there's bound to be some friction or open conflicts, so goes the reasoning. While there is some truth in such logic, an exclusive relationship of two persons need not necessarily be an ideal one in terms of values or ultimate goals which human beings normally strive for. For instance, a person who relates to another in any form of relationship (friendly, contractual, business, spousal, etc.) could be 'befriending the other' simply for selfish, self-seeking and utilitarian purposes rather than for love, selfless giving, sacrifice and in order to ensure the other's growth and welfare. Such relationships can be verified as genuine if it opens out to a so-called 'third'.

Based on the aforementioned reasoning, I hold that: "Two is comfort, but three is either community [if negotiated skillfully] or conflict [if mishandled]." Introduce a 'third' into any twosome, and one is likely to realize whether or not one's other-centeredness and 'befriending' is genuine or not. Let us discuss some instances of this. Take the case of a married couple that enjoys marital bliss for many years. The attention and energy of each spouse is entirely and exclusively directed towards the 'other'. However, the birth of a child could initially be a source of great joy, but could also lead to conflict; because now, besides giving time and attention to each other, the couple must care for the child. There is the possibility of either spouse giving so much of attention to the child so as to neglect the 'other' spouse, leading to resentment and conflict. Or, it could also happen that the husband and wife are so lost in loving each other so as to neglect the child. Seen from anyone's viewpoint—i.e., father or mother or child—it is easier to relate only to just one 'other' rather than to relate to two others at the same time. Indeed, it's not easy to include a 'third'. Yet, it is only when the love of two opens out to a 'third' that true love is tested and 'company' (that can often be self-seeking comfort, at best, or selfish utilitarianism, at worst) blossoms into what I would call 'the first moment of community' with the possibility of either communion (positive) or conflict (negative).

In the fields of drama and cinema, too, we have many instances of the conflict that arises from the proverbial "I-You and s/he" triangular relationship. In Indian cinema—be it in Bollywood, Kollywood or Tollywood—one recurrent theme is the '*Hum-Tuum-Whoh*' [I-You-s/he] when a 'third' enters into a twosome friendship and creates heartache or heartbreak for one or the other of the friends. This 'third' turns what seemed like heaven into hell. Interestingly, Sartre's famous axiom, "Hell is other people" comes from his play 'No Exit' wherein three unknown and unrelated persons are locked together in a room with no possibility of exit or escape.[3] As the play progresses, each one of the three realizes how detestable the company of the 'other' is and how each of them unwittingly becomes 'hell' for the other two: a good example of 'three is conflict'!

We can also think of the theorizing that has been going on in academic circles. For instance, thinkers like Homi K. Bhabha have developed terms like 'Third Space',[4] which refers to a *hybridity*–an 'in-between' that is syncretistic and characterized by negation and silence. This space is that of an apophatic 'undecidability' in the realm of cultural description.[5] Such a position can be reached by a dialectic of thesis, antithesis and synthesis, the third term being a syncretic *hybrid* of the first two. Likewise, the philosopher Martin Buber whose conception of the '*I-Thou*' was extremely influential in existential philosophy reflects upon '*threeness*' or '*thirdness*' in terms of human relationships opening out to a transcendental Third.[6] In all these cases we see that the 'third' has given rise to a new situation which calls for added caution and consideration. Let us now move on to the field of religion and theology.

2. Trinities in Global Religious Consciousness

A phenomenology of religion reveals that many of the world's religions have Trinitarian conceptions of the Divine: (a) Christianity believes that Jesus revealed God as Triune or Trinity; (b) Classical Hinduism has conceptions of *Trimurti* (Brahma-Vishnu-Siva) and *Saccidānanda*; (c) Buddhism understands Buddha as being *Trikāya* (*dharmakāya-nirmanakāya-sambhogakāya*); (d) Zoroastrianism has the trio of Zurvan, the mighty god of time, and his two sons, Ahriman (active force) and Ormazd (passive force) and so on. Furthermore, the Babylonian triad of Anu, Bel and Ea and the Egyptian triad of the Father, Son and Ka-mutef give added credence to the belief that the 'three' is significant as an archetype of divinity or religious consciousness.

Apart from a phenomenology of religions, Carl G. Jung, the founder of analytical psychology hypothesizes that triads are archetypes in the history of religions that provide religious communities pregnant possibilities to discuss divinity. With the help of many examples, he shows how the number 'three' is significant, worldwide, when imaging or conceiving of deity. Without going into details of the many trinities conceived of and worshipped in the world's religions, let us reflect more closely on how we can think of the Christian Trinity as a model or paradigm of communion and community.

3. The Development of Trinitarian Theology for Life in Community

It is not uncommon in Christian circles nowadays to speak about the Holy Trinity—Father, Son, and Spirit—as a 'communion of persons'. Many theologians have been reflecting upon this idea of 'trinitarian communion of persons' in many parts of the world, including India. Theological thinking in this realm is more popularly called 'social trinitarianism'. While the term 'social trinitarianism' is fairly new, the origins of such person/communitarian-oriented theologizing goes far back to the early centuries of Christianity. The earliest proponents of the social analogy were the 4th century Cappadocian Fathers who likened Father, Son and Spirit to three human persons.[7] The social analogy reappeared in a new avatar in the 12th century with Richard of St. Victor's trinitarianism based on interpersonal love. However, the 19th century Russian Orthodox theologian Nikolai Fedorov's (1829-1903) oft-quoted axiom: "The Trinity is our social programme," most clearly sums up the thinking in this sphere.

Today, eminent proponents of social trinitarianism are Joseph A. Bracken,[8] Leonardo Boff,[9] and Jürgen Moltmann,[10] among others. In India, Geevarghese Mar Osthathios initially used the analogy of the nuclear family to explain the Trinity and the consequent demands of establishing a classless society.[11] Though his approach to the Indian situation of inequality and injustice incorporates Marxian insights, the society he envisages is more Gandhian since he sees *sarvodaya* (development of all) as the ideal of classless society.[12] In a later work, Geevarghese develops his trinitarian theology in terms of a 'Sharing God' by using traditional concepts like *koinonia* and *agape*, borrowing from Moltmann and Boff, and incorporating insights from Scripture and Tradition.[13]

Based on my own experiences with the *adivasis* (tribals) of south Gujarat, I earlier attempted to evolve a social paradigm of Trinity by using insights from the tribal worldview.[14] In line with Rahner's "from the economic to the immanent trinity" principle, I argued that doctrine on the Trinity arose and developed not as abstract metaphysical principles about God descending *from above*, but as a process of reflection on communitarian experiences emerging *from below*. The first Christian believers' experiences of calling God *Abba*-Father in prayer, and the power they received from the Holy Spirit, were not only expressed in the creedal confessions of scripture, but also in their ritual and liturgical celebrations now focused upon Jesus Christ. In Jesus' person and life, the early Christian community tangibly experienced the love of Jesus-Father-Spirit, expressed it in word (Jn 3:16; Rom 8:38-39) and emulated it in their everyday living (Acts 2:42-7; 4:32-37). Their focus was on love, service, caring, sharing, sacrifice, solidarity and communion with God and with one another.

Common to early trinitarian confessions is the aspect of their relevance for communion and community life. This new life was possible only through their 'experience of salvation'15 in the Holy Spirit and in Jesus who taught them that God is *Abba*,16 Father—intimate, mother-like, and approachable (Gal 4:4-7; Rom 8:15-16). This relationship of nearness and intimacy animated their own teaching and liturgy (*leitourgia*), as well as their community life (*koinonia*) overflowing into service (*diakonia*). Thus, from earliest times, the trinitarian focus was always soteriological and practical, namely, stressing God's salvation *in practice* of liturgy, sacraments and everyday life, rather than seeking precise articulation in theory or in dogmas.

It is important to note that the trinitarian theology or 'God-talk' that emerged early in the Christian Tradition was developed through analogical thinking and articulated in analogical language;[17] for, "we have no choice whatever but to speak of God in terms derived from our experience of creaturely reality—that is, by analogy."[18] Thus, since the parables, analogies and images that Jesus used for talking about God were drawn from the human person and from the communitarian nature of love. Christ's first disciples and later theologians would speak about God from what they experienced, read and reflected upon the life, love and liberation that Jesus came to bring.[19] Unfortunately, in the later development of trinitarian doctrine, the aspect of love, sharing and true relationship was eclipsed by terms and concepts consonant with the popular philosophies of the times. This often led to aberrations and heresies.

The aberrations and heresies that arose in the Christian Tradition in trinitarian thinking were outcome of steering the trinitarian debate either excessively towards the pole of oneness or towards that of threeness. In the Patristic theology of the East, for instance, the idea prevailed that the one God is God the Father, and that the Son and the Spirit share with him his divine life. Though based on Scripture, this conception led to subordinationist ideas that culminated in the Arian controversy. By contrast, the West conceived of God as the one divine substance comprising Father, Son and Holy Spirit, often losing sight of the distinction and giving rise to modalist tendencies. Consequently, while modalism and monarchianism so stressed the divine unity thereby eclipsing the distinction between the divine persons, subordinationism and tritheism erred by dividing the Godhead into three different beings unequal in rank or entirely separate from each other. One might hold that while the West reflected on the unity, only then to include threeness, the East reversed this: it began with the three different beings (*hypostaseis*) and attempted to understand their unity. Although this East-West typology should not be exaggerated, it prompts us to stay away from theological terminology that arose in bygone contexts, which are very different from those of our day, and to reinterpret the Trinity using the language of person, relationship, community and communion.

4. The Christian Trinity as Triune Being-in-Communion

In countries of the East, and especially in India, although we see a gradual growth of individualism, the family-clan-community holds precedence over the individual. Relationships are given great importance in social life. One's personhood is defined in and shaped by one's relationship with one's family-clan-community. However, there is a difference between saying 'human persons are relational' and 'God is relational'. In the former case, we are referring to the *capacity* or *potentiality* to enter into relationships and thereby to develop 'personality', which is the sum total of the moral, attitudinal and behavioural qualities one imbibes and possesses. Here, the more and better relationships that one '*has*', the more and better are one's chances of actualizing one's personhood into a balanced personality.[20] In this sense, when we speak of anyone being relational, we mean that one *has* relationships or is relational in a secondary sense. But, when we say 'God is relational' and speak of 'person' in God, we assert that being relational is the very *essence* or *nature* of God.[21] Thus, while we *have* relations, God *is* the relations that God has.[22] Or, for God, 'to be' and 'to be in relation' is one and the same thing.

As compared to Western, modern and postmodern societies that foster independence and individualism to a large extent, communities in India that are bound together by relations of interdependence, sharing, caring and community-spirit are more likely to resonate with the image of a God-in-communion. In these communities, while the primacy of the community is stressed over the individual, it does not mean that the individual is unimportant, for there is also respect for the life of all members. This is not exactly so when we speak about the Trinity since, in the Triune God, 'person' and 'community' coincide. This is well expressed by Barry who writes:[23]

> God is perfect community. The three persons are so united with one another that they share everything in common; the only difference between them is their mutual relationships to one another. Hence, in the community that is God there can be no disunity, no separation, and no fear.

The multiplicity of three persons does not in any way imply a division of the divine nature, since the three divine persons coinhere; and, the entirety of divine nature is in each of them.

To conclude our discussion, we can affirm: "God's being is communion"[24] or God is personal *Being-in-Communion*, meaning, God eternally exists as a 'communion of persons'. In other words, God does not exist as some substance or as some abstract principle but as a relationship of persons.[25] Each member of the Trinity "is a person, a distinct person, but scarcely an *individual* or *separate* person. For in the divine life there is no isolation, no insulation, no secretiveness, no fear of being transparent to another."[26] Thus, 'person' becomes a primary ontological category, and the 'being-in-communion' of divine persons becomes a model and a challenge for the being of human community, and for every Christian community, in particular.

5. Pope Francis's Insights into Trinitarian Relationship and Community

One of the world's religious leaders who is immensely influential for his moral integrity, spiritual insights and social teachings is Pope Francis. His recent reflections on: "The Trinity and the Relationship between Creatures," in his Encyclical Letter '*Laudato Si*'' shows us how the Christian Trinity could inspire us to comprehend and commune with 'threeness' not only among human beings, but with God-Others-Nature, which is at the heart of everyone and everything that exists.[27] In other words, Pope Francis takes our discussion deeper by embracing not only all of humankind, but also the whole of God's created universe. He writes:[28]

> The divine Persons are subsistent relations, and the world, created according to the divine model, is a web of relationships. Creatures tend towards God, and in turn it is proper to every living being to tend towards other things, so that throughout the universe we can find any number of constant and secretly interwoven relationships. This leads us not only to marvel at the manifold connections existing among creatures, but also to discover a key to our own fulfilment. The human person grows more, matures more and is sanctified more to the extent that he or she enters

> into relationships, going out from themselves to live in communion with God, with others and with all creatures. In this way, they make their own that trinitarian dynamism which God imprinted in them when they were created. Everything is interconnected, and this invites us to develop a spirituality of that global solidarity which flows from the mystery of the Trinity.

6. Social Trinitarianism Fructifying into Trilogue

Our conceiving of the Christian Trinity as a 'communion of persons' and a model for community building leads us to theologize on what could be practical consequences of such a conception. For purposes of brevity, I merely suggest one: namely, as Christians, we are called and challenged to embark upon a path of '*trilogue*'. Whether in general terms,[29] or as literary form,[30] or in a more technical sense as used in the academy or by the disciplines,[31] 'dialogue' refers to an exchange between two subjects or groups/communities, most commonly identified by the binary *I-Thou*, or *Self-Other*. Even if, at times, more than two persons/parties are involved in this exchange, the 'more-than-two' factor is again either identified as *Thou-Other* or simply as *Plural* or *Many*. In other words, '*Thirdness*', if one might call it that, is not accorded special attention. Barring Bhabha and Buber, whom we mentioned above, and who explain '*thirdspace*' or '*Third*' as *hybridity* or some Absolute, respectively, Henri Lefebvre proposes triadic analysis as an effective way to encounter reality. He writes:[32]

> Triadic analysis distinguishes itself from dual analysis just as much as from banal analysis. It doesn't lead to a *synthesis* in accordance with the Hegelian schema … [it] links three terms that it leaves distinct, without fusing them in a *synthesis* (which would be the third term).

Thus, while the aim of dialogue normally seems to be some Hegelian synthesis or consensus,[33] *trilogue* maintains a *three-one tension* and *always* holds together reality within a *thirdspace*, so to say. Further elaboration from the field of music, might clarify the concept of *trilogue* more.

A 'trilogy' is a combination of *three* dramas, literary works, musical compositions or dance movements *closely related* into a *single* theme. The important words are: (a) three, (b) closely related, and (c) single. One can also think of three *distinct things* like: (a) a piece of wood called 'violin', (b) a length of wire called 'string' and (c) some hairs from a horse's tail drawn into a 'violin bow'. When an accomplished violinist draws the bow over violin strings, the ensuing music is nothing like wood, wire or a horse's tail, but while the audience enjoys the melodious music (One), it can point out where the violin's wood is, what the string does, and how a horse's tail makes good bows (Three). Note that there is *tension* (*conflict*) in this triad, for, if the violinist were to release the tautness of the strings, or the tension in the bow, he would be unable to make music. Though the word '*trilogue*' has been used before,[34] we need to stress three points that distinguish it from mere dialogue, as follows.

First, reality is never black or white, and our opinions are never simply right or wrong, but there is always a 'third' or a 'both-and' way to think, to relate, and to act in any encounter among human beings. In any situation, trilogue neither looks at reality as one-dimensional nor two-dimensional, but as tri-dimensional. Concretely, by looking at reality in its trinitarian complexity, and in seeking solutions with the 'other' and 'another' (persons, events, situations, ideologies, disciplines, etc.), we will be able to resolve our socio-politico-religious concerns animated by deep faith that God—called by any and every name—is at the heart of any 'befriending'.

Second, although we seek perfect community and ultimate communion in all our relationships, while we live here on earth, we will have to face tensions and struggles. Although there is no tension and conflict in the Triune God, God has revealed Godself in Jesus as a self-emptying Being. In theological terms we can say that God is a Kenotic (self-emptying) Being. There is perfect self-giving among the Three Persons, which was revealed to us in the Incarnation: Word made flesh, Jesus. Thus, those who believe in the Trinity and seek to be triloguers must undergo kenotic sacrifice in order to achieve *plerosis* (fullness) of life. Amaladoss writes:[35]

> This fullness is not given, but to be achieved (Eph 1:3-14). In this perspective, we are aware of our own limitedness on the one hand, which makes us open to and receptive of others. On the other hand, we are impelled to dialogue [*trilogue*][36] with others so that through mutual interpenetration we can converge toward unity and reconciliation, purifying in the process what is merely human as limitation and sin, in ourselves and others.

Kenosis is the outcome of love. If one genuinely loves the 'other' and 'another' one will surely be ready to go beyond one's narrow interests and viewpoints in order to embrace the other(s).

Third, in a globalizing world, there are rapid flows of ideas, information, money, markets, skills and personnel. Sadly, while the rich and powerful manipulate and monopolize the world's resources, the big bulk of the world's poor get poorer and weaker every day. Trilogue must therefore be undertaken with an option for the poorest of poor in consonance with God's option for the poor. While 'befriending the other', the trilogue must always keep the poorest of poor as 'another' and ask as Mahatma Gandhi would:[37]

> Whenever you are in doubt, or when the self becomes too much with you, apply the following test. Recall the face of the poorest and weakest man [woman] whom you may have seen, and ask yourself, if the step you contemplate is going to be of any use to him [her]. Will s/he gain anything

by it? Will it restore him [her] to a control over his [her] own life and destiny? In other words, will it lead to *swaraj* [freedom] for the hungry and spiritually starving millions? Then you will find your doubts and your self melt away.

Conclusion: Towards Interfaith Trilogue

The Trinity is not just deity to be worshipped 'up there' but a God who has taken flesh in our midst and shown us what it means to 'befriend the other'. Apart from an 'I-Thou' way of relating to the 'other' triadic analysis and trilogue inspires us to go beyond polarities and dualities and incorporate a triadic approach to life. In the meeting of religions, today, trinitarian trilogue will seek to bridge the apparent tension between the 'prophetic religions' or the 'word religions' (like Judaism and Islam) with a strong focus on the One, and the 'mystic-cosmic religions' (Hinduism, Buddhism and Jainism) accommodative of the Many. Even beyond religions, trilogue is accommodative of those who claim to be atheistic or agnostic. Genuine, triune conversations of this type, I think, will enable and empower us to more concertedly work for a better church, better India, better world.

Notes

1. Existential philosophers like Emmanuel Levinas and Franz Rosenzweig are noted for their philosophies of relationship. See Michael Barnes, *Traces of the Other: Three Philosophers & Inter-faith Dialogue* (Chennai: Satya Nilayam Publications, 2000), 20-22, 50-53.
2. See, for instance, Martin Buber, *I and Thou*, 2nd ed., trans. R.G. Smith (Edinburgh: T & T Clark, 1994), 15-17, who explains the *I-Thou* as the primary word of relation.
3. See Jean Paul Sartre, *No Exit and Three Other Plays* (New York: Random House, 1955).
4. See Homi K. Bhabha, *The Location of Culture* (London & New York: Routledge, 2000), 38.
5. Ibid., 127-138.
6. Martin Buber, *Between Man and Man* (Boston: Beacon Press, 1957), 26, considers human relationship as a spiritual act opening out to eternity.
7. The Cappadocian Fathers are Basil the Great (330–379), who was bishop of Caesarea; Basil's younger brother Gregory of Nyssa (c.332–395), who was bishop of Nyssa; and a close friend, Gregory of Nazianzus (329–389), who became Patriarch of Constantinople. The Cappadocian Fathers advanced the development of early Christian theology, especially the doctrine of the Trinity.
8. Joseph A. Bracken, "The Holy Trinity as a Community of Divine Persons – I & II," *The Heythrop Journal* 15/2, 3 (April-July 1974): 166-182, 257-270,
9. Leonardo Boff, *Trinity and Society* (New York: Orbis Books, 1988) and *Holy Trinity, Perfect Community* (New York: Orbis Books, 2000).
10. Jürgen Moltmann, *The Trinity and the Kingdom: The Doctrine of God* (Minneapolis: Fortress Press, 1993).
11. See Geevarghese Mar Osthathios, *Theology of a Classless Society* (Madras: Christian Literature Society, 1980).

12. Ibid., 132-133.
13. See Geevarghese, *Sharing God and a Sharing World* (Delhi: ISPCK & Tiruvalla: Christava Sahitya Samithy, 1995).
14. See my *God of Our Soil: Towards Subaltern Trinitarian Theology* (Delhi: ISPCK & VIEWS, 2010).
15. See Gordon D. Fee, "Paul and the Trinity: The Experience of Christ and the Spirit for Paul's Understanding of God," in *The Trinity: An Interdisciplinary Symposium on the Trinity*, ed. S.T. Davies et al., (New York: Oxford University Press, 1999): 49-72, for details. In brief, Fee argues that Paul has an 'economic trinitarian' idea of God, and perhaps an 'ontological trinitarian' one, as well, although its philosophical and theological nuances are unclear to theologians. On p.52, he stresses that Pauline trinitarianism emerges out of Paul's 'experience' of 'salvation'.
16. See Luis M. Bermejo, *Abba, My Dad!* (Anand: Gujarat Sahitya Prakash, 2003), for a good scriptural and systematic exposition of God as *Abba* of Jesus and *Abba* of all human beings.
17. Theological language is always metaphorical, symbolic and analogical. Though 'analogy' imputes 'likeness' it also always implies 'unlikeness'; hence, never exhausts the truth contained in *reality-in itself.*
18. William Hasker, "Tri-unity," *Journal of Religion* 50/1 (1974): 1-32, develops this thesis. The quote is from p. 2; see also John A. Thurmer, "The Analogy of the Trinity," *Scottish Journal of Theology* 34/6 (1981): 509-515.
19. See, for how Augustine [354-430] used the analogy of love to explain the Trinity: the Father being 'lover' (*amans*), the Son being the 'beloved' (*quod amatur*) and the Spirit being the mutual love (*amor*) passing between the Father and the Son, proceeding from both, and uniting the three divine 'persons'. See his *De Trinitate*, Book IX, especially ch.8, for this point. See also J.N.D. Kelly, *Early Christian Doctrines* (San Francisco: Harper & Row, 1978), 276-279, and Eugene TeSelle, *Augustine the Theologian* (New York: Herder, 1970), 232-234, for details on Augustine's analogies.
20. See Harriet A. Harris, "Should We Say that Personhood is Relational?" *Scottish Journal of Theology* 51/1 (1998): 214-35, for an insightful analysis of the questions of 'person', 'personhood' and 'relation'.
21. See E. Schillebeeckx and B. Iersel, eds., "A Personal God?" *Concilium* (1977), for aspects of God as person.
22. See Nicholas Lash, *Believing Three Ways in One God: A Reading of the Apostles' Creed* (Notre Dame, Indiana: Notre Dame University Press, 1992), 32.
23. William A. Barry, *Paying Attention to God* (Notre Dame, Indiana: Ave Maria Press, 1990), 72.
24. See also Abhishiktānanda, *Saccidānanda: A Christian Approach to Advaitic Experience* (Delhi: ISPCK, 1974), 98, who writes: "God's life is indeed Communion; Being is essentially Communion." Hence, he coins the word *samsat*, meaning, 'being-with' for the divine existence.
25. See John Zizioulas, *Being as Communion: Studies in Personhood and the Church* (London: Darton, Longman and Todd, 1985), 40-49, who stresses the relational and personal aspects of the Triune God.

26. Cornelius Plantinga, Jr., "The Threeness/Oneness Problem of the Trinity," *Calvin Theological Journal* 23 (April 1989): 50.
27. See Pope Francis's Encyclical Letter '*Laudato Si'*', nos. 238-240.
28. See *Laudato Si'*, no. 240.
29. 'Dialogue' (Greek, *dialogos*, meaning 'through word') commonly refers to a conversation carried on between two or more persons or to a verbal interchange of thought between them.
30. As literary form it is "a carefully organized exposition, by means of invented conversation, or contrasting philosophical or intellectual attitudes." See *New Encyclopaedia Britannica*, 15th ed., s.v. "Dialogue."
31. See, for instance, Sundar Sarukkai, "The 'Other' in Anthropology and Philosophy," *Economic and Political Weekly* 32 (June 14, 1997): 1406-1409
32. Henri Lefebvre, *Rhythmanalysis: Space, Time and Everyday Life* (London & New York: Continuum, 2004), 12.
33. One will immediately think of Hegel's 'synthesis' and John Rawls's 'overlapping consensus', respectively. While not excluding them, *spatial trialectic* transcends these two concepts.
34. For example, Jung Young Lee, *The Trinity in Asian Perspective* (Nashville: Abingdon Press, 1996), 217-218, writes: "The conscientization of religious inclusivity is the beginning of *trilogue*. If all human beings began with the first family on earth, and all religions are part of their cultural heritage, then everyone and every religion is connected to every other just as a great river is connected to many streams. In *trilogue*, many religions are in one religion and one religion is in many religions, because every religion bears the image of the Trinity." This definition appears to mean 'inclusiveness'. I develop *trilogue* differently.
35. Michael Amaladoss, "Syncretism and Kenosis: Hermeneutical Reflections in the Indian Context," in *The Agitated Mind of God: The Theology of Kosuke Koyama*, ed. D. T. Irvin and A. E. Arkinade (New York: Orbis, 1996), 67.
36. While Amaladoss uses the word *dialogue* I hold that this is more in the nature of *trilogue*.
37. Mahatma Gandhi, *Last Phase*, vol. II (1958), 65.

8

Raimon Panikkar's Diatopical Hermeneutics for Befriending the Other: Meister Eckhart's World of Holistic Thinking and the Bhagavadgītā's Experience of the World of Wholeness

Francis X. D'Sa, SJ

Director, Institute for The Study Of Religion, Pune 411014, India

Abstract: The phenomena of interreligious and intercultural dialogue as well as of inculturation and interculturation, so relevant in our context, have to do with understanding religions and cultures other than our own. Most of our efforts in this domain have got stuck here because beyond prayer meetings and even studies of other faith-traditions we have been unable to promote deeper mutual understanding. It is here that Raimon Panikkar's diatopical hermeneutics have relevance. The aim of this paper is to discover a relationship between two different and differing and even mutually contradictory cosmovisions.

In this article, the author wants to show that Meister Eckhart's *World of Holistic Thinking* and the Bhagavadgītā's *Experience of the World of Wholeness* are functional equivalences, i.e., we have argued that the Bhagavadgītā's specific *Experience of the World* and Meister Eckhart's *holistic thinking* of Reality have the potentiality of disclosing a systemic relationship if followed through. What we have done is tried to show *how to go about it*. On the face of it one would not have dreamt of relating these two utterly different worlds but for Panikkar's discovery of the principle of homeomorphic equivalents and their application in the context of his diatopical hermeneutics.

Homeomorphic equivalents are not just any kind of equivalents. They are neither arbitrary nor figments of the imagination. They show an ontological grounding in Reality. Different cosmovisions express this differently. But the three dimensions of Reality (i.e. the Human, the Cosmic and the Divine) are our meeting-points (however we may perceive and express them). "Everything is related to everything but without monistic identity and dualistic separation." The cosmotheandric nature of Reality manifests itself in expressions which in course of time are discovered to be homeomorphic equivalents.

Keywords: Cosmotheandrism, Bhagavadgītā, homeomorphic equivalents, Meister Eckhart, Raimundo Panikkar

Introduction: Diatopical Hermeneutics is about Relating Meaningfully or Befriending Different Cultures and Religions

Today's interreligious and intercultural dialogue is high on good-will and open attitude, and low on how to go about it. Without good-will one can do nothing; and equally without knowing how to go about it we are unable to proceed. Good-will alone cannot make dialogue fruitful, in much the same way that method alone cannot fructify dialogue. Good-will brings people together and but it is method that guides their procedure. Without good-will religions and cultures cannot come together but without some common understanding of procedure it would be difficult for work to progress.

The phenomena of interreligious and intercultural dialogue as well as of inculturation and interculturation have to do with understanding religions and cultures other than our own. Most of our efforts in this domain have got stuck here because beyond prayer meetings and even studies of other faith-traditions we have been unable to promote deeper mutual understanding. It is here that Raimon Panikkar's diatopical hermeneutics have relevance. The aim of the following reflections is to discover a relationship between two different and differing and even mutually contradictory cosmovisions. However the search is neither arbitrary nor a wild goose chase. This version of hermeneutics is built on an analogy of proportionality. it can be put simply like this: The significance that Ishvara, for instance, has to believers in the Bhagavadgītā is similar to the significance that Allah has to believers in Islam. Similarly the significance that Christ has to believing Christians is similar to the significance that Jahweh has to believing Jews. This is not the same as saying Ishvara is the same as or identical with Allah, or Christ is the same as or identical with Jahweh. The focus of such an exercise in diatopical hermeneutics is neither Ishvara nor Allah nor Christ nor Jahweh but the *significance* they enjoy among their followers.

Now how is this supposed to contribute to understanding between different cosmovisions? Aren't these simply parallel lines? In our exposition we are taking for granted that one of the cosmovisions is that of the *believer* who is doing the exercize. This implies that as a believer she knows first-hand or even has experienced the significance of the Mystery of her own faith-tradition. In that case she will be in a position to understand and perhaps even empathise with the position of her dialogue partner. Thus, we who love our parents know what it means to lose them; from that experience we empathise with others when they lose their parents. In an exercise of diatopical hermeneutics falling back on one's own experience is of the essence; otherwise it will become at best an intellectual game or at worst remain an abstract exercise.

More specifically I illustrate this the Bhagavadgītā's world of wholeness and Meister Eckhart's world of holistic thinking. On the face of it the one world does not appear to have anything to do with the other. Diatopical hermeneutics provokes us to think out ways and means of discovering relationships where none seem to exist. This requires familiarity with both the traditions we are trying to relate. I employ the expression "familiarity" intentionally. Familiarity has to do with family and contains the hint of a family relationship. I leave the question "What kind of relationship?" open here with the suggestion that it should exclude *polarization* but at connote *polarity*. Polarity *needs* an Other. A good example is that of the north and south poles where one cannot be without the other!

1. Diatopical Hermeneutics Requires Homeomorphic Equivalences

Gradually our world is coming to the realization that the spiritual treasures of humanity can be shared by all. Here Raimon Panikkar's *homeomorphic* (popularly called functional) *equivalences* could show us the way of going about fruitfully with cultural and religious differences. Panikkar's sophisticated method, *diatopical hermeneutics*, deals with "human *topoi,* 'places' of understanding and self-understanding... which have not developed their patterns of intelligibility or their basic assumptions out of a common historical tradition or through mutual influence".[1]

When, for example, we take avatāra and incarnation then it is not just the single words or concepts that we take up as homeomorphic equivalents but their universes of meaning as well. Panikkar's does not identify avatāra with incarnation and vice versa. For what avatāra signifies in the world of the Hindu Traditions is equivalent to what incarnation signifies in the world of the Christian Traditions. Thus what Krishna signifies in the Krishna traditions is equivalent to what Jesus signifies in the Jesus traditions. In this way each tradition learns a bit the significance of the other traditions.

This of course is only the theory aspect of diatopical hermeneutics. But this comment is not to be interpreted negatively. We need theory to venture out into the unknown and to try out new ways of getting acquainted with the unknown. In what follows we shall attempt to work out the practical side of diatopical hermeneutics. To do this we shall take up two traditions: The Bhagavadgītā from the Hindu Traditions because generally speaking it remains undisputed and it is well known also outside the world of the Hindu Faith; and Meister Eckhart, who compared to the Gītā is a relatively unknown Christian mystic from the Christian Tradition (c. 1260 – c. 1328). The contrast could not be greater. But the choice is deliberate. Is it possible to make a connection across such a vast difference? This is the challenge we have chosen to face here. I am formulating the homeomorphic equivalents thus: The Bhagavadgītā Experience of Wholeness and Meister Eckhart's Holistic Thinking of Reality. When juxtaposing these homeomorphic equivalents I shall make use of smaller paraphrases of both of the which I shall place above the columns.

2. The Bhagavadgītā Experience of Wholeness

For the Gītā the experience of wholeness has to do with perceiving reality as it is. It consists of the dimensions of change, non-change and the depth-dimension. This is a harmonious continuum wherein one dimension dovetails into the other. Clearly this kind of wholeness is anything but uniformity as it does not exclude diversity and multiplicity like the levels of change and non-change on the larger background of an unchanging spiritual Infinite Mystery called Krishna or Vāsudeva.

The fact that I am calling this Mystery wholeness should not cause surprise that it speaks the I-Thou language of a personal God like in the Bible. Elsewhere I have argued in detail that the I-Thou language of the Gītā is employed heuristically as its Divine Mystery is more in the nature of a Cosmo-Theos rather than an Anthropo-Theos.[2] The revelation is *cosmic*, the major symbol here being the Cosmos and not Krishna. Whatever revelation is made is not by the man Krishna nor as a man Krishna but through the Divine Presence Krishna in the Cosmos, in the cosmic elements, not in historical events. This is not said negatively but descriptively. Revelation is always a subject of faith through the mediation of history in the western christian tradition and through the mediation of the Cosmos in the Gītā tradition. Accordingly I have called the Divine Mystery Anthropo-Theos in the former case and and Cosmo-Theos in the latter case. Neither better nor worse but different.

However in the faith-world of the Gītā human beings are incapable of perceiving reality as it is because of *rāgadveṣa*, that is, deep-seated likes and dislikes which misguide human beings in every way. Because of their Ego (Ahamkāra) they are rendered blind to the depth-dimension (their Ātmā, the principle of wholeness). The Ahamkāra binds, whereas the Ātmā liberates one from the negative effects of likes and dislikes in the areas of the understanding, the mind and the senses. At this point the quitessence of the Gītā revelation comes into sharp focus and is expressed through the threefold Yoga of Cosmic

Service (Karmayoga), of Communion with the Divine Mystery in the Cosmos (Bhaktiyoga) and of In-Sight into the nature of the Cosmos (Jñānayoga).[3]

Karmayoga when performed selflessly and for the welfare of all is authentic action because it is cosmic action for *lokasangraha*, no more selfish action. In an age that is gradually becoming ecologically more conscious its relevance should be obvious. Bhaktiyoga leads to the realization that it is not a collection of objects, that it is a living reality, inviting us to participate in its life because we have emerged from it and that we shall return to it and that if we discover its personal and transpersonal dimensions we shall be rewarded with corresponding discoveries also in our Communion with the Cosmos. Christians are used to equating higher life mostly with human life; that the Universe could be a living reality does not resonate in our consciousness. Bhaktiyoga acquaints us with Divine Presence at work in the Universe. Finally Jñānayoga enables insight into the real nature of the Universe. The Universe is the Body of the Supreme Mystery, states Chapter Eleven of the Gītā.

When we speak of the Gītā's experience of Wholeness we are in fact speaking of the Highest Mystery; that is the Gītā's unique way of speaking of the Divine, more specifically of Divine Presence which is the taste in the waters, brilliance in the sun and the moon, wisdom in the wise, strength in the strong, the beginning, the middle, and the end of all being, and the Ātmā, the principle of Wholeness, established in heart of all beings!

3. Meister Eckhart's Holistic Thinking about Reality

Ours is an intercultural age in a global world. We can no more live secluded in our own world, affected as we are on all sides by other cultures in the form of intercultural eateries, entertainment, films, plays, literature, fashion and even intercultural philosophy and hermeneutics to say nothing about the ubiquitous presence of science and its derivatives in our life and world. Modern science is a product of a culture that is a double-edged sword and is receiving easy, free and uncritical access every where.

But whereas plundering of our treasures has taken place in colonial times, sharing of our mutual treasures is an important aspect of the human race which has not played the role it should have played in human history. We are talking of mutual sharing. We could begin with our spiritual treasures which unlike material treasures has the unique characteristic of increasing, not decreasing, when shared.

While agreeing to this idea of sharing, still one might question in this context the wisdom of resuscitating this obscure Dominican mystic Meister Eckhart of the 13-14th century who escaped censure by the Catholic Church merely due to the accident of his death. To us Indians he might appear obscure. Two years ago I was invited to a huge international conference in Munich by the International Meister Eckhart Society. On the agenda was a section called

Meister Eckhart: Interreigious Perspective. I understood the significance of this title only when I heard a delegation of Muslim scholars speaking on Eckhart's influence on their traditions already in his life time. That is, Eckhart was not obscure then; and he is not obscure now judging from the number of publications that are appearing. Eckhart's interpretation of Christianity is finding even today more resonance than ever.

Meister Eckhart's thinking has been called holistic because he argues that the reality of God's unity stands out as an eternal and unlimited giving of his own being/existence to creatures, a giving that is in fact a gifting that neither oppresses nor lets them down.[4] This is basic to Eckhart's argument about God's unity and the unity of reality are not two different things. Eckhart's thinking, one could call it, vision is about unity. The existence of creatures does not militate against the unity of God.

Unlike human giving which is accidental God's giving, according to Meister Eckhart, belongs to God's very nature. "God's Being consists mainly therein not to be] alone or to be for himself alone but to communicate himself fully and exclusively."5 Divine self-communication is of the essence; hence it is not half and half but complete self-communication. Furthermore: "Because of God's plenitude God is free from power-claims, and keeps back nothing for himself of what he has and is."[6] Eckhart's God is a God of plenitude who in his self-communication empties himself totally. Plenitude and *kenosis* go together! "At the same time because of this he makes it possible for everyone to have their own proper being and gives them support and the ability to open up."[7]

Such a God has to be a perfectly loving personal Trinitarian unity. "To speak of "[God's] Unity is to remove all borders [which is brought about by] perspectives, that is, it reveals that the understanding of [God's] being is not like that of a thing. This is the same as being and relationship".[8]

Such an understanding of "[God's] unity could be interpreted as absolute Openness towards others. In that case dialogical relation and difference would no more stand directly opposite to the concept of unity".[9] A concept of unity like this leads to a understanding of God that goes beyond the traditional trinitarian understanding of God.

"All creatures", says Eckhart, "are a pure nothing. I do not say, they are worthless or they merely exist: they are pure nothing. What has no being, that is nothing. Now all creatures have no being, because their being depends on God's existence."[10] It is a mystic who sees things as they are that is speaking here. "For Eckhart the concept of creatureliness implies that no creature is *mere* creature but lives without ceasing [to be] already from the fact that it-is-in-God."[11]

For Meister Eckhart, reality as we experience it, is "manifold, partial and multidimensional." So too are all our statements and truths. But: "They all aim at one common reality that makes them possible in the first place, the reality of God. This, Meister Eckhart calls Unity, because it transcends all perspectives."[12] Again, it is the mystic that is speaking, drawing our attention to the one common dynamic at work in every single being, a dynamic which leads to the one centre of the inner unity of all reality. This is the centre of all meaning that creatures seek everywhere and in every being.

As an aside but more relevantly, Eckhart's bold and unique understanding of Christianity could give a filip to Indian/Asian efforts to interprete the Christian Message in the context of the Asian Religions employing languages of Asian cultures.

It is an astonishing fact (at least in the context of western theology) that Meister Eckhart does not speak of or make use of the redemptive value of the sufferings and passion of Jesus Christ, thus ignoring Paul's injunction of preaching the crucified Christ alone. My reflections on the Hindu Cosmovision have led me to the conclusion that suffering does not have any salvific significance there. Hence however much Hindus may admire the suffering Christ he can not save them from Punarjanma, re-birth – which in the last analysis is the goal of all Hindu yearning.

4. Homeomorphic Equivalences between Meister Eckhart's *World of Holistic Thinking* and the Bhagavadgītā's *Experience of the World of Wholeness*

Table 1: Eckhart's World of Holistic Thinking — The Bhagavadgītā's Experience of the World of Wholeness

God allows time to flow out from the eternal duration, that is from eternity itself or directly from the now of eternity so that time and eternity appear similar to that which mutually touches and enters into the other. Thus time flows always out of eternity.[13] For God is the one who does not divide/separate but unites what is divided/separated.[14]	Eightfold divided is my Nature - thus: earth, eater, fire and air, space, mind, and also soul, and the ego. This is the lower: but other than this I have a higher Nature; this too must you know. [And this is Nature] developed into life by which this world is kept in being. To all beings these [two Natures] are [as] a womb; be very sure of this. Of this whole universe the origin and the dissolution too am I. Higher than I there is nothing whatsoever: on Me this universe is strung like clustered pearls upon a thread.[16]

Therefore it is appropriately said, that God has created not *from* the originary foundation [Urgrund] but *in* the originary foundation. For what was in the beginning and whose end is the beginning, originates always, will be born always and is born always.[15]	By Me, Unmanifest in form, all this universe was spun: in Me subsist all beings, I do not subsist in them. And [yet] contingent beings do not subsist in Me, - behold my sovereign activity: my Self sustains [all] beings. It does not subsist in them; It causes them to be-and-grow. As in [wide] space subsists the mighty wind blowing [at will] ever and everywhere, so do all contingent beings subsist in Me: so must you understand it. All contingent beings pour into material Nature which is mine when a world-aeon comes to an end; and then again when [another] aeon starts, I emanate them forth. Subduing my own material Nature ever again I emanate this whole host of beings, - powerless [themselves], from Nature comes the power.[17]

Time (symbol for the non-eternal) flows from the Eternal (Symbol for God). The Eternal unites the disparate non-eternal. *In* and not *from* the originary foundation God created, says Eckhart. On the other hand, the Bhagavadgītā states that all beings are "in Me", the Absolute.

Table 2: Eckhart's World of Holistic Thinking — The Bhagavadgītā's Experience of the World of Wholeness

I state truly that this Light (called the soul) is not satisfied being unified with the fruitful bosom of divine Nature. Yes, I shall say something which sounds more astonishing: I state standing in the truth, in the eternal truth and in the truth that always remains truth that it is not enough for the same Light [to be] at the simple, still standing Divine Being, that neither gives nor takes: rather it wants to know whence this Being comes; it wants to look inside the simple foundation, in the still desert, in the by- no-means-Differentiation (die nie	None knows from whence I came, - not the gods' celestial hosts nor yet the mighty seers: for I am the beginning of the gods [themselves] as of the mighty seers and all in every way. Whoso shall know Me as unborn, beginningless, great Lord of [all] the world, shall never know delusion among men, from every evil freed. Intellect, wisdom, freedom from delusion, long-suffering, truth, restraint, tranquillity, pleasure and pain, coming to be and passing away, fear and fearlessness as well, refusal to do harm, equanimity, content, austerity, open-handedness, fame and

Unterschiedenheit), neither Father nor Son nor Holy Spirit; in the very interiority, where no one is at home, there only is it enough for that Light, und therein is it more interior than in itself; for this foundation (Grund) is a simple stillness, which in itself is immoveable; however all things are moved by this immoveability and all those receive Life who live reasonably in themselves.[18]	infamy, - [such are] the dispositions of contingent beings, and from Me in all their diversity they arise. The seven mighty seers of old, likewise the Manus four, sharing in my mode of being, were born [the children] of [my] mind; from them [arose] these creatures in the world. Whoso should know this my far-flung power and how I use it [whoso should know these] as they really are, is [truly] integrated; and this his integration can never be undone. Herein there is no doubt. The source of all am I; from Me all things proceed: this knowing, wise men commune with Me in love, full filled with warm affection.[19]

Meister Eckhart's expressions are striking: "unites what is separated/divided", "unified", "that it is not enough for this same light to be with the simple, still Divine Being", "it wants to see into the simple ground, in the still desert, in the never-undifferentiatedness of the Father and of the Son and of the Holy Spirit", "because this foundation is a simple stillness". On its side the Bhagavadgītā stresses that the material aspect of the universe re-presents the lower nature and the spiritual aspect the higher nature of the Absolute Mystery (Krishna): These do not need to be unified because they are organic parts of whole Body of Krishna.

Eckhart: Man knows so little what God is, [in much the same way that] the mouth knows what colour is. The goal of the Soul is to reach there where the perfection of all creatures is undivided and without difference. Clearly this is a pointer to unity, to a unified reality. The Bhagavadgītā: With those whose ignorance was cleared away by knowledge of the Self, [this knowledge] allows them to see the Highest that is like the Sun. This leads to equanimity and equanimity is the path to the Highest (Brahman). Clearly this is a pointer to wholeness/integrity.

Table 3: Creatures: A pure Nothing — I would cause Chaos

All creatures are a pure nothing. I am not saying that they are less worth or they are something: they are a pure nothing. What has no being, that is nothing. All creatures have no being, because their being depends on God's presence.[20]	For if I were not tirelessly to busy Myself with works, then would men everywhere follow in my footsteps. If I were not to do my work, these worlds would fall to ruin, and I should be a worker of confusion, destroying these [my] creatures.[21]

Creatures do not have their own being, they merely participate in God's Being. That is why Eckhart is consequent when he speaks of Unity, since there is only one Being, that is, God's Being. This is different in the Bhagavadgītā: The totality of all entities finds itself in the Highest Mystery. This totality is able to act because the Total Mystery is active in the first place. Would this Mystery cease to act, so too would the totality of all entities be unable to act.

Table 4: Divine Unity of Being — Divine Integration of Totality

No [single] vessel can hold two kinds of linquids. It wine is to be contained then water has to be perforce thrown out: the vessel has to be empty and single. Therefore: you must take up Divine joy and God so that you perforce throw out creatures.[22]	From anger comes bewilderment, from bewilderment wandering of the mind, from wandering of the mind, destruction of the soul: once the soul is destroyed the man is lost. But he who roves among the objects of sense, his senses subdued to self and disjoined from passion and hate, and who is self-possessed [himself], draws night to calm serenity. And from him thus becalmed, all sorrows flee away: for once his thoughts are calmed, his soul stands firmly [in its ground].[24]
Where two have to become one, there one has to lose its being. It is like that when God and the Soul have to become one, the Soul has to lose its being and life.[23]	As the waters flow into the sea, full filled, whose ground remains unmoved, so all desires flow into [the heart of] man: and such a man wins peace - not the desirer of desires. The man who puts away all desires and roams around from longing freed, who does not think, 'This I am'. or 'This is mine', draws near to peace.[25]

Since neither water nor Soul have their own [private] being, Eckhart's argument is based on everyday life. Self-emptying, *kenosis* is the presupposition for being filled up by God, says Eckhart. The Bhagavadgītā however speaks differently: Being freed from passion, hate, etc leads to peace. Both these are spiritual paths The former leads to Divine Being/Unity of Being, the latter to Divine Totality/Integration.

Table 5: God's Unity is guaranteed by God's Uniqueness - God's Wholeness is guaranteed by the indestructibility of the Divine

...note that the One is higher, earlier and simpler than the Good and stands nearer to Being and God or corresponding much more to the name one Being with the Being itself[...] Due to that God is overly rich because of the fact that he is one. For he is the First and the Highest because of the fact that he is one.[26] Would one take away being from all creature of this whole world which God give, then they would remain a pure nothing, bleak, worthless and odious.[27]	Yes, indestructible [alone] is That -know this- by which this whole universe was spun: no one can bring destruction on That which does not pass away. Finite, they say, are these [our] bodies [indwelt] by an eternal embodied [self], -[for this self is] indestructible, incommensurable. Fights then, scion of Bharata.[28]

Eckhart: God's unity is thematic here because of a unique reason, namely, because of the uniqueness of his Being. "For he is the First and the Highest because of the fact that he is one." Entities do not disturb God's Unity because they do not have being. The Bhagavadgītā: The plurality of mortal bodies and of immortal Souls also do not militate against the ontological integrity of the Divine, because they are "part" of the Divine integrity.

Table 6: The One [climbs down] into everything...and unites what is separated - The brilliance in the moon, in the fire...know that it is mine

That is why the One climbs down into everything and in every single thing and [still] remains always the One and unites what is separated. [29]	The splendour centred in the sun which bathes the whole world in light, [the splendour] in the moon and fire,- know that it [all] is mine. [Thus] too I penetrate the earth and so sustain [all] beings with my strength; becoming [the moon-plant] Soma, I, the very sap [of life], cause all healing herbs to grow. Becoming the [digestive] fire in [the bodies of] all men I dwell in the body of all that breathes; conjoined with the inward and out breaths I digest the fourfold food. I make my dwelling in the hearts of all: from Me stem memory, wisdom, the dispelling [of doubt]. Through all the Vedas it is I who should be known, for the maker of the Vedas' end am I, and I the Vedas know. [30]

Again, we encounter here the thematisation of Unity and Integrity. The task of unity consists in in unifying what is separated and that of integrity in the fact of indwelling of the Divine "I" in every single "part" so that every single part develops its specific identity.

Table 7. God's Being consists essentially in his complete self-communication — I have no yearning for the fruits of my actions

Pr. 9, DW I, S. 149,?-12; Übersetzung S. 463:) God is the one who is the most communicative. No thing communicates of its own. For all creatures are not of themselves. Whatever they communicate, they have it from another. Also they do not give themselves. The sun gives its light but it remains at its place. Fire does give heat but [still] remains fire. God communicates what is his, because he exists by himself; what he is, and in all the gifts he gives he first gives himself. He gives himself as God as he is in all his gifts in as much as is possible for the one who would like to receive him.[31]	In the three worlds there is nothing that I need do, nor anything unattained that I need to gain, yet work [is the element] in which I move.[32] Bear Me in mind, love Me and worship Me, sacrifice, prostrate yourself to Me, so you will come to Me, I promise you truly, for you are dear to Me. Give up all things of law, turn to Me your only refuge, [for] I will deliver you from all evils, have no care.[33]
RdU, *Von der wâren pênitencie und sæligem lebene*: Many people think, they have to do great works externally like fasting, going barefoot, etc. which one call works of penance. However the true and best penance consists in that one turns away totally and completely from all that is not God or Divine in oneself and in creatures and turns to one's loving God completely and perfectly[...]."	

Eckhart: God is the most communicative of all. He does this in all his gifts. His unity with all his creatures operates and manifests itself in his gifts. What brings us closer to Him is not *human deeds* but giving up all that is not God's in our lives. The Bhagavadgītā: Though God has nothing to achieve or attain he works out of love for his creatures.

Conclusion

Our thesis in this paper has been: Meister Eckhart's *World of Holistic Thinking* and the Bhagavadgītā's *Experience of the World of Wholeness* are functional equivalences, i.e., we have argued that the Bhagavadgītā's specific *Experience of the World* and Meister Eckhart's *holistic thinking* of Reality have the potentiality of disclosing a systemic relationship if followed through. What we have done is tried to show *how to go about it.* On the face of it one would not have dreamt of relating these two utterly different worlds but for Panikkar's discovery of the principle of homeomorphic equivalents and their application in the context of his diatopical hermeneutics.

Homeomorphic equivalents are not just any kind of equivalents. They are neither arbitrary nor figments of the imagination. They show an ontological grounding in Reality. Different cosmovisions express this differently. But the three dimensions of Reality (i.e. the Human, the Cosmic and the Divine)[34] are our meeting-points (however we may perceive and express them). "Everything is related to everything but without monistic identity and dualistic separation."35 The cosmotheandric nature of Reality manifests itself in expressions which in course of time are discovered to be homeomorphic equivalents.

Notes

1. Raimon Panikkar, *Myth, Faith and Hermeneutics*, Cross-Cultural Hermeneutics (New York: The Paulist Press, 1979). 9.
2. See F. X. D'Sa, "Zur Eigenart des Bhagavadgītā-Theismus", in: W. Strolz/S. Ueda (Hrsg.), *Offenbarung als Heilserfahrung im Christentum, Hinduismus und Buddhismus*. Schriften zur großen Ökumene Bd. 8 (Herder: Freiburg, 1982), 97-126.
3. For a somewhat more detailed exposition see F. X. D'Sa, „The Yogi as a Contemplative in Action", in: *Studies in Formative Spirituality. The Journal of Spiritual Formation* XI:3 (Nov. 1990), 289-302.
4. Christine Büchner, *Die Transformation des Einheitsdenkens Meister Eckharts bei Heinrich Seuse und Johannes Tauler*. Meister-Eckhart-Jahrbuch Beihefte, Heft 1 (Stuttgart, Kohlhammer, 2007), 25. In the following cited as *Die Transformation.* My translation.
5. Christine Büchner, *Die Transformation*, 25.
6. Christine Büchner, *Die Transformation*, 25.
7. Christine Büchner, *Die Transformation*, 25.
8. Büchner, *Gottes Kreatur - "ein reines Nichts?"*, 24-25. Einheit Gottes als Ermöglichung von Geschöpflichkeit und Persönlichkeit im Werk Meister Eckharts (Innsbruck/Wien:Tyrolia, 2005), 24-25. In the following cited as *Gottes Kreatur.* My translation.
9. Büchner, *Gottes Kreatur - "ein reines Nichts?"*, 24-25.
10. Büchner, *Die Transformation*, 9.
11. Christine Büchner, *Gottes Kreatur - "ein reines Nichts"?*
12. Büchner, *Die Transformation*, 20.
13. In Ioh. n. 216, LW III, S. 181,15-182,1: deus iubet tempus descendere immediate ab ipso aevo, quod est aiteritatis ipsa vel nunc aeternitatis, ut tempus et aeternitas sint quasi

quaedam continua et contigua sibimet mutuo, ut scilicet semper ab aeterno tempus ab aevo fluxerit. The original quotations from Meister Eckhart's works have been supplied by the publishers of a lengthier contribution in German I made at an international Congress on Meister Eckhart in Munich, Germany in 2014 which is forthcoming. The translations into English are by me. The present article is an independent piece. For the abbreviations for Meister Eckhart's works see Christine Büchner, Die Transformation, 119-121. See foonote 4 above.

14. In Ioh. n. 267, LW III, S. 222,8: Deus enim, utpote unus, nihil dividit, sed divisa unit.
15. Prol. gen. n. 17f. (Rec. L), LW I,2, S. 25,8-22 (Rec. CT, Lw I, S. 162,2-163,1): P*ropter quod siganter (significanter CT) non dicitur (a*it *CT) a principio, sed in principio* deum *creasse [...]. Quod enim est in principio et cuius finis principium, semper oritur, semper nascitur, semper natum est.*
16. Bhagavadgītā 7:4-7. All translations from the Bhagavadgītā are from R.C. Zaehner, The Bhagavad- Gītā (London/Oxford/New York: Oxford University Press, 1969.)
17. Bhagavadgītā 9:4-8.
18. Meister Eckhart, Sermo 48 from Sermones et Lectiones super Ecclesiastici c.
19. Bhagavadgītā 10:2-8.

20 Pr. 4, DW I, S. 69,8-70,3: *Alle crêatûren sint ein lûter niht. Ich spriche niht, daz sie kleine sîn oder iht sîn: sie sint ein lûter niht. Swaz niht wesens enhât, daz enist niht. Alle crêatûren hânt kein wesen, wan ir wesen swebet an der gegenwerticheit gotes.*

21 The Bhagavadgītā 3:23f.

22 BgT, DW V, S. 28,3-6. Vgl. Auch RdU, DW V, S. 269,5-7; Pr. 80, DW III, S. 386,5-387,2; Pr. 103, DW IV, 1, S. 487,113-119: kein vaz enmac zweierleie trank in *im gehaben. Sol ez wîn haben, man muoz von nôt wazzer ûzgiezen; daz vaz muoz blôz und îtel warden. Dar umbe, soltû götlîche vröude und got nemen, dû muost von nôt die crêatûren ûzgiezen.*

23 Pr. 65, DW III, S. 101,8-10: Swâ zwei ein suln warden, dâ muoz daz eine sîn wesen verliesen. Alsô ist: und sol got und diu sêle éin warden, sô muoz diu sêle ir wesen und ir leben verliesen.

24 Bhagavadgītā 2:64-68.

25 Bhagavadgītā 2:70f.

26 Sermo 29 n. 299, LW, S. 266,4-8; Übersetzung ebd.: [...] nota...(lat. Text wird noch von den Hg. e*rgänzt).*

27 BgT, DW V, S. 50,19f.; Übersetzung S.491: Benæme man allen crêatûren aller dirre werlt daz wesen, daz got gibet, sô bliben sie blôz niht, ungenæme, unwert und hezzeclich.

28 Bhagavadgītā 2:17f.

29 Sermo 29 n. 299, LW IV, S. 266,8f.; Übersetzung ebd.: *unum descendit in omnia et singula, manens semper unum et divisa uniens.*

30 Bhagavadgītā 15:12-15.

31 *Got ist daz aller gemeineste. Kein dinc gemeinet sich von dem sînen, wan alle crêatûren von in selber niht ensint. Swaz sie gemeinent, daz hânt sie von einem andern. Sie gebent sich ouch niht selben. Diu sunne gibet irn schîn und blîbet doch dâ stânde, daz viur gibet sîne hitze und blîbet doch viur; aber got gemeinet daz sîne, wan er von im selber ist, daz er ist, und in allen den gâben, die er gibet, sô gibet er sich selben ie zem êrsten. Er gibet sich got, als er ist in allen sînen gâben, als verre als ez an im ist, der in enpfâhen möhte*

32 Bhagavadgītā 3:22f.

33 Bhagavadgītā 18:65-66.

34 Panikkar, *The Cosmotheandric Experience. Emerging Religious Consciousness*. S. Eastham (Ed) (New York: Orbis, 1993).

35 Panikkar, *The Rhythm of Being*. The Gifford Lectures (Maryknoll/New York: Orbis Books, 2010), 404.

9

Befriending the Other: Building Solidarity through Reconciliation

Joseph Mattam, SJ
Professor (Emeritus) of Systematic Theology, Gujarat Vidya Deep, Vadodara, Gujarat

Abstract: Reconciliation is an important dimension of "Befriending the other." The recent missiological literature emphasizes "Mission as loving relationship". If we look at Mission as the proper loving human relationship that enriches and empowers every one, then reconciliation is an essential component of this process. For we live in a divided world, causing and suffering from various forms of divisions. In this paper we shall look first at the world of division, then see the attempts at reconciliation in various cultures and religions, and then look at the essentials of this process of reconciliation and the areas that need reconciliation, and finally relate reconciliation to mission as relation and to "Befriending the other".

First the author looks at some forms of divisions existing in the world due to various causes; the tendency to divide the States in India, the conflicts between two groups in the same country, for example, in Ireland, Iraq and Rwanda. Then the author examines some of the attempts at unification and reconciliation in various African cultures, as an example of such attempts, in religions and finally in the Catholic Church. The Church has the sacrament of Reconciliation precisely for reconciling the erring members to the community.

The author examines the main theme of what happens in reconciliation. The basic truth behind the process is that each understands the other side from his/her point of view. Reconciliation can happen only when one understands the other from his/her point of view.

Following Jesus' wall-breaking ministry, we must recognize that in the past our mission work has often caused divisions by taking some people out of their groups to be Christians. The Churches have to recognize that their mission is not primarily geared towards increasing the number of members, but being a channel of the working of the Spirit gathering all people into one family of God, into the Kingdom of God, irrespective of their religions, cultures, gender and races.

Keywords: Reconciliation; Kingdom of God, Solidarity; Justice, Unification.

Reconciliation is an important dimension of "Befriending the other," the theme of the Diamond Jubilee of Jnana-Deepa. Besides, the recent missiological literature emphasizes "Mission as loving relationship". When we understand "Mission as relationship," the proper loving human relationship that enriches and empowers every one, then reconciliation is an essential element or component of this process. For we live in a divided world, causing and suffering from various forms of divisions. In this paper I shall look first at the world of division, then see the attempts at reconciliation in various cultures and religions, and then look at the essentials of this process of reconciliation and the areas that need reconciliation, and finally relate reconciliation to mission as relation and to "Befriending the other."

1. A Divided World

Our world is characterized by many forms of conflicts and divisions. There are divisions between cultures, nations, peoples and religions. There are divisions at the personal, national and international levels. Today one notices more and more divisions taking place in the world, especially due to growing religious fundamentalism in different parts of the world. Exclusivist and triumphalist claims by any one religion also lead to divisions and conflicts. Terrorism is also another factor that causes divisions among peoples and nations. The bloody conflicts in Rwanda between two tribes caused the murder of over 100,000 people in a short period of time; the Serbian trouble too is basically between two groups of the same country where people had lived in amity for centuries suddenly turned violent. One knows about the violence in Ireland between two Christian groups and the thousands who lost their lives. In Israel the on-going clash between the Israelites and the Palestinians has resulted in the loss of thousands of lives; only too recently did more than 650,000 people died in Iraq due to the war imposed on them by the Americans. In Iraq conflict continues between two Islamic groups: the Sunnis and the Shiites. In Sudan, Sri Lanka, Somalia, Lebanon and other places the daily death counts are increasing. In almost no part of the world can we find today people living in total peace and harmony with one another.

In our own country we notice moves to divide the States. Only recently have Uttaranchal, Chhattisgarh and Jharkhand been formed; now just recently the government has created a Telangana State by dividing Andhra; there are demands for a Bodo Land, Gurkha Land and so on. In the North Eastern States there are also movements towards division and separation. There the clash between the military and the freedom struggle outfits continues unabated. There are the Naxalite movements in the Southern States and also in Bihar, MP and Jharkhand. The Churches too experience divisive factors: new Pentecostal splinter groups carry away many followers form mainline Churches, causing opposition and antagonism. In some parts of India this is becoming a serious concern for the churches.

2. Efforts at Unification

While moves to divide are alive, there are also efforts for reconciliation. People instinctively feel that division is not helpful for humans, and hence the move towards reconciliation and harmony is also natural. All cultures and religions have ways of reconciling people to the community; sanctions and rewards are ways used by different groups. National and international groups try ways of Reconciliation; South Africa had set up a Truth Commission for the explicit purpose of Reconciliation after the Apartheid was dismantled. That has certainly helped to move people from mutual suspicion and hatred to some sort of harmonious existence. In recent times, East and West Germany were unified; North and South Korea are also trying to unify; there are similar movements in every part of the world. In the Churches too Ecumenical movements, though not as strong as in the post Vatican II period, are alive. Some recent rapprochement efforts have been made between the Orthodox and Catholics.

Religions see sin as a divisive factor and have worked out ways of reconciliation. The New Testament is quite familiar with this phenomenon: the gospel of Matthew takes up the issue explicitly in chapter eighteen. Matthew suggests mutual correction, the community involvement in correcting one erring member and finally excommunication (18.15ff). The Catholic Church, for example, has the possibility of private individual confessions to reconcile the erring members back to the community. The Orthodox too follows a similar pattern. Similar customs are found also in various tribal societies, and cultural groups. Ways of reconciliation in various tribes of Africa are well known. I may mention just a few.

Among the *Luo* people there takes place a dialogue among elders from both sides; they communicate the decision to the offended parties; they kill an animal; its blood is sprinkled on the two parties; they share a meal and drink beer from the same pot with straws; pour libation for the ancestors; herbs are used for sprinkling both parties; they dance and shake hands; women break the news to all those not involved.

In Zambia the *Bemba* tribe follows a similar custom. Both parties assemble and relax; no one may speak about the matter until the leader announces the time for discussion; in major or minor cases, dialogue comes first; a leader and a few witnesses or observers are present; after reaching a conclusion, the parties embrace each other and shake hands and finally they share a meal.

The *Luhyia* community in Kenya: after discussion, the elders hold a calabash filled with water; both the sides wash hands, shake hands and share peace with the whole group; both drink a medicinal drink from the same calabash; a chicken is cut and the gizzard is shared by the disputing parties; and finally there is a meal together.

In general the offended and offender meet with their people to know their feelings and mood; both parties send their messengers to the other side to decide on the date for reconciliation and about the things to be provided by both the parties (white bull, goat and brewed beer); on the fixed day both the parties, their representatives and elders assemble; the two parties are questioned as to what happened; all comment; the offended and offender accept the verdict of the group; they shake hands; both parties are involved in the slaughtering of an animal; they are the first to eat the meat together; the elders sprinkle the animal's blood on both the parties; they eat from the same dish; after these they agree the matter discussed is not to be revealed to anybody. The assembly is officially dissolved. Similar patterns are followed by various tribal groups in India too.

3. The Process of Reconciliation

While these and similar efforts are worthwhile and often bear fruit, what is it that ultimately happens in reconciliation between two persons or two groups? The basic truth behind the process is that each understands the other side from his/her point of view. I shall describe this process at some length. Reconciliation can happen only when one understands the other from his/her point of view. One needs to look at what the other is looking at, i.e., understand the other as s/he understands self when s/he does something. It is often said: you must accept/understand the other as s/he accepts/understands herself. This is impossible as we do not know how the other accepts herself. Hence, I have added: 'when s/he does something', for we know from our own experience that when we do something, we have a justifiable reason for doing it, and so, we see ourselves as blameless, even if the action may be wrong. My contention is that we do not act primarily and intentionally against another just for the sake of being against the other, or just for doing harm to the other. I do not say that all our actions are done with an explicit justification. In merely thoughtless, instinctual and impulsive actions and mob behaviour, one does not have an explicit justification before acting. However, if confronted or opposed, we defend the action as justifiable, as was clear in the case of the Mosque demolition, attack on Iraq and the like. (Actions of psychologically abnormal persons are a class by themselves).

People can easily remember the times when *someone has hurt them*; they can also remember the times when *someone claims to have been hurt by them*. But no one owns up that s/he has done something *in order to hurt* another, *just to cause harm* to another without any advantage for oneself. "I did not do it purposely," or "I did it in order to teach him/her a lesson, to prevent further harm" or "I did it as retaliation". Just to do evil to the other is not the *primary and explicit intention of the person*. We may be conditioned by prejudice, past experiences, fears, the need to protect ourselves, self-interest, and the urge to prevent future harm, profit, ignorance, partial or wrong information, mistaken identity, wrong judgement and the like. In whatever we do, we normally see only what is good for ourselves, or for the group, and other aspects are ignored. If any harm is foreseen, it is justified as called for by the situation. Later on we may become aware of the unconscious motives and may even apologize for the harm done as if it were done purposely. One may do something very harmful from an unconscious need to protect oneself, without seeing the harm done to the other. And because of our conditioning, we may see only one aspect, namely, what appears good and so we defend our action as justifiable and blameless.

This happens not only in individual, interpersonal situations, but also in general. Caiaphas held that he was serving the cause of religion by killing Jesus. "You do not understand that it is better for you to have one man die for the people than to have the whole nation destroyed" (Jn 11.50). President Bush was convinced that it was his duty in the cause of fighting terrorism to bomb and destroy Iraq. When terrorists kill innocent people, they seem to argue that it is the only way for them to bring pressure on the Government or to get what they want and thus justifying their brutal behaviour. I do not say that because the doer has a justifiable reason, the action is right and good; the action can be quite wrong, as in the above examples. Here I am not talking about the morality of the action, but about our approach to bring about reconciliation between people, the attitude with which we ought to live, the way we need to look at the other person if we want to be reconciled to people. That means a person is not equated with what s/he does, as our normal interactions imply, but we see the person as good, even when his/her action is wrong and is opposed.

Such an attitude of understanding the other is what leads to forgiveness without which there cannot be true reconciliation. Understanding the other as s/he understands self is forgiveness. Forgiveness, it seems to me, is the same as unconditional love. For many years I have helped people to forgive one another referring to the example of Jesus praying for His enemies. These days there are many books and seminars dealing with 'healing of memories'. After years of reflection and by analysing many incidents I have come to realise that if one had not misunderstood, misjudged the other, there would be nothing to forgive, no memory to heal. If a person acts with a justifiable reason, even when wrong, that person is not against me and is not to be blamed. To forgive is not to allow the action of the other to affect my relation to him/her. It is like the sun that would not turn away from your windows just because you have closed them and put thick curtains across. True forgiveness means that my attitude to the person remains unchanged, even when I oppose his/her action and demand reparation for the material harm done. The material harm done cannot be repaired by forgiveness, which rectifies only the personal relationship.

I agree that the word forgiveness may be meaningful in certain situations, for example, a mother forgiving the murderer of her son or daughter, even if the murder was done in a moment of passion, anger, revenge and self defence. Even in such situations, understanding makes a great difference.

This means, in other words, we must avoid judgement of the other person, even when we oppose the action of the other. When you listen to people talking about others, you realise that they pass many judgements as 'truths': "I know s/he is like that," implying a value judgement. Jesus said: "Do not judge" (Matt 7.1). Seeing the other as the other sees him/herself in what s/he does is "not to judge" the other. In judging another, one imposes on the other one's own criteria of what is right and wrong, and thus claims superiority over the other, one looks at the event from one's own point of view and refuses to see it from the other's point of view. This creates a wall between the two. Whenever we judge another, we are wrong, for we can see only the external action, while the person's intention and interpretation is known only to that person. By not judging, I do not mean that I approve of the action, or that it is right. There are actions which are wrong and need to be opposed. What I mean is that the person is not judged and blamed; my attitude to the person remains unchanged. If one starts with the assumption that, right or wrong, the person has a justifiable reason for what s/he does, and is not against me intentionally, then there will be no misjudgement against the person and no hurt feelings, even when I have to oppose the action. Jesus seems to do precisely this when He tells the woman caught in adultery: "Neither do I condemn you. Go your way, and from now on do not sin again" (Jn 8.11).

One often hears, "I forgive, but I can't forget". Here it is not just a matter of memory. The judgement against the other remains and it interferes with the proper relationship between two persons. I suggest that instead of trying to "heal memories" we should eliminate the bad memory caused by the wrong judgement of the other. There is nothing to heal: we must see that we have been wrong in our judgement of the other's motive. If we were in the same position and under the same conditionings as the other person, we would have acted in the same way. I have come across hundreds of cases when a hurt person honestly tried to understand the 'offender' from his/her point of view, the problem ceased. For as I said earlier, no one is doing harm to the other intentionally, just for doing harm (Have you done it anytime?). This compassionate understanding has to be cultivated through a lot of awareness, so that interpreting the other favourably becomes a sort of second nature. True love (forgiveness) is capable of transcending all sorrow, breaking down all barriers that separate and disunite and bring about true harmony.

Though what I have said above is useful primarily for interpersonal relationships, the approach is valid also for groups. Hence salvation for societies in conflict is reconciliation and forgiveness.

Even if one holds, for arguments sake, that one does harm intentionally, what has happened is happened; nothing can be done about it by anyone; the only reasonable thing in that situation is to forgive, as Mrs Staines did. If one does not forgive, then she or he suffers, and uselessly carries along a dead weight. The presumed "wrong doer" does not even know that the other is suffering, as s/he had not intended offending the other. If on the other hand, one responds to that situation with understanding/forgiveness, then the person is free of the past. The only sensible thing to do about a past event is to forgive. Here most people seem to fail and hold on to past hurts which are caused by their own misunderstanding. Hence in conclusion, we must forgive everyone from our heart unconditionally, and bring about reconciliation between people.

Once I was visiting a family in Nairobi. Roland, his mother and his two small children (3 and 5) were there. I was told that Isabel, the children's mother, had run away with a married man; they spoke at length about how wicked she was and so on. When I asked them if I could contact Isabel, they strongly dissuaded me, telling me that she had abused so many priests who had tried to contact her. However at my insistence they gave me a contact number. I called the number and left her a message; she called me back immediately. I began by saying: "Isabel, I believe you have had a hard time which forced you to take such a drastic step of leaving your children; I would be happy to meet you". Soon after her office hours she came over. She narrated her side of the story; most of the incidents were the ones told me by Roland. I agreed that given her way of seeing things, how much she was hurt. Then I explained to her how Roland would have seen those incidents; then she saw the point and said, "Now it is too late; if this was done in the beginning, I would have gone back to him". Roland saw everything from his point of view, he had his interpretation; Isabel from hers, she had her interpretation. They said they "loved" one another, but not in reality, they failed to understand the other from the other's point of view.

The priests, who contacted her earlier, saw everything from Roland's point of view alone – hence she opposed them.

Another example is of Sister Bertha. During a retreat she said that she could not pray as something was deeply disturbing her. She had this distraction for the last five years or so, and had discussed it with many counsellors, had made four or five retreats. She shared her story. She was very angry with her Mother General and her team for dismissing her sister from the congregation. She spoke for a long time about her pain, hurt and anger. As Bertha works in the office of the General, it was a daily hell for her. When she finished I asked: "Are you saying that they sent her away without any reason?," "they made no investigation, but believed all that was said against her?," "they knew the accusations were false and yet threw her out?" to all these and a couple of other questions, she answered "No". I asked her: "Then what are you complaining about? They did all they reasonably could and acted the way they thought best for the congregation; you would have done the same if you were in their position". Then Bertha saw and it changed her; she could thank God during the mass that day that she was free from five years of suffering. She had suffered for five years because she refused to understand the others from their point of view; she had misjudged them, and so was against them and she suffered immensely.

What I have said above is useful primarily for interpersonal relationships; it can also be useful in relations between groups, peoples and nations. Our mission is to enable people to come to proper relationship; hence the importance of reconciliation in mission cannot be over emphasised.

4. Reconciliation with Justice

True reconciliation cannot happen without justice. Various Governments have set up Commissions of reconciliation in order to help the process of reconciliation. In India, the North East is an area that needs a lot of reconciliation; the conflict between the Military and the people is becoming worse daily. The Military will have to recognize the rightful grievances of the people; the militants will have to see that ultimately violence is not an answer to any problem. In the North East often missionaries are accused of instigating violence and sectarian divisions. Though there is often no truth in this accusation, what is important is that we ought to actively contribute towards a process of reconciliation between the various groups.

Another area in which Christians can be actively involved is to bring reconciliation between Hindus and Muslims. We are affected by both, yet we can stand sort of "above" the factions and mediate a process of reconciliation, help both the groups to accept the mistakes of the past without being defensive about the past; there is no denying that mistakes have been made by every side. The prejudices, the conquering mentality and fear that affected the relationships in the past need not be carried over into the present day. Similarly, in the conflict between the Israelis and the Palestinians, for example, reconciliation cannot happen until the wrongs done to the Palestinians are recognized, corrected and justice is done to them. The olive trees in Palestine were planted by Palestinians many years before the Jews established settlements in the area; when the Jews marked roads "for Jews only," and took control of the springs and closed off the area with checkpoints the Palestinians have been wronged. They will need to want to have a future in which the Jews and Arabs will be able to harvest olives together without fear. They have to look to a future in which Jews will not have extra privileges. Earlier, when talking about understanding, I said that by not judging I do not mean that I approve of the action of the other; the wrong done to the Palestinians has to be acknowledged and rectified. People will have to want peace and want to be reconciled. Our mission is to help to bring about such attitudinal changes in people, so that, people giving up their hatred for one another, come to understand the other and see that it is better for all if they live in harmony. A future based on the recognition that, as the Universal Declaration of Human Rights puts it: "All human beings are born free and equal in dignity and rights. They are endowed with reason and conscience and should act towards one another in a spirit of brotherhood".

We do not need more inquiry committees; we need truth and reconciliation committees, like those established in South Africa and other countries that chose the way of conciliation, of requesting forgiveness for the past and attempting to build a better and more just future. St John Paul II had shown that asking forgiveness also leads to reconciliation and proper relationship. He had the courage to acknowledge that injustice had been done to Galileo and other scientists, and the Pope asked forgiveness for such injustices. However, the Pope has not acknowledged that the Church had made mistakes in the past, but very ingenuously said: "Another painful chapter of history to which the sons and daughters of the Church must return with a spirit of repentance is that of the acquiescence given, especially in certain centuries to intolerance and even to the use of violence in the service of the Church" (John Paul II 1994, in Fiedler 1998: 50). Many more areas are there that need an apology: the dealings with heretics and schismatics, "witches," sorcerers, crusades, the Inquisition, the suppression of free thoughts and expression, like in the case of the Modernists, theologians like Tissa Balasuriya of Sri Lanka, Boff, Curran, Dupuis and many others. The Church has also to revise its self-understanding of itself as the only guardian of Truth and the assumed authority from Christ to suppress any opinion contrary to theirs. An honest acknowledgement that mistakes have been committed in the past will help heal more wounds than all these beating around the bush will do. Justice, however, must not be set against forgiveness, as the case of the good thief also shows. Even after forgiving him, Jesus does not free him from the cross, that is, from the punishment that the wrongdoer himself considered "just". Thus, we must forgive everyone interiorly while we demand that justice be done. Pope Francis has done right when recently he asked forgiveness for the crimes against children committed by clerics during many years. He has also asked for forgiveness when he visited Bolivia, though in the US he did not ask forgiveness from the original inhabitants of the country for the harm done to them by the invading Europeans.

5. Reconciliation at the Service of Mission as Proper Loving Relationship

Following Jesus' wall-breaking ministry, we must recognize that our work as evangelizers is to help to build solidarity among people, to bring people together, to enable them to live in harmony. In the past our mission work has often caused divisions by taking some people out of their groups to be Christians. There is an element of truth in what Jesus says that he has come to cause divisions (Lk 12.52ff). Even when this happens, namely, some in a group or family decide to become Christian, and others are opposed to it, our efforts would be to help people understand each other's point of view and respect each other's stand and allow each one to follow his/her conscience and path. A proper relation can be preserved even when such divisions are inevitable. Another aspect is to recognize that a difference of opinion need not necessarily lead to antagonism and opposition, if each side approaches the situation through understanding of the other side, which leads to reconciliation, even when each one follows a different path in religion, politics or in personal matters. The Churches have to recognize that their mission is not primarily geared towards increasing the number of members, but being a channel of the working of the Spirit gathering all people into one family of God, into the Kingdom of God, irrespective of their religions, cultures, gender and races.

In order to move in this direction, obviously there is need of a rethinking about the understanding of mission itself, which earlier was understood primarily in terms of Church expansion and numerical growth of the church. While this may still be valid this cannot be the primary understanding of mission. Mission has to be, following the wall breaking ministry of Jesus, geared to building human communities of love, fellowship, justice and mutual respect for each other's rights. Here humans and their concerns come first; they take primacy of place in our mission efforts. Our mission will be to join hands with all those who are concerned about human well-being, freedom, justice and respect for human rights, not minority rights, but human rights of all. If we follow what was mentioned earlier about understanding the other from his/her point of view that will enable us to be mediators of reconciliation between peoples and groups. I mentioned above some of the ways people use in their search for Reconciliation; in every region and culture people have various 'local' ways of handling conflicts and bringing about reconciliation;

we will have to familiarize ourselves with these and make use of them for our mission; if we start with people's own ways, then they are more open to it, than if we import something from outside.

For the theme of JD's Diamond Jubilee Celebration and Conference, namely "Befriending the Other," reconciliation is an important dimension; in every relationship conflicts and misunderstandings are bound to arise; but if one has the spirit of reconciliation as we have developed it earlier through understanding the other, there will be no situation which leads to break up of a relationship; people can continue as friends and contribute to building up of communities of love, fellowship and cooperation.

References

Fiedler, Maureen and Linda Rabben (1998): *Rome Has Spoken, A Guide to Forgotten Papal Statements and How They Have Changed Through the Centuries*, A Crossroad Book, New York.

John Paul II (1994): *Tertio Millennio Adveniente*, Pauline books, Mumbai.

Mattam, Joseph (2015): *Weaving Solidarity: Reflections on Mission Today*, GSP, Anand.

10

Pre-Christian Inter-Personal Values Practised by Africans as a Means of Befriending Others: Cultural-Religious Contexts

Teresia Tarimo, HSS

Principal, Rauya Theological Pastoral Centre, Kilimanjaro, Tanzania

Abstract: This article is an attempt to bring into light the African religious cultural values used to befriend others in the society. The historical account of missionaries about Africa shows that before Christianity the indigenous were pagans in a strict sense. That means the idea of a supreme and personal God did not exist in the African continent. However, various researches have proved the contrary. It is undeniable truths that even prior to Christianity Africans were profoundly religious. They had traditional religion which exerted big influence upon manners of living. Kofi Busia in his book *Africa in Search for Democracy* noted that "Africans' cultural heritage is intensely and pervasively religious and that in traditional African communities; it was not possible to distinguish between religious and non-religious areas of life."[1]

This religion is rooted in the ethos and belief system of people; and developed experientially as a response for their questions concerning the world and daily life situations. It dominates human life and set up a specific tone in his relationship with nature and his fellow people through values observed. The work aims at seeing the convergences of these values to Christianity and how they created congeniality in the society.

Keywords: African theology, Culture, Cultural values, Hospitality, Greeting rituals, Solidarity.

Introduction

The historical account of missionaries about Africa shows that before Christianity the indigenous were pagans in a strict sense. That means the idea of a supreme and personal God did not exist in the African continent. However, various researches have proved the contrary. It is undeniable truth that even prior to Christianity Africans were profoundly religious. They had traditional religions which exerted big influence upon manners of living. Kofi Busia in his book Africa in Search for Democracy noted that "Africans' cultural heritage is intensely and pervasively religious and that in traditional African communities; it was not possible to distinguish between religious and non-religious areas of life."[2]

This religion developed experientially as a response for their questions concerning the world and daily life situations. Religion provided them with important answers and authentic interpretation of the physical world. Distinct from Christian religion, African Tribal Religions (ATR) developed out of *experiential encounter* with the vastness, complexity and orderliness of the universe. One of the elements found in the five proofs of existence of God by St. Thomas Aquinas. Nothing could impart the possibility of a Supreme Being more on the minds of African ancestors than the large sea, the rising and setting sun, the rains, the high blue sky and the big high mountains. It was a natural religion rooted in the ethos and belief system of a people. It dominates human life and set up a specific tone in his relationship with nature and his fellow man. These twenty pages intend to analyse some of the values practiced by Africans as a means of befriending others. Although they exercised them not on the basis of Christianity, but they later proved to be the essential values of Christianity.

1. Semantic Description of Terms

a. Culture

Culture is the totality of a people's way of life which differs from tribe to tribe or nation to nation. It is the characteristic of a particular group of people, defined by everything from language, religion, cuisine, social habits, music and arts.[3] All are interwoven to form their very life. It is therefore very difficult to draw a clear-cut line of demarcation between where their ethical life ends and where their religious life begins.

A culture is a social system that shares a set of common values, in which such values permit social expectations and collective understandings of the good, beautiful, constructive, etc. Culture shapes the way we see the world. Culture is that complex whole which includes knowledge, belief, arts, morals, laws, customs and any other capabilities and habits acquired by man as a member of a society.[4]

b. Religion

Indian theologian Nigel Kumar defines religion as a human activity in response to God's activity in the context of God's reconciliation of humanity to himself. Religion is a combination of a religious view of the world and religious actions in the world all directed in honour of God.[5]

No single definition can be ascribed to the word religion due to its diversity. Many people considered religion as an organized system of beliefs, ceremonies, practice and worship that centre on one supreme God or the deity value that provide groups of men with solution to the question of ultimate meaning.[6]

Religion is also considered to be "collection of cultural systems, belief systems, and worldviews that relate humanity to spirituality and, sometimes, to moral values. Religion is not only a necessary but a very significant part of our lives. Most people would find it very difficult to live without religion or spirituality. Most religions shared wholly or partially some characteristics which include: belief in God or deity, a doctrine of salvation, a code of conduct or ethics, the usage of sacred stories, rituals or religious acts and ceremonies. We cannot exclude the word religion from culture since religion is defined as a collection of cultural systems.

c. Inter-personality

Generally inter-personality means relating to or involving relations between people. It is the way people interact in the society. In the context of this paper it refers to the ways in which Africans associate themselves to each other and in the society. African cultural worldview is such that no one lives by himself or herself; every person belongs to one another in the community.[7] A good human relationship based on inter-personal communication has always been emphasized in the African Community. Biko observed:

> Ours has always been a man-centred society. Westerners in many occasions have been surprised at the capacity we have for talking to each other not for the sake of arriving at a particular conclusion but merely to enjoy the communication for its own sake. But the discussions must respect individuals' sentiments; hence conversations that may cause misgivings are avoided. Intimacy is a term not exclusive for particular friends but applying to a whole group of people who find themselves together whether through work or residential requirements8

d. Values

The word "value" comes from a Latin word '*valere*' means be strong, be well; be of value, and be of worth. Values are principles, standards or qualities that an individual or group of people hold in high regard. These values guide the way we live our lives and the decisions we make. A value may be defined as something that we hold dear, those things/qualities which we consider to be of worth.[9] It also refers to an ethical precept on which we base our behavior. Values are shaped by the culture in which we live and by our experiences. However, there are values that are held high by most cultures. These include fairness and justice, compassion and charity, duties and rights, survival of human species and human well-being.

Values can be related to the norms of culture but they are more worldwide and abstract than norms. Norms provide rules for behavior in specific situations, while values identify what should be judged as good or evil. While norms are standards, patterns, rules and guides of expected behavior, values are abstract concepts of what is important and worthwhile. Flying the national flag on a holiday is a norm, but it reflects the value of patriotism. Wearing dark costume and appearing solemn are normative behaviors to manifest respect at a funeral. Different cultures reflect values differently and to different levels of emphasis.

Values are set of personal or social principles, standards, concepts, beliefs and ideas that can be used to make everyday decisions. Hospers easily distinguishes three senses of 'value' namely as "a liking or preference, that which promotes a goal (end) independently of one's liking or preference' and 'that which has value or worth in itself without reference to any end.[10]

2. The Principal Cultural Values within Which Africans Befriend Others

Human cultural values in the world differ significantly despite some similarities they may share. Some of the reasons which lie behind this is the geographical setting and racial differences. This automatically leads us to talk about European cultural values, Asian cultural values, African cultural values etc. Different scholars proved that most people's cultural values take their essence from manifold elements; such as ethics, religion, politics, economics, esthetics, etc. You can agree with me that one's personality constitutes part of his/her culture. Cultural values can be defined as commonly held standards of what is acceptable or unacceptable, important or unimportant, right or wrong, workable or unworkable in a community or society.[11] It is implicitly in the definition that cultural values are meant for the common good of a society.

Africans' cultural values have been discredited by many (especially missionaries) as completely flabby and uncivilized one. So, more to the point of evangelization, uprooting Africans' culture and imposition of European ones had been a second project of missionaries. This negative attitude affected and deprived Africans of their identity. Up to now majority of Africans are not at home with their cultures. There is always a struggle to become like Europeans. But is it an actual fact that African culture is useless and uncivilized? The late president of Tanzania Julius Kambarage Nyerere once remarked "Of all the crimes of colonialism there is none worse than the attempt to make us believe that we had no indigenous culture of our own, or that what we did have was worthless or something of which we should be ashamed, instead of being a source of pride.[12] Our point here is to unveil the truth that, besides the defects found in African culture, (which may also be in other cultures) there are also positive values in African society which had great impacts to Christian religion.

African values are found in various categories such as Moral values, Religious values, Economic values, Political values, Aesthetic value and Social values. Nevertheless, social values seem to be fundamentally the cardinal. African values are humanistic in the sense that they take human person prior, central and end-point in techno-development valuations and engagements.[13]

Therefore, we would focus precisely on how these values played a considerable role on befriending others. African values were based on the so-called policy of "live-and let –live" that presupposed inter-personal and intercommunity relationship realized in the interaction between individuals of the same community and different communities. Values which nurtured this life setting were the following: hospitality, solidarity/mutual assistance, respect, exchange of greetings, reconciliation and forgiveness. Let us analyse each individually.

a. Hospitality

For Africans 'To be' is to be related. The term humanity in Africa is not just an anthropological term; it is also a moral term when it comes to considering the relations between members of the human species. If we are human, we are (must be) brothers, in a comprehensive sense of the word 'brother.' So any human person has the right to be recognised by everyone and the society at large. The phrase *'All men are equal'* is used to instill in Africans' mind the spirit of brotherhood and friendship in their daily life.

The Akan people in Ghana summarize the idea of hospitality with the proverb "*honam mu nninhanoa*" that means humanity has no boundary. Literary is that:

> In human flesh there is no edge of cultivation—no boundary. The maxim can be interpreted as meaning that 'all humankind is one species', thus, that 'Humanity has no boundary.' When the farmer cultivates his land, he does it up to a limit, an edge where he has to stop; otherwise he would trespass on another farmer's land. There is, thus, a limit to the area of cultivation of land. But the maxim invites us to realise, it is not so in the cultivation of the friendship and fellowship of human beings; the boundaries of *that* form of cultivation are limitless. For, humanity is of one kind; all humankind is one species, with shared basic values, feelings, hopes, and desires.[14]

Though Africans are divided into different tribes, they consider humanity as universal value that constitutes one human family which surpasses the ethnic boundary. Hospitality or generosity is therefore extended to all people regardless of race, culture or religion. Mbiti shed more light on this by saying "It is held to be a moral evil to deny hospitality even to a stranger. Therefore, when people travel they may stop anywhere for the night and receive hospitality in that homestead. They should not be molested unless of course they abuse the hospitality they have received"[15]

This generosity is exercised in every aspect of life. For instance, in Africa one does not need to inform a person whom s/he is planning to visit that one will eat or not. It is in the Africans' tradition that a visitor should never leave without eating something from his/her hosts. Due to this tradition, an African woman will always make sure she prepares enough food for the family and little surplus for whoever may come. Women who cook food without a surplus can sometimes be considered as greedy or selfish.

African culture forbids one to ask a visitor whether s/he wants something to eat. It is considered bad manners. When a visitor arrives after a warm welcome, is served with any edible thing then the decision to eat or not is left upon him. Refusal is the rare case. If s/he took something before his/her coming s/he takes a small amount as a sign of appreciation. Asking a visitor if s/he likes something is translated as not having the will to give and the answer one is expecting to get if such a question is asked is always negative. In this context therefore, an African is sure of food and accommodation among his/her fellow Africans.

Sharing is encouraged no matter how little the food is; keeping a prey for one's own family when the catch is big enough for the extended family was considered as violation of customs and it has to be vehemently reproached. Afolayan Funso compares greedy people with a lion saying "to be generous in heart is to be human, to take food only for oneself reduces one to be the level of the animals, just like lions take food only for themselves. Only the light-hearted and those whose bellies are like bags without openings think only of their appetite and of meeting their own needs at all cost."[16]

The late President Mwalimu Julius Kambarage Nyerere once said "One of the achievements of our African society was the universal hospitality on which members of the community and others could rely."[17] Several writers, including European travellers to Africa in the nineteenth and early twentieth century, have also remarked upon these virtues as practiced in African social and moral life. Briton who spent about three decades in Central Africa from the latter part of the nineteenth century to the early part of the twentieth century made the following observation, "Hospitality is one of the most sacred and an ancient custom of Bantu land, and is found *everywhere.* A native will give his best house and his evening meal to a guest, without the slightest thought that he is doing anything *extraordinary.*"[18] It is even believed that mistreating or refraining from generosity to a stranger can lead to misfortunes or a curse on that family.

Encouragement of hospitality in people's lives is expressed by the maxim "human being is more beautiful than gold."[19] That the goodness/value of man cannot be compared by anything else; and that he is a being which has to be enjoyed in spite of any defects one may have. According to Ifeanyi Menkiti, a beautiful object is enjoyed for its own sake, not for the sake of anything else. Therefore, human being is to be enjoyed for his or her own sake; and to enjoy a human being for his/her own sake means you should appreciate his value as a human being and demonstrate that appreciation by showing compassion and hospitality. It means to be open to the interests and welfare of others and to feel it a moral duty to offer help where it is needed; it also means to recognise the other person as a fellow individual whose worth as a human being is equal to yours and with whom you undoubtedly share basic values, ideals, and sentiments.[20]

However, African hospitality is dispensed in moderation and in prudence. This is demonstrated by the Akan proverb that cautions on foolish dispensation of hospitality saying 'Visitor is a visitor for several days, and then put the person to work.'[21] It agrees with the Swahili proverb which says that 'A visitor is a guest for two days, on the third day, put him or her to work (by giving him or her a hoe).[22] These proverbs imply that a person is not a visitor forever. At one stage he or she will be accepted as one of us who now needs to work like the rest of us in various forms to promote the economic well-being of the hosting family, the entire community and justly earn his livelihood.

A few malicious people who pretend to be visitors with bad intention have resulted the diminishing of Africans' generosity. Besides that, it is crucial to highlight the fact that such attitudes are changing very slowly in our modern day Africa due to the fact that supply in proportion to the people in our modern world is less. Surely, one cannot afford to cook so much food that used to be cooked for the entire extended family and beyond. Growth of population has resulted into scarcity of land which do not produce enough food for the family. Additionally, the change of attitude that is weakening our hospitality can also be attributed to the mushrooming of commercial places like hotels, restaurants, bars and lodgings which have replaced the many social gatherings for refreshment purposes such as local beer drinking sessions that used to be there.[23]

b. Greetings

In African setting, the exchange of greetings symbolizes one's acknowledgement to the dignity and value of the other person. It is inconceivable for two people to meet on the way or anywhere else without greeting each other. Saying hello to whoever you come across is an impression of a well-formed person (though this may not be absolute).

Although this practice binds every member in the society, "when two people meet, the younger one usually starts off the greeting session giving the other the same title that he or she would give to his/her parent or elder of the same group".[24] Greeting is accompanied with some gestures such as shaking hands and half genuflecting, stopping if one was walking; standing if one was sitting; or kneeling depending on the culture and tradition of that particular tribe. Elder people greet those in authority by taking off their hat while shaking their hands regardless of their age.

At times exchange of greetings serves as starting point of dialogue and conversation. It is an art cherished in African relations. In African scenery questions like: did you sleep well? How are your children? Or how is your family form part of greetings and are asked in *bonafide*. Extension of greeting to that extent lies on the fact that Africans freely discuss and express their problems. You may wonder where do they get time to extend greetings in that way. This is possible because majority of Africans go to their place of work on foot (can be to school, farm areas, market etc). If those who meet are taking the same direction they can discuss a lot of things before they depart one another. It is highly important to note that Africans believe that he who discusses his affairs with others hardly runs into difficulties or makes mistakes in the execution of his plans.

Africans, particularly Tanzanians, believe that to greet a person is to wish him/her well, it shows that you value him/her and it is a sign of recognising him as a person and not as an object. Passing somebody silently is a sign of hatred, enmity or disrespect. Certainly, there should be something incongruous or abnormal. If one passes silently s/he can immediately be asked "what have I done to you that you pass me like a stone"? It is a fundamental question which solicits a concrete response from the interlocutor or counterpart.

c. Solidarity and Communality

Akan people have a proverb which goes: "It is the human being that counts; I call upon gold, it answers not; I call upon cloth, it answers not; it is the human being that counts."[25] This adage insists the uniqueness of human being among the created beings. No matter how rich one is, solidarity and mutual assistance takes precedence in the sphere of social life. We may have everything but still we need each other in life. Life is more than richness and what counts in our lives is good relationships.

Relationship between individuals recognizes their worth as human beings and not only what they possess or what can they do for each other. Nevertheless, these can come as secondary considerations, in terms of reciprocity and in terms of inter-personal relationship. People help one another without demanding immediate or an exact equivalent remuneration.[26] Everyone is mindful that each person has something to contribute to his welfare, some time and somehow. Another Hausa proverb illustrates this point clearly. It says: "Friendship with the ferryman right from the dry season means that when the rains come, you will be the first to cross". This proverb emphasizes constancy in friendship. In it, the worth of the ferryman, as a human being is not determined solely by what he can offer during the rains, hence he must be befriended right from the dry season when his occupation is not in strict demand.[27]

Yet, the claim that 'it is human being that counts' does not imply that African social ethics disregard the importance of earthly goods. The point is that, these goods should not detach us from others or community. Earthly goods have value only in relation to human beings. Think of a man who has big companies and no one goes for employment even for high payment. Think also of a sick rich man; can his wealth take him to hospital? No matter how many cars he has, it is only his fellow human being who can drive him to hospital since the car itself cannot. We can give so many other examples but the point stressed here is that mutual relationship, solidarity and affection towards other people has to be promoted by each one in the community.

A person is defined in a way s/he relates in the society. According to Polycarp Ikuenobe the term person in African tradition has dual standards of recognition: normative recognition and descriptive or metaphysical. Normatively, a person is defined or described based on the recognition s/he has acquired from the society due to his/her conformity to the social and moral norms. Metaphysical recognition is based on what constitutes a person. It is recognition based on the ontological analyses of the person; his/her make-up, the nature. It is normative standards that define a person in Africa and one has to prove so practically. Yet, one cannot be described as a person normatively without the metaphysical features.[28]

The arrangement of human relation is that of being one's brother's keeper or caring for each other's welfare. A way of life emphatically centred upon human interest and values; a mode of living evidently characterized by empathy, and by consideration and compassion for human beings.[29] Life is a shared reality hence togetherness and cooperation are praised. Gerald Tanye affirms this saying:

> Solidarity is expressed in work, helping one another to build or repair their houses, in funeral celebrations, in farming and education of children as a corporate responsibility and general involvement in one's another's life. The value of solidarity is expressed concretely through sharing at the heart of daily life where everyone feels to be truly at home.[30]

Onwubiko pointed that the African idea of security and its value depend on personal identification with and within the community. An authentic African is known and identified in, by and through his community.

d. Forgiveness and Reconciliation

It is within Africans' mind that people are unique with their own likes and dislikes, even temperaments differ from one person to another. Hence, misunderstandings and conflicts may arise at any time between individuals, in family or society. The spirit of forgiveness and reconciliation is always insisted to construct and maintain peace and good relationships in the community. For instance, people were warned about the tendency of berating others for their failings with this maxim *a cow falls despite its four legs.*[31]

A cow is not expected to fall easily precisely because it has four legs, these help it to have balance and be stable, but the possibility to slip and fall is there. If that is the case with stable creatures what about two-legged creatures? The message here is that, we do not expect to have infallible people in society. No matter how virtuous a person is, to err is human. Therefore, we need to bear other people's failures and be ready to forgive regardless of how many times they failed.

Africans consider forgiveness and reconciliation as moral obligation in order to maintain solidarity and community ties which bring peace and harmony in the society. Regardless of other elements, blessings and success in one's life in Africa is associated with the good relations one has towards the community members. In the book *Truth and Reconciliation* we read that forgiveness does not mean to forget but an emphatic recognition of the moral vulnerability of human beings. This is by being ready to make a change from the way we remember our traumas and the way those traumas and hatred have defined our relationships with others.[32]

To bring back true peace and inner healing to the ruptured relationship, reconciliation is significant where the two conflicting parties must expose the root causes of the problem one after another. "For if the causes of suffering are not addressed, suffering is likely to continue and the wheel of violence keeps turning."[33] After hearing from both sides the mediator with her wisdom reconciles the two.

In most of African societies the party found guilt, after apologizing publicly, has to pay something as a fine (is usually an edible thing) which is eaten by those who gathered for that purpose (elders) or part of it can be given to the victim or offended family. Regardless of the seriousness of the case, forgiveness and reconciliation is obligatory and there is no way the offended person can refuse. In some tribes there is a particular leaf the offender uses when asking forgiveness to show a heartfelt apology. The motive behind the reconciliation is the fact that it is an imperative duty to build a united community and eradicate roots of division, isolation and build friendship between a person and a person or between neighbour communities.

3. The Convergences of African Values to Christianity

Despite the transgressions found in African culture, a number of values practiced in the society exerted great force in evangelizing process. The Christian values such as respect to elders, hospitality, welcoming foreigners, forgiveness, reconciliation, solidarity and mutual assistance were not new in African land. Unknowingly the Africans lived the gospel message within their culture. To some extent this reflected the evangelizing work.

African hospitality is that extension of generosity, given freely without strings attached. It is a readiness to share gratuitously. It is, thus, the willingness to give, to help, to assist, to love and to carry one another's burden without necessarily profit or reward as the driving forces. African hospitality created the spirit of brotherhood and sisterhood 'between the members of the same family group, same clan and even strangers. Hospitality is perceived and practiced by Africans as open-handed, instinctive and the most natural thing in the world.[34] This is to say hospitality in Africa is not an academic theory that is simply exercised by 'arm-chair' practitioners but a practical way of life on how people live their lives on a day-to-day basis as this study seeks to show.[35]

Analogously, from biblical context hospitality is intended to make human being enter into fellowship with one another and practice Christ's commandment of love. Jesus pointed that, the very credibility of our witness to the gospel is at risk when our ministry of evangelism fails to cross boundaries; when it is limited to those who are culturally or racially similar to ourselves. The real nature of the gospel is contravened when our witness is not extended to those who are far from our ethnic or racial boundaries (Lk. 6:32).

Hospitality is more than simply a context for evangelism; it is integral to the gospel. In fact, the whole life of Jesus was that of hospitality, as Pohl suggests: "Jesus gave his life so that persons could be welcomed into the Kingdom."[36] Koenig puts it this way: "When Paul urges the Romans to 'welcome one another . . . just as Christ has welcomed you' (15:7), he is revealing something close to the heart of his gospel."[37]

The uniqueness of African hospitality can be argued on the basis that, unless you are invited for a meal or dinner by a westerner, you do not expect a treat. In ancient Kikuyu hospitality, it was more distinctive than it is today in that, a hungry person, a passer-by or a stranded stranger could go to the garden, in a strange land, and if he was genuinely hungry, he would get into somebody's garden and consequently eat as many ripe bananas, sugar cane or any ripe fruit but was not supposed to carry it with him (or her) outside the spot. The danger of this rule is that it could encourage parasitism whereby when a person does not want to work, he moves to a strange corner where he is not known and enjoys their hospitality like any other genuinely stranded stranger. However, it is imperative, at this stage, to underscore the fact that such attitudes are changing very slowly in our modern day Africa. This can be attributed to the fact that supply in proportion to the people in our modern world is less.[38]

On the whole, both Western hospitality and African hospitality have something to learn from the ideal of Christ's hospitality which is too sacrificial. Since none of us is perfect before God, we should therefore avoid being judgmental on whose hospitality is more Christ-like or less Christ-like. Rather, we should simply let Christ perfect us.

To wind up this subsection we can rightly argue that rather than African hospitality being seen as unique when we compare it to the hospitality of the rest of the world, it is Christ's hospitality that is clearly and ideally unique and worth of imitation by all nations of the earth

> Solidarity and mutual assistance in African life is grounded in the fact that no one is an island in himself or herself, rather each and every one is part of the whole. Mbiti's dictum, 'I am because we are and since we are therefore I am' sums up the basis on which African hospitality and solidarity is built. The emphasis is put on interdependence, which is in accord with Pauline theology on the need to recognise other people's gifts and talents in order to edify the Church and society in general.(1 Cor. 12.)[39]

Scriptures requires us to practice hospitality and mutual assistance by recognising the equal worth of every person. In African culture hospitality and mutual assistance "both reflect and participate in God's invitation of welcome to all."[40] The African values under discussion are thus characterized by the emphasis on interdependence. It is in agreement with Pauline theology, which is echoed from Christology, especially on the assertion that we are one body, one people of God and this touches the African emphasis on interdependence. According to Paul, the many different gifts, and talents that are bestowed upon each and every one of us by God our maker makes us one in diversity.

The Gikuyu tribe insists interdependence using the proverb 'The hornless animal leans on the one that has them.'[41] The proverb can be connected with what the New Testament implies by fellowship among the believers in Christ. The hornless animal could be equated with someone who is a doctor but cannot teach his children because he does not have that training. Even though his/her profession is noble, he or she needs the services of a teacher and vice-versa.

Africans' sense of community is expressed in innumerous proverbs such as 'One log does not make a bridge' 'one finger does not kill lice, unity is strength', etc. All these proverbs emphasise that by himself or herself, an individual cannot do something substantial. One needs others for advice, teaching, rebuke, correcting and training above other things (See 2 Tim. 3:16).

One cannot give advice to himself; nor rebuke his own wrongs; nor correct or train himself; nor can he see his or her back. This calls us to share whatever talents and gifts we have for the sake of God and the general prosperity of our society as a way of encouraging one another. For 'we ought to encourage one another for the Day of the Lord is coming' (Heb. 10:25).[42]

The interdependence which exists among human being is like that which exists between cattle and cattle *egret* (Latin *bubulcus* means shepherd). Cattle *egret* is a type of a bird which accompany the grazing cattle and other large mammals as if it is the shepherd. The logic of doing so is that as the cattle moves in the grazing land, grasshoppers and other nutritious insects are disturbed and exposed and the bird gets the chance to feast them easily.

In this analogy, we realise that both the cattle and the bird need one another in that the bird helps to remove the ticks that cling to the body of the cow to suck its blood, with the danger of infecting the animal with East Coast Fever and other diseases; while at the same time, the bird depends on the cow, which exposes insects from their hiding places thereby giving it a chance to feast them.

This symbiotic behaviour clearly expresses the ideal African solidarity where we see one another as possible assets at all times. It agrees with St. Paul who echoes Christ when he says that the body is a unit of many parts which need one another at all times. For 'the body is not made up of one part but of many. If the foot should say, "Because I am not a hand, I do not belong to the body," it would not for that reason cease to be part of the body....If the whole body were an eye where would the sense of hearing be? If the whole body were an ear, where would the sense of smell be? But in fact, God has arranged the parts in the body, every one of them, just as he wanted them to be...' (1 Cor. 12:12-26).[43]

The philosophy behind exchange of greetings in Africa is to acknowledge the deep sense of affinity in society. Greeting someone in Africa has the following connotation: telling somebody 'I am at peace with you', 'I do not have anything against you'; 'we are brothers', 'I wish you well being', 'all is well' etc.[44] This idea is expressed in 2 Sam.18:28; a messenger arrives to David to announce the victory over Absalom. He begins with *shalom* "all is well". Often in greetings the use of the word *shalom* is an assurance to the person spoken to of one's good intentions that is one pledges oneself to keep peace.[45]

Existence of hatred between individuals in Africa is immediately discovered by absence of salute. A greeting offers and creates a sense of unity and avoids enmity. Similarly, theologically greetings symbolize token of mutual love and friendship. For instance the implication of epistolary greetings of Paul's letter goes beyond identifying writer and addressees; it is more than saying hello. The author's salutation manifests the nature of the relationship between the author and the audience and even draws lines around the conversation being carried on by the letter in hand. Meanings are more readily and rightly determined in terms of this "rhetorical relationship" formulated by the letter's opening words.

In 2 Cor.13:12 when Paul says "salute each other with holy kiss" he does not necessarily say Christians should kiss each other even when culture does not allow. But the passage recommends the cultivation of the spirit of love by being affectionate to one another. It means: show affection by hugging, smiling, shaking hands and being overall warm and affectionate to others. These are exterior manifestations of a strongly founded element of congeniality within families and the entire African I-Thou relationships well reflected within multiform of social realities.

Africans observe reconciliation as a value and part of social norms. Due to the fallible human nature, an emphatic recognition of the moral vulnerability of human beings call for the virtue of forgiveness and reconciliation to refurbish conflicts that would cause a rupture of relationship as insisted by Jesus Himself in his teaching. (Eph. 4:32)

4. Divergences Found within African Cultural Values

Having established some convergences of African values with Christianity, it is worthwhile also to see a few divergences within their culture. Africans were aware of the existence of a Supreme Being to whom they attributed all power and life. However, they believe that this God is very far from them and therefore they considered their ancestors as their intermediaries. This background makes them seek help and direct their prayers to ancestors than God their Creator. Sacrifices, rituals were offered to these ancestors. Automatically this made them to be recognised as polytheists and ancestral worshippers.

Other appalling cultural traditions practiced by some of the African tribes include severe punishment for those who broke social norms like killing or sending them to exile, suppression of women, killing of twins because of the belief that they bring bad fortunes, etc. So, despite the fact that good values exist in traditional African society, Christianizing Africans was substantially necessary to bring changes in those unbecoming cultural rituals and to evoke conversion to authentic Christian life based on strong ethical values.

For Christ's Gospel to be firmly rooted in the African soil would indeed mean a reversal of many traditional values and practices long cherished by the African. It would mean also a new ethical reference point, Christ's own love ethic as his new commandment. In practice this new faith with its new morality means to the African a higher idea of God and more perfect rules of human conduct.

Conclusion

As regards the reasons of the aforementioned African practices is that "the Africans find it difficult to conceive a man as a purely contemplative being; for them human qualities presuppose a world of human relations. It is only within our relationship with others that we can actualize our humanity. We believe strongly that isolation make our potentialities become inert, static and dormant. Relationship therefore is a crucial element and it needs to be cultivated by any means in every society. The above discussed values make Africans a single family; everyone feels at home wherever s/he is. This is all to do with the communality of African society where one person's happiness is happiness for all, and one person's sorrow is a sorrow for all.

Notes

1. Kofi A. Busia, *Africa in Search of Democracy,* Praeger, New York, USA, 1967, p. 1. Commenting on the intensity of religious attitude in African society, Leonard G. describing Igbos life says "they are, in the strict and natural sense of the word, a truly and a deeply religious people, of whom it can be said, as it has been said of the Hindus, that they eat religiously, drink religiously, bath religiously, dress religiously. In a few words, the religion of these natives as I have all along endeavoured to point out is their existence in their religion." A.G. Leonard, *The Lower Niger and Its Tribes,* Frank Cass, London, 1968, p.429.
2. *Ibid.*
3. Hugh Barber, *Crazy Revolution: Living Outrageously in Faith for the one who gave everything,* Xlibris Corporation, Bloomington Indiana, 2012, p. 35
4. Jerry D. Moore, *Visions of Culture: An Introduction to Anthropological Theories and Theorists*, Rowman Altamira, California- USA, 2004, p. 5.
5. Nigel A. Kumar, *What is Religion? A Theological Answer,* SAIACS Press, Bangalore-India, 2014, p.293.
6. Odejobi Cecilia Omobola, http://ijsse.com/sites/default/files/issues/2014/v4-i3-2014/Paper-4.pdf accessed on 9th July.
7. George A. Phiri, Social-*Cultural Anthropology: Communication with the African Society*, Wipf and Stock Publishers, Eugene Oregon, USA, 2009
8. Biko in Yosefu Waghid, *African philosophy of Education: On being human*, Routledge, Taylor, London, 2012, p. 27
9. See https://sielearning.tafensw.edu.au /MCS/CHCAOD402A/chcaod4 02a_csw/knowledge/values/values.htm
10. William Frankena, "Value and Valuation," *The Encyclopedia of Philosophy*, vol. 8, New York: MacMillan, 1967, pp. 583-584.
11. Gayle Cotton, Say Anything to Anyone, Anywhere: 5 Keys To Successful Cross-Cultural communication, John Wiley & Sons Publishers, USA, 2013, p.45.
12. Macaulay A. Kanu, The *indispensability of the basic social values in African Traditional: A Philosophical appraisal,* p.150 in file:///C:/Users/teresa/Downloads/57930-101933-1-PB.pdf accessed on 9th July,2015.
13. *Ibid.*

14. Ifeanyi A, Menkiti, "*Person and Community in African traditional thought" African Philosophy: An Introduction*, 3rd edition, University Press of America, Lanham, Maryland, 1984 p. 176
15. John S. Mbiti, *An Introduction to African Religion,* East Africa Educational Publishers, Nairobi, Kenya, 1991, p.176. (Hereafter referred to as Mbiti, *Introduction to African Religions*). Fr. Joseph Israel comment about this saying a visitor in Africa is not seen as an interruption; people are happy to see visitors and they welcome them wholeheartedly because hospitality is a cultural and social value which is promulgated by each community. Cf. Joseph Israel, *The Church as a Family: A Theological Pastoral Study With Reference to the African Synod*, Pontificia Universitas Lateranensis, Rome, 1998, p. 52. Also Pope John Paul II in his pastoral address in Congo said "Nor can I pass over in silence the deep impression made on me by the vitality of that continent, which preserves intact a good many fundamental moral values, such as those of hospitality, the family, the community sense, life as a precious gift, which is always given a generous and happy welcome." John Paul II, in Tanye, *The Church as Family,* p. 30. Africans believe visitors bring blessing to their hosts and are considered as divine agents. Sybertz observed "....when a visitor comes to someone's home, family quarrels stop, the sick cheer up, peace is restored and the home is restored to new strength. Visitors are therefore social healers. They are family doctors in sense." Sybertz D. & Healey J., *Toward an African Narrative Theology*, Maryknoll: Orbis, New York, USA, 1996, p. 174.
16. Afolayan, *Culture and Customs of S. Africa*, Pp. 221-222.
17. Julius K. Nyerere, *Ujamaa: Essays on Socialism,* Oxford University Press, Dar es-salaam-Tanzania, 1968, p. 5.
18. A. Briton, *In the Heart of Bantuland: A record of twenty-nine years in Central Africa among the Bantu Peoples*, Dugald Campbell, London, 1922, p. 45.
19. Kwame Gyekye, *African Cultural Values: An Introduction*, Sankofa Publishing Company, Accra, Ghana, 1996, p. 25.
20. Menkiti, *Person and the Community,* p. 189.
21. Healey and Sybertz 1996:173
22. Ibid. p.172
23. Julius Mutugi Gathogo, *African Hospitality: Is it Compatible with the Ideal of Christ's Hospitality?* in http://churchsociety.org/docs/churchman/120/Cman_120_1_Gathogo.pdf accessed on 21July, 2015. (Hereafter referred to as Mutugi Gathogo)
24. Sambuli, *The Heartbeat,* p. 95.
25. Philip Higgs, *African Voices in Education*, Juta and Company Ltd, Cape town, South Africa, 2000, p. 183.
26. See http://www.emeka.at/african_cultural_vaules.pdf accessed on 25th July,2015
27. *Ibid.*
28. Polycarp Ikuenobe, *Philosophical Perspectives on Communalism and Morality in Africa Traditions*, A division of Rowman & Littlefield Publishers, Inc., Lanham, Oxford, UK, 2006, p. 52. (Hereafter referred to as Ikuenobe, *Communalism and Morality in Africa*).
29. Macaulay A. Kanu, *The Indispensability of the Basic Social Values in African Tradition: a Philosophical Appraisal* in file:///C:/Users/teresa/Downloads/57930-101933-1-PB%20(1).pdf accessed on 26th July, 2015.
30. Tanye, *Church as a Family*, p. 28.

31. Rose R. Korir, *An Analysis of the Nandi Proverbs and its place in critical psychology* in www.discourseunit.com/arcp/5. Accessed on 20th Sept. 2013.
32. Charles V. Vicencio & Fame Du Toir eds., *Truth and Reconciliation in South Africa: 10 Years On,* New Africa Books Ltd, Cape town, South Africa, 2006, Pp. 75-76.
33. Robert J. Schreiter, *Reconciliation Mission &Ministry in Changing Social Oder*, Orbis Books Maryknol New York, USA, 1992 p. 20.
34. See Mutugi Gathogo.
35. *Ibid.*
36. Christine D. Pohl, *Making Room: Recovering Hospitality as a Christian Tradition* (Grand Rapids, MI: Eerdmans, 1999), xi.
37. John Koenig, *New Testament Hospitality: Partnership with Strangers as Promise and Mission* (Philadelphia, PA: Fortress, 1985), p. 11. Koenig also states in his recent study on the missionary dimensions of the church's Eucharistic rituals: "Answering the command to join Christ's mission becomes possible only when we can savor the eager and compassionate welcome that he extends to each of us personally (Matthew 11:28f.; Romans 15:7ff.)." The Feast of the World's Redemption: Eucharistic Origins and Christian Mission (Harrisburg, PA: Trinity Press International, 2000), p. 220.
38. See Mutugi Gathogo.
39. *Ibid.*
40. Christine D. Pohl, *Making Room: Recovering Hospitality as a Christian Tradition* (Grand Rapids, MI: Eerdmans, 1999), p. 172.
41. Julius G. Mutugi, *The Truth about African Hosipitality: Is There Hope for Africa?* Salt Productions, Kenya, 2001, p.21.
42. *Ibid.*
43. Julius G. Mutugi, *African Hospitality: Is it Compatible with the Ideal of Christ's Hospitality? Part 1* in http://churchsociety.org/docs/churchman/120/Cman_120_1_Gathogo.pdf accessed on 26 th July 2015.
44. Unfortunately nowadays things are contrary. Malicious greetings exist almost everywhere. Many people do not want to show they are in bad term with somebody; they will exchange greetings as usual. But what happen behind this you cannot imagine. People are even killed by those whom they think is a friend without knowing.
45. Martin F. Baasten, *Hamlet on a Hill: Semitic and Greek Studies*, Peeters Publishers, USA, 203, p.156.

11

Friends for a Purpose: South Africa's UDF as a Model for the Environmental Movement

Peter Knox, SJ

Dean of the Jesuit School of Theology, and Deputy Principal – Academic, Hekima University College, Nairobi, Kenya

Abstract: Multiple serious threats face Earth as a home hospitable to the human race and the myriad species that inhabit this planet. Nine of these are named in the 2009 "Planetary Boundaries" theory of Rockström et al. Pope Francis discusses many of these threats in his highly spiritual, accessible, groundbreaking 2015 environmental encyclical *Laudato Si'*. In the encyclical, Pope Francis calls for political action to pressurise governments to legislate and enforce sound environmental policies. Such action to limit environmental degradation entails sustained strategic citizen mobilisation at national, regional and municipal levels.

In this paper the author maintains that the United Democratic Front (UDF), which contributed to the toppling of apartheid in South Africa in 1992, might serve as a model for such multi-level sustained strategic citizen mobilisation. What the author dubs the "United Environmental Front" should involve every citizen of planet Earth, and operate internationally, regionally, nationally and locally. Alliances of concerned citizens should challenge the hegemony of vested political and economic interests which pollute, strip landscapes, dump radioactivity, contribute to global climate change, etc.

Having undergone a personal conversion, activists will educate others to avoid ecologically harmful lifestyles. Shouldn't people in religious life be at the forefront of this global and intergenerational solidarity?

Keywords: Environment, UDF, South Africa, *Laudato Si'*, Activism

Introduction

South Africa (hereafter, SA) had a history of alliances to topple apartheid. For instance, the multiracial Congress Alliance was founded in the 1950's and included the SAIC - the SA Indian Congress - founded in 1924, (of which Mahatma Ghandi was an important member).[1] The Congress Alliance led to the writing of the Freedom Charter in 1955. A larger political tripartite "strategic alliance" was forged later between the African National Congress, the SA Communist Party and the Congress of SA Trades Unions. This alliance persists till this day in SA parliamentary politics, preventing the communists and largest trade unions from effectively challenging the policies and candidates of the ruling party.

1. The United Democratic Front

Arguably the most effective of the alliances to challenge apartheid was the United Democratic Front (UDF), launched in 1983 in opposition to P.W. Botha's proposed changed constitution and tricameral parliamentary system. This was designed specifically to co-opt "Indian" and "Coloured" minorities to prop up SA's faltering apartheid government. The tricameral parliament was mere window-dressing. It offered no executive powers to the House of Representatives ("Coloureds") or House of Delegates ("Indians"). The purpose was to keep the majority Black population disenfranchised with no share of power in SA.

The UDF brought together members well over five hundred anti-apartheid groups, civic, student, political, labour, and ecclesiastical movements. Based on non-racial principles, the UDF brought under one umbrella members of "Black, White, Coloured and Indian" organisations.[2]

The front operated countrywide, incorporating movements from all the ethnic groups scattered around the country. The UDF brought together people who did not have a natural affinity to each other, e.g.

White madams of the Black Sash movement who were initially and primarily concerned for their domestic servants' welfare.

Congress of South African Trade Unions - an umbrella body of mostly "black" (meaning everybody not identified as "white") trade unions.

Conscientious Objectors: End Conscription Campaign - young white men who refused to do four years of military national service. Many of the members of the ECC were labelled "homosexuals" – in those days a grave insult – because they were either pacifists or strongly objected to SA's military adventures in the neighbouring states and in the townships of the country

Black student activists, members of the Congress of South African Students (COSAS) at secondary and tertiary level, protesting the scandalous apartheid educational system

Yet participating together in the struggle for democracy, calling one another "comrade," and learning about and undergoing the trials and persecutions meted out by the apartheid government helped people to forge friendships and understanding despite their vastly disparate backgrounds.

2. Reason for Such a Front: Apartheid as a Totalitarian Ideology

Why was there a need for such a broad front? As an ideology, apartheid touched every dimension of SA life, segregating people from birth to the grave. Opposition to apartheid was equally needed at every level of SA society. The grand vision of apartheid was of keeping Members of the racial groups completely separate and affording them (read: "whites," and particularly Afrikaner whites, descended from Dutch colonialists) "separate development." The strategy was to "other" – i.e. alienate – members of different racial groups to the extent that they believed in the need and the logic of apartheid. With its accession to power of the Nationalist Party in 1948, a whole raft of legislations was enacted to entrench white domination of the economy, codifying what had existed in many instances since the British colonial period, and from 1910 when the Union of SA became independent from Britain.

With the Immorality Act (1950) and Prohibition of Mixed Marriages Act (1949), (sexual) relationships were prohibited across colour lines. The Reservation of Separate Amenities Act (1953) assigned different amenities to different "communities" - e.g. municipal facilities like benches, buses, libraries, swimming pools, beaches; provincial facilities like hospitals, schools; and national facilities like post offices, universities, etc. The Bantu Homelands Citizenship Act (1971) assigned different parcels of the country to different Bantu tribes. These were tiny tracts of land like pieces of a jigsaw puzzle which amounted to a fraction of the country, and were intended to deprive Bantu people of the natural richness of the land. Four of the tribal "homelands" took so-called "independence" (Transkei, Ciskei, Venda and Bophutatswana) and became separate "states" with their own laws, borders, passports, citizens, etc. and diplomatic representation in SA - the only country in the world that recognised them. The homelands policy was designed to deny SA citizenship to the Black majority. The Bantu Education Act (1953) was enacted to provide inferior education to keep black people as hewers of wood and drawers of water - so that they would never be suitably qualified to participate as significant wage earners in SA's rapidly industrialising economy. Indian and Coloured schools and universities were allocated considerably less funds per student than white schools. White universities were world-class and black universities were no more than overpopulated "bush colleges" - some of which, however, contributed to the education of famous leaders like Nelson Mandela, Robert Mugabe, Steven Biko, etc.[3]

Each race was to have its own space and facilities, and there was no need for any group to mix socially or politically with another. The lie, of course, was that the white economy was completely dependent on the labour input of every other race. And so the government created labour pools within commuting distance of each white urban centre. There were Black, Coloured and Indian townships "out of sight, and out of mind" of the white suburbs, and further afield were the so-called homelands, enormous impoverished labour reserves, from which labourers were allowed to come to service the white economy – provided they had the right stamps in their "pass book."

3. UDF's Achievements

The UDF co-ordinated rallies, marches, political protests, student unrest, intellectual ferment – all around SA and abroad. Through its various labour union branches, it organised mass action for improved working conditions and remuneration. This was widely supported by other branches of the UDF. The front argued for disinvestment and sanctions, thereby contributing to the growing international isolation of SA.[4] The UDF challenged apartheid education, health, economy, job reservation, etc. to the point where the President P.W. Botha believed there was a "total onslaught" against white domination. He met this with his brutal "total strategy," bringing the army into the townships to suppress any protests. Students were arrested, children were killed, activists were detained without trial, tortured, "disappeared." Spies were deployed everywhere. Against enormous opposition, the UDF continued its activities, eroding the legitimacy and gradually wearing down the resolve of the SA government. On 2 February 1990, the political parties were unbanned, some political prisoners were released, some exiles were permitted to return, the State of Emergency was partially lifted, executions were suspended, and restrictions on the UDF were lifted. This created a climate in which, negotiations could be held for a new constitution, and ultimately democratic elections could be held with universal franchise on 14 April 1994. After that, the UDF naturally disbanded. The political landscape had obviously changed over the decade of the UDF's existence. Having come together from very disparate backgrounds into a single struggle, many comrades in arms found common ground to continue their journey towards greater justice, equality and freedom, even in the new democratic dispensation.

4. Environmental Threats

There are multiple serious threats to the wellbeing of every person on this planet, and to the survival of the human species.[5] "Planetary boundary" theory outlines nine threats to human existence on the planet. The theory shows that everything is interconnected. Our planet is not a collection of disparate cycles. But rather it is an "earth system." Interfering with any set of factors may tip our planet beyond the point at which it can support human life. The 2015 version of this research lists these factors as: climate change, stratospheric ozone depletion, atmospheric aerosol loading, ocean acidification, freshwater use, biogeochemical flows, land-system change, biosphere integrity and novel entities.[6] Trained as a chemist, Pope Francis deals with five of these threats in his ground-breaking encyclical *Laudato Si'* (LS).[7] But I argue that he barely scratches the surface of the environmental threats facing human life on the planet.

The welfare of every citizen, and our descendants for generations to come is threatened by these ecological factors. To face such threats will require concerted effort from every member of every layer of human society if our species is to survive. Francis is aware that the environmental threats are global in their scope. Thus he makes a break from previous encyclicals and teachings of the church which are addressed to Catholics or to "all men and women of good will." He breaks out of traditional partisan teaching, and writes "I would like to enter into dialogue with *all people* about our common home."[8] In his section on "justice between the generations"[9] he urges cross-generational solidarity – to the point of befriending the generations that are yet to come, and preserving a home on Earth for them.[10]

Francis writes that we need to wean ourselves from our "throwaway culture."[11] To do this, we must think of the origin and destination of everything we buy, including every piece of packaging and the rubbish we generate. We need to participate in climate demonstrations, such as are taking place around the planet. We need to disinvest and call for disinvestment from fossil fuel companies – no matter the cost and inconvenience to us. We need to expose the lies and hypocrisy of industrialists, and also be prepared to have our own moral compromises exposed. We need to educate our children and all adults about the harmful effects of our transport and fuel choices. We need to begin to invest heavily in more renewable sources of energy. We need to block the further development of nanoparticles if no environmental impact study has been done on them – even if our brothers and sisters, our spouses and uncles are involved in these industries.

LS is not just a pious reflection on our common home, with a touch of St Francis Assisi to make us feel good. It is a battle cry to save our planet. To heed the call, every person needs to be involved. It is commendable to pressurise governments to carry out their responsibilities towards the environment. Pope Francis writes:

We cannot fail to praise the commitment of international agencies and civil society organizations which draw public attention to these issues and offer critical cooperation, employing legitimate means of pressure, to ensure that each government carries out its proper and inalienable responsibility to preserve its country's environment and natural resources, without capitulating to spurious local or international interests.[12]

While this is a very good place to start, environmental activism is not justabout cleaning up the local river or sidewalk. Francis is clear that it involves political and strategic mobilisation at the national, regional and municipal levels. *Laudato Si'* tells us:

Because the enforcement of laws is at times inadequate due to corruption, public pressure has to be exerted in order to bring about decisive political action. Society, through non-governmental organizations and intermediate groups, must put pressure on governments to develop more rigorous regulations, procedures and controls. Unless citizens control political power – national, regional and municipal – it will not be possible to control damage to the environment.[13]

Francis does not condemn governments for placing their priorities on short-term, visible projects, which bring returns within the immediate election cycle – particularly when resources are limited. Rather with a dose of realism, he writes: "Results take time and demand immediate outlays which may not produce tangible effects within any one government's term. That is why, in the absence of pressure from the public and from civic institutions, political authorities will always be reluctant to intervene, all the more when urgent needs must be met."[14]

5. A Similar United Front is Required for the Ecological Challenge

It is no exaggeration, thus, to say that Pope Francis is calling for a co-ordinated approach to environmental threats along the lines of the UDF – not just groups of "environmental" activists, but every citizen of Planet Earth.15 The breadth of the environmental threats calls for a worldwide "UEF" – a United Environmental Front. There are world-wide networks and alliances of activists challenging the hegemony of vested political and economic interests which strip our forests bare, which pump pollutants into our air, water and land, which extract minerals and fossil fuels as though there were no tomorrow, leaking chemical by-products and fossil fuels in precious water reserves, which produce radioactive waste and dump it in Africa, which develop nanotechnology with no thought for its environmental impact, etc. Similar to the strategies of the UDF, these networks need education to enhance our personal conversion.[16] They need to promote intellectual ferment, so that other ways of problem solving and new models of development might be conceived. These networks will thrive with some kind of co-ordination at grassroots level. We need to disinvest funds from all kinds of environmental demons. We will see larger and more intense protests, marches and demonstrations. Ultimately it is conceivable that this might lead to civil disobedience and occasional acts of industrial sabotage.

For people in religious life, environmental advocacy must become a constitutive dimension of all our ministries. We should discover all sorts of new friends: Jesuits should learn from Franciscan tradition. Men must sit at the feet of women theologians who are at the forefront of Christian environmental concerns.[17] Christians can take a leaf out of Buddhists' behaviour with their "tread lightly" philosophy. People "in the world" would benefit from the wisdom of monastic movements and live more in tune with natural cycles. Theologians can learn from agriculturalists so that our speculation is not in some ethereal beyond, but rooted in the vital concerns of everyday life.

The trouble with living in emerging economies like India and Africa is that our compatriots have such high aspirations. Everybody wants to live the capitalist dream, ignoring that this is a distorted, unsustainable model of development. Telling people that this lifestyle is neither possible nor desirable is a sure way to "lose friends and influence over people."[18] As we lose friends, we form new friendships and alliances, collaborating with like-minded people, including people who are not-so completely different to ourselves – even those on other ends of the planet.[19]

Notes

1. About 152,000 Indians arrived in SA from 1860 to 1911 to work mainly in the sugar fields of Natal, as indentured labourers (a sanitised version of slavery). See Padraig O'Malley "The Indian Community in SA" - https://www.nelsonmandela.org/omalley/index.php/site/q/03lv02424/04lv03370/05lv03414.htm .
2. These are the four largest race groups identified under apartheid. At one time, the classification included Griquas, San, etc. (e.g. Japanese were regarded as 'honorary whites.' Yet Chinese were in a group of their own.)
3. I have no wish to disparage the dedicated and (in some cases) highly qualified academics who taught there, selflessly committed to providing black students the best education they possibly could.
4. Jawahrlal Nehru led international isolation of SA because of its apartheid policies when he opened the discussions that finally saw the expulsion of SA from the Commonwealth in 1961.
5. See Johan Rockström, et al., "Planetary Boundaries: Exploring the Safe Operating Space for Humanity," *Ecology and Society*, 14, no. 2 (2009).
6. Like nanoparticles and radioactivity.
7. Pope Francis, *Encyclical Letter Laudato Si' on the Care for Our Common Home* (Vatican City: 2015).

8. Ibid., 3. Italics mine.
9. Ibid., 159-162.
10. In LS 53, Francis specifically picks up on the UN's notion of sustainability which implies that the present generation not compromise the ability of future generations to meet their own needs. See United Nations World Commission on Environment and Development, *Our Common Future* (Oslo: 1987), 27. He has a great ally in the Brundtland Report which decries that "We borrow environmental capital from future generations with no intention or prospect of repaying." See ibid., 25. This is not original to Pope Francis in Catholic Social Teaching. In his annual peace message for 2010 Pope Benedict quotes the concept of intergenerational solidarity from his predecessors John Paul II and Paul VI. See Benedict XVI, *If You Want to Cultivate Peace, Protect Creation*, Message for World Day of Peace (Vatican City: 1 January 2010), 8.
11. See Francis, *Laudato Si'*, 20-22.
12. *Laudato Si'* 38.
13. *Laudato Si'* 179.
14. *Laudato Si'* 181.
15. Particularly the most powerful - businesspeople who can make the difference to the way industry is conducted. But the likelihood is that they will be the last to act - having such strong investments in the current way of conducting business. A case in point is the 2015 disclosure of industrial-scale cheating on Nitrous Oxide emission results on diesel vehicles manufactured by Volkswagen. There is no doubt in my mind that this is not reserved to one German motor manufacturer, but it betrays industry-wide deception to get around inconvenient legislation designed to protect the environment from nitrous oxides. These carcinogenic air pollutants are particularly virulent contributors to the greenhouse effect.
16. For a very accessible online textbook go to the Jesuits' Healing Earth: http://healingearth.ijep.net/.
17. Pioneering 'ecofeminists' like Rosemary Radford Reuther, Sallie Mc Fague and Evone Gebara come to mind.
18. As opposed to Dale Carnegie, *How to Win Friends and Influence People* (New York: Simon and Schuster, 1936).
19. There are many global networks such as Global Catholic Climate Movement (GCCM), AVAAZ and 350.org which enhance the sense that we are all citizens of one world, with common concerns and a united voice. Visit https://avaaz.org and www.350.org and https://catholicclimatemovement.global/.

12

Befriending the Other: A Paradigm for Re-Building Relationships

Eugenia Thomas, HSS
Former Superior General, Society of Holy Spirit Sisters, Germany

Abstract: Africans believe that life is a complex web of relationships. "Befriending the other" in an African context aims at rebuilding relationships that are broken and distorted due to slave trade, religious fundamentalism, tribalism, and all sorts of gender and cultural inequality that destroy human life. In the Old Testament God revealed himself in constant relationships by rebuilding the community of Israel through His own Spirit and in the New Testament Jesus makes the theme of relationship central through his vision of "who the other is" and how one should respond to the other. Pope Francis invites us to share our lives as a symbol of God's love with the marginalized and the poor and Jean Vanier insists that "each one is carrying the capacity to be, to become, to love and to be loved. The goal of 'befriending the other' is to transform our relationships in all spheres of life. It is to make our entire cosmos a better place to live in. The various efforts of our Inter-religious Dialogue invariably aim at building bridges with the other and to learn to accept others with all their differences. Befriending the other indeed is a process of radical opening of oneself up to God and to the 'other towards the fullness of humanity.

Keywords: Befriending; Bridge-building; Relationships: Interconnectedness; Harmony; Africa

Introduction

Have you ever been an alien, a foreigner, or a stranger? I have and I thought I was going to die. I felt I was losing my identity; no longer sure of who I was, as if the 'me' I thought I knew had been steamed off. I understood however, that I was different. Still the question of who the 'other' is might seem useless because in some way we are all the 'others' to someone, and everyone else is 'other to us. We can never fully know 'the other' and even if we strive to do so, 'the other' is constantly changing. At the same time, there can be no 'I' without relation to the concept of the other.

The concept of the 'other' is considered to be an individual or a group perceived as not belonging, as they are culturally constructed as being fundamentally different in some way, those we usually do not want to see or those who pretend do not exist and are excluded.[1] The other is also seen as a lesser or inferior being and is treated accordingly in a society having fewer or no legal rights or may even be regarded as sub-human. The paradox of our times is that the drastic process of 'othering' is accelerated in an apparently 'unifying' world through unitive processes of globalization and information and communication explosion.

Befriending the Other means treating human as "human" and giving them due respect. It is veritably the need of the hour as the panacea to various conflict situations both national and global such as socio-political-economical-cultural-ethnic tensions, religious rivalries, terrorist violence, ideological differences, dehumanizing elements, selfishness, individualism, egoism, oppression of women, the poor, the orphan, sexual abuses, deforestation and ecological unawareness.

We meet many people every day. We might have often looked at them but without seeing them because we think that they are different. Befriending the other in the society is to understand them, to respect them and accept them as they are and treat them with dignity and justice rather than belittling them because they are created in the image and likeness of God, the Ultimate OTHER.[2] It is to cause someone to be your friend. It is a means of reducing the isolation (*Ecclesia Africa* 79) and build up bridges to maintain close relationships, nurture confidence and trust. It is the best gift to the world, a spiritual nova in our midst exerting a force stronger than vengeance, stronger than racism, stronger than discrimination and hate.

Hence each relationship is effectively a union of what the referred person needs and that which the other can offer. Certainly, this demands a lot of effort on all sides, as it encourages being open and walking step by step - towards building a compromise where the world views/feelings and needs of each member have a place. We are shaped by those who love us and by those who refuse to love us. Befriending has the potential to rip through the processes of 'othering' and accentuate the processes of 'building bridges'. Most relationships can begin with a simple greeting offered sincerely. It can begin a conversation, which in turn starts a friendship that can powerfully affect lives and relationships. Learning to be quick to befriend the other, ready to accept them, and join them in their life journeys begins the process of rebuilding relationships with others around us and offers to them a soft place to fall,3 shares stories, cry together and forgive.[4]

1. Befriending the 'Other' Is a Bridge Building

Human beings are beings for others. Befriending is a state of genuine well-being of an entire community, of which human relationships form the core. Befriending the 'other' in Africa aims at rebuilding relationships that are broken, due to slave trade, colonialism, tribalism, corruption, gender discrimination and religious fundamentalism that has destroyed human life, culture and human possibilities.

Jean Vanier presents a radical way to embrace the 'other' when he says, "each one is carrying the capacity to be, to become, to love and to be loved."[5] We are all called to share our lives with people in dehumanising ambiences and pain, and place them in a position where they can grow toward authentic humanity in all its fullness of life.[6] Befriending the other challenges us to venture beyond our boundaries towards wider horizons, where the rest of the human family may be encountered and appreciated, learn to share, build spaces[7] and relate because each person is a house where God resides.[8] Pope Francis in his *Evangelii Gaudium* invites us to share our lives with the marginalized of the society "because God's heart has a special place for the poor,[9] those we consider the 'other'.

The African Philosophy of *Ubuntu*[10] (humanness) insists on the inter-connectedness of all humankind, an all-inclusive nature of community in which every individual is befriended. The Zulu expression of '*Umuntu ngubuntu Ngabanye Bantu* means 'a person is a person through another person', insists on interconnectedness of humankind and an all-inclusive nature of a society in which every individual is valued and appreciated. Archbishop Desmund Tutu tells us that "if at all we are to prosper it will only be together."[11] This is also stressed in GS 25 where human beings are essentially social and interdependence by nature. Community building values of love, generosity, reconciliation, freedom, justice, peace and trust should be everywhere cultivated.

2. Areas in Africa Crying for Befriending the Other

Relationships can be messy. When they are good, they are really good, but when they turn sour nothing can be more painful. Being hurt by others can make us so judgemental and so protective of ourselves that it is difficult to invest in new relationships.[12] It is not just the interpersonal relationships between individuals that requires reconciliation, healing and befriending but the social and cultural relations as well. The socio-historical experiences of othering in Africa have left profound and evident scars in communities and persons, and they require the healing touch of 'befriending'. Those areas are:

a. Slavery

People are considered slaves when others have total control on their life and they are used, forced to work either by mental and physical threat instead of being loved. Human beings were reduced to commodities ('other') a category that sanitizes the high level of violence and mass murder that inflicted on the Africans and their societies.[13]

Between 16th and 19th centuries about hundred million people were uprooted from Africa by this physical and social violence.[14] Of these millions only 10 million arrived America, Europe and Asia. Many were killed individually or collectively in various brutal and vicious ways.[15] In 2001 Pope John Paul II in Senegal asked for forgiveness and said "Christians may never again become the oppressor of the other brethren."[16] Sad enough this evil is still going on in some parts of Africa. Global Slavery Index 2014 shows that out of 35.8 million enslaved people in modern world 6.4 million are in African Continent.[17]

Wars and political instability have forced many African citizens to move to other parts of the continent and abroad which makes them vulnerable. In South Sudan for example, there are 800,000 people currently enslaved citizens.[18] The country's decades of civil war between the North and the South has enslaved thousands and resulted periodic raids on villages. Many local residents were subsequently enslaved to work as local domestic field workers, many women forced into marriages, boys and men forced to join armed groups.[19] In this context of deplorable social cleavages and bruising historical experiences of dehumanizing slavery, the Africans are called to be agents of befriending the other which Christ our peace (Eph.2:14) offers to humanity and rebuild our embittered relationships.

b. Gender Inequality and Cultural Barriers

Many women in Africa are not perceived as equal citizens as they have few rights and no decision-making in the families, religions or societies.[20] They are often denied access to health care, property, education and information and are affected by religious and cultural oppression.[21] Women are often considered the 'other' especially in the patriarchal system[22] and not "treated as person and sister in humanity."[23] The working paper on the African Synod, "*Instrumentum Laboris*" clearly outlines some of the types of discrimination as:

- Some aspects of marriage laws and customs in Africa which are oppressive against women and really dehumanizing e.g. polygamy,[24] dowry system, virginity rituals and child bearing force.
- Clan consciousness which is exclusive.
- In some societies a girl of 13-16 years is given in marriage to a man she does not know and is much older than herself. This can be a very sad experience for the young bride.
- Customs of widowhood which are generally oppressive of women, e.g. widow's disproportionate exclusion from property ownership.
- Cultural practices such as female genital mutilation/cutting.[25]
- The role of women within society is something unduly restricted.
- In some societies women are practically reduced to beasts of burden and are subjected to untold suffering and inhuman treatment.

This has been part of the fate of the African woman. But befriending the other will show that it is not her destiny. Despite all these a woman in Africa remains the source of strength and the backbone of the society. Her spit remains a fire that flares stronger and higher with each attempt to extinguish it. Her smile lights up the darkest night and the warmth of her embrace heals the worst wounds. This strength is for the well-being of the whole community rather than for the woman herself.

In those countries where there is war, women and girls are targeted of conscious shocking brutality and sexual violence and being taken to slavery. Every day they face threats from armed militias, the military and even the police who are supposed to protect them. Where are the 220 school girls of government secondary school Chipok Nigeria kidnapped by Bokoharam in 2014?[26] Parents say the girls are being sold to their Islamic extremist abductors for 2,000 naira ($12) and married. If numbers could scream,[27] the world would understand how women are silent sufferers in a society we now live and it is more dangerous to be a woman today than a soldier.[28] It is in such situation St John Paul II once said, "Men must be taught to love in a noble way; they must be educated in depth in this truth, that is, in the fact that a woman is a person and not simply an object of adultery."[29]

Women as primary caretakers of the family are afraid to work in the fields or gather firewood from the jungle or collect water even in a group as it puts them at a greater risk of attack. They have to care for children and try to earn money with no social safety net. Women are silent sufferers. How to befriend the 'other'? How do we equalize oppressive power relations through the process of befriending? We are in dilemma!!

Befriending the other will provide an atmosphere for women to be loved, to be listened, to be appreciated and to be treated with absolute ease and a sense of friendliness that hold no trace of embarrassment or inappropriate familiarity.

It will change the mindset of the Africans and "study further women problem in cooperation with the government and church agencies whenever possible" (*Ecclesia in Africa 121*) and create inclusive conditions on which we relate and accept 'the other" for we are all one in Christ (Gal. 3:28)

c. Religious Fundamentalism

Relationships in Africa are at stake. There are groups based on Religious Fundamentalism (known as "*Born again fundamentalists and fanatics*)[30] e.g. *Bokoharam* – Nigeria, *El Shabaab* – Somalia, Brotherhood – Egypt, and *Uamsho*[31] – Tanzania and more others. In these countries, Christian-Muslim relationship is at its lowest ebb. Fundamentalist's activism is nothing if not youthful, and its young disciples are most urban, unemployed and profoundly unhappy with the politics they have known. The 'other' who is my sister and brother is seen by the religious as *'Kafir'* – infidel who deserves only to be killed. Such groups and more others have forgotten that human life is sacred and valuable and each has the right and freedom to live and worship. The sanctity and dignity of life which has been preserved and adored by all cultures and religious traditions in the past, seems now to be weakened. This is challenging the *Ubuntu* understanding.

Religion must touch upon the deepest level of identity. It is a relational identity because religion in its purest sense is about relationship. It challenges the believer to grow into an 'I' – 'Thou' relationship with the Divine and resonate its dynamics in the relationship with the 'other'. Here the 'other' is not an object or an 'it' but a 'thou' a subject, a person.[32] However, the existence of such extremist groups shows that the main groups have failed to give meaning and identity to their people especially the young. Many see life as meaningless because of sufferings, hardships and unrealized goals in life. They are hoping for eschatological satisfaction and promises. African values of family, generosity, protect life, care the other, freedom to worship and religious pluralism are losing meaning.

It is in this context that we have to understand befriending 'the other' as a paradigm for rebuilding relationships for "the greatest needs of human being are the needs of fellow human beings."[33] You recognise me in my sameness when you acknowledge me as a human among humans. Therefore befriending 'the other' is a vision of both an on-going process to establish a community of love and care in which conflict and injustice, though still present, are actively being addressed, and the eschatological goal of cosmic communion in love being definitely achieved."[34] A call for religious pluralism will lead us to transcend the borders in a radical way by fashioning an agenda for dialogue,[35] and make all aware that no matter what religion one is believing we are all "fellow-travellers searching for life, light and truth.[36]

d. Tribalism

Within the borders left by the colonial powers, the coexistence of ethnic groups with different traditions, languages and even religions[37] often meets obstacles arising from serious mutual hostility (*Ecclesia in Africa* 49). It is common in Africa to find people of the same tribal supporting each other. The problem begins when this 'standing together' is exclusive. This malaise is spiritually, emotionally and socially crippling and social and religious communities, thus making them unspiritual, unhappy, unloving, unfruitful and unfriendly. Divisions due to tribalism have been a scandal to witness the Gospel as many live unfulfilled life in the society and Church as chances to fulfil their dreams are blocked.[38]

Although Bujo Benezet reminds us that Jesus Christ, the Proto Ancestor is the foundation of a new tribe/clan community and culture. Such a culture is challenged by the culture of Christianity and of *Ubuntu* that celebrates the spirit of unity in diversity which upholds an inclusive solidarity as opposed to exclusiveness: "All people are called to belong to the new People of God to promote peace" (*LG 13)* and "Christians cherish a feeling of deep solidarity with human race in its history" *(GS 1*). Unfortunately, in many parts of Africa, stress on ethnicity, tribalism and regionalism have threatened living together in amity. Ethnic antagonism can be very disastrous. The worst case of genocide in 1994 took place in Rwanda where about a million Rwandans died. "The Hutu saw the 'elimination of Tutsi sisters and brothers as a practical solution to their political problems."[39]

Befriending the other protects our relationships from the damage of the past. It frees others from demand of perfection as it overlooks faults and offenses. When the Africans learn to share the journey together they will be able to transcend tribalism that has enchained the mentality of many. This challenges us to venture beyond our ethnic or regional boundaries towards wider horizons and open spaces where the rest of humanity will be encountered and befriended.[40] Africans must energetically combat tribalism, which is a poison, a social scourge that is Africa's misfortune today.

3. The Biblical Call to Embrace the Other

As scriptural image of befriending, shalom, peace addresses the fundamental order of relationships with physical world, other persons both individually and collectively, oneself and God. Befriending the other reigns when the whole world and its parts are in right relationships. It evokes an image of harmonious interrelationship order and cooperate for independence.

Living in God's love is the first step of befriending. Befriending the other is the covenant relationship of Yahweh and the people: they shall be my people and I will be their God with faithfulness and justice (Zechariah 8:8).

The chapter ends (vv 20-23) with the image of God's dwelling among the people. In Is. 2:2-5 it is the word of Yahweh which instructs the nations to beat their swords into ploughshares and their spears into punning hooks (Hos. 4:1). For Hosea, one cannot claim to have experienced God as a covenant partner if one does not maintain the same relationship with one's fellow human partner.[41]

When relationships are broken, we see God repairing with his own Spirit (Ez. 37:23). Thus, relationship with God seems prerequisites to befriending the other and its fulfilment is to live the life in fullness – live in God and God in us (Jn. 5:20). The entire biblical narrative can be read as the consistent, persevering attempts of befriending from an unconditionally loving God to a people who constantly rebel, distance and seek to retreat to their own selfish shells. God doesn't give up! This can be a paradigm for all our initiatives of befriending.

Service to other person flows from fundamental openness to a personal reality. Human persons are being for others. Prophets Amos 5:10-12; Isaiah 1:21-23 measured the quality of community life by response to the concrete needs of those who were powerless to demand a response, namely the poor, the widow and the orphans. Prophet Amos has strongly insisted "Where there is no justice the society suffers, and where there is no righteousness the society dies"[42]

The New Testament presents a recurrent cluster of ideas in its descriptions of befriending the other and of bringing people together.[43] The breaking-in of the reign of God in Jesus' mandate connected to some specific signs (Lk. 4:18-19) reveals the whole idea of befriending. This liberation means wholeness on socio-political as well as personal level. In Lk. 19:1-10, Jesus risked ruining His own reputation by befriending Zacchaeus and called him in the world of love. The simple act of offering lunch and conversation rocked Zacchaeus entire world and transformed him.[44] The call of befriending the other comes from Jesus himself in the form of command: "love one another as I have loved you, so you must love one another" (Jn. 13:34.35). "There is no greater tool for touching the world than simple demonstrations of love".[45]

Befriending the other is God's action through Jesus Christ (Rom 5:1-8); Eph. 2:13; Col.1:20). The whole ministry of Jesus proclaimed this reality of befriending the other and particularly his death on the cross and resurrection. He gave us the divine response to human sufferings as well as injustice and violence.

By His incarnation where "God himself in Jesus goes out in search of the "stray sheep," a suffering and lost humanity,"[46] God raised the dignity of human beings beyond creatures to a higher and more noble level of children of God "by adoption" with the possibility of inheriting from God as from a father (Gal. 4:4-7). He overcomes the historically accrued divisiveness between God and human persons, between groups as well as between human persons

(Jn.10:35-37) and how we should respond in case of a need. It is in this dignity and respect of the other as fundamentally equal and origin in needs which the story of Good Samaritan salutes. This Samaritan saw the robbed victim an equal whose specific needs called for corporeal works of mercy.

4. Befriending is Cosmic

Seeking God is the universal human quest. It is common to all cultures. It is the fundamental human longing and ultimate to all human activities.[47] We can find God in everything; we can commune with God in and through all things. Creation and other people in particular, not only regain their true light, given to them by God, the Creator, but, so to speak, they lead us to God himself the way that God will to reveal himself to us. Human persons are fundamentally equal in originality (*GS 29*). This equality calls for an end to discrimination or violations of basic human rights. The other is also knowing, willing, feeling, acting subject just as the "I". The other is neighbour, colleague and equal. One cannot exist without the other.[48]

Human person lives in relationships and is equal in God's sight.[49] The human person is fundamentally open to external reality that involves dialogue with reality. The human person is in relationships to the material world, to other persons, to the group of persons and to God. These relationships can be characterized as associations of solidarity (a being with), of creation (a being by) and of service (a being for). There is solidarity with the material world in that human person and the material world share the same earth, and labour under the same needs and laws.

All are related to the whole created order (Gen 1). Dominion over creation is the capacity to love, to nurture and to develop into wholeness and any human approach towards this material world needs to be a posture of service in contrast to exploitation. We Africans hold that the world and nature are gifts that entrusted to us to provide: nourishment and security. Nature was altars and temples. It was under the big trees where people used to meet for reconciliation, sacrifice offering and plan for building the communities.

God in Africa is a relational being who is known through various levels of relationship with creation, a cosmic wholeness.[50] In relation to humanity, God is the great ancestor of the human race. This is what also moved intimately Pope Benedict XVI in his call for peace to exhort humans to make 'heaven on earth.' "Our use of creation and human development in general should be for the development of the whole human being and all people," he said. (*Sollicitudo Rei Socialis* 30). The same idea is strongly stressed by Pope Francis in his *Laudato Si'* "to work together in building our common home".[51] Therefore befriending the 'other' is on-going process to establish a community of love that the eschatological goal of cosmic communion is definitely achieved and "together form a kind of universal family, a sublime communion which fills us with sacred, affection and humble respect."52 Thus the heavens, the land and the animals contribute to a befriending the other rebuilding of all the relationships. When Yahweh is the God of the nations, then befriending the other can be known in personal well-being, in social-political and in the cosmic world (*GS 39*).

5. Encounter the Other as Neighbour in Inter-Religious Dialogue

Africans believe that life is a complex web of relationships that may either enhance and preserve life or diminish and destroy life. The goal of religion is to maintain those relationships that protect and preserve life. *Ad Gentes Divinitus*, Decree on the Church's Missionary Activity' recalls God's universal plan of salvation of mankind and the sending of His Son, in order to establish a relationship of peace and communion with himself and in order to bring about brotherly/sisterly union among people.[53]

Interreligious Dialogue in Africa is particularly necessary because people are literally surrounded by religions. It is the way with which mutual relationship can be made possible. Often religious pluralism cuts across nation, tribe, and at times even family lines. Moreover, the dialogue the "primary importance should be given to getting involved with the life of the neighbour next door"[54] Cardinal Arinze tells us that "Interreligious Dialogue is a meeting of sincere believers who want each to listen to the other and identify areas to study together what they can do together."[55] The unity of all united humanity is the will of God (*Ut Unum Sint* 27). It creates and revives relationship in all religions. The act of befriending the other challenges and opens hearts, heals wounds of divisions and creates communion.

The pain and cost of the broken relationships in our world and the frequent use of violence as a tool for achieving happiness is a draw to any process of befriending the other. Change of hearts and minds will re-enforce befriending as a process that brings healing. Mahatma Gandhi once said, "It is easy to be friendly to one's friends. But to befriend the one who regards him/herself as your enemy is the quintessence of true religion."[56]

For it is the harmony and stability that provides good relationships, that create the conditions for well-being and wholeness. Inter-religious Dialogue in Africa is a tool for peace and language for befriending. It "is a meeting of hearts and minds across religious frontiers who want each one to listen to the other and identify areas of convergence and divergence and to study together what they can do together[57] to build trust and understanding of the world of the other. Religious Dialogue in Africa is particularly important and indeed necessary for relationships. This is because people are literally surrounded by other religions among which they live, witness to and work for the Kingdom of God. Often religious pluralism cuts across nation, tribal and, at times even family lines. We seek dialogue with persons of other religions not because we tolerate their beliefs out of courtesy but a specific mode of being and a way of life in view of forming one communion of communities. Fr. Arul Swamy Kaspar is reminding us that "We shall not live in our own petty narrow worlds of hatred and violence against those who do not belong to us but rather we shall imagine the greatness and uniqueness of everyone and revere them as sons and daughters of God."[58] Each religion is called to a critical appropriation on its own tradition and also to openness to the truth and grace in other traditions and no religion shall hinder us to befriend the other for there are no strangers and aliens in our common Earth. Julius Nyerere, the first president of Tanzania and the Father of the Nation, during his time of ruling (1961-1985) not only tolerated, but respected other people's beliefs.[59]

Inter-religious Dialogue is "building bridges to others who do not share our faith. "In this way we learn to accept others and their different ways of living, thinking and speaking."[60] It is the transformation of human existence from self-centeredness to reality centeredness." It leads to mutual conversion, removes prejudices; brings greater understanding and it leads to communion, peace, harmony and integrity of nation. When some of us in Africa have lost courage to hope, dialogue becomes an invitation to solidarity in a challenging hour of sufferings. "We cannot truly call on God the Father of all, if we refuse to treat in a sisterly/brotherly way anyone created as image of God" (*NA* 5). Africans must respond to the signs of the time and see the human race as a complex whole (*GS* 5) and make the "joy and hope, grief and anguish of people especially of those who are poor and afflicted to be theirs (*GS* 1). Change of heart and mind is what reinforces befriending, a process that brings healing.

Conclusion

Jesus came to give life and life in abundance (Jn. 10:10) and announces the kingdom that brings life. It is this Kingdom where people 'the other' are embraced and experience life, love, freedom and justice we are called to build in order to befriend the other.[61] We are today in an age of befriending. The age of rivalry is over and the world is taking different turns. In this context religions and politics have the responsibility of coming together and working hand in hand and solve the world issues and give meaning to the life of people.

We are now called upon "to promote together for the benefit of all humankind social welfare and moral welfare, as well as peace and freedom" (*NA* 3). Dialogue is a tool for peace and language of befriending. Befriending remains an important bridge for us to cross into the other[62] as it involves both listening and replying. Befriending therefore is a radical opening up to God, to the 'other' and to the cosmos. It is a process in which there is a transition from brokenness to fullness of humanity that leads to true relationships.

Bibliography

Achermann, Eduard. *Cry Beloved Africa: A Continent Needs Help*. Munich: African University Studies, 1993.

Anderson, Bernhard. *The Living World of the Old Testament.* London: Longman, 1966.

Appiah-Kubi, Kofi and Torres Sergio. (eds). *African Theology en Route.* Orbis: New York, 1979.

Arinze , F.C. *Church in Dialogue: Walking with the Other Believers*, 333.

Baum, Gregory. and Wells Harold (eds.), *The Reconciliation of Peoples Challenge to the Churches.* Geneva: WCC Publications, 1997.

Benedict XVI. *Deus Caritas Est*. Mumbai: St. Pauls, 2006.

Benezet, Bujo. *African Theology in Its Social Context.* New York: Orbis Books, 1992.

Buber, Martin. *Ich und Du.* Stuttgart: Philipp Reclam jun., 1995

Carr, Anne. *Transforming Grace: Christian Tradition and Women's Experience.* San Francisco: Harper and Row, 1988.

Catechism of the Catholic Church. New Delhi: Theological Publication, 1995.

Chittister, Joan OSB. *The Fire in These Ashes: A Spirituality of Contemporary Religious Life*, Kansas City: Sheed & Ward, 2001, 46.

de Menezes, Rui. *Voices from Beyond.* Mumbai: St. Paul's Publication, 2005.

Djerekee, Jean-Claude. "Peace and Reconciliation in Rwanda Today: What can the Church Do?" *The Month 28, No. 6* (June 1995): 230.

Evert, Jason. *Saint John Paul The Great: His Five Lovers*. Lakewood: Totus Tuus, 2014.

Francis, Moget. "Pope John Paul 11: "A Model of Reconciliation in the World Today," *Indian Journal of Spirituality*. 6/2 (2001): 186.

Gandhi, Mahatma. *Worte des Friedens.* Gandhi Herder: 1990.

Israel, Selvanayagam. Gal-ed Versus Peniel. "True Reconciliation in the Essau-Jacob/Israel Story," *Reconciling Mission, 22.*

Jacobsen, Wayne and Jacobsen Clay, *Authentic Relationships*. Michigan: Baker Books, 2003.

John Paul II. *Ecclesia in Africa*. Nairobi: St. Pauls: 1995.

Kappen, Sebastian. *Tradition, Modernity, Counter Culture: An Asian Perspective. Bangalore*: Visthar, 1998.

Kaspar, Arul Samy. *Towards the Community: A Portrail of the Christian Community in the Acts of the Apostles.* Eluru: Good News Press, 2007.

Kemdirim; Protus. "The Need to Empower Women Through Theological Education." *African Ecclesia Review,* 41/1 (February 1999): 41-49.

Kobia, Samwel. *The Courage to Hope: The Roots for Vision and Calling of the Church in Africa*. Geneva: WCC Publications, 2003.

Magesa, Laurent. "Will Africa Ever Stand Tall and Walk?" *African Ecclesia Review* 34/2 (April 1992):95

Magesa, Laurent. Am I not a Human Being and a Brother/sister? *African Ecclesia Review* 34/2 (April 1992): 96-114.

Magesa, Laurent. The Atlantic Slave Trade and Economic North Today, "African *Theological Review* 37/1 (February 1995), 192.

Magesa, Laurent. The Atlantic Slave Trade and Economic North Today, *African Theological Review* 37/1 (February 1995), 192.

Mandela, Nelson. *Long Walk to Freedom*. New York: Abacus, 1994.

Maurin, P. The *Case of Utopia in The Green Revolution, Easy Essays on Catholic Radicalism*. MA, 1961.

McCullum, Hugh. *Africa's Broken Heart: The Land the World Forgot*. Geneva: WCC Publications, 2006.

Ndiokwere, I Nathaniel. *The African Church Today and Tomorrow* Vol.: Prospects and Challenges Osina: Effective Key Publishers, 1994.

Nouwen, Henri J. M., *Life of the Beloved: Spiritual Living in a Secular World. New* York: The Crossroad, 1993.

Oduyoye, Mercy Amba. *Daughters of Anowa: African Women and Partiachy.* New York: Orbis, 2003.

Oduyoye, Mercy Amba. *Introducing African Women's Theology*. Cleverland: Ohio Pilgrim Press, 2001.

Okure, Teresa. "The Ministry of Reconciliation (2 Cor. 5:14-21): Paul's Key to the Problem of 'the Other' in Corinth," in *Mission Studies: Journal of the international Association for Missions Studies*, 23/1 (2006): 112.

Padinjararekuttu, Isaac. *Challenges to Religion; Church and Theology*. Mumbai: St. Pauls,

Pope Benedict XVI. "The Human Person the Heart of Peace: Message for the Celebration of the World Day of Peace – 2007." *L'Osservatore Romano* (20-27): 6-7.

Pope Francis, *Evangelii Gaudium*. Trivandrum: Carmel International Publishing House, 2013.

Pope Francis, *Laudato Si'*. Bangalore: Claretian Publications, 2015.

Porutur A., "A Decade of Dialoguing: Non-Elitist Approach," in *Mission Today*, II (2000) 4, 485-490.

Rathinam, Selva. "Universalism in Amos," *Vidyajyoti Journal of Theological Reflection*, 66 (June 2002), 730.

Rodney, Walter. *How Europe Underdeveloped Africa.* Dar es Salaam; Tanzania Publishing House, 1976.

Second Vatican Ecumenical *Council Lumen Gentium*, Dogmatic Constitution on the Church, 7 November 1964, in AAS 56 (1965): 5-71. Text: Flannery A., (ed.) *Vatican Council II. The Conciliar and Post Conciliar Documents*., St. Pauls Publication, Bombay 1995, 320-397.

Second Vatican Ecumenical Council; *Gaudium et Spes,* Pastoral Constitution on the Church in the Modern World, 7 December 1965, in AAS 58 (1966): 1025-1120. Text: Flannery A., (ed.) *Vatican Council II. The Conciliar and Post Conciliar Documents*., St. Pauls Publication, Bombay 1995, 794-891.

Shorter, Aylward. *The Church in African City.* New York: Orbis Books, 1991.

Thannickal, Dr. Joe SDB. *Gifted Journey: Search for your Meaning Transcend Your Limitations Partner with Your God.* Bombay: Pauline Sisters, 2012.

Tutu, Desmond. *God Has a Dream: A Vision of Hope for Our Time.* New York: Doubleday, 2004.

Vanier, Jean. Befriending the Stranger. New Jersey: Mahwah Paulist Press, 2005.

Vanier, Jean. *Encounter the 'Other'*. New Jersey: Mahwah Paulist Press, 2006.

Websites

"As I know Nyerere," http://www.juliusnyerere.org/news/ assessed on 10 January 2016.

"If numbers could scream," http://commcgi.cc.stonybrook.edu/assessed on 15 January 2016.

"Issues affecting women," https://www.sheissafe.org/category/assessed on 15 January 2016.

"Millions of Africans continue to live as slaves," http://www.com/slave trade abolition is celebrated/ assessed on 16th January 2016.

"Nigeria Girls abducted," http://edition.cnn.com/ assessed on 15 January 2016.

"Nigeria school girls sold as brides," http://www.cbsnews.com/news/assessed on 15 January 2016.

"Tribalism is a poison in the Society," https://www.siyandawrites.com/ /on-Africa-day/ assessed 10 January 2016.

Notes

1. Jean Vanier, *Befriending the Stranger* (New Jersey Mahwah: Paulist Press, 2005), 54.
2. Dr. Joe Thannickal sdb, *Gifted Journey: Search for Your Meaning, Transcend Your Limitations, Partner with Your God* (Bombay Society, Pauline Sisters, 2012),34.
3. Wayne Jacobsen and Clay Jacobsen, *Authentic Relationships* (Baker Books, Michigan, 2003), 36.

4. Philip Yancey, *What's so Amazing about Grace?* (Secunderbad: OM Books, 1996), 105.
5. Jean Vanier, *Encounter the 'Other'* (New Jersey Mahwah: Paulist Press, 2006), 29.
6. Mercy Oduyoye, *Hearing and Knowing* (Maryknoll: Orbis, 1986), 98.
7. JeanVanier, *Encounter the 'Other,'* 37.
8. *Catechism of Catholic Church,* (Theological Publications in India, New Delhi), 1995.
9. Pope Francis, *Evangelii Gaudium* (International Publishing House Trivandrum, 2013), 152.
10. The traditional values of *Ubuntu*: to live and care for the others, to act kindly towards others, to be hospitable, to be just and fair, compassionate, trustworthy and honest, have good morals and assist those in distress. It is the essence of being human. An offence breaks a relationship, ruptures interconnectedness, a harmony that is so essential for full existence. *Ubuntu* seeks to heal a breach, to restore relationship, to forgive. It is interrelatedness
11. Desmond Tutu, *God has a Dream: A Vision of Hope for our Time* (USA: Doubleday, 2004) 28.
12. Wayne Jacobsen and Clay Jacobsen, *Authentic Relationships*, 40.
13. Laurent Magesa, "Will Africa Ever Stand Tall and Walk?" in *African Ecclesia Review,* 34/2 (April 1992): 95.
14. Laurent Magesa, The Atlantic ,Slave Trade'and Economic North Today, "*African Theological Review,* 37/1 (February 1995): 192.
15. Hugh McCullum, *Africa's Broken Heart: The Land the World Forgot* (Geneva: WCC Publications, 2006),1.
16. Francis Moget, "Pope John Paul 11: A Model of Reconciliation in the World Today," *Indian Journal of Spirituality*. 6/2 (2001): 186.
17. Global Slavery Index-http://timesofindia.indiatimes.com/articleshow/assessed on 28 January 2016
18. Issues affecting women, https://www.sheissafe.org/category/assessed 15 January 2016.
19. Millions of Africans continue to live as slaves, http://www.com/slave trade abolition is celebrated/ assessed on 16th January 2016.
20. Jean Vanier, *Befriending the Stanger*, 52.
21. Mercy Amba Oduyoye, *Introducing African Women's Theology* (Cleverland:Ohio Pilgrim Press, 2001),75.
22. Mercy Oduyoye, *Daughters of Anowa: African Women and Patriarchy* (New York: Orbis Books, 2003), 4.
23. Jason Evert, *Saint John Paul the Great: His Five Loves,* (Lakewood: Totus Tuus Press, 2014), 111.
24. Pedua Huston, *Third World Women Speak Out* (New York: Praeger Publishers, 1979), 58.
25. Alice Walker and Pratibha Parmar, *Warrior Marks: Sexual Genitalia Mutilation Sexual Blinding of Women* (New York: Harcourt&Company 1995), 51.
26. "Nigeria school girls sold as brides," http://www.cbsnews.com/news/assessed on 15 January 2016.
27. "If numbers could scream," http://commcgi.cc.stonybrook.edu/assessed on 15 January 2016.
28. "Nigeria Girls abducted," http://edition.cnn.com/ assessed on 15 January 2016.
29. Jason Evert, *Saint John Paul the Great: His Five Loves*, 111.

30. Nathaniel I. Ndiokwere, *The African Church Today and Tomorrow* Vol. 1: Prospects and Challenges (Osina: Effective Key Publishers 1994), 61.
31. Nathaniel I. Ndiokwere, *The African Church Today and Tomorrow Vol. 1: Prospects and Challenges*, 70.
32. Martin Buber, *Ich und Du*, (Stuttgart: Philipp Reclam jun.,1995), 3.
33. Sebastian Kappen, *Tradition, Modernity, Counter Culture: Asian Perspective* (Bangalore: Visthar, 1998), 98.
34. Anne Carr, *Transforming Grace: Christian Tradition and Women's Experience* (San Francisco: Harper and Row, 1988), 187.
35. Isaac Padinjarekuttu, *Challenges to Religion, Church and Theology* (Mumbai: St. Pauls), 2008, 82.
36. Henri J.M. Nouwen. *Life of the Beloved: Spiritual Living in a Secular World*, (New York: The Crossroad),21.
37. Aylward Shorter, *The Church in African City* (New York: Orbis Books, 1991), 30.
38. Remember Hutu-Tutsi Genocide 1994 in Rwanda.
39. Gregory Baum and Harold Wells (eds.), *The Reconciliation of Peoples Challenge to the Churches* (Geneva: WCC Publications, 1997), 49.
40. Jean-Claude Djerekee, "Peace and Reconciliation in Rwanda Today: What Can the Church Do?" *The Month 28, No. 6* (June 1995): 230.
41. Rui de Menezes, *Voices from Beyond* (Mumbai: St. Paul's Publication, 2005), 112.
42. Selva Rathinam, "Universalismus in Amos," *Vidyajyoti Journal of Theological Reflection*, 66 (June 2002), 730.
43. Jean Vanier, *Encountering the 'Other'*28.
44. Jean Vanier, *Befriending the Stranger*, 22.
45. Wayne Jacobsen and Clay Jacobsen, 31.
46. Benedict XVI, *Deus Caritas Est*, (Vatican City: Libreria Editrice, 2006), 30.
47. Joan Chittister OSB., *The Fire in These Ashes: A Spirituality of Contemporary Religious Life*, (Kansas City: Sheed & Ward, 2001), 46.
48. Teresa Okure, The Ministry of Reconciliation (2 Cor. 5:14-21): Paul's Key to the Problem of 'the Other' in Corinth," in *Mission Studies: Journal of the International Association for Missions Studies*, 23/1 (2006): 112.
49. Israel Selvanayagam, Gal-ed Versus Peniel: True Reconciliation in the Essau-Jacob/Israel *Story In Reconciling Mission, 22.*
50. Nelson Mandela, *Long Walk to Freedom* (Abacus, 1994), 15.
51. Pope Francis, *Laudato Si'*, 13.
52. Pope Francis *Laudato Si'*, 66.
53. Cf. AG.3
54. A. Poruthur, "A Decade of Dialoguing: A Non Elitist Approach," *Mission Today*, II (2000) 4, 490.
55. Francis Arinze, *Church in Dialogue: Walking with Other Believers*, (San Francisco Ignatius Press, 1990), 332.
56. Mahatma Gandhi, *Worte des Friedens*, (Freiburg Herder, 1990), 119.
57. Francis Arinze, *Begegnung mit Menschen anderen Glaubigens: Den interrreliösen Dialogue vestehen und gestalt:* Verlag Neue Stadt, Munchen, 1999,10.

58. Arul Samy Kaspar, *Towards the Community: a Portait of the Christian Community in the Acts of Apostles*, (Eluru: Good New Press, 2007), 121.
59. "As I know Nyerere," http://www.juliusnyerere.org/news/ assessed on 10 January 2016.
60. Pope Francis, *Evangelii Gaudium*, 183.
61. Bernhard W. Anderson, *The Living World of the Old Testament*, (New Jersey, Longman Group Limited), 11.
62. Francis Arinze, *Church in Dialogue: Walking with the Other Believers*, 333.

13

Befriending the Other as Nature's Recipe for Greater Stability and Prosperity

Job Kozhamthadam, SJ
Director, Indian Institute of Science and Religion, Delhi

Abstract: Perhaps the most baffling trait of the universe is its stability, despite its long history of almost 14 billion years, despite its almost limitless size and innumerable constituents, despite its state of continuous motion and complex interactions. This paper points out that mother nature achieves this extraordinary feat by using the strategy of befriending the other. It identifies some of the principal constituents and conditions involved in this strategy, and studies with concrete scientific examples how this strategy is applied at different levels of cosmic beings: human/rational (science-religion dialogue), biological (human body, carbon cycle, photosynthesis), and physical (solar system). The paper concludes by reflecting on what lesson we can learn from mother nature in this regard.

Keywords: Interconnectedness, Science-religion dialogue, Stability of the universe, Carbon-cycle, Photosynthesis, Stability of the solar system.

Introduction: Interconnectedness as a Fundamental Feature of the Cosmos

Interconnectedness is one of the most fascinating features of our universe. For a long time our sages and mystics had come to notice this intuitively. Fortunately, in recent times contemporary science has been confirming this fact scientifically. Not only are the different constituents of the vast universe interlinked, within each individual member of the universe also we can see amazing interconnectedness. This observation has convinced thinkers like Immanuel Kant to look upon our universe as a unified whole. True, there are certain instances of disconnectedness and disharmony; there are also occasions of discord and dissonance. But it seems to me that in the vast ocean of order and harmony these should be taken as puddles of exceptions. It is important to recognize that this cosmic interconnectedness is not something peripheral and merely cosmetic – not something the universe can easily dispense with. Rather it is something fundamental and deep, substantial and essential for the universe since, as I shall point out, the universe depends on it in a significant way for its existence, preservation and smooth functioning. For instance, we know that the different planets and other heavenly bodies in the solar system are closely interlinked. Disturb any segment of it, the whole system goes out of step and eventually collapses. This interconnectedness is not confined to the physical world only, it is applicable also in the biological as well as rational/human world. Again, interconnectedness is found not merely between beings of the same type. It is found also among items which appear to be different and unrelated – at a deeper level these dissimilar beings are found to be deeply and intimately related. Often this discovery of the deeper linkage and unity between apparently dissimilar candidates can serve as a source of growth and enrichment since this process involves tapping the resources from different sources. For instance, at first glance it may look that science and religion have hardly anything in common, but, as will be discussed later, deeper interaction and reflection can show that they have much in common, and pooling these resources can trigger greater growth and enrichment. It is in this kind of context that 'befriending the other' becomes a successful strategy for mutual growth and enrichment. This paper is a detailed study of some of the salient features and benefits of 'befriending the other' at the different levels of existence – rational/human, biological and physical. At all these levels it will be seen that befriending the other is an effective way for greater growth and development. It will also study some of the implications of this strategy and practice.

1. Befriending the Other – Exploring the Concept

It may be useful to deal with this issue from various perspectives.

a. Some Features of Befriending the Other, Particularly at the Human Level

Befriending the other is a process, a complex process, involving many aspects. It is important that we unpack this rich concept in the beginning itself. First of all, as mentioned already, we need to keep in mind that this process is not limited to the rational, human level only. It is universal, embracing the different levels of existence: the rational level in humans, the biological level in living beings and the physical level in the physical nature. However, the process of befriending the other is most commonly and frequently studied and practiced at the level of humans. Hence now we will enter into a short discussion of what it means to befriend the other at the human level.

We can befriend the other at the human level in many different ways. Jean-Paul Sartre, for instance, has a very negative and pessimistic view of the other when he says: "hell is other people." Jesus Christ, on the other hand, asks us to consider the other as our brother and sister. In fact, he goes much further to identify the other with himself: "When you did it to the least of my brothers and sisters, you did it to me." For Jesus and his genuine followers the principle and practice of befriending the other is very positive; it takes the other as a friend, not as an alien.

Again, the spirit of befriending the other looks upon the other as a person, who is an end in himself/herself. It can never look upon the other as an object to be used. The other is a person with rights and privileges, duties and obligations, freedom and limitations, likes and dislikes. Befriending the other means recognizing all these different dimensions and taking them into serious consideration while dealing with him/her.

The other becomes a close collaborator in the context of befriending the other. It means that the other is considered an equal partner having something valuable to contribute. It means also having confidence in the sincerity and seriousness, competence and capability of the other. It involves listening to the other with care and attention.

The attitude that should animate the spirit of befriending the other is one of openness and positiveness. It involves accepting the limitedness of one's own resources, and being ready to welcome the almost unlimited resources available in others outside. This positive attitude does not mean uncritically acquiescing to the other, rather it means a willingness to agree joyfully and a readiness to disagree gracefully.

The benefits one can reap from the positive approach of befriending the other are many. It leads to greater efficiency by dividing the labour and multiplying the benefits. It can be a source of joy and consolation since it often involves dividing the pain of the struggle and multiplying the joy of the reward. It results in the redoubling of the resources since the resources of the other also become available for the common good.

b. Some Important Conditions of the Process of Befriending the Other

In general to render the process of befriending the other an enriching experience a number of conditions or requirements can be of help, some of which are given below.

- The process of befriending involves a complex issue having many essential components or partners.

- The components or partners often differ significantly from each other.
- The outcome cannot be achieved by any one of the components or partners alone.
- Each component or partner brings in something essential for the outcome, which the others cannot.
- The outcome achieved benefits the whole system.

As has been mentioned already, the process of befriending the other is universal, cutting across all forms and levels of being. Furthermore, this can take place at different levels and in different forms. It can take the form of interaction among the different partners; it can take the form of dialogue between the different parties, etc. In all these cases, it is expected that the attitude taken and the spirit animating is one of mutual respect, mutual understanding, genuine openness and creative concern for the general good. Also in this context special effort is made to focus on what is common to all, what unites all with a common goal.

To substantiate our claim that the process of befriending is universally applicable, and exercised at all levels, we will take up different cases from the three realms of existence – the human/rational, the biological and the physical.

2. Befriending the Other at Different Levels

We may talk of befriending at various levels.

A. The Human/Rational World – Science-Religion Dialogue (SRD)

i. Science and Religion and Their Need

Science and religion arguably are two most powerful influences in our world today, having vast resources and affecting our lives most profoundly. In some significant ways they shape our worldviews, set our goals, form our value system and control our ambitions and aspirations. Since they are very different from each other, there may not be any natural tendency to pool their resources together. At the same time, it is well known that they both have much to offer to humans, and the human race will be far better off if their vast resources can be brought together for the betterment of humans and society. This is what science-religion dialogue attempts to achieve.

ii. Science-Religion Dialogue – Its Nature and Significance

Although science-religion dialogue is as old as science itself, it is quite recent as a systematic, interdisciplinary field, particularly in the academic circles. Inherently general and interdisciplinary, it is open to many forms and interpretations. I look upon it as an attempt to bring together the latest findings of modern science and the deepest insights of religions in order to build up a better humanity in the multireligious, multicultural and multiracial context of our globalizing world. Obviously, it is open to all religions and all branches of modern science, including social sciences. It is based on the belief that both science and religion are the most powerful influences in our society today, wielding tremendous power in shaping our attitudes, meaning-system, value-system, etc. A well-informed approach to issues with mutual respect for the perspectives of each other, openness to new possibilities, and readiness to change are the trademark of this field. Although the initial stages of science-religion interfacing were marked by unsureness about its feasibility, uncertainty about its capability and doubts about its success,[1] today this field has undergone a quantum leap, moving to the central stage of academic research and study, engaging many outstanding scientists, philosophers, theologians and other thinkers all over the world, thanks, to a great extent, to the substantial support and encouragement, especially monetary, it has been receiving from generous patrons like the John Templeton Foundation. It seems that almost every month a new book is out on the subject; frequent conferences, seminars and symposia are held in various parts of the world as a matter of routine. India has been making its share of contribution, particularly at the Indian Institute of Science and Religion (IISR), Delhi, Jnana Deepa (JD) Centre for Science and Religion (JCSR), Pune, Institute of Science and Religion, Aluva, Kerala, Science and Religion Samgam, Goa, etc. For instance, on the average once every month IISR has been conducting programs in this field in some college or academic institution in India, and the response has always been very positive and encouraging.

iii. Different Models of Science-Religion Interaction

Although there is near unanimity concerning the importance of science and religion as the two most powerful influences in our world today, with regard to the relationship between the two no such unanimity is forthcoming. The pioneering work of Ian Barbour identifies 4 different models: Conflict, Independence, Dialogue and Integration. John Haught, on the other hand, suggests Conflict, Contrast, Contact, and Confirmation. Ted Peters goes on to present eight different models to account for the complex relationship between science and religion. My own study and reflection on the matter has identified mainly[3] different models: Conflict, Compartmenting and Complementarity. It seems to me that the many models suggested by various scholars can, with appropriate adaptation, be shown to be different variants of these three basic models. When we come to certain specific cases, this relationship can be highly complex, defying any attempt to reduce it to a single model. For instance, my own study of the relationship between Catholicism and modern science over the centuries shows that the relationship went through three different stages: Encouragement, Estrangement and Engagement[2] When modern science was in its infancy, the Catholic Church encouraged it enthusiastically. However, later on a period of estrangement ensued, the classic instances being the unfortunate and avoidable Galileo episode and the Darwinian controversy. Later on this period of estrangement gave way to the period of engagement, the state the dialogue between the Catholic Church and science is in today.

a. The Conflict View

The fundamental idea of the conflict view is that science and religion are not only radically different, but also are antagonists constantly at war with each other, with science mostly at the winner's seat. Over the years science has been winning, and it is only a matter of time before it attains total victory, while religion gets vanquished.

"The boom of science is the doom of religion" is the standard slogan of this view. In the past this model was considered almost the standard view on the relationship between science and religion. Even today this remains the most common popular perception on the matter, thanks mainly to the popular cliché-driven media which often uncritically presents this view. This view has been propounded by Logical Positivism and other atheistic systems of thought.

John William Draper (1811–1882) in his book of 1874, *The History of the Conflict between Religion and* Science, and Andrew D. White (1832-1918) in his book of 1896, *A History of the Warfare of Science with Theology in Christendom,* contributed considerably towards popularizing this view. However, in recent times this view has come under severe criticism, in light of serious study and research in the history of science by eminent scholars.[3] It is true that in the context of religious fundamentalism and scientific materialism this view may get some support, but these cannot be considered legitimate representatives of religion and science. Today very few scholars subscribe to this view. My own study and reflection on the matter reveals to me that this conflict view is more the creation of certain historians of science with vested interest than of historical data.[4]

b. Compartmenting View

The basic idea of this model is that science and religion are two valid, legitimate systems, but they remain independent and do not interact. The claims they have and the statements they make are legitimate and worthy of respect and acceptance in their own respective domains, having no significant impact on others. Classical statements like "When Faraday opens the door of his oratory, he closes the door of his laboratory," bring home the spirit and substance of this position. In the past many scientists used to subscribe to this view, particularly since it avoided most forms of controversy and consequent tension. In recent times Stephen J Gould in his *Rocks of Ages: Science and*

Religion in the Fullness of Life has brought back this view under the title NOMA (Non-Overlapping Magisteria).[5]

c. Complementarity View

The complementarity view, which I consider the best to describe the complex relationship between science and religion, respects and accepts both science and religion as very important and legitimate areas of importance in our world, particularly in the life of humans. Each has very valuable and even necessary contribution to make. Each is legitimate, but differs substantially from the other. The two are complementary in the sense that one brings in something important and necessary which the other does not and cannot. It is also found that for the fullness of human life both are needed since human life will be incomplete and impoverished if either one is missing. It may be noted that the complementarity relationship takes place not so much at the level of a particular theory or law in science, or a particular belief or dogma in religion as at the level of human life – they complement each other at the level of the lived life and deep experience of humans. For human life to be complete and fruitful the contribution from both is needed. Some representative statements illustrating this relationship are: "Science without religion is lame, religion without science is blind." (Einstein). "Science can purify religion from error and superstition; religion can purify science from idolatry and false absolutes." (Pope John Paul II). "Science does not need religion (mysticism); religion does not need science; but man needs both." (Fritjof Capra). It seems to me that today many scholars, particularly scientists, are becoming more and more inclined to embrace this complementarity view.

B. Befriending the Other at the Biological Level

i. Befriending of the Different Components (interconnectedness) of the Human Body

The human body is a miracle of coordination and collaboration of the constituent parts. It has been estimated that an average human body has 100 trillion cells. We know that in each cell there is a DNA molecule with about 3.1 billion base units, each of which is made of many atoms. From atomic theory it is known that each atom comprises many elementary particles like proton, neutron, electron, etc. Now the remarkable point is that all these are constantly moving and carrying out important functions. The movements and activities of such an incredible number of particles will have to be carefully coordinated and harmoniously blended to make the human body function normally. These innumerable components will have to adjust, accommodate and collaborate. This is a beautiful illustrative instance of befriending the other taking place all the time in the biological world, which ensures the stability and healthy functioning of the biological world.

ii. The Carbon Cycle – Photosynthesis-Respiration Cycle

a. Different Natural Cycles

Our universe is blessed with a series of natural cycles – Carbon Cycle, Nitrogen Cycle, Phosphorus Cycle, Water Cycle, etc. A natural cycle is a phenomenon involving the use and reuse of a limited quantity of resources for an indefinite length of time. It involves several stages which are arranged in such a way that the end of the first stage becomes the beginning of the second, etc. Also what is remarkable about this process is that the waste product of one stage becomes the principal raw material for the next stage. This phenomenon is indeed an ingenious master-stroke of our mother nature wherein the minimum amount of resources is used to get the maximum output to carry out very vital functions. The natural cycle is a supreme display of nature's uncanny wisdom, unmatched economy and amazing efficiency.

b. The Carbon Cycle

Carbon cycle is a process in which carbon moves from one stage to another in a cyclic way performing important functions. Carbon is essential for life and living beings. But there is only a limited supply of it in nature. The carbon cycle process enables nature to carry out all these functions with this limited supply. The carbon cycle process can be considered a very interesting illustrative case of befriending the other in action in nature because it involves the participation of different levels of beings – physical world, plant kingdom, animal kingdom and even humans. All these different partners contribute and collaborate, mutually ensuring that the life functions are carried out efficiently and smoothly for the common wellbeing. To illustrate the point, let us consider photosynthesis, a process in which plants prepare sugars or carbohydrates by using carbon dioxide from the atmosphere as well as water in the presence of sunlight. In this process oxygen is also produced. Next comes respiration in which oxygen is taken in by animals and humans and carbon dioxide is produced which is discharged into the atmosphere to start the cycle all over again. Thus we see in this process the different items collaborate and mutually adjust to produce results for the common good. Here one item in nature befriends another apparently unrelated item to produce results that are beneficial for all the parties concerned.

C. Befriending the Other at the Physical Level

i. In the Astronomical World

Although contemporary science offers many pieces of evidence for the finiteness of the universe, there is no consensus with regard to the number of galaxies or the total number of stars in the universe. Some reliable estimates say that there are 100 billion galaxies, and in each one of them there are about 100 billion stars, thus putting the total number of stars at 1022. Each star has its own star system, just like our solar system, with planets, satellites, comets, asteroids, etc. The total number of heavenly bodies is simply mind-boggling. Even more amazing is the fact that none of them is stationary; all are moving constantly in complex motions. And yet they do not seem to be getting in the way of each other or disturbing the stability and normal functioning of the universe! They must be moving and interacting with each other in a highly coordinated and collaborative way to allow the smooth functioning of this vast universe. This is another magnificent display of befriending the other in nature, in the physical universe.

ii. The Stability of the Solar System

According to some calculations, it is about 5 billion years since the solar system was born, and it may be another 5 billion years before the sun dies. The solar system is expected to remain stable for all practical purposes for this long span of time, although recent studies show some difficulties in the long run in this regard. The stability of the solar system was a major puzzle for Newton. He studied this problem at considerable length in 1687 and could not find any natural, scientific explanation for this stability. Since he was a firm believer in the rationality of nature, according to which all natural phenomena should have a genuine cause, he invoked the periodic divine intervention to explain this stability. According to him, God periodically intervened to ensure that the solar system was maintained in its original condition. However, Laplace, building on the works of Euler and Lagrange, showed the dispensability of any such outside divine intervention. Laplace studied the motion of Jupiter and Saturn and found certain anomalies in their motion: Jupiter's orbit appeared to be shrinking, while that of Saturn was expanding. He showed that this was due to "the gravitational attraction of each planet upon the other." He found that any two planets and the sun must be in mutual equilibrium. Generalizing the results of his investigation, Laplace pointed out that the total eccentricity of the planetary orbits of the solar system had to remain constant. This meant that the eccentricities of planets would have to be balanced. If the eccentricity of any one planet increased, then that of the other planets should decrease such that a balance would be maintained. It was also found that the same balancing arrangement would hold in the case of the inclination of a planet's orbit to the plane of the ecliptic. In short, mutual cooperation and mutual adjustment was the secret of the stability of the solar system. According to Gerald James Whitrow, the work of Laplace was "the most important advance in physical astronomy since Newton."[6]

It may be noted that in light of more recent studies on the solar system, the findings of Laplace are found to be only approximate, and can ensure only limited stability for a limited time. Recent studies lead scientists to conclude that the solar system is chaotic, although it happens to be somewhat stable. My point, as far as this discussion is concerned, is that this remarkable stability, albeit limited, of the solar system has come about because it has been exercising the strategy of befriending the other. This stability is the end result of mutual collaboration and adjustment by the different partners for a common good.

A similar process is responsible for the stability of the earth's orbit around the sun. Primarily two forces are involved here: The gravitational force between the sun and the earth because of which the earth is pulled in and the centrifugal force due to the curved motion of the earth because of which the earth holds out. The stability is achieved by the mutual adjustment of the two forces: If the earth is too far out, gravity pulls it back; if it is too close, the centrifugal force pushes it back out. Similar is the case with other bodies going around the sun. The way our nature operates is indeed amazing, and in these situations the process of befriending the other is going on.

3. Some Significant Implications

a. Stability and Prosperity Achieved through Befriending the Other

The brief study above shows that the strategy of befriending the other carries with it many welcome rewards. The cases we discussed show that nature has used it to achieve much-needed and hard-to-get stability and smooth functioning. It can be a reliable path to growth and prosperity. Nature teaches us in this context that the universe and beings in it can draw strength and stability through collaboration and partnership, while they collapse and destroy themselves if they remain in isolation.

b. Further Evidence for the Deeper Unity of the Universe

The process of befriending the other is not limited to a small part of the universe, rather it is found at all levels of being: human/rational, biological and physical. It seems to be a fundamental feature of the universe, thereby offering further evidence for the deeper unity of the universe.

c. Everyone Counts, Everyone Has a Definite Role to Play

In this strategy of befriending everyone counts. For it to be successful everyone has to contribute, everyone has to play a definite role. Hence none can be bypassed or ignored. Everyone needs to be taken seriously and respectfully.

d. Need to Develop Skills in Interpersonal Interaction

One of the lessons we can take home from this study and reflection is that to befriend the other successfully the right way of interacting is necessary. At the human level this calls for developing skills in interpersonal interaction.

Conclusion: Befriending the Other in a Globalizing World

We live in a world that is globalizing continuously. This naturally calls for interacting with people of different cultural, racial, religious, educational and personal background. Only by learning to befriend them creatively and constructively can one get ahead in this globalizing world. As the world gets more and more globalized, the need for befriending the other becomes more and more necessary.

As Jnana Deepa is celebrating the Diamond Jubilee of its new home in Pune, it can proudly recall its own contribution to the process of befriending the other. For the last 122 years in general and for the last 60 years in particular JD has been serving as a catalyst in the process of befriending the other – bringing peoples together, religions together, cultures together, disciplines together, binding them creatively and harmoniously to be ambassadors of love, joy, peace and harmony. May it continue this noble mission in the years to come! May it continue to inspire and guide men and women from all corners of India and abroad in this great art of befriending the other!

Notes

1. I remember in 1980 when I told a few eminent professors of the universities in New York that I was planning to do my doctoral dissertation in the area of science-religion dialogue, they gave me a wide look of surprise and discouragement. In their verbal communication they told me that the subject was too vague and unsystematic, and so no good work could come out of it. But the non-verbal communication was loud and clear: This Indian must be living out of this world, with no knowledge of what he is talking about!
2. For a detailed discussion of this point see Job Kozhamthadam, "The Changing Face of Science-Christianity Dialogue: Encouragement, Estrangement and Engagement," in Job Kozhamthadam, ed., *Science, Technology and Values: Science-Religion Dialogue in a Multi-Religious World* (Pune: ASSR Publications, 2003), pp.3-34.
3. See Stephen J Gould, *Rocks of Ages: Science and Religion in the Fullness of Life* (New York: Ballantine Publishing Group, 1999).
4. For instance, see Job Kozhamthadam, "The Galileo Episode Revisited," *Vidyajyoti* 58 (1994), 337–358.
5. See note 2.
6. See https://en.wikipedia.org/wiki/Pierre-Simon_Laplace accessed on 2/11/2015.

14

Befriending Nature: The Leaf That Smiles

M. Arif* and Rehana Arif
**Adjunct Professor in Life Science,
Pemraj Sarda College, Ahmednagar, Maharashtra*

Abstract: We live with trees, are surrounded by them, yet just how often do we stop to consider how important they are to all life on earth? Perhaps it's because they have become such a common element of our lives that we often take them for granted. But doing so is increasingly at our peril. Things like extensive deforestation and invasive species are just some of the many threats to flora across the planet...threats we can neither ignore nor sustain.

If it weren't for plants and trees, the history of Human race would read differently. And yet, we have no reservations about bringing them down. Because they are primeval, they outlive us, they are fixed, trees seem to emanate a sense of permanence. And though rooted in earth, they seem to touch the sky. For these reasons it is natural to feel we might learn wisdom from them, to haunt about them with the idea that if we could only read their silent riddle rightly we should learn some secret vital to our own lives; or even, some secret vital to our real, our lasting and spiritual existence.

Keywords: Life, Trees, Deforestation, Renewable natural resource, Aesthetically pleasing, Spiritual existence.

"The wonder is, we see these trees and we don't wonder more."
– Ralph Waldo Emerson

We live with trees and are surrounded by them, yet just how often do we stop to consider how important they are to all life on earth? Perhaps it's because they have become such a common element of our lives that we often take them for granted. But doing so is increasingly at our peril. Things like extensive deforestation and invasive species are just some of the many threats to trees across the planet...threats we can neither ignore nor sustain. Unless we befriend the trees together with the forest and nature, our future remains threatened.

1. The Grandeur of Trees

A tree is essentially the opposite of the way we breathe. A tree in fact takes what we exhale and use it for its own purpose, and it exhale what we need most- the oxygen. One tree can support ten people, so if you were to put a cover over this tree along with ten other people, you wouldn't need oxygen to be pumped in that would already be taken care of by the tree itself.

This giant that towers 50 feet or more above your head and has a rustling green canopy the size of a circus tent started life as a miniscule seed, a fragile sapling. In almost total silence, over a period of almost 50 years or more, it grew drawing only carbon-di-oxide from the air and sunlight to construct its graceful cathedral like structure. And in the process, sustained a host of other life forms; ants that cruise back and forth like traffic on highways, myriads of beetles, bugs and grubs buried under the bark, birds and mammals that help themselves to succulent leaves, delicious berries, yummy fruits and nutritious seeds. And build homes in them. Bees and wasps busy foraging nectar making honey and splendid job of pollination and generations of children who take joy in swarming up them.

All the while the trees get on with its own business- pumping up water from deep underground, its leaves producing food, starch and sugars, through the magic of photosynthesis–while emitting oxygen as waste product (a waste product of a plant is life sustainer element of all animals) enabling us to live, its mesh of roots holding the very earth together.

Its flowers, often dazzling and fragrant, attract insects and a wide array of life with treats of nectar and pollen. Fruits, busting with sweet juice, are dangled enticingly to tempt birds, bats and other animals which in return, scatter its seeds far and wide. On top of that it air conditions and purifies the environment too and provides shade on blistering days.

And nearly every part of it – roots, leaves and bark has some medicinal value. Remember Quinine the drug that saved mankind from the epidemics of malaria or the leaves of Holy basil that takes care of your blood pressure.

2. Environmental Impact

Can any human made factory emulate that? Can we produce anything at all, without making an ungodly din or fouling our surroundings?

The arboreal impact on the rest of environment too is of vital significance. They provide food, help prevent soil erosion and flooding and filter water. The economic footprint on human society is also remarkable. A relatively young tree of 50 years can have a big impact. A tree is an incredible natural resource humanity have inherited.

Even in death, trees provide life for many species of insects and animals. Trees eventually die, they fall down and they decompose. And that makes an environment for, whether it be insects on the ground or debris for animals, they derive food from it, can make their nests and things like that. It just works hand in hand, it's a lot better with trees. If you didn't have trees, you wouldn't have a lot of animals. They are the excellent example of plant animal association, an ecosystem that make possible life to prosper and evolve.

Trees also provide intangibles. They're aesthetically pleasing, just good to be around. This is something that artists and writers have extolled for centuries, the effect on the human soul that a simple walk in the woods can provide. Remember William Wordsworth 'The woods are lovely dark and deep and I have promises to keep and miles to go before I sleep'. You feel much better, you see in a walk through the woods, you see animals interacting with vegetation, birds you know and things like that. It just makes that a much more peaceful situation, instead of walking through a parking lot and there's nothing there at all."

Trees are a renewable natural resource and on an individual level, it's easy for anyone to plant a tree. This little action alone, just putting a tree that might have a two-inch wide trunk in the ground is a huge, huge thing that you're doing. And you just don't even think of it that way. You think, OK, I put that tree in the ground, some day it will get big, that's great, move on. But what you've just done is you've created an incredible amount of value back to the environment by what you've just done."

So the next time you pass a tree, take pause and consider the deep roots that bind the soil and add fertility to it, the branches reaching the sky saturating the immediate surrounding with oxygen and moisture , the leaves displaying their beauty...and say a little thanks for all they give.

Conclusion

We need to look at trees as part of the human element. It shouldn't be a separate situation, where you live your life and the tree lives its life. We have co-existed on this planet since time immemorial and must we co-exist now, and for this we don't need to do anything special, just be benign to it. Trees contribute so much to our lives; we really have to give it something back.

Because they are primeval, they outlive us, they are fixed, trees seem to emanate a sense of permanence. And though rooted in earth, they seem to touch the sky. For these reasons it is natural to feel we might learn wisdom from them, to haunt about them with the idea that if we could only read their silent riddle rightly we should learn some secret vital to our own lives; or even, some secret vital to our real, our lasting and spiritual existence.

Such spiritual existence will lead us back to nature, to wonder at the trees and locate ourselves in the larger web of life. Such a befriending will enable human beings to flourish, together with the rest of life-forms.

Reference

Ahmad, Raja. (2010) *Ten Reasons Why Trees Are Valuable*. KitabGhar, Mumbai.

Choubal, Devyani. (1997) *Save Trees*. Vision Publication, Jaipur.

Grimm, William Carey. (2001) *Illustrated Book of Trees*. Stack pole Books; Rev Sub edition.

Silverstein, Shel. (2015) *The Giving Tree*. HarperCollins Pub.

Taplin, Kim. (2015) *Tongues in Trees*. www.pinterest.com

15

Befriending the Other: Use and Abuse of Social Media

P. T. Joseph, SJ

Director, Marian International Institute of Management, Kuttikanam, Kerala

Abstract: The proliferation of smart phones and expansion in wireless connectivity form part of the pattern of our increasingly persistent virtual presence on social media services that has all but collapsed the boundary between being online and offline. Befriending the other used to happen off-line. Now with the proliferation of mobile devices and internet connectivity , befriending the other can happen online. There are more than two billion active social media users worldwide, representing a global penetration rate of 28 percent. This ability to engage so readily with digital media and online networks is empowering but our actions can also make us vulnerable. As the social networking is being increasingly used as an education and information resource, we have to decide how to make it a non-abuse place for our society. Pornography, violence, obscenity and hatred lurk in unexpected places, and innocent children stumble upon them all too frequently.

Keywords: Social connectivity, Cyberbullying, Online communities, Social media addiction, Surveillance society, Commodification of identity, Global village, Abuse of Social media

Introduction: Proliferation of Social Media

The proliferation of smart phones and expansion in wireless connectivity form part of the pattern of our increasingly persistent virtual presence on social media services that has all but collapsed the boundary between being online and offline. Befriending the other used to happen off-line. Now with the explosion of mobile devices, befriending the other can happen online. The virtual and the real form a seamless space in which many of us live out our daily' lives. We fashion the self through social interaction, community, and network affiliations, and in these ways we construct our identities as well as interpret the identity of the others we interact with. The age of social media and networks and the ease with which individuals can now produce, reproduce, and distribute digital content has powerfully shifted the ways in which we think about personal and global connectedness, distribution of artefacts and access to media, social action, and the production of knowledge.

There are more than two billion active social media users worldwide, representing a global penetration rate of about 28 percent. This ability to engage so readily with digital media and online networks is empowering our ability to befriend the other, but our actions can also make us vulnerable. Social media make us suffer the pressures of information overload and time management. The Internet has shifted from a set of static objects to a dynamic network of connected, interacting subjects. The term digital identity is broad. It stretches from the 'certification of an individual to partake in authentication based transactions such as managing an online bank account' to 'online personas that are made visible through selective acts of self-disclosure, such as writing a blog or sharing our Facebook profile'.

There are millions of people on the internet who are looking to meet other people and to gather and share information and experiences on a variety of topics. Because of this, hundreds of social networking sites have been created, and they have attracted millions of users in the few short years that social networking has become a phenomenon. Whatsapp is one application which is expanding exponentially . As of October 1st 2015, there are 700 million daily users of Whatsapp. The estimate is that every day 1 million users are added to Whatsapp. Today there are more than 1 billion users of Whatsapp. There are many such applications in use these days. Most of the key features of these sites are very similar, yet the cultures that form around the social networking sites vary in many different ways. Some of the sites target diverse audiences, while others attract people based on common language, race, sexual preferences, religion, or nationality. The sites also vary the ways in which the show and incorporate new information and communication tools, like mobile access, blogging, and photo and video sharing.

In recent years, digital media and networks have become embedded in our everyday lives, and are part of broad-based changes to how we engage in knowledge production, communication, and creative expression.

1. Need for Social Connectivity and Community

Social connectivity is part of being human and there has never been a time in human history when people have been able to connect to one another with such ease. Social connections are no longer restricted to the people in our immediate surroundings, instead electronic media , such as smart phones, emails, and online social networks, have enabled us to connect with those both near and far. Specifically, the use of online networks have come to be an integrated part of people's daily routines.[1] While feeling socially connected is important for our health there are still uncertainties about the implications of online connectedness.

Indeed, people are wired to socially connect. They are social beings who strive to connect and form bonds with each other, which is termed social connectedness.[2] The broad concept of social connectedness refers to the desire people have to create and maintain relationships, the social bonds they have with others, and the feeling of belongingness that results from these bonds. Social connectedness can be expressed through various needs fulfillments and social behaviors, such as seeking out other individuals to avoid feeling lonely, to ask for advice, or simply to socialize. Furthermore, people do not simply strive to create bonds they also resist dissolving relationships.

It is not until fairly recently the internet has exploded as a venue for social connectedness. Specifically, online social networks have emerged as a new way to socially connect, and in a short period of time connecting through these sites has become as common as other social phenomenon such as grabbing a tea/coffee with a friend. The media format allows for easy and convenient interaction among individuals, independent of their physical location. Thus, these online social networks have become a common way for people to share, communicate, and gather information. Indeed, several studies indicate that online social networks are now a common part of daily life, particularly among young adults all over the world.[3]

Social psychology recognizes the need for connectedness of human beings where the pursuit of connectedness represents one of the basic motivational principles that underlie social behavior. Connectedness can be described as the feeling of belonging to a social group and implies the creation of bonding relationships. The concept of "connectedness" can be defined as "a positive emotional appraisal which is characterized by a feeling of staying in touch within ongoing social relationships."[4]

According to self-psychology theory,[5] a sense of social connectedness develops early in life and extends throughout the life span. In childhood, for example, parent-child attachments provide an initial sense of security and likeness with others. In adolescence, peer affiliations and group memberships allow individuals to identify with others who share similarities in appearance, interests, and talents. By adulthood, the aggregate of these past and present relationship experiences are gradually incorporated into one's overall sense of self, providing a relatively stable psychological sense of connectedness that is not susceptible to vacillations in relationships, such as the loss of a friend or social exclusion from a group. People with high connectedness tend to feel very close with other people, easily identify with others, perceive others as friendly and approachable, and participate in social groups and activities.

The notion of community is at the heart of the World Wide Web. The psychological need for connectedness could therefore explain the popularity of social networks such as Facebook.

Social media and online communities offer increased possibilities for connection, interaction and participation but also new media with tools for self-presentation and identity management.

Social media such as Twitter, Facebook, MySpace, YouTube, Flickr, and others have been growing at a tremendous rate and the adoption rate of such media has been skyrocketing which, in turn, has delivered astronomical numbers of users in less than 15 years. As a consequence of this astounding phenomenon involving both the rapid emergence of this cutting-edge technology and its adoption, social media have become an integral part of the contemporary classroom, of advertising and public relations industries, of political campaigning, and of numerous other aspects of our daily existence.

Originating from the Internet, different online communities pervade the public and private life.

Being part of a community or group fulfils one of the basic human needs, that of belonging. Nowadays the use of the Internet to build different interest-based and self-identified communities evidently stresses that communities do not necessarily need to interact face-to-face. The development of the Internet resulted in the increase of different online com munities since information and communication technologies enabled geographically disperse groups and individuals to connect.

Online communities cannot just be built. It can only be facilitated in order to provide people with inter-action platforms where people could come and participate in or form a community of their choice. This alone emphasises the human factor within the design of cyberspaces. Online communities do not have physical borders but social life within these communities does have expression boundaries as well as norms and rules for behaviour on-line and sometimes also off-line. These boundaries for social actions and behaviour are either inherited by the structure of a certain e-space or different social media, i.e., discussion forums and social networking websites, or imposed by the designers and users of e-spaces. In order to be successful, online communities, e-spaces and other electronic congregations need regular users. Cyberspace does not exist without electronic inhabitants; otherwise it is a deserted cyber place. The sense of community is one of the important social features that shape both the social qualities of an online community as well as activities and behaviour of the community members. Sense of community is often described as a set of subjective experiences of belonging, mutual respect, and commitment that can be gained only through interaction and participation.

The degree of success and functionality of virtual communities is incorporated and built through trustworthy group interaction. The rise of social software and online social networks impose new challenges for law, security and trust, identity and interaction. The challenges go sometimes as far as to raise questions related to democracy and citizens' degree of participation in private or public online communities.

Entering cyberspace concerns issues of both identity and identification. The possibility to anonymously participate in online communities may ease the entrance to online communities. Some participants, though, may dislike anonymous people. They may however, gravitate towards digitally eponymous people welcoming them in an electronically-mediated social environment.

There is a multiplicity of people in online communities: e-learners, visitors of different chat rooms, participants of interest groups, and members of support groups and e-communities, as well as users of social media. All share different needs and have different aims. In cyberspace, group and community formation as well as identity building, testing and maintenance comprise the social, cultural and psychological aspects of behaviour with communication technologies.

The phenomenon of the digital identity has been referred to by many different terms including: online identity, online personality, digiSelf, virtual identity, avatar and online persona.

Marshall McLuhan, a communications theorist, philosopher and media guru, prophesied his visions of the future long before the world wide web existed. In McLuhan's iconic 1962 media analysis, *The Gutenberg Galaxy: The Making of Typographic Man,* he introduced the idea of the 'global village'.6 The term global village described a phenomena in which the world would become more closely interconnected like a village, and where the movement of information would instantaneously transmit from one point of the earth to another. McLuhan predicted the global village would happen with the rise of electronic technology and mass-media. The global village is now used as a metaphor for the Internet, as the movement of information has become instantaneous, connecting the world and people to an intense degree that was not possible before.

As McLuhan prophesised the current reality of the 'global village', an online identity can be likened to be the global village's citizen or 'netizen'. The birth of a digital identity can start as easily and simply as creating a name, account or handle to register on an Internet website, and can be as elaborate as an online existence that spans over many different websites, including a multi-media trail that can include anything from photographs, text, videos, music and even live webcams.

2. Social Media Driving Changes in the Society

Social media's quick development into an important way to influence society is part of the advancement of information and communication technologies. The following eight aspects of social media are driving changes in the society.[7]

The first change specific to social media is the anonymity of its agents, which means that those who write and comment often use nicknames or aliases. Even though anonymity provides an opportunity to comment on delicate issues, it can also sometimes lead to "flame wars" and avoiding responsibility.

The second change is the richness and diversity of information social media provide. Users are no longer dependent on a single source for their news and other data any more, but can flexibly use several different media side by side. The modus operandi can be thought of as remediation, where media use, modify and reorganise contents gathered from other media. Also connected to this changed information environment is the fact that it is not possible to participate in every conversation.

The third change is omnipresence – there are no longer any isolated places or hiding holes. The private and public lives of society's most influential figures have merged and become public space. Many a politician has had to face the fact that a phrase taken out of context or a joke they told during a private conversation has been recorded by outsiders and quickly made public on the Internet.

The fourth change is speed. News and information are spread more quickly than ever before, and the demand for speed can also lead to reports without any confirmation.

The fifth change is the multitude of roles that users assume, and their relationships to each other. The lack of a clear hierarchy is characteristic of social media. A good example is the online encyclopedia, Wikipedia, which doesn't really have a main editor, but an army of tens of thousands of writers, inspectors, and editors. So, if inaccuracies are found, to whom at Wikipedia should complaints be directed? The answer to this: don't complain! Instead, supplement the article in question and correct perceived mistakes alone.

The sixth change is the move from objectivity to subjectivity. For example, in the United States, some of the so-called traditional mainstream media have abandoned the promotion of equality and pluralism.

The seventh change is the new ability to combine different kinds of recorded information in very flexible ways.

Social media isn't just text, pictures, audio, video, and animation, but all of these combined. With today's compact video cameras, sound recorders, laptop computers and other mobile devices, combined with affordable soft ware, one can easily create and edit impressive presentations.

The eighth change is the near absence of traditional methods of regulation. A government can attempt to restrict the content of social media, but traditional censorship cannot keep up with ever-changing web pages.

3. The Social Media and Marketing

With over 1.2 Billion active users, Facebook provides a virtual reality in cyberspace where users can enact identities for their friends, acquaintances, and a larger passing public. The social media revolution has given consumers around the world the most powerful voice they've ever had. It has also forced companies to think about how they can be more transparent and responsive. Social media, along with a global recession, has led companies, organizations, and governments to figure out how to accomplish more with less money—to get their messages out there and talked about, without spending as many dollars on declining media like television, radio, and print.

Word-of-mouth marketing has always been considered the purest and best form of marketing, and social media has continued to prove this fact in many ways. People like to share with and feel connected to each other, brands, organizations, and even governments they like and trust.

Facebook's Like button, introduced in April 2010, has already been added by more than three million distinct websites. The Like button allows Facebook's more than one billion users, with one click, to express approval of companies, organizations, articles, or ideas. Whether it's a friend's picture of her baby you like, an article shared from the New York Times, a video from a local organization, or a contest from a global brand, the Like button gets more than two billion clicks per day.

Yet, as astounding as these numbers are, it's the new personalization of the Web that matters most in the social media revolution, both to companies and consumers. It's Facebook's ability to show you exactly what your friends and friends of friends like that makes the like function such a powerful tool. If you have a new baby, for example, you don't care what stroller is advertised on television, and, in fact, you probably don't care if 50, 500, or 5,000 people like a new stroller on Facebook. But if a friend of yours likes that stroller, you are more likely to feel that you can trust the company that made the item and are comfortable buying,

Facebook isn't the only social network to adopt a "like" feature, either. YouTube, Linkedln, Pinterest, Instagram, and foursquare have all added their own functionality that allows users to express approval of content, and Twitter has a Favorite button that allows users to approve of specific tweets. Content, companies, products, and ideas judged likeable by people you know and trust can be easily found throughout today's Internet. Companies and professionals who are worthy of people clicking their Like button will, in the short term, build trust and, in the long term, win the new Web in their respective categories.

4. Matrimonial Sites as Channels to Befriend Couples

Almost around the same time as the Internet boom began in India, the online matrimonial portals also came into existence. Contrary to expectations and surpassing the apprehensions, online matrimonial portals clicked. Online matrimonial portals were just the most needed oxygen for young boys, girls and their families. The space was more democratic when compared to the tedious route of matchmaking through uncles, aunties and neighbours. Matrimonial sites were conveniently anonymous, and could turn familiar when things moved from one stage to another.

Soon, the data analytics companies entered the fray. Online matrimonial sites became data-mining sites and spaces which gave deeper meaning to the 'fields' to collect data. For, when the match was made, or the recommendation would be sent, the final result was the human meeting where a thousand things could go wrong. And, if they went right, the success would belong to the website that brought a good pair of individuals together. A country that believes in marriages are premeditated coming together of couples, their stars, their horoscopes and their families, has to rely on highly precise data to make this happen on the Internet. Online portals such as shaadi.com, bharatmatrimony.com, secondshaadi.com, jeevansaathi.com, shubhlaabhmatrimony.com among a few thousands of such dedicated spaces, started their journey much earlier and learnt along the way. They were dynamic and open for learning along the route.

As a result of this, today matrimony has turned into a huge business opportunity for budding e-entrepreneurs. The sector, right now, has a Rs 520-crore market, which will soon see a huge expansion in the coming days. For, it is clocking a compounded growth rate of 65% annually, according to ASSOCHAM survey conducted in 2013.

Apart from single men and women registering themselves online, the challenge of matchmaking is huge both in terms of data and logistics. With about 8,000 new members registering themselves every day, the number gets more tedious and difficult for mining and matching, if the technology used remains dated. As a result, both economics and technology of this matchmaking business constantly undergo changes, and mostly for better with more number of users entering the Internet space. One of the main reasons attributed to the growth of online matrimony business is the time efficiency and convenience that's a boon for those in search of partners for self or others.

The reason behind the success and the need of matrimonial websites is more predictable than any other social concept that prevails across countries. Arranged marriage has always been a norm in India, with love marriages upsetting the social equilibrium. Culture and mutual understanding between the couple hold keys to a lot of situations which can blow up in the face.

Moreover, marriage in India is never between two persons. It is always a give-and-take relationship between two families of similar background and economic status.

5. Social Media in Elections

Barack Obama's 2008 US presidential campaign has often been described as the first electoral campaign in which the use of social media had a decisive impact. The 2008 US presidential campaign had a huge presence on social networking sites. Barack Obama, a virtually unknown Democratic candidate, utilized 15 different social media websites to form relationships with the millions of American citizens who utilize those networks. His social networking profile pages were constantly being updated and interacting with followers. By the end of his campaign, Obama had 5 million social media network supporters. The use of social networking sites in his marketing campaign gave Barack Obama's campaign access to e-mail addresses, as posted on social network profile pages. This allowed the Democratic Party to launch e-mail campaigns asking for votes and campaign donations.

The "Arab Spring" uprisings in Tunisia, Egypt, and Libya, have proven that social media can be used to transform society and politics on a global scale. These uprisings used social media to organize protests, highlight injustices and government crackdowns, and sway public opinion at home and abroad. The effects spread to other nations, as even now, several nations in the Middle East find the status quo challenged by youths and social activists who use social media to rally others to their cause. In response, some countries have tried, often unsuccessfully, to limit access to social media sites, but these efforts just go to prove the staying power of the internet and social media as a tool for social change.

For generations, if a person wasn't at an event alive, the only way they would hear about it would be from the news media. This worked well enough when you consider how things were before, but the side effect was that a few gatekeepers controlled what images people saw, what news stories were covered, and from what angle. Now that social media sites let people from all over the world share their story through videos and images, it has changed the way people get their news and think about news in general. It has become a big issue for governments or organizations that want to hide the truth behind the veil of official secrets. Exposes from behind closed doors and aired on channels like YouTube have forced changes in ways that traditional media couldn't because they lacked access.

6. Abuse of Social Media

As the social networking is being increasingly used as an education and information resource, we have to decide how to make it a non-abuse place for our society. Pornography, violence, obscenity and hatred lurk in unexpected places, and innocent children stumble upon them all too frequently. It is not the problem of parents and their children only, but employees viewing and trading pornographic, offensive or otherwise unproductive material has also emerged as a key concern of many business managers. Not only are these activities wasteful of time and resources in themselves, they may also involve the employer in legal issues. The ease of access and distribution of these materials makes these issues all too common in daily business.

It is clearly evident that social media is a very powerful means of exercising one's freedom of speech and expression. However, it is also been increasingly used for illegal acts which has given force to the Government's attempts at censoring social media. Some of the misuses of social media are listed below:

a. Social Networking Addiction

Social networking addiction has become increasingly debated among experts. With recent abilities to become even more connected with user-friendly platforms, the ability to become addicted to social networking sites is becoming even more plausible. In a PDF research document entitled "Always Connected, How Smartphones and Social Media Keep Us Engaged," Facebook and IDC tracked the habits of almost 7,500 U.S. smartphone users over a week in March 2013. In just a short space of time, these users now find Facebook as an almost as popular and meaningful way of staying connected with friends and family as using the phone to talk or send texts. Some 84% of communication is done through text, email or social means, leaving the phone bit of the smartphone at only 16%.

In the case of social media websites, what hooks people is the rush they get from social recognition, the thrill of getting a 'like' or a re-tweet. That 'social high' causes addictive personalities to check their Facebook, Instagram and Twitter timelines every few minutes. But as soon as they hit one level of social recognition, they want to go one level higher. Suddenly, it's no longer enough to have five friends laugh at your clever turn of phrase or status on Facebook; it has to be at least 50. And when you hit 50, then it has to be 100. And so it goes.

But what's wrong with all this, you might ask? At the end of the day, nobody gets hurt if somebody spends too much time on Facebook, Instagram, Snapchat or Twitter. Unfortunately, people do get hurt — just not visibly. In the obvious sense, a person who is so obsessed with their Facebook status that they have to check it every few minutes is not going to be very productive at work.

There are other losses as well. Take, for example, the selfie obsession that has taken social media by storm. Unattractive and equally unnecessary, these selfies are taken anywhere and everywhere.

Social networking addiction is a behavioral addiction. Because social networking interaction can lead to elevation in moods, one may make the connection that social networking addiction is a disease. According to Rose, "the following are some of the most categorized symptoms of social networking addiction:[8]

> Your social networking activities cause you to neglect your obligations such as housework, school work, and work.
>
> You hide the truth about how much time you're online.
>
> You lose track of time when you're on sites like Twitter.
>
> Your social networking activities have caused negative issues at work or school, yet you continue those activities.
>
> Updating your Facebook status (how you're feeling) replaces 'talking it out' with friends or family.
>
> You sleep less, and avoid sleep regardless of fatigue, too spend time on sites like Facebook.
>
> Your discussions (offline) tend to include your posts, or the post of others, more than conversations about the other aspects of your life.
>
> You have gnawing feelings of guilt and shame over the amount of networking use.
>
> You become agitated or have mood swings when you're forced to spend periods of time away from social networks.
>
> You devote increased thoughts to what activities are, or could be going on, on Friendster or Twitter when you are not on them.
>
> You create an enhanced online personality-unrelated to your real person.
>
> You increasingly share information or become apart of online activities and discussions you KNOW are dangerous.
>
> You create an enhanced online personality-unrelated to your real person.
>
> You lie about relationships or children to encourage more interaction online by other users.
>
> You spend more time socializing online, and begin to avoid person to person interactions.
>
> You prefer interactions on social networking sites over various intimacies with your partner.
>
> You are too preoccupied with the posts of those you follow.
>
> You begin to lie in order to add excitement to your Facebook and Twitter wall.

You define yourself, or feel inflated and deeply saddened, by the number of friends or followers you have collected.

b. Cyberbullying

One problem with social networking is that it can lead to cyber bullying, which affects students in and out of school. Cyber bullying is a hard concept to define as more and more technology becomes available to children.

Cyber bullying is also complicated because there is direct cyber bullying, which most of us think of when we think of cyber bullying, but there is also cyber bullying by proxy, or indirect cyber bullying. The proxy bullying involves using other people to help cyber bully a victim, sometimes without the accomplice actually knowing what they are doing. It essentially is getting someone else to do the dirty work in bullying. Cyber Bullying by proxy also can occur when someone hacks into a victim's account of some type and uses it to send out inappropriate content to the victim's friends and contacts.

What really distinguishes cyber bullying from "playful teasing" is the aggressive intent behind the bullying. But again what makes it complicated is intent can be in the eye of the beholder, and someone can always claim they "were just joking." But a basic definition of cyber bullying is when someone bullys someone else through the use of technology. The cyber bullying exists on a continuum of severity. When the bullying is on the lesser end of the spectrum it is very hard to identify that it is bullying. But on the more extreme end cyber bullying has led to murder and suicide.

Types and Methods of Cyber Bullying[9]

Flaming - Flaming is a brief, heated exchange that happens between two or more people using some sort of communication technology. It usually happens in a public space like chat rooms or discussion groups, rather than in private discussions like emails .

Harassment - These are words, conduct, or actions being directed at a specific person with the intent to annoy, alarm, or cause emotional distress in that person. It is usually repeated messages or actions against one person.

Denigration - This is information about someone that is derogatory and untrue. Online it can be posted to a website, sent via email, or messaged to someone else. This also included sending or sharing photos of someone that portrays them in a sexual or harmful manner. Online "slam books" which are created in order to make fun of others are also forms of denigration.

Impersonation - This is when a person pretends to be another person, usually by using the victim's password to gain access to their accounts. They then send communication to others that is usually cruel, negative, or inappropriate, posing at that person. In more extreme cases, impersonation has lead to someone giving out where a person lives to the wrong people, in order for them to be track down by said people.

Outing and Trickery - Outing is sharing personal, and sometimes embarassing, information with others who were not meant to learn that information. Trickery is tricking someone into revealing personal information, and then sharing that information with others.

Exclusion/Ostracism - Children, like most people, just want to be a part of a group and fit in with others. Being excluded can be seen as "social death," and people can be excluded using online methods. The online exclusion could be being locked out of a password protected chat space, or just being de-friended on Facebook.

Cyber Stalking - This is stalking via the use of electronic communication using repetitive harassing and threatening communication.

Happy Slapping - This is a fairly new method of cyber bullying that has become popular in England. People, usually teens walk up and slap someone, while another person uses a phone or camera to record the incident. The video is then put on the internet for others to see, even though the victim may not be aware of it.

c. Commodification of Identity

In today's economy, identity information often is viewed as a valuable commodity. Businesses desire to advertise their products to the markets most interested in them, and may even retool their products to be more appealing to certain segments of a market. Knowing the preferences of individuals allows a corporation to target perfectly their products to those who would prefer and, thus, be most likely to purchase, them. Making a detailed survey of an individual's preferences, though, is very difficult, if not impossible. Often an individual cannot specify the exact motivation for her purchase of a particular product. From the seller's perspective, determining which questions to ask purchasers can be a daunting task. Further, certain questions, despite their potential usefulness, are not likely to be answered by a purchaser. To work around this problem, businesses use identity information as a proxy for preferences.

As a result, many businesses collect information about identity as part of its transactions. A purchase order form may ask for an address, occupation, and income level. Stores may ask individuals to relinquish portions of their identity in exchange for goods and services. For example, customers may be offered special discounts or free products if they complete a survey. Similarly, a customer may be asked to complete a registration form detailing her reading and television-viewing habits in order to receive a card entitling the customer to a discount . The business creates a database using the information from these forms and the names of the products that were purchased. Hoping to develop a more accurate profile of their customers -- in essence, hoping to learn the full identity of the average consumer, businesses sell or rent portions of their databases to other businesses. Conceivably, if enough vendors collaborate, a "profile" of buyers may be created without the consumers express permission or knowledge. The information is then used to guide the direct marketing of other products to customers or the retooling of current products. It also could be used to identify those people who have a high probability of not paying their bills. Such databases stand to threaten the privacy interests of consumers, especially for those purchasing legal, but socially stigmatized, products like pornography.

d. Surveillance Society, Transparent Society

While concealing one's identity might be easy to do online, it is a feeble defense against the predations of government and corporate power in real life. Though the digital identity might go to great extremes to protect their real identity when they are online, the real world they live in is becoming a surveillance society. With the belief that surveillance is synonymous with security, the world could enter into a surveillance society. The appetite for information and willingness to be monitored seems to characterise the modern world as an information society.

The rise of the surveillance society, would seem like a science fiction depiction of the future; however the surveillance society already arrived some time ago. Many civil rights activists fear that the power and authority can be misused, and can take away civil liberties formally enjoyed by citizens of democracies. However not all interpretations of the surveillance society are negative, some theorists have optimistic views on the surveillance society. The opposite of a transparent or open society is a secretive society that protects not only citizens but the larger powers, such as world governments, businesses and the criminal underworld.

e. Manipulation of Social Networking Sites for Commerce

Social networking websites allow individuals and businesses to interact with one another and build relationships and communities online. When companies join these social channels, consumers can interact with them directly. That interaction can be more personal to users than traditional methods of outbound marketing and advertising.

Social networking sites act as word of mouth or more accurately, e-word of mouth. Social networking sites and blogs allow followers to "retweet" or "repost" comments made by others about a product being promoted, which occurs quite frequently on some social media sites. By repeating the message, the user's connections are able to see the message, therefore reaching more people. Because the information about the product is being put out there and is getting repeated, more traffic is brought to the product/company. They allow consumers to express their needs, wants and values, online. Social media marketing then connects these consumers and audiences to businesses that share the same needs, wants and values.

Through social networking sites, companies can interact with individual followers. This personal interaction can instill a feeling of loyalty into followers and potential customers. Also, by choosing whom to follow on these sites, products can reach a very narrow target audience.

Social networking sites also include much information about what products and services prospective clients might be interested in. Through the use of new semantic analysis technologies, marketers can detect buying signals, such as content shared by people and questions posted online. Understanding of buying signals can help sales people target relevant prospects and marketers run micro-targeted campaigns.

Social networking is used by 76% of businesses today. Business retailers have seen 133% increases in their revenues from social media marketing.

Conclusion

Social media has come as a blessing for be-friending the other in many areas of life- for building community, for sharing interests, for selling and marketing, for political activism, for getting help in need, for teaching and learning, etc. On the other hand, it has generated new problems and challenges which can alienate others. Some of those challenges are :

Networking addiction which can be harmful for the user , Cyber bulling which can destroy the other, Mislead unsuspecting persons for predation, Create a surveillance society where privacy is lost and Misuse social media for commodification.

Notes

1. Boyd, D. M., & Ellison, N. B. (2008). "Social network sites: Definition, history and scholarship." *Journal of Computer-Mediated Communication, 13, 210-213*
2. Baumeister, R. F., & Leary, M. R. (1995). "The need to belong: Desire for interpersonal attachments as a fundamental human motivation." *Psychological Bulletin*, 117(3), 497-529.
3. Whiting, A., & Williams, D. (2013). "Why people use social media: A uses and gratifications approach." *Qualitative Market Research: An International Journal*, 16(4), 362-369.
4. Van Baren, J., IJsselsteijn, W.A., Markopoulos, P., Romero, N., de Ruyter, B. (2004). "Measuring Affective Benefits and Costs of Awareness Systems Supporting Intimate Social Networks." in: A. Nijholt, & T. Nishida, (Eds.), *Proceedings of 3rd Workshop on Social Intelligence Design. CTIT Workshop Proceedings Series WP04-02* (pp. 13-19).
5. Baker, H. S., & Baker, M. N. (1987). "Heinz Kohut's self-psychology: An overview." The American Journal of Psychiatry, 144, 1-8.

6. Marshal McLuhan. *The Gutenberg Galaxy: The Making of Typographic Man*, University of Toronto Press, 1962.

7. "Social Media - The New Power of Political Influence," Centre for European Studies, www.thinkingeurope.eu.

8. Rose, S. (2009, August 2). *Social Networking Addiction: Do you need detox from facebook and twitter?* http://www.associatedcontent.com/article/2014392/social_networking_addiction_pg3.html?cat=72.

9. Kowalski, R., Limber, S., and Agaston, P. (March 17, 2008). *Cyber Bullying: The New Moral Frontier*. http://onlinelibrary.wiley.com/book/10.1002/9780470694176.

16

Intellectual Challenges to Christianity

Isaac Padinjarekuttu
Oriens Theological College, Shillong, Meghalaya, India

Abstract: In this article, the author explores the intellectual challenges facing Christianity today. According to Ernst Troeltsch, the most important intellectual challenge to Christianity was the growing lack of appreciation of the essential content of the Christian message: the ethos of love, the view of the human person, the communitarian cult, and the centrality of Jesus Christ. If we reformulate these challenges for today's secularized and secularizing world, they are: the intellectual hegemony of values and cognitive assumptions that make the love ethos of Christianity unintelligible; an understanding of personality that contradicts the Christian understanding of the uniqueness of the person; an increasingly individualistic perception of spirituality; and the loss of the idea of Transcendence without which the notion of Jesus Christ as mediator between human and divine is impossible.

The author holds that the Catholic Church is best equipped to face all these challenges. But for that it must come out of its defences which is the case in many countries or it has withdrawn from public life. The Church must show that it can articulate its message afresh, the message about the Holy, the Messiah, the Prophet, etc. Only then will it continue to be relevant morally and spiritually. If the task of the Church is to accompany people on their pilgrimage as they search for the True, the Good and the Beautiful, in every age and place, there is no way of doing this without believing in reason, and reasoning together, posing difficult questions and searching for new answers.

Keywords: Ernst Troeltsch, *intellige ut credas,* Love ethos, human dignity, Transcendence.

The Roman historian Tacitus called Christianity "one more contemptible superstition, an additional evidence of the sad capacity of human beings to believe strange things."[1] But Christianity turned out to be something quite different, in fact, a substantial astonishment for everyone. That a movement beginning with a breakaway group within Judaism should end by capturing the imperial palace could hardly have been foreseen by anyone. One reason for it was the intellectual power of Christianity which the great Fathers of the Church convincingly proved to their contemporaries. As the great theologian Origen maintained, there is a precise distinction between the *dogmata* of the Church's tradition which had to be maintained and the *problemata* which needed to be discussed.[2] The intimate relationship between faith and reason was summed up by Augustine's famous sayings: *crede ut intelligas*, because understanding was a reward of faith, and *intellige ut credas*, for one is not able to believe without reason.3 No one in fact believes "if he has not first thought it necessary to believe. It is reason which shows "who is to be believed" and thus "even faith has eyes with which it sees that what it does not yet see is nevertheless true."[4] Therefore, in *De Trinitate* Augustine defined theology as "the science which generates, nourishes, defends and fortifies faith…for it is one thing to know only that which must be believed in order to obtain the blessed life…and another to know it in such a way as to be able to place it at the service of the good and to defend it against the bad."[5] So a fundamental principle of Augustine's theological method was the ardent desire to arrive at an understanding of the faith and the employment towards this end of all human resources. The history of theology is the history of the attempt to understand the faith and enjoyment of the Truth, which constitutes the highest good for human beings.

That it is an important task today is clearly stated by Pope Francis: "Proclaiming the Gospel message to different cultures also involves proclaiming it to professional, scientific and academic circles. This means an encounter between faith, reason and the sciences with a view to developing new approaches and arguments on the issue of credibility, a creative apologetics which would encourage greater openness to the Gospel on the part of all. A theology – and not simply a pastoral theology – which is in dialogue with other sciences and human experiences is most important for our discernment on how best to bring the Gospel message to different cultural contexts and groups."[6]

Everybody will agree that the world has changed, and so has the Church's place in the world; to dream of a return of the world and the Church of the "good old days" is a decoy, an illusion, and it rests on the sacralization of one historical form of the Catholic Church. During the Synod of Bishops on New Evangelization, 2012, one of the participants said: "Our beautiful Christian faith is too complicated: the terms, their content and their explanation. We bathe in an ensemble of dogmas, of mysteries: the Holy Trinity, the Incarnation, Redemption, the Sacraments...These dogmas must be interpreted in a form capable of touching upon daily life, human aspirations, happiness and prosperity, the daily realities of our faithful."[7]

In many Catholic and Christian countries, to the question, "to what Church do you belong," one gets increasingly the answer, "none." Many people have come to believe that what they learned as children about the nature of God can be erased as fairy tales. The culture that surrounds us focuses on science, growing out of the long history of Copernicus, Darwin, Freud, Einstein and Hawking. Still, most people are not atheists but agnostics, still searching even as they entertain doubts about God. There is need for a new conversation about God, one that shows people that God is not an old man with a long white beard. God is infinite and unlimited. God is incomprehensible to our finite minds. This is not easy to grasp. We surmise that God is spirit, straddling the universe and parallel universes. At the same time God is intimate to each of us. We cannot prove his existence by reason, nor can science disprove God's existence.

Many people say that they relate to God personally and do not need a Church. We applaud this personal relationship, but it is also truly human to do things in community. But there is a reason for the rejection of the Church. They ask what caused the Church over the centuries to underestimate the Gospel's core messages, love and compassion. People also have other serious issues that loom large on their horizon: the morality of world economics, spiritual life, human sexuality, peace and war, the poor and their suffering, etc. So the main challenge the Church faces today is to relearn how to communicate a deeper, more intelligent and more relevant religion that leads to a life of love, compassion, justice and peace. How to remain in contact with the millions of people who look for God but not come to Church? This is the background of my reflection on the intellectual challenges to Christianity today.

A century ago, the German Philosopher Ernst Troeltsch published an article about the future of Christianity.[8] In fact, he spoke not only about the future of Christianity but of religion in general. Against all pessimism, Troeltsch saw the possibility of a reformed and revitalized Christianity provided it addressed the intellectual challenges facing it. According to him, the most important intellectual challenge to Christianity was the growing lack of appreciation of the essential content of the Christian message: the ethos of love, the view of the human person, the communitarian cult, and the centrality of Jesus Christ. If we reformulate these challenges for today's secularized and secularizing world, they are: the intellectual hegemony of values and cognitive assumptions that make the love ethos of Christianity unintelligible; an understanding of personality that contradicts the Christian understanding of the uniqueness of the person; an increasingly individualistic perception of spirituality; and the loss of the idea of Transcendence without which the notion of Jesus Christ as mediator between human and divine is impossible.[9] A few words about each of these would be in order.

1. The Love Ethos of Christianity

The world today is characterized by increasing individualism and there are mainly two types of individualism. The first is "utilitarian individualism" which is a utility-oriented understanding of life and relationships. Everything is judged by its utility for immediate and often material profit and personal enjoyment, and therefore, life is basically making clever choices and developing strategies to achieve these goals. The second type of individualism is "expressive individualism" which maintains that the goal of life is self-expression and self-realization of the individual and the satisfaction of one's material and emotional needs. According to the American Sociologist Robert Bellah, the two sociological types that symbolize these two types of individualism are the American "Manager" and "Therapist."[10] According to him, there can be serious conflicts between these two types of individualism. One example was the revolt of the 1960s and 1970s by the expressive young generation in the West against the utility oriented worldview of their fathers. Another option is not to make a choice between the two types of individualism but to try to harmonize them, symbolized by the "Yuppie Culture" of the 1980s. Self absorbed, rich, given to demonstrably high consumption, they are out of touch with most of the challenges and concerns of others and live their life unperturbed, concerned only with the fulfilment of their desires. The entire financial system of the capitalist world, its business philosophy and strategies, its banking system, and indeed, the whole science of economics are dominated by these types of individualism. The crises in the financial markets during the last few years did offer some occasion for a rethink, but now, business is as usual once again.

As against these two types of egocentric or even narcissistic individualism Robert Bellah proposed two other types of individualism, the "Republican" and the "Biblical." The word "Republican" has nothing to do with the political party with that name, but refers to a political tradition which goes back to the city-state republics of Athens and Rome and the Italian city states of the Middle Ages. The citizens played an active role in political life and had a say in its affairs. It was expected from them that they act virtuously which meant they should not do anything which goes against the common good, because the common good is more important than personal benefits and individual self-realization. Although such an attitude was very commendable, it was unmistakably clear that the common good of my republic was more important than that of the other.

The alternative to this is the biblical notion, which has its origin in the Judeo-Christian tradition. According to the biblical tradition, human beings are morally obliged in their decisions to look beyond their family, city, republic, country, religion or class. That is what the Bible means by "love your neighbour as yourself," irrespective of whether one belongs to one's group, class, religion, family or country. That is the core of Christian morality. Of course it is yet to be demonstrated satisfactorily why human beings should be motivated to act in this way in order to live a morally correct life or why one is not acting morally when one acts in pure self-interest. It is also not shown why one should be sensitive to the sufferings of others, which does not belong to the sphere of rational arguments.

Herein lies the superiority of the Christian love ethics over other moral systems and the different forms of individualism discussed above. But it is an intellectual challenge to show to the utilitarian, egocentric and expressive individualisms their limits, to the republican individualism its parochialism and to a purely rational global ethical system its irrelevance for concrete human life. No discussion on morality will be able to avoid the discussion on justice and love as its central components and both are foundations of the Christian moral teaching. The Christian concepts of unconditional love and justice are based on the concept of a God who loves human beings unconditionally and acts justly. The intellectual challenge to Christians today is to present all these as matters of great relevance and urgency for the globalized world today, and show that Christians are not, in the words of Max Weber, representatives of an "a-cosmic" love ethos. They believe in love and justice in the here and now, and both are indispensable for a new social and political order.[11] But it is a difficult task today to prove the superiority of Christian morality when the credibility of the Church's teaching on moral goodness is questioned on many counts.

2. The Human Person

Perhaps the most spectacular intellectual challenge to Christianity today is confronting the reductionist naturalism that is propagated vigorously. Researches in Neurosciences, Genetics, Socio-biology, etc. claim to establish that there is no difference between human and animal behaviour, that human life is a purely biological and chemical phenomenon, thus challenging the religious world view of the vast majority of human beings. This reductionist naturalism rejects such concepts such as freedom, symbolization, etc. The debate has been with us since the nineteenth century but now it finds greater echo in the public.[12]

Such a worldview has consequences for the Church and its understanding of the human person. There is need for a new articulation of the Christian understanding of personality. Christianity believes in the unique dignity of the human person who is created in the image and likeness of God and is endowed with an immortal soul. Unfortunately, history shows that respect for the human person and his dignity were the fruits of hard struggles by other institutions than the Church. The human person was not the yardstick of the Church's actions, which is clearly shown in its opposition to democracy, human rights, etc. for centuries. These were the achievements of anti-Christian movements like the French Revolution, the American War of Independence, etc. It is good to ask what role the Churches played in the history of human rights, abolition of torture, abolition of slavery, discrimination against women, discrimination against sexual minorities, etc. Did not Christianity justify the upholding of structures which were against the Christian understanding of the human person? This is a major secular criticism against Christianity. The idea of the person as unique, created in the image of God, with dignity and inalienable rights is not what we see in the history of the Church with its brutal suppression of the rights of people in the name of truth, authority and obedience. The intellectual challenge for the Church today is to investigate self-critically and objectively the inter-relationship between Christianity and the sacralisation of the human person and draw appropriate conclusions for our engagement in the world today and put the dignity of the human person at the centre of its teaching and ministry.

3. Spirituality

Modern person has an understanding of spirituality that is at odds with that of the Church. Many people candidly confess that they have spiritual experiences where we least suspect it: in art, aesthetics, erotic love, confrontation with existential crises, like illness, death, loss of loved ones, etc. Modern person spares no energy in his/her search for exotic spiritual experiences and rituals. S/he believes that spirituality is a very personal affair and the Church is nowhere in their scheme of things. The Church is even seen as a hindrance to spiritual growth.

Believing and practicing Christians, in fact, encounter the incomprehension of their contemporaries for their continuance in the Church in spite of their having serious problems with it. This incomprehension is the result of the view that is almost taken for granted today that social organizations must be based on free association of the members, and therefore, anything that places the institution before or above the individual should be rejected. The claim of the Church that it is a supra-personal reality capable of leading people to faith and self-realization contradicts the individualistic tendencies of our age.

Those who hold this view do not understand what the Church is, that it is not a "cultic club," an organization merely meant for the communal celebration of rituals, and that it has a transpersonal character. It is true that even within Christianity, there are different understandings of community,

with some, like the Catholics, Anglicans and Orthodox Christians having a more universal community consciousness, while some Protestants, like the Free Churches and Congregationalists have less of it. Let us take the Catholic Church. Historically it stressed for a long time an authoritarian, hierarchical and excessively centralized form, although the theological core of the Church as a community of agape or love was not totally forgotten. The Christian Creed speaks of the Church as "one, holy, catholic and apostolic," one but not uniform, holy but also sinful and so in need of reform, missionary like the apostles and catholic which means trans-cultural, transnational and so concretely universal. In spite of all the differences, the Christians have something in common.13 Charles Taylor, in his book *A Secular Age* called the Church a *Network of Agape.* According to him, the lifeblood of the Church is agape and not a set of rules and regulations. It is nourished by relationships and when it is extended to the other a network is established. In this sense, the Church is a Network-society, but of a special kind, because the relationship that its members share is not that of a family, clan or tribe. In the Church, relationships exist that transcend familiar categories, like the family, clan or tribe. The only basis of relationships in the Church is agape. It is a special experience that binds the members together in the community.14 The challenge before the Church today is to make this community attractive once again, as a place of spiritual experience which satisfies the individual and does justice to the community and show that spirituality and community do not exclude each other as many people tend to think today, that spirituality in its different hues and colours is possible also in a community, particularly in the Church.

4. Transcendence

The next challenge is to face the loss of the idea of Transcendence, not the watered down understanding of Transcendence by which we mean anything that goes beyond the ordinary, but the Judeo-Christian understanding, the total otherness of divinity, a radical desacralization of the present and its political and social structures, as the Prophets of the Old Testament proclaimed it which the Christian faith continues to uphold. This understanding of Transcendence is integral to the Christian faith. Here we are faced with two challenges: the first is the conflict between the specifically Christian understanding of Transcendence in the form of the Trinity and the Jewish and Islamic understanding of pure monotheism and the need for a dialogue which calls for great intellectual acumen; the second is to go behind the open and conscious assault of philosophy, culture and politics to de-transcendentalize reality and to offer possibilities of human self-realization in political and cultural ideologies as we experienced in National Socialism, post-revolutionary Communism, etc. That such ideologies are at work again is clear to everyone and it is the task of a post-totalitarian Christianity to confront such trends intellectually.

Karl Jaspers has traced the origin of the idea of Transcendence to the so-called Axial Age, the period between 800 and 200 BC.[15] Its potential for challenging a one-sided anthropocentrism and absolutisation of this worldly structures and institutions was emphasized by the Prophets of the Old Testament. The Abrahamic religions have continued this tradition. He also discussed the similarities and differences between Semitic and Eastern religions, like Buddhism and Confucianism. So in spite of the popularity of the theory of the "Clash of Civilizations" which the present day context tends to endorse, there is still need for a rediscovery of the commonalities of all religions and an alliance of all of them against all forms of narrow-mindedness and exclusivism, including the blanket rejection of Transcendence. The political and moral potential of this idea in the contemporary world for resisting political, religious and cultural ideologies and in combating radicalism, fanaticism and fundamentalism needs to be explored and that is an intellectual challenge addressed to the Church.

Of course there are other challenges, too, but these touch upon the core of the Christian message. The ecological crisis, the grave danger posed by an unregulated financial market, the immensely destructive potential of science and technology, the scandal of world hunger and malnutrition, the injustice inherent in international politics, etc. should concern the Church, indeed all religions and all human beings.

One could ask why the whole question of sexual morality is not presented as one of the serious challenges before the Church. If Christianity takes the love commandment seriously, all problems of sexual morality can be resolved. When the law of love takes the backstage and questionable anthropological and legal postulates take the centre stage problems crop up. Then in sexuality procreation of children will be given a false priority to expression of love. Homosexuality will become a sin instead of an expression of love between two human beings. Celibacy of priests will not be misunderstood as enmity towards sex but as liberative asceticism for the service of others.

Then there is another alleged challenge, the so-called dictatorship of relativism popularized by Pope Benedict XVI. It is to be genuinely doubted whether there is such a danger as dictatorship of relativism. The number of people who theoretically profess an epistemological or moral relativism is arguably very small and so a dictatorship of this small group over the vast majority of human beings is not a serious danger. What is true is that pluralism of philosophical, epistemological and moral systems is a fact of reality. There will be competition among them in their claim to truth. In this context it must be said that the Church also has the duty to critically analyse its own truth claims. The standpoint of the Church for a long time that faith is equal to obedience to a set of doctrines of a highly institutional and authoritarian Church was a mistake. This sacralisation of institutions instead of measuring

everything against the holiness of God cost the Church dearly. The Church has to face the challenges from competing ideologies and religions through the attractive and convincing power of the Good News of Jesus. This is a serious intellectual challenge. The church cannot function like a quasi state and still lack the guarantees of a constitutional state. It is not transparent, is bureaucratically top heavy, without many of the guarantees for the protection of individual rights and structures of institutional self-reform.[16] This has cost the Church much in terms of credibility in recent times.[17]

Conclusion

The Catholic Church is best equipped to face these challenges. In order to do so, it must come out of its defences which is the case in many countries or it has withdrawn from public life. The Church must show that it can articulate its message afresh, the message about the Holy, the Messiah, the Prophet, etc. Only then will it continue to be relevant morally and spiritually. If the task of the Church is to accompany people on their pilgrimage as they search for the True, the Good and the Beautiful, in every age and place, there is no way of doing this without believing in reason, and reasoning together, posing difficult questions and searching for new answers.

Notes

1. John McManners, ed., *The Oxford Illustrated History of Christianity*, Oxford, 1990, 60.
2. Hans Küng, *Christianity: Essence, History, and Future*, New York, 1995, 164.
3. Johannes Quasten *Patrology*, vol. IV, Allen, Texas, no year, 403.
4. *Ibid.*
5. St. Augustine, *De Trinitate*, 14, 1, 3.
6. Pope Francis, *Evangelii Gaudium*, 132-33.
7. Intervention of His Beatitude Grégoire III Laham, B.S., Patriarch of Antiochia of the Greek-Melkites, Head of the Synod of the Greek-Melkite Church, Syria.
8. "Die Zukunftsmöglichkeiten des Christentums," *Logos* 1 (1910/11) 165-185.
9. Hans Joas, *Glaube als Option*, Freiburg, 2012, 203-218.
10. Robert Bellah, et al., *Habits of the Heart. Individualism and Commitment in American Life*, Berkeley, 1985.
11. Hans Joas, 206; also see Paul Ricoeur, *Liebe und Gerechtigkeit*, Tübingen, 1990.
12. See Matthias Jung, *Der bewusste Ausdruck. Anthropologie der Artikulation*, Berlin, 2009.
13. See Karl Lehmann, "Das katholische Christentum," in: Hans Joas/Klaus Wiegandt, eds., *Saekularisierung und die Weltreligionen*, Frankfurt am Main, 2007.
14. Charles Taylor, *Ein säkulares Zeitalter*, Frankfurt am Main, 2007, 480
15. Karl Jaspers, *Vom Ursprung und Ziel der Geschichte*, Zürich, 1949.
16. Franz Xaver Kaufmann, *Kirchenkrise. Wie überlebt das Christentum*, Freiburg, 2011.
17. Ernst-Wolfgang Böckenförde, "Das unselige Handeln nach Kirchenraison," *Sueddeutsche Zeitung*, 29.4.2010, 2.

17

The Otherness in the Other

Victor Ferrao

Dean of Philosophy, Rachol Patriarchal Seminary, Goa

Abstract: The hierarchy and structuring of India maybe viewed in logocentric linear manner. Such a view often legitimizes reining hierarchies and regimes of oppressions. It imposes a static lens of sameness on the entire process of that formed and is forming our society. In contrast to this view, we take up a non-linear, non-hierarchical, horizontal and immanent view in this study by critically scrutinizing otherness. To enter this dynamic terrain, we take a walk into the ecology of thought of Gilles Deleuze and Pierre-Félix Guattarri. We shall first study the material processes and discern the relation between repetitions, resemblance and equivalence. Then we deepen our study through a scrutiny of Immanence. Next we deal with three ecological registers: the environment, society and subjectivity. Finally we discuss the dynamic flows of our Indian society in a rhizomatic way.

Keywords: Other, Otherness, Repetition, Resemblance, Plane of immanence, Territorialisation and Deterritorialization, Desiring Machines, body-without-organs, Rhizome

The structural and cultural complexities of India maybe viewed in logocentric linear manner. Such a view often legitimizes reining hierarchies and regimes of oppressions. It imposes a static lens of sameness on the entire process of that formed and is forming our society. In contrast to this view, we take up a non-linear, non-hierarchical, horizontal and immanent view in this study by critically scrutinizing otherness. Otherness is not static. It is important to understand how the other emerges from as dynamic and multiple flows of otherness. The other is an emergent property of the unstable otherness. This unstable otherness reaches some level of unstable stability in the shape of being other. The ontic other that we experience irrupts from an ontological dynamic volcano. It is from the depth of otherness that its other emerges which then in relations to its dynamic 'out bursting' otherness leads to a new level wherein another other bursts on the scene and the process marches on as the multiple possibilities open the dynamic otherness that reaches a kind of unstable closure. The logocentric underpinnings of our thought comfortably essentialize sameness and privilege it against difference. Unfortunately, this difference is constructed in the horizon of sameness. Hence, in this context I find that Deleuzian rendering of sameness and difference in a dynamic mould of repetition can untie these knots and allows the dynamics of sameness and otherness shine to its full potential. Hence, it is important to understand how both difference and repetition rises from a dynamic interiority which operates only in the multiple and determines multiplicities. Hence, the other of otherness is an effect or a product of mobile relations.

We cannot black box sameness and difference in a static mould and then relate them mathematically so to say. There is no stable sameness or difference. There is only a dynamic repetition and differentiating difference. Sameness is not a subtraction of otherness. We need to step into the dynamic dance of intensive flows and multiple energies that allow repetition and difference to burst on the scene. It is in this dance that always spreads from a decentred centre and displaced periphery that we can trace the zone of the other in the otherness. To enter this dynamic terrain, we take a walk into the ecology of thought of Deleuze and Guattarri. They offer a new thought that strives to bring a new materialism that does not begin from an imposition of human values, meaning and culture upon material processes. They explore the role of material processes in the emergence of three ecologies: the environment, society and subjectivity.

We shall first study the material processes and discern the relation between repetitions, resemblance and equivalence. Then we deepen our study through a scrutiny of Immanence. Next we strive to deal with three ecological registers: the environment, society and subjectivity. Finally we shall try to discuss the dynamic flows of our Indian society in a rhizomatic way.

Repetition, Resemblance and Equivalence

There is irreducibility in repetitions. Repetitions are not resemblances. There is a radical difference between the two. The equation of repetitions to resemblance is a subtraction of difference. It is based on the calculus of exchange or substitution. This apparent exchange or substitution is possible

only if one views repetition though a static and generic terms. Often resemblance and difference is thought in a cyclic mode of thought. Although, it brings dynamism to resemblance but it exterminate difference, it's other. Hence, the logocentic thinking of identities and their relations to alterities has to be deconstructed.

Repeating the Unrepeatable

Repetitions are concerned with relations that are non-exchangeables or non-substitutable. There is a paradox in repetition in as much as it seeks to repeat the unrepeatable. This is why repetitions are non mathematical, economy of exchange. Repetitions are different in kind. Psychoanalytically repetition is born out of insatiability and a sense of incompleteness. Even a simple human act cannot fully reduplicate itself. That is, there is somehow a counterfeit dimension in all repetitions. In other words repetition is repeating the unrepeatable. That is why resemblance does not belong to nature but is a second nature. It is a habit of our thinking and speaking and hence acquired at the cost of the murder of dynamism of being. Therefore, we need to put metaphysic in motion. Movement is repetition. Repetition cannot be represented. In repetition, we experience pure forces, dynamic lines in space act in a manner we cannot really describe. It acts without intermediary. It is like language which speaks before words or gestures which develop before organized bodies, or masks before faces, sceptres and phantoms before characters. Repetitions produce movements or leaps. This means it escapes fixation. David Hume had already shown that repeated series such as AB, AB, AB....themselves produce something new, namely a habit and expectation. Hence he says when A appears we habitually expect B (Smith 2013).

Repetition as Singular

Repetition cannot be replaced. It is singular. Delezue uses the metaphor of a gift or theft to draw the singularity of the repetition. Repetition is about unexchangeable and unsubstitutable singularities. For instance, one cannot exchange one's soul. Exchange is the criterion of resemblance and equivalence. Hence, there is economic difference between repetition and resemblance and singular (Deleuze, 1994: 1). Deleuze states that to repeat is to behave in a certain manner but in relation to something unique and singular which has no equal nor equivalent (Deleuze, 1994: 1). Thus, festivals do not add the first time to the second time to the first but carry the first time to the nth power. Therefore it is on 15th August that commemorates the Independence of our country. But it is the independence that repeats and celebrates on every 15th August. There are two types of languages. The language of science is dominated by the symbol of equality and hence each term may be exchanged by another while in a lyrical language every term is irreplaceable and can only be repeated (Deleuze, 1994: 2). The law belongs to the order of resemblance while transgression of the law belongs to the order of repetition. It puts all law, including the law of nature into question. It denounces its nominal and general character in favour of more profound and more artistic reality (Deleuze, 1994: 3). Delueze succinctly teaches this when he says, 'expecting repetition from the law of nature is the 'Stoic' error.'

Differential Fields as the Ground of Repetition

Differential fields are structures that are conditions of genesis of creative transformation of things. The differential fields are inhabited by multiple flows and intensities that produce mutual re/de territorialisation. The differential fields are constituted of multiplicities. Multiplicities give rise to thresholds that lead to the emergence of singularities. Thus, for instance, in a game of football it is differential relations of the ground, sphere, players and rules that lets the a sphere emerge as a football or the players as footballers and field of play as a football ground. It is the differential relations and intensities that open the virtual (possible) to become actual as the players move, advance and retreat in the course of the game. These relations can be seen as strewn singularities that led the ball move from players to players across the football field. But football is just one actualization of the differential relations. Change the rules slightly and you have hand ball or rugby etc. Thus, it is the distribution of the flows and intensities in the differential fields that becomes the ground of difference as well as unrepeatable repetitions. The unrepeatable difference is (un)substitutable. Thus, my reflection in the mirror is a repetition of me but cannot substitute me. My friends will not relate to my reflection but would need me. Repetitions express persistence of difference that can be viewed as immanent variability or cadence. The harmonious musical composition (cadence) is a result of differential fields of intensities of the dance of notes that makes it possible.

Thinking Immanence

Deleuze reads philosophers like Spinoza and Bergerson through the lens of immanence. Immanence is a complex notion and is at play at several levels in Deluzian thought. It is an ontological notion that forms the basis of Deluezian thought. It becomes the horizon from where thinking takes place. It constitutes the internal condition of thinking. Thinking produces concepts which Deleuze calls intensive events where thought crystallizes into a specific formulation responding to specific problem at stake for a thinker . All thinking emerges from what he calls the plane of immanence.

Plane of Immanence and Thinking

Deleuze teaches that the main task of the philosophers is the generation of concepts. He notes that concepts are always composite and multiple. Thus, for instance Cogito is composed of a certain idea of thinking, being and the self. Concepts not only attempt to provide us solutions to specific problems, they become tools rendering possible the elaboration of the problem in question. Precisely because they have to be created and are not found, they require a milieu out of which they can be created. Deleuze calls it the plane of immanence. The relation between the concept and the plane of immanence is one of mutuality. No concept can be generated without the plane of immanence which grounds them, yet, the plane of immanence cannot be thought without the concept that inhabits it. That is why the plane of immanence is often thought as pre-philosophical, not in terms of something pre-existing philosophy but as that which constitutes the unspoken, the unthought internal conditions of thinking itself. Each plane of immanence is outlined in such and such a way depending on the nature of question. Being pre-philosophical, it cannot be thought as such yet it constitutes thought. Deleuze terms it as an image of thought

The Plane of Immanence, Thought and Chaos

Emerges within the plane of immanence that provides consistency to it. The counterpoint of the plane of immanence is not transcendence but chaos. The plane of immanence makes consistency possible while chaos is that which has no consistency and is that which constitutes a continuous dissolution of consistency. Chaos is perpetually chaotizing where nothing has yet taken form neither as thought or nature and in the same way threatens to dissolve all that is formulated and wrought into form. Thus, chaos is not static, inert or in stationary state. It is in a constant mode of chaotizing. While still being immersed into the chaos that thought begins by precisely instituting the plane of immanence which is nothing but a section of chaos. This means what we call thinking occurs as tensive relation between chaos and immanence where chaos ungrounds thought and immanence makes it possible to ground it and yet maintains chaotic speed. By letting thought be formulated as a continuous tension relation to chaos, we have an essential groundlessness of the thought or philosophy itself. This means there are no fixed points and no given questions, concepts or problems for thought. The very absence of givenness, of world, subject, consciousness or God constitutes the horizon of thought. The plane of immanence enables the creation of meaning against the background of chaotic non-meaning that underlines all life.

Plane of Immanence, Territorialisation and Deterritorialization

Territory is an ethological sense is viewed as an environment of the group that cannot be objectively located but is constituted by the patterns of interaction which enables the group to acquire a certain stability and location. Hence, a territorial process is continuously going on everywhere. The Plane of immanence continuously becomes the earth or deterritorialization on which it creates its concepts. The plane of immanence provides us two sides: extension and thought. It means it provides us the power of being and powers of thinking. Hence, the plane of immanence is in a continuous process of deterritorialization. It is phase space of a system. The plane of immanence has multiple layers that sometimes knit together and sometimes separate. The plane is never given as such but it is given only in through what it gives. This means it can only be inferred in what it gives. What it gives is differential actualizations that come from the world of virtual tendencies (phase space). The virtual constitutes a domain that is much larger and is teeming with potentials. This means that plane of immanence is never given and is never present. The differential calculus formalizes the virtual into the actual. That is, the plane of immanence is a ground of morphogenesis. It is on the plane of immanence under which intensities that tend to cancel each other are brought into actuality. It has the power to organize infinitely. This infinitely complex process brings the locking of intensities (intesitisties may be viewed as pints of attractors, bifurcators, zone of sensitivity that based the theory of selforganizability) into system of resonance and redundancy. Always there is a loss of something in the process of actualization (deterritorializations).

The Ecology of the Environment

Matter and form do not exist in isolation but are intimately intertwined. They express themselves by stratifying themselves. Every strata expresses without signifying anything because it is based in to the power to organize infinitely. We attempt to primarily listen to the dance of Differentiation. (difffrenciation in the Heideggarian sense)

Differentiation and Differenciation

In *Difference and repetition* and the *logic of sense*, Deleuze argued that the virtual is self-differentiating or difference in itself. The virtual realm is not undifferentiated chaos but is a realm of regional ontologies laying out the multiple possibilities for 'a' society, 'a' language and 'an' animal, and so forth can exist. Deleuze calls triggering of a bifurcator as an Event that unleashes an 'emission of Singularities' (Protevi, 2001). It means a bifurcator provides for the new set of attractors or patterns of behaviour. This process is named as differentiation by Deleuze in contrast to diffrenciation which names the process of actualization (Protevi, 2001). Actualization is a process of becoming of exclusive disjunctions which involves the selection of a series of singularities whose actualization precludes (prevent from happening) the simultaneous actualization of others. These would then have the status of 'road not taken' (Protevi, 2001). Within this train of thought, we are challenged to view phase space as dynamic and virtual as creative or productive. Scholars like Stuart Kaufmann of Santa Fe Institute positions a 'mutual bootstrap' effect between the 'landscape' of a particular phase space and specific trajectories inhabiting it (Protevi, 2001). In this way the actual agents serve to transforms the virtual field creating new singularities, 'fitness peaks' or attractors that will let diffrenciation reach a new level of emergence (Protevi, 2001). Hence, the virtual is not static but a differentiating chaotizing .

Selective Accumulation

The intensive flows at the level differentiation are permeated with unstable, unformed, open and nomadic singularities. Thus, for instance at the scale of geological stratification, it consists of process that inhabits territorialisation, sedimentation and fixation of intensities and singularities- through which structures (or stable forms) emerge and molar assemblages (Substances) take place. At the level of sedimentation, cyclical sediments are laid whose homogeneity is a result of 'sorting out mechanism' through which a highly improbable distribution is achieved. Within this complex mechanism of sedimentation, we can understand the role of rivers , which bring rocky materials from the mountains to the ocean. During this process of transit, pebbles of different weight, size and shape are variously affected by water that transports them. It is these effects in the context of moving water that sorts them out with the smaller pebbles reaching the ocean faster than the larger ones. Ones this laying out of the pebbles takes place, a second process sets in and transforms the loose pebbles into sedimentary rocks. This process is carried out by soluble substances like silica that penetrate the sediments through the pores in the pebbles. This process steadily lets the pebbles emerge as more or less permanent architectonic structure that evolves into a new entity, the sedimentary rocks (Beistegui, 2010: 55-57).

Isolative Consolidation

Besides the phenomenon of accumulation, coagulation and sedimentation, we have to draw our attention to a process of isolative consolidation. To understand this important process, let us take the example of morphogenesis of genes. Neo-Darwinists teach that a species is formed by gradual accumulation and selection of genes. Genes are not distributed or deposited at random but are sorted out by variety of selection pressures like climate change , the action of predators, parasites and effects of male and female mating choices. Thus like the geological stratification the genetic accumulation also goes through the process of consolidation. The genetic consolidation occurs as a result of reproductive isolation. Reproductive isolation is a process that leads to the closure of a gene pool, when a given subset of population becomes incapable of mating and reproducing along with the rest. It is through the dual process of selective accumulation and isolative consolidation, a population of an individual organism emerges as a species. It is within what we have called the plane of immanence that where alluvions, sedimentations, coagulations, foldings and recoilings that lead to the emergence of an organism (Beistegui, 2010: 58-59).

Ecology of Society

From the Freudian point of view society, desire and sexuality revolve around the oedipal event. This Freudian oedipal triangle is questioned by many thinkers today. The social codes come along with its base desire in what is prohibited or something that is lacking. For the boy it is the mother that is prohibited so he would seek substitutes for her and for the girl what is lacking is the Phallus and she would seek those who may give her one. Desire here is a desire for the forbidden fruit. Deleuze and Guattari turn desire on its head. They develop the notion of desire that does not feed from its representation in terms of an object that we want or something the subject lacks. Deleuze teaches that one never simply desire a person or an object. What one desires is an entire scenario, landscape, mode of existence or episode expressed in the person or the object. Desire is productive and has connective abilities.

Unconscious as a Site of Production of Desire

Deleuze and Guattari abandon the Freudian notion of unconscious as a site of repression of oedipal desires. They present the unconscious as rhizomatic rather than arborescent . It operates as networks or fields of operation rather than as a site that is steeped in repressed desires that are created after the resolution of the Oedipus Complex. The new notion of unconscious allows us to open the possibilities for a multiplicity of desires that may be oedipal, non-oedipal and beyond oedipal. This brings us to the possibility of living beyond the law of the father. Beyond the oedipal and oedipalized territories (Family, Church, School, Nation, Party) , particularly the territoriality of individual, and the new notion of unconscious evoke deterritorialized flows of desire, the flows that have not been reduced to the oedipal codes and the neuroticized territorialities and as such can escape these codes through lines of escape that lead elsewhere. Desire as productive connects desire (desiring machine) an object to some other object giving us the possibility to discern desire in everything and everywhere.

The Desiring Machine

Deleuze and Guattari use the term desiring machines not in its literal sense but in a metaphorical sense. They are not discussing machine as configuration of pre-existing parts nor do they think of them in a mechanistic sense. Machines to them are some things that connect that do not necessarily belong together, things that were not necessarily designed for each other. Thus, for instance, the pianist uses his hands to connect the keys of the piano and uses his feet on the pedals to produce music. The flow of music is produced by a music machine that consists of hands, feet, pedals, and the sheet of music that is being read. The desiring machine does not operate linearly and does not have specific task or time line. Desire connects objects to other objects (the pianists to piano, writer to books and paper, and writing tools) and is not limited to Oedipus complex and can break away from the oedipal triangle. Desire leads us to become body without organs by shunning away the organized, hierarchized and pre-given pre-existing body. Desire rides an attempt to become-molecular (not molar which presupposes a pre-given identity). Becoming molecular is not unified and cannot be identified because it has no identity and is rhizomatic

Desire as Schizophrenic

Deleuze and Guattari teach that schizophrenia reveals the profound nature of desire. While developing a positive and immanent of desire, they found a blueprint in Spinoza and were compelled to engage with the dominant discourse on desire. In their work, Anti-Oedipus, they attempt to render, desire or unconscious immanent. They suggest that unconscious is the faculty of desire and venture into an immanent critique of its powers and uses and establish philosophy as Schizoanalysis. They teach that the faculty of desire does not relate to its own object through correspondence, conformity or what phenomenology calls intentionality but through a relation of causality. This means they hold that the representation of the object is the cause of that object. Therefore, they argue that desire cannot be said to be missing anything or lacking in anyway. Besides, they do not link desire with pleasure or satisfaction. They view desire as productive, what we can do and the extent to which we can express through action, thought and creation. It is the infinite power of substance in Spinozian sense. Hence, unconscious becomes a site of production and not representation. Desire does not express anything in linguistic-semantic sense (it is not a signifier). It does not express in myths, tragedies and dreams which has to be carved out through interpretation. Desire is an engine that drives history. It is not wrapped and hidden in the Interest of class. It is not limited to oedipal triangle but is social and even cosmic. Desire is schizophrenic. It moves to become body without organs. Body without organs is the site that records the production of desire. It is on the body without organs that everything glides where connective and disjunctive energies collide resulting into a production or emergence of higher intensities and singularities.

The Body Without Organs and Indian Society

The body without organs is a field of immanence of desire. It is the plane where differentiation sets in the process of dynamic actualization the social sphere of our country. This brings us to the dynamism and fluidity of morphogenesis of everything that makes India. The India that we are living in is in the making. This process of actualization has not and will not follow a readymade path but is a product of spontaneous organization of several contingent factors that led the process of territorialisation, de-territorialisation and re-territorialisation.

The Rhizomatic flow of Indian Civilization

The evolution and development of Indian civilization can be viewed as rizomatic flow. Our civilization did not develop merely in a linear hierarchical fashion as some ultra-nationalists think. India has emerged on a rhizomatic lines of flights. There is no point on a rhizome but only lines. Rhizome ceaselessly establishes connections between semiotic chains, organizations of power etc., which forms assemblages that form plateaus. Deleuze and Guattari call plateau any multiplicity connected to other multiplicities by superficial underground stems so as to form or extend a rhizome. The multiple points of intersections, overlaps, convergences, twistings and infinite folds have collectively produced our society. Hence, rhizomatic flows take us into horizontal overflows and not in a vertical hierarchical mode of social formation. The interweaving of our civilization has not occurred in isolation as the essentialist modes of thought makes us to believe but in a Rhizo–India way in connection with its various flows both from within and from outside. The Rhizo-India mode, makes us to accept the geological flows, the formation of the Himalayas and the formation of Indian peninsula coupled with the human habitation resulting in the deforestation, the great Indus valley civilization, the migration of the Aryans and Vedic tradition, the rise of Sanghas leading to the birth of Magadha, the tribals and their cultures , the religious movements like Jainism, Buddhism in conflict with Brahminism, the invasion of Alexander, the great, the rise of the Mauryas, Asoka and the spread of Buddhism , the Gupta age, Harshavardhana, Rajputs and the Afghan-Turkish Sultans, Mughals, Marathas and the kingdoms of the south like the Pandyas, the Vktakas, Ikshvakus , the Kadambas, Chalukyas, Rashtrkutas, the Pallavas, the Bhamani Kingdom and the Vijaynagara has their share in the making of our country. Besides, the colonizers from the west: the Portuguese, the British and the French, the freedom movement, the cultural churning of RSS, and reformers of Hinduism, the two nation theory and the Hindu-Muslim conflict, the partition of Indian, the democratic rule, the birth of Bangladesh, along with the caste, religions, languages, sacred and secular literature and art forms, economic and political ideologies led to the formation of plural and vibrant India (Dalal, 2014). All this have to be seem in an emergent rizomatic way. Thus, for instance, if colonization was not to take place we out not have Hinduism or India of this shape.

The Death Drive and Indian Society

Body without organs has the death drive. It is a castrated body. Deleuze and Guattari teach that body without organs is a synonymous with Freud's death instinct. Body without organs is what desire desires not as an object but as a state of being. It is the direction and the way in which desire moves. Indeed, the body without organs come into being as an effect of desiring. Hence, it does not pre-exists desire. It is a desire to be in a state of organless body. The desire is governed by the unconscious and hence the body without organs is also a product of the unconscious. It can be best thought of as Being Degree Zero: that which stubbornly remains resisting all negation even when positive quality has taken way. It is neither an integral whole nor emptiness but rather remains an undifferentiated fluidity. It produces nothing but has to be reinserted in the production. Within this scheme of things, we can understand the logic of body without organs at play in the making and unmaking of Indian society. It becomes the 'socius', the full body of social production. In our country the 'socius' is the plural ethos that sustains the life and breath of our society. Upon this plural ethos that plurality and multiplicity in our country evolves and produces our social life. But there is the reverse movement that occludes the vibrant plural ethos of our country which homogenizes, essentializes part of it and leads us into the illusion of being nationalistic and more Indian than others. Thus, body without organs becomes a surface on which both the forces and agents of plural affirmation as well as negation are at play. The forces of negation of the plural ethos of our country become a clear expression of the death drive that can eventually destroy the vibrant plural ethos of our country. Thus, the champions of Hindutva and Hindu Rashatra become the visible portrayal of desire that is attempting to convert India into a body without organs. But there are secular forces that constantly de-territorialize and check the death drive injected by the Hindutva forces.

The Schizophrenic Desire and Indian Society

Deleuze and Guattari place desire in the social formation of production and production in the unconscious psychological realm of desire. This form of desire has no subject that causes production but it is production that causes further production. Such production results in the production of collective subjectivity of us Indians. Indian subject is an enduring self but is constantly changing and forming connections with the collective subjectivity. This means self of Indians are psychically and socially continuously de-territorialised. Thus, in several ways, we are 'schizophrenics'. Some of us are Christians, Goans, and Indians all at the same time. This is the case of every Indian. Schizophernia is seen as a line of escape completely free from constrains of social representation and based entirely on experience. We can see how some cultural police are trying to impose what they selectively deem as Indian culture and position it as noble and national. These powers are erecting the law of the father to all of us. Those who do not accept their version of culture and nationalism are orphaned and denationalized. But a schizo has the strength to disown all of it. He is an anti-Oedipus and refuses to be disowned by the several laws of fathers erected in our society. In fact an Indian is challenged to disown the 'father' and continuously invent his /her Self. This means we Indians are challenged to become anti-Oedipus and save the plural ethos of our country. We have to resist the voices and forces that force us to oedipalize. This is the way the minorities in particular can liquidate and de-territorialize the powers that attempt to orphanize and de-nationalize them.

Conclusion

The dynamic metaphysic of difference of Deleuze and Guttari leads us away from linear, vertical and hierarchical understanding and leads us to a non-logocentric, horizontal and rihzomatic way. We are enabled to view an Rihzo-India that can liberate us from intolerance, hate and violence. This can enable us to understand the otherness of the other, which necessarily constitutes the 'non-other' self of the subject.

References

Smith, Daniel W. (2013). Review of James Williams, Gilles Deleuze's Philosophy of Time: A Critical Introduction and Guide, Edinburgh University Press, 2011. http://ndpr.nd.edu/news/42146-gilles-deleuze-s-philosophy-of-time-a-critical-introduction-and-guide/ accessed on 30th Sept. 2015.

Deleuze, Gilles. (1994). *Difference and Repetition*, Trans. Paul Patton.New York: Columbia University.

Protevi, John. (2001). The Geophilosophies of Deleuze and Guattari. SEDAAG (Southeastern Division of the Association of American Geographers). http://www.protevi.com/john/SEDAAG.pdf accessed on 28th Oct. 2015.

Beistegui, Miguel de (2010). *Immanence : Deleuze and Philosophy* (Endinburg: Endinburg University. 2010), pp. 55-57.

Dalal, Roshen (2014). *The Puffin, History of India*, Vol. 1. Gurgoan: Puffin Books.

18

Befriending the Complex Other with Multiple Identities: Towards Creative Dialogue to Befriend the Other in Their Otherness

Kuruvilla Pandikattu, SJ

Dean, Faculty of Philosophy, Jnana Deepa, Pune 411014

Abstract: The author is convinced that other begins with my own self. We are in fact not one monolithic self, but a multiplicity of even contradictory and ambiguous selves. At the postcolonial level, we can speak of the multiple discourses (conflicting and entangled narratives) governing us and so the othering of the other starts with the othering of my own self. For this we take two authors, Arundhati Roy and David Malouf, who will show the complex and nuanced identities of oneself. After realising this complex identities, we can try to enter into dialogue with the other, who is equally complex. This will help us to befriend the other.

Keywords: Arundhati Roy, David Malouf, Multiple Citizenships, Remembering Babylon, Multiple Identities.

Inspired by *Intimate Enemy: Loss and Recovery of Self Under Colonialism* (Nandy, 2015), I want to reflect on the fact that the other begins with my own self. We are in fact not one monolithic self, but a multiplicity of even contradictory and ambiguous selves. At the postcolonial level, we can speak of the multiple discourses (conflicting and entangled narratives) governing us and so the othering of the other starts with the othering of my own self. For this we take two authors, Arundhati Roy and David Malouf.

Multiple Citizenships and Commitments

Going beyond hybridity and identities, we study the committed to multiple citizenships drawing insights from Arundhati Roy and David Malouf. This section will enable us to appreciate the role played by the people who are marginalise and disprivileged in the post colonial discourses.[1]

a. Arundhati Roy: Globalising Dissent

Arundhati Roy is one of the most familiar faces of India. Though her book *The God of the Small Things* has made her famous, her later writings have made her controversial. "Contested and upheld, denounced and defended, global change wrought by the globalization of neoliberal economic doctrine has come to mean different things in different contexts—the promotion of world integration and opportunity for growth, as well as the reproduction of inequalities old and new" (Grewal, 2009: 143). The latter has provoked local–global activism from players with varying agendas, which in turn has enabled spirited debate in university classrooms and academic journals, international board rooms, and local communities, raising deep questions of human agency, social justice, and equity. We can situate Arundhati Roy's work as part of the wider response of civil society, at local, state, and global levels, whose aim is to "mediate between government and the power of capital" in order to "claim and retain the rights and entitlements of state and global citizenship" (Grewal, 2009: 143).

Roy's is a voice from the global South purposefully undoing Sanctioned ignorances, crossing borders of gender, caste, and class, of the nation state, of the South/North divide. Breaking taboos against complicating the lives of the haves and the have-nots—breaking the decorum of the institutionalized academy—Roy's writing lays bare the workings of power without permission from "the experts." A feminist, but no bourgeois one, she gives herself to the cause of the people while expressing her wariness of the "traditional, mainstream" and "strangely unbending" Left with its rigid ideology. No wonder Roy ruffles so many feathers and is often looked down by the bourgeoisie.

What makes Roy compelling in our context is that she stakes her claim in multiple citizenships and in the accountability or responsibility that attends them—Indian citizenship; global capitalist citizenship (or as a "subject of Empire"); and a democratic feminist–humanitarian people's citizenship of the world. Few have *publicly* claimed multiple citizenships so flamboyantly, claiming all of her citizens' "rights to express dissent" (Roy, 2001: 87). It is no surprise that she is the acclaimed writer of the growing global justice movement: she has staged herself as a global citizen voicing the discourse of human rights in a bold, lyrical, and impassioned way.

It is insightful to trace how the author of *The God of Small Things* (Roy, 1997) become the advocate of big things like democracy and justice? According to Gurleen Grewal, there is a continuity between these two aspects of Roy. In fact it is by continuing to do "in the public sphere what she had done with the private sphere of home and family in her novel," (Cited in Grewal, 2009: 144) that Roy has given voice to the colonised. Uma Narayan's definition of the feminist daughter's political enterprise, to "retell the story of a mother-culture in feminist terms," is highly appropriate for understanding Roy's work as a whole: "It is a political attempt to tell a counter-story that contests dominant narratives that would claim the entire edifice of 'our Culture' and 'our Nation' for themselves, converting them into a peculiar form of property, and excluding the voices, concerns, and contributions of many who are members of the national and political community" (Grewal, 2009: 144).

It may be noted that Roy is the latest among an increasing number of global feminist voices that have interrogated the neoliberal policies of economic globalization. For Roy, the questions are basic and important: who benefits? Who pays the cost? "What is it [globalization] going to do to a country like India, in which social inequality has been institutionalized in the caste system for centuries? In which three hundred million people are illiterate" (Roy, 2001:13–4). Roy's analysis of the predicament of the poor in India has been preceded by that of feminist scholars who have worked in the areas of development for over two decades: the work of Gita Sen, Peggy Antrobus, Rajni Kothari, Bina Agarwal, Vandana Shiva, and others (Grewal, 2009).

In the epigraph to *The God of Small Things,* Roy quotes John Berger: "Never again will a single story be told as though it is the only one." In a sense, Roy's novel is about the ecology of being, showing how everything and everyone is interconnected, and how each life is shaped by what happens to others. The novel is moving because it gives nearly all the characters, even the oppressive ones, a vulnerability and humanity: a character may be twisted, but not inherently evil.[2]

The author of *The God of Small Things* has become a passionate critique and a powerful voice for the subaltern and for the marginalised in a post-colonial situation. This takes us to a more powerful story situated in Australia.

b. David Malouf: Remembering Babylon

Another unique approach to the use of cultural hybridity in a postcolonial text has been utilized by David Malouf, in his novel *Remembering Babylon* (Malouf 1993). Malouf writes of the formative years of an Australian settler colony, and he uses a very unique character, that of Gemmy, to illustrate the vast differences between the settlers and the aboriginals, and, eventually, between the settlers themselves. Gemmy is a white man who has grown up amongst the aboriginals. He has been away from Western society for so long that he is unable to communicate competently, or effect legitimate social discourse with the other whites. He comes to live with a young settler colony, and Malouf uses him to illustrate differences between all members of this colony. As each member of the colony tries to analyze the differences between themselves and Gemmy, they come to realize fundamental differences amongst them all. As Mr. Frazer writes in his logbook, "We must rub our eyes and look again, clear our minds of what we are looking for to see what is there" (Malouf, 1993: 130 and Hybridity, 2010).

Surely, each member of a postcolonial society would love to encounter one specific voice which could articulate their particular suffering and oppression under the colonial institution--one voice which would articulate their own sense of national identity. But exploration of these societies, and the literature produced by postcolonial authors and poets illustrates that there is a veritable infinite number of differing circumstances inherent in each postcolonial society, and, consequently, in each piece of literature produced by postcolonial writers. If one is to read this literature in a way which will shed some light on the postcolonial condition, one must understand and adopt the theory that we are all walking amalgamations of our own unique cultures and traditions. We are all always struggling with our own identities, personal and national. We must understand that there is no "one true voice" representing an easily identifiable postcolonial condition, but, instead, each author is his or her own voice and must be read as such (Hybridity 2010).

The story takes place in the mid-19th century in a remote settlement of Queensland, Australia. One day as a group of children are playing at the edge of the village, a remarkable figure stumbles out of the bush. This dark, unkempt person (Gemmy) turns out to be a white man who fell from a ship 16 years earlier (when he was a 19-year-old sailor) and has lived with an aboriginal tribe ever since (Coulehan, 2012). He hardly remembers English, and his culture and sensibility have become those of his adopted people.

At first Gemmy creates a sensation in the settlement and people want to help him, despite his obvious savage mentality (after all, he isn't even embarrassed by nakedness!). He goes to live with the McIvor family, whose daughter, Janet, and nephew, Lachlan Beattie, were among the children who found him. While Mrs. McIvor accepts Gemmy with Christian love, her husband Jock is sceptical (Coulehan, 2012).

In fact, it soon becomes clear that there are major tensions in the village regarding Gemmy. Has he really become "one of them" (a black)? Can he be trusted? He seems harmless enough--almost a pleasant imbecile--but perhaps it is all a subterfuge. Perhaps he is in contact with THEM (Coulehan, 2012).

Among the European settlers, there are two views of how to handle the blacks. One group believes they should simply be wiped out--every one of them killed--because they are savage, worthless, and couldn't possibly become (real) Christians. A second group has a more romantic view. They think the black people could be "tamed" and become their servants. They envision themselves as owners of large plantations (as in the southern United States) worked by multitudes of happy and harmless black servants (Coulehan, 2012).

Representatives of both groups try to win Gemmy's confidence and obtain information regarding the whereabouts and plans of the black tribes. He, however, remains silent about these matters, although pleasant and deferential toward everyone. An uneasy truce holds until one day two aboriginal people are observed visiting with Gemmy on McIvor's property. This creates an uproar, which eventually leads some of the God-fearing whites to commit acts of vandalism and to injure Gemmy (Coulehan, 2012).

To preserve the peace, the McIvors send Gemmy to live with Mrs. Hutchence, an eccentric woman who lives on the margin of the settlement. However, he soon disappears into the wilderness, but not until he retrieves--and destroys--what he thinks are the seven pieces of paper on which Mr. Frazier, the minister, had written Gemmy's life story soon after he had emerged from the bush (Coulehan, 2012).

Reflections

This novel portrays a cultural chasm, rather than a cultural clash. Gemmy, imbued with the mysticism and earth-centeredness of the native Australians with whom he has spent 16 years, is (precisely as the settlers fear) no longer "white." Gemmy cannot identify with the European culture that was once his by heritage. No wonder he can hardly remember how to speak the English language (Coulehan, 2012).

The Europeans, secure in their conviction that the aboriginal people are sub-human savages, cannot even consider treating them as persons. Some of the settlers want to eliminate the blacks completely (genocide), while others would prefer simply to rule them. Gemmy slowly comes to the realization that to save himself he must return to his aboriginal "roots." Ironically, this escape doesn't work--an epilogue to the story implies that Gemmy comes to a bad end.

How much goodness is there in the human spirit? This novel primarily explores the casual, unthinking darkness that threatens to engulf us all. Yet, the story also reveals glimmers of light in many individual persons (Coulehan, 2012).

Remembering Babylon, as its title suggests, shares the earlier novel's preoccupation with language, and both explore what happens when a stranger, reared in totally other cultural circumstances, is introduced into a small, beleaguered community held together largely by a common fear of all that surrounds it (Taylor, 1993: 123-25).

Remembering Babylon's title remains an enigma until its final chapter. The bulk of the novel is set in a tiny settlement of Scots immigrants in Queensland north of Bowen in the middle of last century (Taylor, 1993: 123-25). They are surrounded – and threatened – by rainforest inhabited by hostile Aboriginals. Everything about them is creepy, and at night they sleep as close to their guns as they do to their spouses.

And then, in a page of breathless, seemingly endless prose which it would be murder to condense, something balances on that crucial dividing fence at the edge of the rainforest, balances there for a moment, confronted by a white child with a stick aimed like a rifle, and tumbles out of the terrifying unknown into the white settlement.

Gemmy Fairley is a London slum child who survived the appalling conditions of the Industrial Revolution by becoming the "boy" (we are left to imagine some of his duties) of a London rat catcher. Escaping to sea, he is thrown overboard near the Queensland shore and lives for ten years with an Aboriginal tribe. He can neither read nor write, and can barely speak any English, but is induced to tell his story to the local parson and schoolmaster who, to his fascination, write it down.

Taken in and cared for by the family of the child who "discovered" Gemmy, he is given work, taught again to speak English, and partially integrated into the community. This is helped along by two strange women who have built a real house – as distinct from the crude shacks of the Scots – and who establish a kind of genteel "salon" which includes not only the young school teacher and some of his pupils, but also Gemmy (Taylor, 1993: 123-25).

It all falls apart. Fear grows – and violence with it – that Gemmy might be an infiltrator and spy for hostile Aboriginals. He disappears, taking with him a handful of the children's school exercises which, being illiterate, he thinks is his appalling life as it was written down by the teacher on his arrival. And the novel leaps, for its final chapter, fifty years or so (Taylor, 1993: 123-25).

This is where the novel's title makes sense: *Remembering Babylon*. Gemmy Fairley was another language injected into the settlers' world: he was once Cockney, he was more particularly Aboriginal, above all else he was Threat. Having proved that he could exist there, he came out of Nowhere and, therefore, demonstrated that others could too. He divided the unanimity of the settlement, made them argue amongst themselves. He set tongue against tongue, and created Babel. And remembering? One of the children who encountered Gemmy that day was a girl who became a nun. The boy with the stick, her cousin (like Gemmy, an orphan, but a luckier one), became a member of State Parliament. His career is compromised, during the Great War, by the revelation that his cousin has been corresponding with a German.

The topic? How bees communicate, a subject that she has been researching in her convent. The authorities think she may be dealing in code (Taylor, 1993: 123-25).

The sudden leap in time near the book's conclusion is only one of its audacities. Some may find it unsettling; others utterly compelling. Another is the actual conclusion, as positive as anything in modem fiction in English. But then Malouf has never been afraid of the grand statement so few of his contemporaries would dare. He can do it gently, subtly, with the force of a revelation rather than a pronouncement.

Malouf's reputation is so secure nowadays that he might almost get away with anything. The real reason why he can get away with what he does is because he gets it right. *Remembering Babylon* is yet another demonstration of how right he gets it. Truth and language do not fit so well as Kant hoped they would. But in a language of great subtlety and beauty, Malouf suggests that there may be another way of bridging the gap between our minds and what we are trying to understand, so that the world can be "in touch now with its other life". Of discovering, in other words, the truth about itself.

Two Features of Post-Colonial, Multiple Identities

From our discussion above we pick up just two features of postcolonial identities: hybridity and utopian vision with a view to appreciate an elaborate, complex and even conflicting identities. For this we base ourselves mainly on Malouf.

Hybrid Identities through Difference

Resistance or response from a member of a colonised community: David Malouf's *Remembering Babylon* strictly speaking, a post-colonial text. Most would agree with Malouf it is certainly not an example of resistance or response from a member of a colonised community in the same vein as, several themes running through the novel which constitute elements of post-colonial discourse, leading to a possible empowerment of both the colonisers and the colonised.

The power of language: The construction of this new identity would both privilege and discriminate against the other smaller (elite) communities, who in turn took advantage its opportunities and resisted its constraints. So the identity is tied to language, which has unimaginable power.

Hybrid culture: There is a pervasive sense of colonial guilt throughout *Remembering Babylon*, an awareness of the suspect morality of the colonial process. Like *Great Expectations*, *Babylon* recognises Australia as a potential utopia for the industrious European immigrant – unlike Dickens, however, Malouf asserts that the success of the project rests not on merely exploiting the resources available (while ignoring or displacing the indigenous people), but on reaching a kind of harmony and exchange with the landscape and with the colonised. This hybrid culture represents, for Malouf, the ideal ultimate outcome of the colonial process (Dunlop, 1997).

Concluding Remarks

"Our first business will be to supervise the making of fables and legends, rejecting all which are unsatisfactory; and we shall induce nurses and mothers to tell their children only those which we have approved." – Socrates in Plato's *Republic*

For generations, humans gathered around hearth and fire to tell and retell stories. Much of cultural transmission was in the form of storytelling. Today, people are more likely to gather around the cool glow of the television, but we are no less storied creatures. Some imaginary calculations of the amount of time and money spent on the entertainment, news, and publishing industries should give us pause to think about how central storytelling is to our humanity. To this add the everyday interactions with friends and families in which people recount events and share gossip. By my rough estimation, perhaps fifty percent or more of our waking hours is involved in storytelling. In the words of sociologist Christian Smith, humans are "animals who make stories but also animals who are *made* by our stories" (Smith, 2003: 64).

Stories always have normative content, describing what is important, what is unimportant, what is better, what is worse, what is good, and what is bad. Charles Taylor argues that stories about self and society are how humans construct the "horizons of meaning" that form the critical background for social relations and life choices. Narratives always represent a kind of movement in moral space. Narratives are the way that humans have of constructing coherence and continuity in our lives. (Taylor 1989). So they help us fashion our selfhoods through differences.

It is important to emphasize that humans can hold multiple narratives, sometimes mutually exclusive. We mix and match. The conservative Roman Catholic narrative is incompatible with the narrative of Liberal Democracy, but that does not prevent most conservative Roman Catholics from being enthusiastic supporters of Liberal Democracies. The Christian narrative appears incompatible with capitalist virtues, but that does not prevent Christians from living the bourgeois life. The eco-romantic narrative appears incompatible with much of modern technology, but that does not prevent environmentalists from using soon to be obsolete laptops and flying around the world to enjoy ecotourism. Each generation reinterprets these narratives in different situations, even as each generation is also constituted by these received stories. People are not passive recipients of these narratives, but active reinterpreters.

The idealized past narrative above contrasts sharply with progressive, future oriented narratives, for instance the Scientific Enlightenment narrative or the Capitalist Prosperity narrative. This nostalgia narrative is woven into many of the fundamentalist religious movements today whether in the East or West, the North or South. One can argue with this nostalgia narrative, but evidence alone cannot compel someone to believe otherwise. Like all of the narratives listed and described by Christian Smith, it involves a certain reading of history and a certain set of assumptions about what really matters in life (Smith, 2003).

As contemporary philosopher William Grassie shows the greatest untruths will always be the unconscious lies that we tell ourselves, the mistaking of our own limited perspectives with the Absolute. Reinhold Nicbuhr summed it up, when he quipped "The doctrine of original sin is the only empirically verifiable doctrine of Christianity" (Niebuhr 1941). To avoid sin, we should be humble, rigorous, courageous, and creative in pursuing truth (and beauty and goodness), wherever it leads. And the goal of intellectual nonviolence and postcolonian assertion of identities is to set out in as many different directions as possible, to be multiply converted to diverse metanarratives, inhabiting their truths, forgiving their failures, taking the best, and leaving the rest. This enables us to fashion multiple (even conflicting) selfhoods, respect differences and so understand ourselves – colonisers, colonised and their hybrid children – deeper.

The paradoxical observation of William Butler Yeats (1865-1939) is apt here (Yeats: 1919):

> Things fall apart; the centre cannot hold;
> Mere anarchy is loosed upon the world,
> The blood-dimmed tide is loosed, and everywhere
> The ceremony of innocence is drowned;
> The best lack all conviction, while the worst
> Are full of passionate intensity.
> Surely some revelation is at hand…

Drawing from the multiple postcolonial identities, can we still reduce the individual and collective violence – both real and imagined – we inflict on ourselves and others due our imaginary identities, constructed selfhood, derived self-fashioning and amplified differences? So the challenge now is to realise our own multiple and conflicting identities of the self and those of the other. Then we can enter into a creative and complex dialogue between them, enabling us to befriend the "others" in the Other and "Otherness".

References

Bhabha, Homi K. (1994). *The Location of Culture*. London ; New York: Routledge.

Coulehan, Jack (2012). "Malouf, David, Remembering Babylon," Literature Annotations of New York University accessed at http://litmed.med.nyu.edu/Annotation?action=view&annid=1339, retrieved on Sept, 2, 2012.

Dunlop, Nicholas. (27 May 1997). Post-Colonial Themes in David Malouf's Remembering Babylon http://www.qub.ac.uk/imperial/austral/babylon.htm. Retrieved on June 23, 2012.

Dunlop, Nicholas. (May 27, 1997). Post-Colonial Themes in David Malouf's Remembering Babylon http://www.qub.ac.uk/imperial/austral/babylon.htm. Retrieved on June 3, 2012.

Grassie, William. "Entangled Narratives: Competing Visions of the Good Life." *Transdisciplinarity in Science and Religion*, 2008/4 339-365. See also http://www.scribd.com/doc/17922700/6/Entangled-Narratives-Competing-Visions-of-the-Good-Life. Retrieved on June 8, 2012.

Grewal, Gurleen. (2009). "Home and the World: The Multiple Citizenships of Arundhati Roy," Ghosh, Ranjan, and Antonia Navarro Tejero (eds). *Globalizing Dissent : Essays on Arundhati Roy*. Routledge Studies in Social and Political Thought. New York: Routledge.

Hobsbawn, Eric. (1997). *On History*. London: Abacus.

Hybridity. (Aug 20, 2012). "Hybridity and National Identity in Postcolonial Literature." 123HelpMe.com. <http://www.123HelpMe.com/view.asp?id=6743>. Retrieved on June 14, 2012.

Malouf, David. (1993). *Remembering Babylon*. 1st American ed. New York: Pantheon Books.

Nandy, A. (2015). *The intimate enemy: Loss and recovery of self under colonialism*. New Delhi : Oxford University Press

Roy, Arundhati. (1997). *The God of Small Things*. New York: Random House.

Roy, Arundhati. (2001). *Power Politics*. Cambridge: South End P.

Roy, Arundhati. (2004). *An Ordinary Person's Guide to Empire*. Cambridge: South End P.

Said, Edward W. (1978). *Orientalism*. 1st ed. New York: Pantheon Books.

Sen, Amartya. (2006). *Identity and Violence: The Illusion of Destiny*. New York: W.W. Norton, 2006.

Smith, Christian. (2003). *Moral, Believing Animals: Human Personhood and Culture*. New York, Oxford University Press.

Taylor, Andrew. (1993). David Malouf, Remembering Babylon Journal: Westerly: 1993, Volume 38, No. 3, Spring.

Yeats, William Butler. (1919). "The Second Coming". http://www.online-literature.com/yeats/780/ . Retrieved on June 9, 2012.

Notes

1 This article is adapted from my paper published in Ferrao, V., & In Ponniah, J. (2013). Identity, difference and conflict: Postcolonial critique : papers presented at the ACPI Annual Research Seminar held at Jnana-Deepa, Pune, 26-29 October 2012.

2 Grewal, 2009: 146. Arundhati Roy is not only an accomplished novelist, but equally gifted in unraveling the politics of globalization, the power and ideology of corporate culture, fundamentalism, terrorism, and other issues gripping today's world. This volume – featuring prominent scholars from throughout the world – examines Roy beyond the aesthetic parameters of her fiction, focusing also on her creative activism and struggles in

global politics. The chapters travel to and fro between her non-fictional works – engaging activism on the streets and global forums – and its underlying roots in her novel. Roy is examined as a novelist, non-fiction writer, journalist, activist, feminist, screenwriter, ideologist, and architect. This volume presents Roy's interlocking network of the ideas, attitudes and ideologies that emerge from the contemporary social and the political world.

19

Psychospiritual Perspectives on "The Other"

Konrad Noronha, SJ
Pastoral and Moral Theology, Jnana Deepa Institute of Philosophy and Theology, Pune

Abstract: Social sciences' and theological understandings of the "other" or the *anawim* have moved beyond traditional and conservative understandings. Understandings differ according to academic disciplines and thus there are various definitions, approaches and ways of knowing the "other." The *anawim* in today's literature include immigrants, the homeless, LGBTQ, and the elderly. Issues of domination, discrimination and exclusivity arise when considering them, in opposition to values of equality, unity and inclusivity. This article discusses two of the *anawim* - the "missing" girl child and the elderly. The "missing" girl child is a person with rights right from the moment of conception. The elderly are considered in terms of quality of life, isolation and meaning making. Psychospiritual dimensions are touched upon and a theology of action explicated.

Keywords: The other, Domination, Discrimination, Girl Child, Elderly

When we consider "the other," it means there is a difference; either two persons or two groups. It could be a majority group, minority or smaller groups, groups with more voice, money, power and those with less. The understanding of "the other" has been studied across various scientific disciplines including, anthropology, sociology, psychology, neuroscience, medicine, and theology. All these disciplines have their definitions, approaches and understandings.

In considering groups as separate, elements of domination, discrimination and exclusivity arise, in opposition to values of equality, unity and inclusivity. Noort and Noort (2012) give us an understanding of the relationship between the "I" and "the other." They state: "Our uniqueness, defines our personal and social identity. But it is in the social relation that the "other" defines me, and "I" define the "other." By recognizing difference and setting boundaries we construct the identity both of the other as well as ourselves" (p. 503)

Social sciences' expanded understanding notwithstanding; theological understandings of the "I" and "the other" too have crossed borders. Scientific and empirical research has expanded this understanding by going beyond traditional and conservative understandings. Also, the human personality is dynamic, constantly evolving, whether emotionally, physically, mentally, or spiritually. Religious and spiritual affiliations define a lot of who the person is and how a human functions in the world. In a world where more and more people are making choices of their form of religion and spirituality, these understandings are being expanded and explored.

In the Christian understanding, a term for the "other" would be the *anawim*. The *anawim*, are many, and include women (Lk 8:1-3, NRSV), children (Lk 18: 15-17, NRSV), widows (Mk 12:41-44, NRSV), the poor (Lk 13:10-17, NRSV), the Samaritan (Jn 4:1-45, NRSV), the gentiles (Mt 4: 15, NRSV), and orphans (Jas 1: 27, NRSV). In today's world, with a broader understanding of the context, we add immigrants (Esses, Medianu, Hamilton, & Lapshina, 2015), homeless (Ahmed, Chaudhry, Afzal, Farooq, 2015), LGBTQ (Johnson, Amella, 2014), persons with disability (Swinton, 2011), and the elderly (Das, 2011). This presentation is in light of the expanding understandings of the "I" and "the other," utilizing biblical understandings of *anawim,* in the light of scientific research and "sensitivity" ("Pope Francis," 2013). This is so that the *anawin* might have a clearer voice, face less discrimination and have an equal status, in a multicultural and diverse world.

Multiculturalism and Diversity

Some issues of multiculturalism and diversity are not easily spoken about in mainstream society. Most considerations take place with the majority in mind. Whether it be human right abuses, marginalization, or biases with regard to skin color, caste groups, age or economic backgrounds; the majority, the dominant, powerful, those with voice, men become the bases for examining these issues. These issues need to be addressed not only to build awareness but also from the point of societal integration.

In India gender-based violence is one such issue. It includes feticide, rapes, honor killings and sexual abuse. These have taken on insidious forms that are justified in the name of faith, community, even development. Intolerance of other faiths, through attacks on places of worship is significantly on the rise.

The target groups include Christians, and Muslims who are among the religious minorities in India. People of alternate sexuality too are prone to violence in a society not open to persons of diverse sexualities and orientations. Similarly, there is a profound shift in the understanding of what is happening to older Indians-in the context of changing family relationships, values and severely limited old-age income support.

This article examines some questions that arise out of these now common issues in society. This article is restricted to two of "the other"- the 'missing' girl child, and the elderly. Psychospiritual dimensions are touched upon. The questions considered are (1) Who is the "other" for us today? (b) What is the understanding of the "other?" (c) How can "the other" be understood and integrated better in society today? These questions are examined, and a theology of action explicated.

The 'Missing' Girl Child

This section is on the unborn child, or the newborn child. It situates the violence done to women, not just from the time the girl child is born, but while even in the womb. Rights of the unborn are trampled upon; they have no voice. Giving voice to the voiceless, to those who are not even born, is something that is not considered in a country, where value is placed on the male child. Patriarchal religious traditions celebrate girls as young wives and mothers, not as the girls they are and is a key component of girls' disempowerment (Stith, 2015). There is a triple injustice here - to the unborn, the girl child, and to the voiceless.

Globally an estimated 100 million women have been eliminated from population statistics (Stith, 2015). Survival chances of girls in parts of south and East Asia have been adverse. Female feticide, infanticide, abandonment, under-reporting of female births, and selective neglect of girls leading to higher death rates have contributed to this adversity. Female feticide has increased by 49.2% in India between 1999-2000, ("National Crime Records Bureau") especially in the north and north western parts of India (Dey, Nambiar, Lakshmi, Sheikh & Reddy, 2003). The United Nations Children's Fund, estimated that upto 50 million girls and women are 'missing' from India's population because of termination of the female fetus or high mortality of the girl child due to lack of proper care and that as many as 10 million female fetuses were aborted in India over the past two decades (Chunga & Das, 2011). Punjab epitomizes the growing phenomenon of feticide, and sex-selective abortion of girls (Sarkaria, 2009). In India, the most plausible explanation for fewer female than male births seems to be prenatal sex determination (Sahni, Verma, Narula, Varghese, Sreenivas, & Puliyel, 2008) followed by induced abortion of female fetuses. The differences in sex ratios between slum and elite areas is also significant (Bhardwaj, Nagargoje, Jadhao, & Khadse, 2011). The question that arises is how to give voice to those who cannot speak.

Much has been written about the girl child in scriptures. In the Old Testament, this discrimination, domination and inequality is evident. We see an apparent preferential option given to the girl child in Exodus 1: 16, which is not really a preferential option, as the Egyptians did not want Hebrew male children, and so would kill them. They let the girl child live, as girls and women, were not considered of any importance then. We do hear the prophet Zechariah express positivity when he says "The city streets will be filled with boys and girls playing there (Zech 8:5, NRSV)." The Old Testament also presents a strong woman like Naomi, who put the welfare of her daughters-in-law ahead of her own and Ruth her daughter-in-law, who stood by her (Ruth1:16, NIV). There are also examples of strong wives like Sarah (Gen 21:26), Rachel and Leah (Gen 21:26).

More and more equality and concern is brought in by Jesus, and his option for the *anawin* is seen when he raises the dead girl (Mat 9:18, NRSV). That women had a voice and spoke directly with men and even confronted them is seen in Mt 26: 69, and Mat 26:71, when Peter was confronted by the servant girls. The role of the Marys' and other women in the New Testament, cannot be underestimated e.g. Mary the mother of Jesus (Acts 1:14, NRSV), Mary of Magdalena (Mk 16:1, NRSV), and Mary the sister of Lazarus (Jn 11:1, NRSV). Jesus did not reduce women to the background, he portrayed them as strong. Similarities and dissimilarities notwithstanding, power needs to be given to the *anawim*, for a more real status in a world that Jesus conceived.

We as Christians need to remove any boundaries that have been created through patriarchal structures, and bring in thinking more in line with Jesus' way of living. That is important for a healthy spiritual health and development. We also need to recognize that men and women understand and express their love for God differently (Hoffman, Knight, Boscoe-Huffman, & Stewart, 2008), and that elements of superiority and inferiority are present. Experientially, females perceive God as loving and caring, and men as a God who is dominating and controlling (Hoffman, Knight, Boscoe-Huffman, & Stewart, 2008).

Jesus went beyond cultural, ethnic and gender barriers. He did not treat anyone based on what others say, their accomplishments, possessions, or appearance. For Jesus, gender was irrelevant in his offer of salvation. In terms of spiritual authority all God's people are equal (Stith, 2015). Society in general, and some Indian states in particular, need to learn to value the girl child so that we do not have any more 'missing' girl children. They need to acknowledge that the girl child is a full person with rights, from the moment of conception. She is a child of God, part of his kingdom of love, peace and hope.

The Elderly

The size of the elderly population is increasing over time. By 2050 there will be almost 2 billion people over 60, around 22% of the forecasted total world population (Flynn, 2009). In India from 5.6% in 1961 it is projected to rise to 12.4% of population by the year 2026. The problems and issues of its grey population have not been given serious consideration (Das, 2011), although the government has come out with a number of acts and policies with regard to the aging population. One of them is "The Maintenance and Welfare of Parents and Senior Citizens Act, 2007" which provides for,

> maintenance of Parents/senior citizens by children/relatives made obligatory and justiciable through Tribunals, revocation of transfer of property by senior citizens in case of negligence by relatives, penal provision for abandonment of senior citizens, establishment of Old Age Homes for Indigent Senior Citizens, and adequate medical facilities and security for Senior Citizens.

Also, the National Policy on Older Persons (NPOP), 1999, envisages "state support to ensure financial and food security, health care, shelter and other needs of older persons, equitable share in development, protection against abuse and exploitation, and availability of services to improve the quality of their lives." These two acts and policies among the many others address some of the problems that confront the elderly in India, today. They set the tone for what the government is doing; the rest needs to be done at the grassroots level. A significant consideration is the mental health of older adults.

Ignorance, loneliness, negligence and social isolation in older adults are major problems these days (Ahmed, Chaudhry, Afzal, & Farooq, 2015). Transitions can significantly affect quality of life. Participation in some sort of activity is crucial for psychosocial health and well-being as they help improve life satisfaction, social isolation, and loneliness. This results in greater life satisfaction and lower levels of social isolation. Forming alliances and group identities is the key for building new relationships and maintaining relationships in the community (Winstead, Yost, Cotton, Berkowsky, & Anderson, 2014). There is a need to identify the positive aspects of growing old and what is gained during this time period rather than what is lost. This is necessary to avoid disease, maintain high cognitive and physical function, and active engagement with life (Aldwin & Igarashi, 2015). This would result in an improved quality of life (Winstead, Yost, Cotten, Berkowsky, & Anderson, 2014).

The Old and New Testaments are quite clear about the roles of the elderly in society and family. They talk about the need for the elderly, the needs of the elderly and of fertility (Gen 5:32; 21:5, NRSV) of the elderly. That respect has to be given to the elderly, is clearly stated in Lev 19:32 and that a long life brings understanding (Job 12:12, NRSV). In the book of Proverbs, we read that children's children are a crown to the aged, and that parents are the pride of their children (Prov 17:6, NRSV). The difficulties and infirmities of the elderly are addressed in Matthew 8:17. The role that the elderly played in the early Church is emphasized and thus their importance, as is heard in the letter to James (5:14-16, NRSV):

> Is anyone among you sick? Let them call the elders of the church to pray over them and anoint them with oil in the name of the Lord. And the prayer offered in faith will make the sick person well; the Lord will raise them up. If they have sinned, they will be forgiven. Therefore, confess your sins to each other and pray for each other so that you may be healed. The prayer of a righteous person is powerful and effective.

Discussion

When considering the "other" it is necessary to reflect on "who is the other is for me?" It makes us consider the relationship between the "I" and the "other." This is related to the question, "who is the God we worship?" The answer is revealed to us through the life, death and resurrection of Jesus Christ (Swinton, 2011) and in this revelation from Him, we realize his options. Having thus considered this relationship, we check for prejudicial understandings, considerations that need to be worked at, or understandings that have changed, with regard to the 'missing' girl child and the elderly. It implies an explicit and implicit response to include the "other" into the very fabric of society; not as an afterthought, but fully.

An acknowledgement of prejudices is necessary in order to respond after reflection. With regard to the 'missing' girl child and the elderly, it brings up the need for giving voice to the voiceless, power, dependencies and the absence of equality. If Jesus came for all peoples, then it must be Society, including Christian society that imposes conditions, sets in barriers, so that groups get separated from each other. Differences exist and although it is not necessary to agree with another's worldview, it is important to recognize the tension between different world views and belief systems and the imposition of one on the other (Hoffman, Knight, Boscoe-Huffman, & Stewart, 2008). This occurs only through the creation of equal structures and the realization that openness works better than self-centeredness. Thus issues of equality (as opposed to discrimination), unity (as opposed to domination) and inclusivity (as opposed to exclusivity) need to be addressed.

Women

The role of women in history has been constructed and reconstructed. At one time it was thought that women were originally for the purpose of reproduction and survival of the species. Later on other aspects of relationships and intimacy also began to be considered. This process has been paralleled in the Catholic Church's understanding. At times during the history of Christianity, sex was considered to be solely for reproductive purposes. The church has now placed sex in the context of a broader relational understanding. For married couples, sex is now understood to be, part of a healthy intimate relationship and enhances mental health." It is only when one affirms that women are an essential part of society, not just sex objects or objects for procreation, will their full worth in society be realized, and the killings of the girl child stopped.

The critical areas of concern are the human rights of women, specifically the girl child. This has been spoken of globally at the UN as well as nationally, to ensure equality and non-discrimination under the law and in practice. The drop in the sex ratio of girls in India, in the 0-6 age group from 945 in1991 to 927 in 2001, indicates that the preference of society is for sons. This means that parents and their partners are actively involved in not allowing the girl child to be born, especially in certain communities in India. There are very specific laws framed to prevent such crimes. Some of the laws are: crime against children – murder ("Indian Penal Code" Section 302), infanticide ("Indian Penal Code" Section 315), and feticide ("Indian Penal Code" Section 315, 316). In considering the 'missing' girl child, women, advocates, families, health professionals and researchers need to rethink and improve existing protocols and interventions for children (Bonilla, 2005). Protective measure like the pre-natal diagnostic techniques act (PCPNDT), 1994 and the medical termination of pregnancy act (MTP), 1971, should be strictly implemented with regard to their regulation and prevention of misuse.

The Elderly

Successful aging is meaning related. It involves self-acceptance, self-contentment and engagement with life. Self-acceptance includes "realistic self-appraisal, a review of one's life, and focusing on the present, and engagement with life including openness to experience, generativity, social interactions, and positivity" (Aldwin & Igarashi, 2015). Although healthy individuals would be more likely to participate in community activities, even those who believe that they are less healthy have greater life satisfaction when they do participate. This is what Pope John Paul II in his address to the 2nd World Assembly on Aging, 3 April, 2002, said:

> The elderly should never be considered a burden on society, but a resource which can contribute to society's well-being. Not only do they show that there are aspects of life—human, cultural, moral and social values—which cannot be judged in terms of economic efficiency, but they can also make an effective contribution in the work-place and in leadership roles. In short, it is not just a question of doing something for older people, but also of accepting them in a realistic way as partners in shared projects—at the level of thought, dialogue and action.

With the elderly population increasing it is important that their maintenance and welfare be considered. The health care, shelter and other needs of older persons need to be looked after so that they have an equitable share in development, protection against abuse and exploitation. Services to improve the quality of their lives might have to include care of the elderly by children and relatives under pain of the law. Property transfers might have to be revoked in case of negligence, and abandonment should result in penal provisions. These areas of concern are necessary so that financial and food security of the elderly are ensured. For the aged, interventions to promote optimal aging, cognizant of the characteristics of the target audience must be considered. Life review, wisdom enhancement, and mindfulness-based interventions may be effective in promoting greater well-being. A combination of therapies that include wisdom enhancement therapy should be developed for application (Aldwin & Igarashi, 2015). Spirituality, and other spiritually related coping strategies should be considered for those with relevant spiritual and religious concerns along with the resources that spirituality may offer.

Conclusion

Minority groups offer opportunities to challenge theological and political perspectives and actions that cause pain and distress (El-Khoury, Dutton, Goodman, Engel, Belamaric, & Murphy, 2004). The bible clearly states that God sent his only son for "all peoples" to complete his work, and the work of Gods people is, "to believe in the one he has sent." This belief implies, that Jesus came for all kinds of people, children, (Lk 19: 15-17, NRSV) the poor, and the Samaritan (Jn 4: 1- 45, NRSV), the girl child, the elderly and that all groups and peoples have access to him. There are many *anawim* today. These oppressed groups welcome interaction with those with greater voice, money and who are dominant. Interaction, dialogue, and listening are essential starting points for attitudinal changes. They help in breaking down subtleties of behavior, action and thought.

References

Ahmed, A., Chaudhry A. G., Afzal, M. I., Farooq, H. (2015). Loneliness and Diseases Prevalence: A Gerontological Perspective of Elder's Disease Status. *Professional Medical Journal. 22*(3). p. 343-348.

Aldwin, C. M.; Igarashi, H. (2015). In: APA handbook of clinical geropsychology. *Chapter Vol. 1: History and status of the field and perspectives on aging.*[Lichtenberg, Peter A.; Mast, Benjamin T.; Carpenter, Brian D.; Loebach Wetherell, Julie (Eds.)]. American Psychological Association: Washington DC, USA. pp. 331-359.

Bandyopadhyay, Mridula. (2003). Missing Girls and Son Preference in Rural India: Looking Beyond Popular Myth. *Health Care for Women International. 24*(10). p. 911. doi: 10.1080/07399330390244220

Bhardwaj, S. D., Nagargoje, B., Jadhao, A., Khadse, J. (2011). Missing Girls: Low Child Sex Ratio – Study from Urban Slum and Elite Area of Nagpur, India- A Cross Sectional Study. *National Journal of Community Medicine. 2*. p. 477

Bonilla, Z. E. (2005). Including Every Woman: The All-Embracing "We" of Our Bodies, Ourselves. *NWSA Journal. 17*(1) (2005), pp. 175-183

Cantelmo, Gregg. (March 8th 2006). "*How Jesus Ministered to Women.*" https://bible.org/article/how-jesus-ministered-women#P110_43452

Chunga, W., & Das, Gupta, M. (2011). Factors Influencing 'Missing Girls' In South Korea. *Applied Economics*. *43*(24). p. 3365. doi:10.1080/00036841003636284

Das, S. K. (2011). Part-I Chapter I, Introduction. Situation Analysis of Elderly in India. *Central Statistics Office Ministry of Statistics & Programme Implementation Government of India*. p.1

Dey, S., Nambiar, D., Lakshmi, J. K., Sheikh, K., & Reddy, K. Srinath. (2003). Missing Girls and Son Preference in Rural India: Looking Beyond Popular Myth. *Health Care for Women International. 24*(10). p. 922. doi: 10.1080/07399330390244220

El-Khoury, M. Y. Dutton, M. A., Goodman, L. A., Engel, L., Belamaric, R. J. & Murphy, M. (2004). Ethnic Differences in Battered Women's Formal Help Seeking Strategies: A Focus on Health, Mental Health, and Spirituality. *Cultural Diversity and Ethnic Minority Psychology. 10*(4):383-93. doi: 10.1037/1099-9809.10.4.383

Esses, V, M., Medianu, S., Hamilton, L., Lapshina, N. (2015). In: APA handbook of personality and social psychology, Volume 2: *Group processes*. [Mikulincer, Mario (Ed); Shaver, Phillip R. (Ed); Dovidio, John F. (Ed); Simpson, Jeffry A. (Ed)]. *American Psychological Association*. pp. 423-445.

Flynn, John. Aging's Impact on the Economy. (2009). *ZENIT International News Agency*, http://www.ewtn.com/library/ISSUES/zflynnbmbst.

Hoffman, L, Knight, S, Boscoe-Huffman, S, & Stewart, S. (2008). Diversity Issues and the God Image. *Journal of Spirituality in Mental Health. 9*(3-4), p.271. doi: 10.1300/J515v09n03_13

Indian Penal Code: Sections 302, 303, 315, 316. http://www.indianpenalcode.in/ipc-506/sec.

Johnson, M. J., Amella, E. J. (2014). Isolation of lesbian, gay, bisexual and transgender youth: a dimensional concept analysis. *Journal of Advanced Nursing. 70*(3), p. 523-532. doi: 10.1111/jan.12212

National Policy for Older Persons. http://pib.nic.in/newsite/PrintRelease.aspx?relid=108092

National crime records bureau. http://ncrb.nic.in/CD-CII2012/Home.asp

Noort, G and Mark C. Noort, M. (2012). The "Other" Contributes Equally: Some Theological and Psychological Perspectives on Constructing Inclusive Christian Identity. *The Ecumenical Review. 64*(4), pp. 500–518. doi: 10.1111/erev.12007

Pope Francis. http://www.nytimes.com/2013/07/30

Sahni M, Verma N, Narula D, Varghese RM, Sreenivas V, Puliyel, J. M. (2008) Missing Girls in India: Infanticide, Feticide and Made-to-Order Pregnancies? Insights from Hospital-Based Sex-Ratio-at-Birth over the Last Century. http://dx.doi.org/10.1371/journal.pone.0002224

Sarkaria, M. K. (2009). Lessons from Punjab's "Missing Girls": Toward a Global Feminist Perspective on "Choice" in Abortion. *California Law Review. 97*(3). p.939*PLoS ONE. 3*(5): e2224. doi:10.1371/journal.p002224

Stephenson, H. (2005). Our Bodies, Ourselves for a New Generation: Revising a Feminist Classic. *Birth. 32*(3). p. 181. doi: 10.1111/j.0730-7659.2005.0379a.

Stith, Jennifer. (2015). Child Brides to the Patriarchy Unveiling the Appropriation of the Missing Girl Child. *Journal of Feminist Studies in Religion*. 31(1), p.95-96

Swinton, John. (2011). *Who is the God We Worship? Theologies of Disability; Challenges and New Possibilities*. IJPT. *14*. pp. 273 – 307. doi. 10.1515/IJPT.2011.020

The Maintenance and Welfare of Parents and Senior Citizens Act, 2007. http://india.gov.in/maintenance-and-welfare-parents-and-senior-citizens-act-2007

Winstead, V., Yost E. A., Cotten S. R., Berkowsky R. W., & Anderson W. A. (2014). The Impact of Activity Interventions on the Well-Being of Older Adults in Continuing Care Communities. *Journal of Applied Gerontology*. p. 906. doi: 10.1177/0733464814537701

20

Growing as a Person: From Befriending the Self to Befriending the Other

Keith D'Souza, SJ
Rector, St Xavier's College, Mumbai

Abstract: Growing as a person often entails a long journey from befriending the self to befriending the other. This journey may be depicted in terms of a wide spectrum that consists of numerous states of awareness. One pole of the spectrum is an extreme form of self-absorption, while the other pole is an expansive sense of being other-oriented. There are three broad ranges of awareness on this spectrum: befriending the self, befriending others largely within one's community and befriending others beyond one's community.

Personal growth is an ongoing task and challenge, in order that higher ranges of this spectrum may gradually characterize the general state of one's consciousness. For this to happen, there is need for adequate situational or contextual grounds for growth to thrive, as well as the need for personal discernment, so that higher levels of awareness are experienced at a greater frequency, intensity and duration.

Keywords: Personal growth, Befriending the self, Befriending the other, States of awareness, Transpersonal growth, Trans-community growth.

Human growth entails a long and often tedious journey involving many elements: discovering oneself, relating with others, living in community and being open to transcendent realities and values. Living a wholesome human life thus entails some form of success in processing intrapersonal, interpersonal, communitarian and transcendent experiences in a salubrious manner.

This article will focus on what it takes to live a wholesome personal life, in the larger context of the human, cosmic and divine world. The main thesis proposed is that an optimal trajectory or hierarchy of states of growth extends from a basic mode of befriending oneself at a lower extreme, towards ultimate human fulfillment in some self-transcendent form of befriending the 'other,' at a more refined and wholesome extreme. The operative presupposition is that optimal personal growth needs to factor in community concerns and relationships, as well as the larger cosmic and divine world of meaning and value.

We will first consider a few of the more obvious features – or general conditions or observations—related to the theme of personal growth. We will then identify a few of the more necessary normative principles that govern growth, keeping in mind that personal growth needs to take into account larger realities such as communitarian, global, cosmic and divine dimensions. The main feature of the article then follows, viz., a presentation of ten states of consciousness which delineate this range of possible levels of growth. A brief clarification and explanation of this apparently linear progression of these states of consciousness then follows.

1. Primary Facets of Personal Growth

There are many features and aspects related to the theme of personal growth. Some are more central, while some may be considered to be more peripheral. I will present some of the more obvious features or characteristics of personal growth, as a necessary background in order to understand more adequately the nature and status of the states of consciousness which represent increasingly more wholesome ways of being human.

1.1. Personal Growth is a Mystery

The journey from being born a human animal towards the realization of the fullness of being human may be best described as a "mystery." It does not require much observation or research to realize that while some persons make easy leaps and bounds in terms of growth, others find growth to be an extremely slow and even painful process.

While specific professions, programmes and processes oriented towards personal growth seem to abound, growth is not something that can be mechanically or systematically induced.[1] One of the main theses in Gerald May's insightful book titled, *Simply Sane*,[2] is that professional exercises geared towards engineering personal growth do not typically meet with expected success. This is not for want of good expertise on the part of the diverse professionals employed, but rather because of the nature of the object under consideration and exploration, viz., the human person. The person is more a mystery to be understood wisely, rather than a problem to be examined, explained and experimented with statistically or scientifically.[3]

Those who appear to be delinquent or deviant may often show signs of growth under more salubrious conditions and circumstances,[4] while those who appear to be more integrated and centred may likely have arrived at this point in their personal journeys after long personal and social struggles. This is in keeping with the popular adage that "saints have a past, and sinners have a future." Even the best human beings are influenced by what some theorists like Jung refer to as "shadow" dimensions of the self.[5] There are aspects to human existence that do not easily fit into the categorizations that one understandably employs in the human or social sciences.

When growth is forced towards specific objectives, tragic results may be generated, especially in cases of forced socialization or brainwashing.[6] This often happens in social movements which are ultra right in conviction and orientation. Such programmes and processes often result in violent forms of social expression, and often do untold damage to persons who come within their ambit and influence. This is because the human person cannot be reduced to the same status as an object in the natural realm, or a merely passive recipient of programmes of indoctrination.

1.2. Growth is Contextually Influenced

While there is no doubt that personal growth remains a mystery, it is also quite evident that salubrious social contexts undeniably aid the progress of growth, especially during the first few years of human development. Healthy economic, political and cultural factors are very important as supportive conditions for personal growth. On the other hand, social discrimination and marginalization based on gender, race, class, caste, religion, etc., all have a very important part to play in stunting human growth. A girl child growing up in a heavily patriarchal society hostile to female development has much more of a hurdle to face than one growing up in more egalitarian cultural contexts.

Besides culturally discriminatory and oppressive forces, political instability, economic uncertainty, forced migration and war—all of these leading to physical hardship, deprivation and violence—constitute even more severe conditions for human wellbeing to take place. Some human beings have a privileged start—especially a vast majority of those in materially developed nations—so experience better conditions for growth to take place effortlessly and steadily. However, there is no guarantee that those who live in healthier social climes will *ipso facto* experience better growth trajectories.

1.3. Growth Requires Personal Effort

While extraneous circumstances have a lot to contribute towards the growth of individuals, the disposition and effort that the individual invests in his or her own development has perhaps the most part to play in personal growth. At the beginning of the human journey, unlike other animals, the human animal requires a lot of attention merely for physical survival. At later stages of the human journey, this extraneous support needs to be mirrored by an internal support process, involving consistency and tenacity of effort, resilience or the ability to bounce back from adverse situations.

There are numerous examples of individuals who have suffered tremendous social hardships, yet have bounced back in order to make a personal success of their lives as well as to productively contribute to society. Hence, social context is not the sole category which determines a trajectory of growth. Besides social conditions, individual differentiation has a large part to play when it comes to personal growth. Most parents will easily agree that while the social resources placed at the service of their children were very similar, each sibling turned out quite differently from the others. This is the psychological and spiritual challenge to sociological, anthropological and statistical generalizations. This is also in continuity with thesis 1.1. above, viz., that personal growth is a mystery and not something that can be easily mastered or even fully comprehended.

1.4. Growth may be Measured by Different Parameters

The issue of personal growth is a highly contentious one, with different schools abounding in different social or human sciences, each of them proposing competing parameters or criteria by which growth may be measured. Among the more well-known theories of personal development are the psychodynamic theory proposed by Freud and developed by Erik Erikson, and the cognitive-structuralist theory proposed by Jean Piaget and developed by Lawrence Kohlberg.[7] While some theories give more importance to the experiences of early childhood, others give importance to cognitive capacities, while yet others pay more attention to social adaptability and capacity building, such as the cultivation of emotional and social intelligence.

This divergent approach is mirrored by different cultural estimations with regard to how human beings ought to manifest growth patterns. Some cultures give more importance to conformity with traditional practices, while others value independence and autonomy at an early age of adulthood. Among the former, which stress the communitarian dimension, are tribal or indigeneous societies—and also a growing tendency among right-wing ideologues and activists, which some attribute to a reaction against globalization. Other cultures, which are more influenced by urban and capitalistic lifestyles and attitudes, favour individualism and personal autonomy as more authentic indicators of growth. The former or more traditional focus highlights what the person owes to his or her society, while the latter or more liberal focus highlights what the person achieves or contributes to society, by way of creativity, enterprise and risk.

2. Normative Principles Governing Personal Growth

Determining the criteria governing the issue of personal growth or "human development" is a complex and sometimes contentious process. Among the diverse theoretical schools dealing with personal development, the psychologically influenced ones give importance to personal dimensions of growth, while the sociologically influenced ones give importance to social relatedness and productivity and the spiritually influenced ones give importance to sensitivity towards transcendent and divine reality.

In this exercise we move from the descriptive realm of the 'is' to the prescriptive or normative realm of the 'ought.' While proposing norms—and later, a hierarchy of states of consciousness based on these norms—for determining personal growth, I have taken into consideration various psychological, social, moral and spiritual aptitudes requisite for integral and ongoing development.

At the *personal level*, primary among the indicators of growth is integrity, or having and living by strong and upright moral principles and convictions. This requires emotional and spiritual intelligence and depth. Reliability and consistency of character is a strong indicator of integrity. When these principles and convictions are increasingly autonomous and not only dependent on social convention or pressure, the quality of integrity gets even more refined. Besides integrity, an important quality is resilience, or the ability to bounce back from adverse circumstances. Resilience is generally founded upon a core optimistic or positive outlook towards life. Finally, persons of integrity may be relied upon as being responsible for tasks assigned to them. Also, such persons assume responsibility for their actions and their outcomes, and do not easily attribute blame to others or social situations.

At the *interpersonal level*, integrity is manifested in honesty or truthfulness in communication. The principle of the Golden Rule—present in diverse forms in various cultures and religions—is adhered to, with mutuality and justice given a high premium in relationships. Beyond duty and justice, a spirit of sensitivity and compassion, and a concomitant valuation of mercy above justice are further indicators of a heightened quality of interpersonal relationships.

At the *social level*, personal and professional transparency is esteemed, associated with the value of accountability. The desire to contribute productively to society—and to "give back," especially from a situation of privilege—is also given a high premium. Establishing a social situation that features fraternity and harmony within one's primary communities and with persons of other communities in general is also valued. The idea of the "common good" takes precedence over the narrow, privatized idea of the "individual good."

Finally, at the *trans-human and trans-social level*, respect for nature and natural resources is increasingly gaining ground as a moral imperative today. Beyond and beneath this, a sensitivity, receptivity and collaborative disposition towards the presence and working of transcendent and ultimate spiritual realities are also important factors in furthering personal growth.

3. States of Growth

Growing as a person may ideally be depicted in terms of a trajectory that consists of numerous states of awareness. One pole of the trajectory is an extreme form of self-absorption, while the other pole is an expansive sense of being other-oriented. Beyond a deficient or dysfunctional state of existence in which one is not able to even befriend oneself, there are three broad spectrums of awareness on this trajectory: befriending the self, befriending others within one's community (being at home within one's community's horizon of meaning and purpose) and befriending others beyond one's community (being at home with communities and concerns that transcend one's own and one's community's horizon of meaning and purpose).[8]

3.1. Individually Focused Growth: Befriending the Self

Befriending oneself is not as easy at it seems, given the stresses and strains of family and social life. A primal, yet prevalent state of existence that many human beings find difficult to transcend is that of a nagging self-doubt, self-pity and even self-loathing. Beneath these sentiments lies a range of emotions such as fear, shame and unhealthy guilt. In these circumstances, it is difficult to befriend even oneself, leave aside the other. This state of existence may be characterized as *phobic*, as many of the emotions experienced are related to some form of fear or anxiety.[9] Psychoanalytic theorists pay special attention to early childhood experiences—especially related to different forms of fear—to help explain later dispositions and behaviour patterns. However, besides personal wounded memories and lack of opportunities for freedom and flourishing, there may be various oppressive social situations which cause phobia: economic uncertainty, political strife, cultural marginalization—all of these are factors which do not easily allow people to go beyond this dysfunctional state of consciousness.

The most basic manner of befriending oneself may at first be manifested in *egotistic* or severely self-centred, narcissistic behaviour. This may seem personally and socially dysfunctional, but it is somewhat better than being plagued by powerful negative forces (at the *phobic* level) that leave one psycho-spiritually scarred and crippled.[10] While narcissism may have its origins in personal life narratives, it may also be caused by strong cultural factors. For example, living in a strong capitalistic milieu naturally gives rise to a spirit of competition for goods and services. In such situations, educational institutions and corporate industries encourage pitting oneself against others in diverse fields of productive enterprises.

The next state beyond the egotistic may be termed the *aesthetic*, in the limited and technical sense in which Kierkegaard uses it as a primal or basic stage of human flourishing.[11] This state of consciousness corresponds to a life driven by the pursuits of varied pleasures. There is a need to get out of one's skin in order to engage with the larger world, even though this engagement may largely be characterized by instrumental relationships. It is important to differentiate this form of aestheticism from a higher form of aesthetic enjoyment, in which the focus is not the self but rather the aesthetic object in itself—or even better, the aesthetic experience, which goes beyond subject-object duality.

Beyond the pursuit of pleasure, perhaps the best state of awareness within the limited spectrum of "befriending the self" is that of *authentic* living, understood as strategically planning and achieving one's personal goals, and thus satisfying one's ambitions in life. Some forms of existentialist thought which advocate authenticity—and in a different light, contemporary corporate culture which encourages personal achievement and success—foster this self-oriented outcome of personal choices and achievement as a wholesome goal of human existence. While the thought of the early Heidegger may well represent the ideal of authenticity from an existentialist perspective,[12] the objectivist philosophy of Ayn Rand may best represent the wisdom of living from this type of consciousness at the social, corporate and even ideological level.[13]

When egotism, aesthetic pleasure and personal success are relativized in terms of a more important and wider value or focus, then one's consciousness automatically moves to a higher realm. This may be either furthering the interests of a community or communities with which one is identified, or even beyond, manifesting a concern about the larger human community or the trans-human realm of meaning and value.

3.2. Community-Focused Growth: Befriending the Other as Self

Growing as a person can hardly come to a terminus by merely fulfilling self-oriented goals. The impetus to befriend oneself needs to graduate to a higher level, to include befriending those with whom one shares common interests, a common vision and purpose of life, shared community practices, a collective cultural and religious background, etc. However, while affirming all of these commonalities, there is a movement to befriend the other to a large extent because the other mirrors—or is viewed as an extension of—the self. This type of awareness may then be properly termed, "befriending the other *as self*."

Within this broad spectrum of "befriending the other as self," there are at least three types of awareness. The most basic level is an *organic* awareness, in which one recognizes the need for social, legal and institutional order and one's place in such a shared order. Middle order managers, or those who desire to see that everything is in order and that the system runs smoothly are those who especially appreciate such a consciousness. Such a consciousness also features as a default initial state of mind for a majority of tribal or indigenous communities the world over, in which a collective sense of belonging is valued far above individual attention, pleasure or achievement.

Beyond this basic affirmation of a commonly ordered life is a more refined *moralistic* awareness, where one is convinced of and reifies core moral—and often religious—values associated with law and order. Most culturally and religiously based traditional societies lay great emphasis on the cultivation of such a consciousness. However, there may also be dysfunctional forms of operating from this consciousness, e.g., that which is found among right wing groups, be they religiously bigoted, narrowly nationalistic or culturally chauvinistic.[14]

When one is able to relativize and transcend the narrow observance of the law for its own sake—and for a greater social or moral good—this leads to a more radical understanding of befriending the other. Such a disposition may be termed *empathetic*, as personal compassion prevails over legal, social and moral perfection, and mercy prevails over justice. From such a position, persons are judged to be more important than principles, relationships more important than rules and regulations, and the expression of personal care more important than the mere execution of one's duty.[15]

3.3. Trans-Personal and Trans-Community Focused Growth: Befriending the Other as Other

This interpersonally refined empathetic state of awareness is a threshold towards—and sets the conditions for—an even more evolved state, in which one is able to allow for personal and communitarian differences with one's own horizon of meaning and purpose. It is this level of awareness that may generally be referred to as "befriending the other," but more properly as "befriending the other *as other*." This form of awareness too may be broken down into at least three discrete types. An *altruistic* awareness is the most basic, in which one recognizes the value of "alterity" or "otherness." This entails an admittance that there are persons and communities who live by different values, and are possessed of a different vision and purpose in life, and that all of these have a unique status and value and ought not be reduced to one's own way of life. Based on this consciousness of alterity, contemporary currents of postmodern critique point towards many glaring instances of discrimination based either on a binary polarization (male-female, white-'coloured', clergy-laity) or a hierarchical system (class, caste). This heightened consciousness is able to recognize and affirm the mutual rights of other communities.

However, a mere admittance or recognition of "otherness" does not automatically entail that one has the inclination or the ability to genuinely empathize with people of other communities. This requires a more proactive *agapeistic* awareness—an extension of the empathetic attitude towards the other as other. Compassion and concern for those of other communities and the cultivation of companionship—etymologically, "breaking bread together"—with the other are constitutive elements of this state of awareness. One of the clearest examples of a person operating from such a consciousness is Mother Theresa, who cared for the lowly and the dispossessed from all religious, cultural and national communities. There are many non-governmental and non-profit organizations whose members also operate from such a consciousness, thus transcending the limited concern exhibited by governmental and corporate agencies—the former operating from national interests, and the latter largely from monetary interests.

Beyond even this benevolent disposition lies perhaps the highest state of awareness that humans may reach in terms of personal development. At this level of being, it is quite likely that the awareness of a self which is separate from any other reality breaks down. In this *mystic* state of awareness, one is suffused with an ecstatic experience that may be characteristic of a wide variety of ultimate values—based on one's fundamental spiritual orientation—such as love, beauty, goodness, wellbeing, existential truth and unity (harmony, interconnectedness). Numerous examples of great mystics from the different religious traditions abound: Plotinus, John of the Cross, Sankaracharya, Ramakrishna Paramahansa, Aurobindo. However, there are numerous instances in the lives of ordinary human beings which may also feature flashes of this overcoming of duality between the self and the other, and a momentary experience of some form of transcendent reality, which in many cases may be indescribable or even unable to recall with accuracy.[16]

Beyond these examples of extraordinary and ordinary mystics, are numerous examples of persons who systematically moved beyond individual and community wellbeing, and embraced trans-community or universal wellbeing as their goal, e.g., Buddha, Socrates, Jesus, Gandhi, Mother Theresa. Many such people found themselves living at a heightened state of human consciousness. Unfortunately, some of these—and many others—had to pay with their lives for the novel and radical vision and values they propagated to their contemporaries.

4. The Tenuous Nature of the Different States of Growth

It is tempting to consider these states of consciousness in terms of linear and progressive *stages* of growth.[17] Also, we often assign a "character" to persons who seem to operate from a particular state of consciousness. However, regression to lower states of consciousness is always possible—and likewise, progression to higher states. Even if a person operates from a particular state of consciousness in a regular and sustained manner, it is quite possible that he or she goes through diverse experiences ranging from the phobic to the mystical during the course of a day. This will largely depend on extenuating circumstances and how one decides to respond to these circumstances. Thus, while it may appear to be natural that growth takes place in a linear manner—that is, moving from one state to the next in a steady progression—the extenuating conditions governing human life and corresponding personal responses to them introduce necessary nuance and ambivalence into an otherwise apparently progressive perception of human growth.

People living in urbanized, capitalistic governed societies may largely be driven to live their lives at a more individualistically focused level, while those who live in rural, traditional or indigenous (tribal) societies which value communal belonging and interconnectedness over individual achievement, will by default live at higher levels of consciousness on the normative scale provided. However, a more integral pathway towards a full human life seems to naturally include all these three types of befriending: befriending oneself, befriending others in one's community and befriending the 'other' beyond oneself and one's community. A person living at higher states of consciousness will not ideally negate or repress previous experiences associated with lower states. Instead, he or she needs to build upon the past by organically synthesizing or integrating past experiences at lower states into subsequent experiences at more refined and wholesome states of consciousness.

Conclusion

Personal growth is an ongoing task and challenge, in order that higher ranges of the spectrum of growth proposed may gradually characterize the state of one's awareness. For this to happen, one needs to ensure that there are adequate external or circumstantial conditions for higher states of awareness to thrive. Besides fostering these situational conditions for growth, however, it is also necessary to discern how to respond to external stimuli—especially adverse circumstances—in an enlightened manner, so that higher levels of awareness may be experienced at greater frequency, intensity and duration.

he attainment of consciousness at more refined states is both a task and a gift, and one cannot be assured that such a state persists without conscious effort. There is thus need for regular discernment or some form of ongoing awareness exercise, to sustain a higher level of consciousness and wellbeing. Growing as a person is a lifelong personal project. But it is also a spiritual, moral and social obligation. Because the journey of growth from befriending oneself to befriending the other is not just an exercise in personal or interpersonal growth—it is also a spiritual, moral and social imperative.

Notes

1 Besides professional spiritual directors, counselors, psychologists and psychiatrists, the number of "life coaches"—especially in urban, materially developed contexts—is increasing exponentially, hardly meeting the need and demand of those who are willing to pay exorbitant amounts for the therapeutic mentoring exercises offered by these experts.

2 See Gerald May, *Simply Sane: The Spirituality of Mental Health*, 2nd ed. (NY: Crossroad, 1993).

3 See also Gabriel Marcel, *The Mystery of Being*, Vol. 1, (Chicago: Charles Regnery Co, 1951), 149, where Marcel asserts that, "we must reject the idea of there actually being a legitimate answer, an objectively valid answer, to the question: 'Who am I?' . . . [It is] a riddle that, at the human level, simply cannot be solved: it is a question that does not imply, and cannot imply, any plain answer."

4 This is the wisdom in having growth-oriented remedial programmes in places of incarceration, so that prison inmates may look towards a humane life after serving their term.

5 See Francois O'Kane, *Sacred Chaos: Reflections on God's Shadow and the Dark Self* (Toronto: Inner City Books, 1994), which is an application of Jung's understanding of the shadow to human, and even to divine life.

6 Peter Berger and Thomas Luckmann point out to possibilities of brainwashing in the context of the differentiation between primary and secondary socialization. See *The Social Construction of Reality: A Treatise in the Sociology of Knowledge* (London: Penguin, 1966), 149 ff.

7 See R. Murray Thomas, *Moral Development Theories—Secular and Religious* (Westport, CT: Greenwood Press, 1997), for a summary description of various theories dealing with human development, from a secular as well as religious point of view.

8 See Keith D'Souza, "Levels of Existential Development," in *The Dynamics of Development: Negations and Negotiations*, ed. Keith D'Souza (Bangalore: Asian Trading Corporation, 2014), 301-23, for a philosophically-based schema of these ten states of consciousness, and Keith D'Souza, "Living Faith in a Postmodern World: Principles and Phases of Faith Development" in *The Quality of Adult Faith*, ed. Cleophas Fernandes (Bangalore: NBCLC, 2015), 184-208, for a theologically and religiously-based schema of these states.

9 While the emotions of shame, guilt and grief are apparently discrete from that of anxiety or fear, all of these emotions in some way stem from the imagined possibility of losing something valuable: name and status (in the case of shame), integrity (in the case of guilt) and a significant or prized relationship (in the case of grief).

10 According to Francoise O'Kane, in *Sacred Chaos*, 15, "those symptoms and reactions described as characteristic of a narcissistic personality can also be viewed from a different perspective: they are part of an attempt at survival, a way for the individual to confront despair over a life that, for whatever reason, has been dominated by shadow and destruction."

11 Besides the *aesthetic* or pleasure-oriented stage (exemplified by Don Juan and Faust), the more advanced stages are the *ethical* (exemplified by Socrates) and the *religious* (exemplified by Abraham). See Soren Kierkegaard, *Stages Along Life's Way*, trans. Walter Lowrie (NY: Schocken Books, 1967) and *Concluding Unscientific Postscript*, ed. and trans. Howard Hong and Edna Hong (Princeton, NJ: Princeton Univ Press, 1992), for a description of these three types of stages.

12 See Heidegger's depiction of authenticity (*Eigentlichkeit*) in *Being and Time*, trans. John Macquarrie and Edward Robinson (NY: Harper and Row, 1962).

13 See Ayn Rand, *For the New Intellectual* (NY: Penguin, 1963), for a good overview of her philosophical position advocating individual flourishing.

14 The Pharisees depicted in the Gospels—who considered themselves to be upright or "righteous" (Mk. 7: 1-23; Mt. 15: 1-3)—are a good example of people assiduously living by such a consciousness.

15 The various conflicts over the interpretation of Sabbath laws between Jesus on the one hand and the Scribes and Pharisees on the other (Mk. 2: 1-12, 23-28; Mk. 3: 1-6) are a good example of conflict between one who operates from empathy (Jesus) and one who gives more importance to the adherence of contemporary social and moral codes (the religious leaders who opposed Jesus).

16 See Harvey Egan, "The Mysticism of Everyday Life," in *Formative Spirituality Bulletin* (Duquesne), 10/1 (1989), and James Carse, *Breakfast at the Victory: The Mysticism of Ordinary Experience* (NY: Harper One, 1995).

17 One of the main differences between these stages of consciousness and Lawrence Kohlberg's six moral stages of growth—which has been the original framework which I have worked upon to posit these ten states—is that Kohlberg seemed to have a more rigid cognitive understanding of the nature of these stages, besides not allowing room for regression to take place. For other differences between Kohlberg's six stages and these ten states, see Keith D'Souza, "Levels of Existential Development," in *The Dynamics of Development: Negations and Negotiations.*

21

Befriending Water: A Pathway to Sustainable Development

Arjen Tete, SJ
Jnana Deepa, Pune 411014

Abstract: In the Indian context, nadequate access to clean drinking water and sanitation, increase in water-related diseases and disasters, competition for the resources among different sectors and regions, and the effects of climate change, are presenting daunting challenges to sustainable water-systems, eco-systems, and humanity itself. Exploring the causes and effects of the Indian water crisis, water-related practices, policies, programs, and possibilities, and examining the physical and chemical properties and behaviors of water, I have envisaged friendship with water as an adequate inter-religious response to the current crisis of water insecurity in India. May the life-giving power of water and the Spirit renew the face of the earth, bringing freshness and fecundity amidst the "crisis of existence" or the "cry-for-life" in India. That would be part of befriending our nature

Keywords: Water, Indian situation of water, Befriending water, Urbanisation, Industrialisation

> Water is the most essential element for life, and the future of humanity depends on our capacity to guard it and share it.
> -Pope Francis (Francis 2015)

Introduction

In her national poem *Vande Mātaram*, India is described as the land full of water and fruit. Today, however, the water crisis in India is the most pervasive dimension of the nation's encroaching desolation. Water privatization, poisoned rivers, population increase, rapid industrial growth, urbanization, agriculture, and climate change are putting tremendous pressure on water demand and posing a complex and wide-ranging threat to human survival as well as to the eco-system. Inefficient management is bad enough when the supply is plentiful; it is potentially disastrous when we have diminishing resources. Hence, befriending water will mean both a way of understanding water and a way to help save her. Exploring the mystery of water in the natural world and her essentiality for life, this paper attempts to redeem the sacred status water has enjoyed since life appeared on earth and to divest her of a commodity-driven character, which is only a recent manifestation. It invites us to gaze on water with the eyes of love rather than with arrogant, utilitarian designs.

Indian Situation

India is still considered rich in terms of annual rainfall and total water resources. The annual precipitation of the country is estimated at 4,000 billion cubic meters, including snow-fall, for which details are not available. The combination of rainfall, surface, and groundwater resources seems sufficient for providing adequate water to the Indian population. However, the Indian case is not monolithic but complex. A closer look at India's water resources reveals huge disparities of water availability from region to region. The levels of precipitation vary from 100 mm a year in western Rajaṣthan to over 9,000 mm a year in the northeastern state of Meghalaya (Planning Commission, 2002). Let us now unpack some of the Indian water stressors.

Population Pressure

According to UN-Water, "water use has been increasing at more than twice the rate of population increase in the last century," and the rate of withdrawal is expected to increase 50 percent more in the so-called "developing countries" by 2025 (UN-Water, 2014). India has 18 percent of the world's population but only 4 percent of the freshwater resources and 2.4 percent of the world's land area (NWP, 2012). Today, India's population has grown to over 1.2 billion and per capita water availability has fallen to barely more than 2,000 cubic metres (cm) per year, with the actual usable quantity being around 1,122 cm per year. With the current population, India is projected to become a water-scarce country by around 2025 (NWP, 2012).

Domestic Demand

Domestic water use will increase as the population continues to grow. Economic development is raising the standard of living for many people. As more and more people achieve a level of affluence, more demand is placed on the freshwater supply. Peter Rogers and Susan Leal observe that as the better-educated and higher-paid populations of China and India ascend into the middle class, they are increasing their water footprint (Rogers and Leal, 2010: 6).

Agricultural Irrigation

Indian agriculture, though mostly rain-fed, uses more than 90 percent of the total freshwater due to the unpredictability of the monsoon (Shrivastava and Kothari, 2013: 178). This places greater demands on surface and groundwater resources at the expense of the industrial and the domestic supply.

Rapid Urbanization and Industrialization

The Census 2001 projection report shows that only 28 percent of India's population is urban. However, the urban population in India is expected to double in the first three decades of this century. Indian Prime Minister Modi has announced his vision to set up 100 smart cities across the country. Urbanization generally accompanies industrialization. As the country rapidly urbanizes and industrializes, greater quantities of water will be required.

Climate Change

Climate change will further decrease water availability. In its paper, "The Himalayan Challenge: Water Security in Emerging Asia," published in 2010 (Strategic Foresight Group, 2010) the Strategic Foresight Group has shown that a combination of two factors—rapid glacier melt and erratic, heavy, and intense monsoon patterns—of climate change are already impacting the Ganges and Brahmaputra Rivers. The group foresees that on account of fewer days of rain, adequate amounts of water will not percolate down to the groundwater tables. Increased temperatures will also increase the rate of evapotranspiration. This will further reduce the actual amount of water that is available for human use.

Management of the Water Crisis

Realizing the gravity of the problem, the Government of India has launched a number of policies, acts, and plans for the management of water. I shall highlight some of the key features of the three National Water Policies in order to elucidate the national perspective on water. The National Water Policy (1987) positively recognized water as one, indivisible resource, affirming that rainfall, river waters, surface ponds, lakes and ground water are all part of one interdependent system, which is part of yet a larger ecological system (NPW, 2087: 1:1). There is no mention of private sector participation in the water management.

The 2002 National Water Policy added priorities to include ecology and navigation, and divided industry into categories of agriculture-related and non-agricultural industries. However, this policy encouraged privatization of water (NPW, 2002: 13).

The National Water Policy of 2012 states that water needs to be managed as a community resource, and held by the state under public trust doctrine, in order to achieve food security, support livelihood, and ensure equitable and sustainable development for all. It also upholds the ecological needs of rivers for the first time, stipulating that water be set aside in proportion to a river's natural flow regime (NPW, 2002: 13). At the same time, this policy underlines the need to treat water as an economic good, thus providing flexibility for allocating water for industrial use even at the cost of agriculture. It says that after meeting the minimum quantity of water required for survival of human beings and eco-systems, available water "should increasingly be subjected to allocation and pricing on economic principles so that water is not wasted in unnecessary uses and could be utilized more gainfully" (NPW, 2012: 7:4).

Together, the three National Water Policies have prioritized dam building and extracting underground water while masking the human toll exacted by these industries. The policies have gradually progressed from perceiving water as a national resource to approaching her as an economic good. Although there have been some initial successes, in the long run such policies are unsustainable. A 2005 study entitled "Financing the Water Crises," published in India by Research Foundation for Science, Technology & Ecology, has documented widespread failures of water privatization (Navdanya, 2015). In reality, such shortsighted strategies are inflicting catastrophic environmental and social ruin on the country as a whole, particularly upon the poor, who disproportionately bear the greatest burden of the crisis.

Perception of water as an economic commodity has precipitated a boom in the bottled water industry.[1] Along with bottling plants for fizzy drinks, the industry has contributed to falling water tables, groundwater depletion, and the spread of pollution across many regions of the country. The rise of bottled water has actually come at the expense of public drinking water. The lure of huge profits has attracted big players into the water-bottling business.

Tragically, water management in India has always taken a top-down approach and has become virtually a government monopoly, resulting in the exploitation of additional water resources. Despite efforts of The World

Bank and the Government of India to address the water crisis, development pressures and rise in demand are changing the scenario of water availability and the priorities of water distribution in India today.

Despite our technological mastery, however, we have not managed to create a water-secure India. Technology is useful and necessary, but is merely a tool rather than a solution to the complex water crisis. While it is true that we need more sustainable and effective technologies, policies, and assistance from international and national institutions to prevent and resolve the water crisis, the stresses on our Indian rivers and water supplies are so great and so widespread that along with the implementation of these measures we need a new imagination of reverence and responsibility for water. Thomas Berry has rightly said:

> The pathos of the present is that the human community has lost its capacity to interact creatively with the other components of the planet Earth. This includes the landscape of the planet; the nurturing qualities of the air, the water, and the soil; the energy flow that enables the dynamic powers of the Earth to continue their functioning; the life systems that are integrated in an immense complex of partners beyond full human understanding (Berry, 2009: 81).

Water is perceived variously as a commodity, as a commons (common property), as a basic right, and as a sacred resource or divinity. Fundamental attitudes towards water can also worsen the crisis. Those who see water as a commodity are often blind to the other dimensions of water. Therefore, rejecting the absolute kingship model of relationship with the earth and water, we need to move beyond the stewardship model as well, to a kinship model of relationship to befriend water. The notion of stewardship maintains the structure of hierarchical dualism. In evolutionary history we form one mutually interdependent community of life. We are all kin.

Befriending Water

Friendship implies self-disclosure. Persons, though enigmatic, are revealed by their roots, backgrounds, and biographies. Therefore, in order to understand and appreciate the life-mediating properties of water and to enhance friendship with her, I will first explore the root story of water and her physical and chemical properties. Subsequently, I shall articulate spiritual and ethical implications of befriending water for a sustainable development.

In his work, *Life's Matrix: A Biography of Water*, science writer Phillip Ball writes that "like a person, water has immediate, evident, and familiar characteristics that can be understood only, if at all, by a consideration of its deeper makeup, of the hidden factors that shape its behaviors." Ball continues that "water may remain in some respects a mystery, but is—and has always been—a most fecund mystery, one that provokes us to find new ways of exploring the nature of the physical world" (Ball, 1999: x). Water is a mystery, but water is also a physical reality. Water changes the face of the land, splitting open rock desert like a peach. She is the visible face of climate. Myths and legends have depicted water as the blood that runs through the intricate network of veins and arteries of Mother Earth as rivers and streams, providing sustenance to plant and animal life everywhere.

Origins of Water

Water is a tiny molecule consisting of three atoms: two of hydrogen and one of oxygen. Water molecules cling to each other because of a force called hydrogen bonding. The hydrogen atoms attract the negative charge of oxygen atoms that are part of other water molecules. For this reason water can do amazing things. She "takes the form of droplets rather than spreading out as a thin film. The high surface tension of water is responsible for capillary action, which allows it (and its dissolved substances) to move through the roots of plants as well as through the veins and arteries of the human body" (Altman, 2002: 9).

How did hydrogen and oxygen emerge in our universe? According to Ball, hydrogen originated in the cooling period after the initial Big Bang explosion. Oxygen is said to be the third most abundant element in the universe after hydrogen and helium. Since they are the primordial generation after the Big Bang, they constitute almost every strand of creation. But, helium is unreactive. It remains aloof. Water, the combination of hydrogen and oxygen, therefore, pervades the universe.

Physiognomies of Water

Water is a shape-shifter. She exists in three states on earth: liquid, gas, and solid. Liquid water is a jumbled bunch of water molecules. She comes out of faucets, flows underground and in rivers and oceans, and forms clouds and fog in the air. When water freezes into a solid, she does a strange thing: she floats. Most other solids become denser and sink. If water behaved that way, ice would accumulate on the bottom of the lakes and oceans during the winter, and would have difficulty melting in the spring. This would have serious consequences for aquatic life as ocean is still home to more kinds of life than anywhere else on the planet.

Movements of Water

The Greek philosopher Heraclitus once said that one can never walk through the same river twice because water is in constant flux. Earth water is always in motion. She moves inside the planet, across its surface, and in the atmosphere above. Water in lakes, rivers, and oceans turns into vapor and moves into the air through evaporation. Plants draw water from the soil and return it to the air. Volcanoes release water vapor that is locked deep inside rocks. Water's main, reliable routine forms what we know as the water or hydrologic cycle. This water cycle repeats continuously, which makes it possible for the same water to nourish the earth over and over again. If not for this water cycle there would not be water enough for our planet (Boyle, 1961: 2). Our water system is connected around the world.

Another surprising characteristic of liquid water is that she can absorb and store huge amounts of heat without melting, freezing, or boiling. Water boils at a very high temperature—100 degree Celsius at sea level—compared to similarly sized molecules. If water behaved like other liquids, it would exist as a gas at the temperatures found on earth, and life as we know it could not survive. This awesome characteristic of water affects climate in many ways. Ocean currents move warm water around the globe. At the North and South poles, sea ice forms and melts with seasons. Water vapor in the atmosphere holds the sun's heat like a blanket. Clouds and ice sheets reflect some of that heat back into space. Together, these processes keep our planet from getting too hot or too cold (Chamberlain, 2010: 68).

The Human Body and Water

Just as life began in the primeval seas, human and other mammalian life continues to originate in the water of the womb. Gary Chamberlain rightly affirms, "We begin our lives in uterine water, amniotic fluid. When 'the waters break,' we are born" (Chamberlain, 2010: 74). Our bodies consist of two-thirds water. Yet, we do not wobble like a bulging water-skin. Certainly, some of this fluid gurgles in our guts, surges in our veins, lubricates our palate and our eyelids and joints. Water plays an active role of solvent and carrier for the cellular machinery of our bodies. Ball notes that without her, other biomolecules would not only be left stranded and immobile, they might no longer truly be biomolecules, unraveling or seizing up and losing their biological function in the process. Therefore, Ball concludes that biology starts with water—historically, ontologically, pedagogically (Ball, 1999: 250).

Implications of Befriending Water

We have seen above how the hydrological cycle preserves and communicates life and creates beauty in nature and the human body in mysterious and miraculous ways. Scientists and poets have marveled at the fecund mystery of water. The mystery of water awakens us to attend to the "signs of the times" everywhere life breaks forth and comes into being and alerts us to denounce an economic system built on the cult of commodity and consumerism.

Therefore, friendship with water challenges us to revitalize the fragile hope that is ever present, even where life is being plundered and eviscerated. We are challenged to practice justice, not only to humankind but to non-human creation as well. We are invited to develop a water ethic that conduces to the sustainability of our planetary home.

Contemplative Response

Befriending water necessitates us to contemplate water as God's revelation, to gaze on her with the eyes of love. We will not save what we do not love. A contemplative response engages water with religious imagination. Though there are many things in nature to be contemplated, admired, and enjoyed, they are not ours to pollute or privatize. Water is a sacrament of love and life. We are responsible to uphold water as the source of life without turning her into a source of death and decay.

Ascetic Response

Befriending water challenges us to restrain our rampant consumerism and self-indulgence. This is not a world-denying but a life-affirming asceticism, summoning us to protect and preserve water for life. We do these things not to make ourselves suffer but to ensure environmental sustainability and indeed the very survival of the cosmos itself. Humanness consists in living together, giving life to one another, and sharing water, forest, and earth with all living things. It consists in solidarity with the whole of creation; in making sure that the basic needs of everyone are met, and in the creative possibility of everybody having a share in existing resources and opportunities. There is neither humanness nor authentic happiness apart from the wholeness of the universe and the peace of all things.

Prophetic Response

Friendship with water challenges us to take critical action on behalf of the earth and water, whether politically, economically, culturally, or socially. Contemporary spirituality cannot be seen in isolation from the faith-justice mandate. Christians have an imperative from the Scriptures for a prophetic spirituality. Hence, we counter non-sustainable cultures and the systemic destruction of our world through healing, caring for, and protecting our earth, even if our actions run counter to the political and economic interests of the powerful. We ought to resist the technology, which is born of greed and has proven to be inhuman and death-dealing.

Pastoral-Educational Response

Christians constitute only 2.3% of the population in India, numerically insignificant compared to Hindus. In a society with an overwhelming population of Hindus, Muslims, and other religious groups, the Church in India is a powerful organization with a large network of structures, institutions, and services to educate the people of India.2 Recognizing the water crisis as one of the several challenges to Christian mission, bishops, in their pastoral letters; and pastors, in their preaching, teaching, and retreat direction, could invite people to appreciate more deeply our covenant with creation as central to right relationship with God and one another. They could accordingly articulate a faithful response based on political responsibility, employment, family life and personal lifestyle, calling people to acknowledge their corporate responsibility for the state in which we find ourselves and resolve to pull back from the brink of disaster. Priests, religious, and seminarians are well-placed to register a powerful protest against a wasteful lifestyle devoid of any sense of responsibility to the world of nature.

Re-education in the traditions, scriptures, cosmologies, and spiritualities is central. Through the re-appropriation of the doctrine of creation, incarnation, and a dialectical doctrine of God (balancing transcendence with immanence), Christian education can lead toward a new vision, a holistic worldview conceived for the environment. Such an educational program also demands an appreciation of the way in which scientific understandings complement religious insights and even contribute to a sense of wonder for the marvels of water. Christian universities and research centers could promote studies and practices focusing on the question of environmental improvement. The Ministry of Water Resources has been conducting national painting competitions on water conservation for school children since 2010 (Ministry for Water Resources, (2015). Christian educational institutions could actively engage school children to participate in these competitions and to eventually become creative and active agents of water conservation. There could also be education of the heart through catechesis, sacramental preparations, rituals, prayers, meditation, and mindfulness practices. Mindfulness can lead to creative ways to use water that retains its bounty and purity.

Inter-Religious Response

In each religious tradition, we can find both mystical and prophetic experiences and ideals. Despite diversity of faith, Indians share a common ground of suffering regarding the water crisis. Hence, there are many possibilities for fruitful collaboration.

Thus, all religious traditions of India can enlist their prophetic powers to call for needed changes in water use and management, not only in powerful, prophetic statements but in such actions as boycotts, letter-writing campaigns, lobbying, research, and protests.3 We all need to join and celebrate the efforts of activists diligently working to green the earth by practicing water democracy. We may recall the successful story of Rajendra Singh, the waterman, whose decades of hard work along with people living in the foothills of the rugged Aravallis in Rajasthan is reaping a rich water harvest today. The villages have more than enough water to last the entire year. Groundwater is available at five to six metres and the five dead rivers have become perennial. The transition from sacred texts, ritual practices, and observances to responsible actions toward the environment and water ought to be mediated by individuals and groups who themselves are committed to intimacy with the earth and water.

Conclusion

Contemporary India is in a precarious situation in terms of water. Inadequate access to clean drinking water and sanitation, increase in water-related diseases and disasters, competition for the resources among different sectors and regions, and the effects of climate change, are presenting daunting challenges to sustainable water-systems, eco-systems, and humanity itself. Exploring the causes and effects of the Indian water crisis, water-related practices, policies, programs, and possibilities, and examining the physical and chemical properties and behaviors of water, I have envisaged friendship with water as an adequate inter-religious response to the current crisis of water insecurity in India. May the life-giving power of water and the Spirit renew the face of the earth, bringing freshness and fecundity amidst the "crisis of existence" or the "cry-for-life" in India.

References

Altman, Nathaniel. *Sacred Water: The Spiritual Source of Life.* Mahwah, N.J.: HiddenSpring.

Ball, Philip. (1999). *Life's Matrix: Biography of Water.* New York: Farrar, Strauss and Giroux.

Berry, Thomas. (2009). *The Sacred Universe: Earth, Spirituality, and Religion in the Twenty-First Century.* New York: Columbia University Press.

Boyle, E. Marie. (1961). *Water: Its Form and Motion.* Boston: Beacon Press.

Chamberlain, Gary L. (2010). *Troubled Waters: Religion, Ethics, and the Global Water Crisis* (Lanham, Maryland: Rowman & Littlefield Publishers, 2010), 68.

Francis, Pope. (March 22, 2015). "Sunday *Angelus* Address in Saint Peter's Square." World Water Day.

Ministry for Water Resources, River Development and Ganga Rejuvenation (Government of India), "Kid's Corner: Water Conservation," http://wrmin.nic.in/forms/List.aspx?lid=1106&Id=6, accessed on 17th September, 2015.

Navdanya. (2015). "Financing the Water Crises: World Bank, International Aid & Water Privatization," available from http://www.indiawaterportal.org/sites/indiawaterportal.org/files/water-crisis.pdf, accessed on 9th May, 2015.

NWP, 2012. Ministry of Water Resources, Government of India, *National Water Policy* (2012), http://wrmin.nic.in/, accessed 3rd August, 2015.

Planning Commission, (2002). Government of India, *India Assessment 2002 – Water Supply and Sanitation*, http://planningcommission.nic.in/reports/genrep/wtrsani.pdf, accessed on 3rd August, 2015.

Ray, Binayak. (2008). *Water: The Looming Crisis in India.* Lanham, Maryland: Lexington Books.

Rogers, Peter and Susan Leal. (2010). *Running Out of Water: The Looming Crisis and Solutions to Conserve Our Most Precious Resource.* New York: Palgrave Macmillan.

Shrivastava, Aseem and Ashish Kothari. (2013). *Churning the Earth: The Making of Global India*. New Delhi: Penguin Books..

Strategic Foresight Group (2010). "The Himalayan Challenge: Water Security in Emerging Asia," (A paper published in 2010), http://www.strategicforesight.com/publication_pdf/85801himalayan-challenge.pdf, accessed on 3rd July, 2015.

UN-Water. (2014). United Nations Water. http://www.unwater.org, accessed on 3rd August, 2015.

Notes

1 Other than the market leader, Parle's Bisleri, there is Pepsi with its Aquafina brand. Tata Tea has recently acquired a big stake in Mount Everest. Coca-cola, which sells water under the Kinley label, has bought a part of Glaceau. Even WIPRO has entered the bottled water business with its purchase of the FMCG (fast-moving consumer goods) firm Unza. See (Shrivastava and Kothari, 2012. 2013: 100-106.

2 As of 2011 statistics, Roman Catholics run Colleges and schools: 14,429, Training Institutes: 1,086, Hospitals and dispensaries: 1,826, Publications: 292. Available from http://en.wikipedia.org/wiki/Catholic_Church_in_India, accessed 17th July, 2015.

3 In 2013, in Madhya Pradesh's Khandwa area, 51 people stayed immersed in water for the 14th day in what was being called a '*jal satyagraha*' (Water Resistance). The protestors were demanding compensation and rehabilitation for villagers whose homes would be submerged under water after the state government's order of opening all the gates of the Omkareshwar dam.

22

Beyond an Unscientific Bias towards a Scientific Knowing for the Authentic Befriending of the Religious Other

Chae Young Kim
Sogang University, South Korea

Abstract: The issues related to engaging with the other, or how to welcome the other, or how we let the other feel friendly in our religious pluralistic environment. Actually this subject is not new but has been dealt with recently in many academic and also practical meetings since the encounter of the other persons would have happened frequently. However, comparatively this issue is not strange to Asians but historically deeply rooted in Asian way of life due to the rich experience of living together as a member of the community beyond the indifferent awareness to the existence of the other in the present times. Borrowing the basic insights of Bernard Lonergan, the author explores the unscientific bias towards scientific knowing and encountering the religious other.

In this process, the author transcends a notional or a descriptive apprehension of what we are anticipating or sensing as, now, we move toward apprehensions of meaning that live in an immaterial way within our acts of understanding. That which is not seen and which can never be seen becomes something which is understood through a form of self-transcendence which is endemic to our understanding. It joins us together as we move from a material order of things toward a familiarity that lives with meaning, intelligibility, and spirit towards knowledge societies embracing religious dimension embodied in our contemporary scientific and technological environment.

Keywords: Bernard Lonergan, Religious Other, Scientific Knowledge, Transcendence as faith in human life

Introduction

The general theme of this article is on the issues how to engage with the other, or how to welcome the other, or how we let the other feel friendly in our religious pluralistic environment. Actually this subject is not new but has been dealt with recently in many academic and also practical meetings since the encounter of the other persons would have happened frequently. However, comparatively this issue is not strange to Asians but historically deeply rooted in Asian way of life due to the rich experience of living together as a member of the community beyond the indifferent awareness to the existence of the other in the present times. This experience might be true in many ways in other places of our globe too.

However the general religious perception of the other would be unfortunately emphasized on the negative side of the Western religious world exposing especially violent issues of the crusade or the modern missionary zeal emerging in the context of the three religious traditions, Judaism, Christianity and Islam. The image is still going on the same track with a strong bias. At the same time unfortunately the usual image is also continuously witnessing the right aspect of them also in the present life in Europe. The positive side of them is not yet communicated for the balancing perception of them in the ordinary level of the modern human life.

The Western and Eastern Appoaches to Religion

This is further strengthened in the modern West. Especially when modern "secularism" attempts to deny or eradicate this point, unfortunately a false unscientific bias is conveyed: a bias that faith is not normal in human life, although this kind of diagnosis is both strange and abnormal in the context of global human history. Thus, for the ultimate security of the human life, without a restoration of this point of view in human life, no one can expect that authentic human encounters or fruitful inter-religious dialogue will emerge within the emergent pluralism of our world. Contemporary secular culture does not concern much about our human spiritual security due to disregarding the fundamental principle of transcendence as faith in human life.

In contrast, the perception of the Eastern religious world is quite distinctively intensified in the ideal image in our ordinary way of life. The negative image of the Eastern religious world, especially Hinduism and

Buddhism, is not yet deeply engaged with the ordinary way of life. Unfortunately recently the violent image emerging in Hinduism and Buddhism in Asia is reversing the usual ideal image of the two great traditions. Several examples are witnessing this point sharply in the treatment of religious minority groups, the Hindu, the Christian, and the Muslim in Sri Lanka. Also in India and Burma, the treatment of the Christian and the Muslim would be indicated in the similar way. Apart from these examples, so many cases could be pointed out in Asia.

The Religious Other as Minority

In this situation, we could say that the existence of the religious other as a minority in the major dominant religious context would not be easily accepted not only in the West but also in the East. Unlike the ordinary perception of the Hinduism and the Buddhism, the situation of them is not really telling the key difference from the cumulated image of the three religious relationships, especially the Christian and the Muslim. No matter where they would exist, still in our globe, the existence of other as a minority is witnessing the very similar uncomfortable story in the East and the West.

How could we breakthrough individually or collectively this same scheme of recurrence in our globe? Why is it almost impossible to be transformed further for our human good? Where could we find the some clues to break it apart for the new integration of the existence of other for the further friendly community in our globe? Theoretically many studies have already seemingly accomplished for the solution of the problem in religious studies/theologies, philosophies, economics, political science, sociology, psychology, peace and conflict studies, and other modern academic fields.

Nevertheless the problem is recurring repeatedly. Nowadays it is exposing unimaginable extreme situation. The present international institutions such as UN and NATO and various economic associations are not able to interfere and correct it for the creation of the good order of our world. Rather it is going in further extreme way. The speed does not seem to have any break to be stopped. Many criticisms on the religious extreme matters emerging against the other do suggest a good solution but they are not persuasively compelling. Even religious solutions are suggested diversely but the reality is not changed. The problem is further solidly fixed. For example, doctrinally the Hindu and the Buddhist theory of religious other is superb comparing to the Judeo-Christian oriented theory. The former is more theoretically tolerant than the latter. Historically it contributed much broad perspective in the relation to the religious other. However, in terms of the practice for the religious other, the latter would be seemingly more appealing in modern times about issues of class equality, human right, and gender issues.

Nevertheless, this point could not be totally generalized due to the difference of the various denominations or the different streams of each religious tradition. Still many different aspects could be found in the Judeo-Christian tradition not to welcome the gender issues and also the deeper relationship of the religious other. The opposite aspect of tolerance on this matter could be found in some branches of the Hinduism and the Buddhism. Practically they would reveal the different point as M. K Gandhi and Ven. Thic Nat Han did in their tradition. So in this paper, I would like to approach the matter of the religious other in our pluralistic global times more focusing on the human agent in any activities of our religious life in relation to the other. In so doing, I will not attempt to articulate a doctrinal perspective of the religious other but more emphasize the common anthropological play ground structurally rooted in our human subject as a common foundation for the authentic engagement with the religious other.

Bernard Longergan's Contributions

In this essay I would like to articulate this issue for the appropriate encounter of the religious other with a special reference to Bernard Lonergan's thought of bias and scientific knowing. Lonergan does not deal intensively with this issue on them in relation to the encounter of the religious other. Nevertheless, I think that his insight could be authentically applied to the encountering context of the religious other in a pluralistic environment emerging more distinctively in our present global times due to the impact of the recent immigration labor market.

Especially, in this occasion I will raise the question of religion and science and we speak about a scientific knowledge of religion or, in other words, about how a scientific understanding of things can be combined with a religious understanding of the same things. Some kind of fundamental compatibility towards knowledge societies would seem to be possible if we can determine how determinations of meaning in one discipline or perspective have not to be conflict with determinations that belong to another point of view. Both, in some way, exist together.

As a point of departure, two points constitute a suggestive heuristic with respect to the kind of relation which in fact exists between different human groups if we distinguish scientific groups, on the one hand, from religious or literary groups, on the other hand. Our first point refers to a difference (a contrast); our second, a connection with respect to how one kind of knowledge leads to the other.

Scientific Knowledge as Acquired

As our first point, it is to be noted that scientific knowledge exists as acquired knowledge (Lonergan Institute, 2019: 149). Its catalyst is the asking of questions as we move from what we know to what we would like to know but have yet to know. None of us are strangers to inquiry. We notice ambiguities. We notice tensions or contradictions. What appears to be may not be and so we ask questions and this asking encourages our moving into philosophic and scientific questions. We can also say that the asking of questions encourages us to move into the possibilities of theological understanding and knowledge although no theological understanding can exist, in any real way, apart from our having some kind of religious faith. In distinguishing the being of any kind of knowledge that comes from questions, we speak about *a posteriori* knowledge or, in more metaphysical terms, *a posteriori* apprehensions of being.

Knowledge as Special Intuition

But, on the other hand, the experience of visions is something that is reported to us by many and various persons. It comes to us from testimonies of one kind or another where we encounter a knowledge of things that does not come from the asking of any questions. In an unsolicited way, a knowledge of things is somehow given to us. It is a kind of knowledge that, in some way, we have prior to the asking of any questions, and because we have not sought or worked to have this kind of knowledge, we speak about a kind of knowledge which, in its immediacy, is best described as a species of intuition. It exists as a kind of unmerited gift and, on our side, if we attend to the quality of our subjectivity, we best speak about a receptivity that is purely open and submissive. In this kind of knowledge, we have an *a priori* kind of knowledge or, in more metaphysical terms, an *a priori* apprehension of being (Lonergan Institute, 2019: 145-158).

Turning to point two, in examining the order of our human knowledge, we find that *a priori* kinds of knowledge precede *a posteriori* kinds of knowledge (Lonergan Institute, 2019: 16). If our acquired knowledge of things always move from a knowledge and an understanding of things that we already have and we do not have to acquire it, then, inevitably, we are forced to admit that all acquired knowledge and its acquisition is predicated on the basis of a more primitive, basic kind of knowledge as this exists for us as a kind of gift that comes to us from sources that we might not exactly know or understand. In other words, if we turn our attention of a larger study of *a priori* kinds of knowledge, we discover foundations for scientific and philosophic knowledge that can be traced to the reality and the being of literary and religious roots. If we should refer to the seeing of any visions in a literary or religious context, we refer to condensed, compact apprehensions of meaning and being which have yet to be fully understood. Symbolic apprehensions of meaning and being precede scientific apprehensions of meaning and being and, if we retain this focus and realize its importance, we can begin to understand why literary and religious apprehensions of meaning and being have an importance that is crucial for us as human beings. We begin with these and if we are working with apprehensions of meaning and being which are provocative and suggestive, we can move into the kind of meaning as this exists emerges in the practice of religion and science.

Concluding Suggestions

Furthermore, I would like to point to the fruitfulness of a larger framework which can be identified if we should raise questions about how or why the growth which exists in our human knowledge of things is something that can be joined to the kind of knowledge which exists if we should refer to a second kind of familiarity or a second kind of knowledge which exists for us through the human experience of visions that can be found if we should refer to how, in various literary or religious contexts, persons sometimes speak about a different kind of seeing that mysteriously belongs to them. It differs from the kind of seeing which belongs to their ordinary or common knowledge of things and it also differs from the kind of seeing which belongs to a scientific seeing of things that belongs to the genesis and the growth of scientific knowledge (Lonergan Institute, 2019: 152-154).

In other words, we transcend a notional or a descriptive apprehension of what we are anticipating or sensing as, now, we move toward apprehensions of meaning that live in an immaterial way within our acts of understanding. That which is not seen and which can never be seen becomes something which is understood through a form of self-transcendence which is endemic to our understanding. It joins us together as we move from a material order of things toward a familiarity that lives with meaning, intelligibility, and spirit towards knowledge societies embracing religious dimension embodied in our contemporary scientific and technological environment. That can help us to befriend each other more meaningfully by mutually enriching each other.

Refernece

Crowe, F. E. (1992). *Lonergan*. London: Chapman.

Lonergan Institute. (2019). "Natural Law: Part II," unpublished manuscript. Washington, DC: St. Anselm's Abbey.

Lonergan, B. J. F., & Lamb, M. L. (1981). *Creativity and method: Essays in honor of Bernard Lonergan, S.J.* Milwaukee, Wis: Marquette University Press.

Lonergan, B. J. F., Dadosky, J. D. & Doran, R. M., (2017). *Method in theology*. Toronto: University of Toronto Press for Lonergan Research Institute of Regis College.

23

Walking, Meditating and Rising to Befriend the Other: Transforming the Subjective and the Objective to Transpositional Subjectobjectivity

Ananta Kumar Giri
Madras Institute of Development Studies, Chennai, Tamil Nadu

Abstract: This article is a meditative walk in friendship towards the other in transpositional movements. It calls for transformation of the subjectivity and objectivity as we know including transformation of these from nouns to verbs-meditative verbs of pluralization. It also involves transformation of epistemological and the ontological including work of what I have elsewhere called ontological epistemology of participation and post-epistemological moves. But transpositional subjetobjectivity also calls for a new pragmatics of social communication, social dialogues and contestations. These are also part of our walking and meditating with self and other which is the ground of emergence of friendship.

Walking and meditating with self and other calls for experience of new wisdom about self and other as well as wisdom of relationship and the world. Transpositonal movements give birth to such wisdoms which help us in cultivating transformative friendship with self and the other

Keywords: The Other, Transpositional Subject, Transpositional Subjectobjectivity Transpositonal Movements, Meditation, Walking, Friendship

"Objectivity does not mean detachment, *it means respect*; that is, the ability not to distort and to falsify things, persons and oneself. [..] To be objective is possible only if we respect the things we observe; that is, if we are capable of seeing them in their uniqueness and interconnectedness."
Eric Fromm (1950), *Man for Himself*, p. 105-104.

"Observations are unavoidably position-based, but scientific reasoning need not, of course, be based on observational information from one specific position only. There is need for what may be called "trans-positional" assessment—drawing on but going beyond different positional observations. The constructed "view from no where" would then be based on synthesizing different views from distinct positions. The positional objectivity of the respective observations would still remain important but not in itself adequate. A trans-positional scrutiny would also demand some kind of coherence between different positional views." Amartya Sen (1994), "Positional Objectivity," p. 130.

"What we receive in contemplation, we give out in love." Meister Eckhart.

"If we take eternity to mean not infinite temporal domain but timelessness, then eternal life belongs to those who live in the present." Ludwig Wittgenstein.

"What is it namely, that connects the temporal and eternity, what else but love, which for that very reason is before everything and remains after everything is gone."
Søren Kierkegaard

Introduction and Invitation

Befriending the other calls for being with the other not only in static positions but in dynamic and meditative movements--walking and meditating. Walking and meditating with the other we arise in friendship with other but we may not as well as we might meet some unsurmountable and intractable differences in our journey. We can embrace the challenges of such differences and further walk and meditate instead of turning these into an excuse for a condition of permanent withdrawal, escape or enmity. Befriending the other is a complex process of walking, meditating and further actions, reflections and transformations. It in turn calls for appropriate cultivation of subjectivity, intersubjectivity, transsubjectivity and objectivity. Friendship is not just a spontaneous overflow of feelings. It calls for works of love, labor and mutual learning involving epistemic and ontological works, meditations and transformations. It also calls for transpositional movements, for example, from self to other and other to self and creative, critical and transformative movements in between and across. It also calls for transforming the subjectivity of the self and the other and the structures of objectivity which produce us. In my essay, I bring both these concerns, transpostional movements as well as transforming subjectivity and objectivity as a companion and contribution to our engagement with friendship.

Walking and Meditating with Self and the Other: Transforming the Subjective

Arising in friendship in the context of challenges of life calls for walking and meditating not only with the other but also with the self as one can become a friend to oneself as one can be one's enemy.[1] Walking and mediating with the other, we discover unexplored layers and dimensions of both self and other which can be a source of emergent mutuality or emergent disdain of hatred. In our mutual walk and meditation, we can not put our subjectivity aside as if it does not exist. If as Gadamer tells us that our initial cultural prejudices can not be wished away, similarly our initial subjective biases can not be put under the carpet. They are with us and for a journey of togetherness which involves both communication as well disjunction, commonalty and conflict, we need to work with our subjectivity and cultivate it appropriately.

Subjectivity has a dimension of ego as well as self. In both critical theory and spiritual traditions, there is a distinction between ego and self which is nurtured by the cultivation of a post-conventional self which is not an uncritical reproduction of the existing conventions of society and which has not lost its capacity for creative, critical, autonomous and responsible moral reflections (cf. Habermas, 1990). Our subjectivity has a reality and possibility of post-conventional which is not bound to existing conventions of ego, self, culture and science and this becomes a helpful companion in our striving for objectivity. In a related way, Sri Aurobindo also challenges us to understand that subjective is not reproduction of the typal conventions of society nor is it a case of reproduction of one's egotistic standpoint. In his *Human Cycles*, Sri Aurobindo (1962) characterizes the modern age as the rise of the subjective which goes beyond the typal conventions of society, not only of traditional social order but also of the modern ones which is dominated by conventions of science and society. The subjective in both Sri Aurobindo and Habermas is animated by a post-typal and post-conventional movement which also finds a creative resonance in the work of Alain Touraine who looks at the subjective in terms of a process of critique, creativity and transformation what he calls *subjectivation* (Touraine, 2000). *Subjectivation* in Touraine is different from looking at subjects as just subjected to regimes of subjection as it seems to happen in certain aspects of works of Michel Foucault and Judith Butler and is characterized by the desire, aspiration, capacity and creativity to say no to existing conventions of self, science and society which hinders fuller self-realization. Thus the subjective as subjectivation of saying no to taken-for-granted idols of method, science, epistemology and ontology[2] is crucial for our striving towards our journey of being with others which does not have a fixed *apriori* formula but is a dynamic formation. Walking and meditating with both self and other become multi-dimensional formations and verbs of co-realizations of self, other and the world. Our verbs of togetherness, however, are not only activistic but also meditative; they embody what I have elsewhere called meditative verbs of co-realizations (cf. Giri 2012, 2013).

Transforming the Objective

Being with self and other which becomes the ground and sky of arising in friendship or falling from grace grapples with not only the challenge of transforming the subjective but also the objective. We relate to both self and other many a time with a naïve sense of objectified social categories: both belonging to objectified structural categories such as caste, race, gender or the so-called personality types. Being imprisoned within such objectifying and objectivistic categories does not help us in starting our journey with self and the other. We need to move beyond objectifying categories which produces us as stones and move towards ways of being together and realizations which co-create us as flows. This thus calls for transforming objectivity as we conventionally know and practice and cultivate a new mode of objectivation in our journey and mediation of togetherness.

Here we can build upon some contemporary rethinking of objectivity. Pierre Bourdieu talks (2003) about participant objectivation where the key question is how does an observer observes himself or herself and this is a helpful capacity in our journey of togetheness. Though Bourdieu asks this question he does not really address this as he does not cultivate an appropriate subjectivity where one can simultaneously take part in an activity and observe with some kind of needed distanciation. In Indian spiritual traditions this has been spoken of as developing a witnessing consciousness which while taking part in life nonetheless has a capacity to witness with detachment as evident in the metaphor and realization of two birds sitting on a tree, one eating fruits and the other witnessing.[3] Bourdieu is silent about these issues as he is primarily within a valorized epistemological mode here and does not feel the need to cultivate an appropriate ontological mode.[4] Bourdieu, like Habermas, does not cultivate an appropriate ontological mode as both of them look at ontology primarily from the point of view of limitations of political ontology of Martin Heidegger and their justified critique of Heidegger's early association with Nazism and his subsequent silence over the Holocaust (cf. Bourdieu 1991). But ontological is a multi-dimensional journey of reality and realization and we need to cultivate it further drawing inspiration from both critical philosophy and spiritual traditions. For example, Foucault talks about an ontology of the present and Vattimo (2011) talks about an ontology of actuality[5] which also resonates with what I have called on ontological epistemology of participation. Transforming objectivity as part of a journey of togetherness involves a creative ontological epistemology of participation. In fact, our journey of togetherness can be viewed as a dynamic movement of ontological epistemology of participation in which we strive to know each other truthfully and be together authentically. Such truthful knowing, authentic being and inter-being and loving can help us in our journey of friendship with the other.

Transforming the Epistemological and Ontological in our Journey of Togetherness and Transpositional Movements

Our journey of togetherness has an epistemological dimension as well as ontological dimension but here epistemology is not one of conventional epistemology of certainty and ontology one of mastery. Our journey of togetherness here is related to contemporary post-epistemological movements which go beyond conventional epistemology and links epistemology to hermeneutics (Capurro, 2000). Post-epistemological movements are accompanied by transformations of conventional epistemology through movements such as practical epistemology[6] in which aesthetics plays an important role and virtue epistemology. In the last half century we have witnessed important moves beyond positivism and these post-positivist moves are discernible in linguistic, feminist and ecological turns (cf. Sunder Rajan 1998). But these post-positivist turns are not necessarily aware of the limits of the modernistic primacy of the epistemic and they need to acknowledge the link between epistemology and violence more head on. This then calls us to go beyond epistemology of violence and epistemology as violence in our relations and cultivate non-violence in relations and non-injury in modes of thinking.[7]

Post-epistemological movements are also accompanied by post-ontological movements which take ontology beyond the dualism of subjectivism and objectivity and make it part of a journey of love, care, labor and learning. In moves such as practical ontology characterized by love, labor and learning (cf. Dallmayr, 1987) and practical epistemology we find nurturing support for the interlinked movement of ontological epistemology of participation. Ontological epistemology of participation calls for a multi-valued logic of autonomy and interpenetration and an aesthetics of discovering threads of connections which helps us in our needed journey of the transpositonal, for example moving beyond our fixed positions of ontology and epistemology. Walking and meditating together with self and other calls for such movements.

Transpositional Movements

Transpositional movements build upon movements with and beyond positions and call for multi-dimensional transformative movements in both theory and practice. It calls for a new pragmatics of transpositionality and social communication where subjects from different positions come together and communicate with each other in a spirit of compassion and confrontation. It calls for a new poetics and aesthetics of transpositionality where poetics and aesthetics help us in border crossing between different positions. It also needs a new pragmatics of transpositionality as part of a new aesthetic ethics of responsibility which involves both ethical and aesthetic works, imaginations and meditations. It also calls for a new politics of transpositionality. Boaventuaara de Sousa Santos (2008), for example, talks about trans-conflictual moves while in forums such as World Social Forum participating organizations and individuals move beyond their positions with agreement, disagreement and an emergent trans-conflictual move.

In transpositional movements, there is creative and critical work of a different art of transpositional subjectivation as well as transpositional objectivation. Transpositional subjectivation builds on positional subjectivation which is different from positional subjectivity which is most of the time a positioned subjectivity. Positional subjectivation can be much more than positional subjectivity as it is not just a logic of reproduction. Transpositional subjectivation builds upon positional subjectivation. But our positions are embedded in socio-psychic structures of constitution. Our positions are embedded in psychic and social histories, many time in histories of production of domination, pain and suffering. Moving beyond such positional subjectivity thus calls for courage, *karuna* and mutual adventures. It also calls for transformative forgiveness, healing, reconciliation and forgetting. This is both an act of soul as well as creative institutional experimentation and constitution making in society which is part of transpositional subjectivation.

Like transpositional subjectivation, we also need transpositoinal objectivation. This builds upon both Bourdieu's concept of participant objectivation discussed earlier as well as Amartya Sen's idea of positional objectivity. For Sen, "[..] positionally dependent observations, beliefs, and actions are central to our knowledge and practical reason. The nature of objectivity in epistemology, decision theory and ethics has to take note of the parametric dependence of observation and observation on the position of the observer" (1994: 126). But the objectivity here is that of an observer but as co-walkers in our journey, we are not only observers but also participants but even beyond our conventional understanding of participation—we are co-walkers and co-meditators. Sen talks about the need for transpositional scrutiny but transpositioinal scrutiny is not adequate for the challenges at hand, we need to cultivate transpositinal movements. Sen talks about the need for positional objectivity but once the agents are not only observers but also participants the objectivity that emerges is not only objective but also intersubjective and transsubjective. So in our journey with self and other, we need to cultivate *transpositiona*l *subjectobjectivity*—one which emerges out of pluralization of the subjects, border-crossing transmutations among positions and transformative cultivation of the objective and the subjective including intersubjective and transubjective. It calls for transformation of the subjectivity and objectivity as we know including transformation of these from nouns to verbs-meditative verbs of pluralization. It also involves transformation of epistemological and the ontological including work of what I have elsewhere called ontological epistemology of participation and what Bruno Latour (2013) calls post-epistemological moves. But transpositional subjetobjectivity also calls for a new pragmatics of social communication, social dialogues and contestations. These are also part of our walking and meditating with self and other which is the ground of emergence of friendship.

Walking and meditating with self and other calls for experience of new wisdom about self and other as well as wisdom of relationship and the world. Transpositonal movements give birth to such wisdoms which help us in cultivating transformative friendship with self and the other.[8] Transformative friendship is different from acquiescent friendship where we just adjust to existing status quo even if it not expressing of creative potential of all concerned. In transformative friendship we challenge each other to be more truthful, giving and capacious and generous.

Transpositonal movements involve a new hermeneutics of self, culture and society where we walk and meditate with not only with self but also with the other. Building upon Raimundo Panikkar and Boaventuara de Sousa Santos, we can call this diatopical hermeneutics where we put one feet in one topoi and the other in another. But walking and meditating with self and other also needs to go beyond the double contingency of self and other and embrace the triple contingency and the multiple contingencies of the world. Hermeneutics here is thus multi-topial and such a multi-topial hemerneutics helps us in self-realizations, co-realizations and world realizations in creative ways.[9]

References

Beteille, Andre. (2009). "Sociology and Ideology." *Sociological Bulletin* 58 (2): 196-211.

Beteille, Andre. (2002). *Sociology: Essays on Approach and Method.* Delhi: Oxford U. Press.

Beteille, Andre. (1998). "Comparative Method and the Standpoint of the Investigator." *Sociological Bulletin* 47 (2): 137-154.

Bourdieu, Pierre. (1991). Political Ontology of Martin Heidegger. Cambridge: Polity Press.

Bourdieu, Pierre. (2003). "Participant Objectivation." *Journal of Royal Anthropological Institute* 9: 281-294.

Bussey, Marcus. (2000). "Tantra as Episteme." *Futures* 30 (7)

Capurro, R. (2000). "Hermeneutics and the Phenomenon of Information." In Metaphysics, Epistemology and Technology: Readings in Philosophy and Technology (ed.), C. Mitcham. New York: Elsevier.

Cornelissen, Matthjis. (2013). "What is Human Knowledge? A Reflection Based on the Work of Sri Aurobindo." *Sraddha* 5 (1): 85-114.

Dallmayr, Fred. (1987). *Critical Encounters: Between Philosophy and Politics.* Notre Dame: University of Notre Dame Press.

Fromm, Eric. (1950). *Man for Himself.* London: Routledge and Kegan Paul.

Foucault, Michel. 2005. *Hermeneutics of the Subject: Lectures at the College de France, 1981-82.* New York: Palgrave.

Giri, Ananta Kumar. (2012). *Sociology and Beyond: Windows and Horizons*. Jaipur: Rawat Publications.

Giri, Ananta Kumar. (2013). *Knowledge and Human Liberation: Towards Planetary Realizations*. London and Delhi: Anthem Press.

Habermas, Jurgen. (1990). Moral Consciousness and Communicative Action. Cambridge: Polity Press.

Parker Palmer & Arthur Zajone with Megan (2010), The Heart of Higher Education: A Call to Renewal, p. 107. San Franscisco: Jossey-Bass.

Sen, Amartya. (1994). "Positional Objectivity." *Philosophy & Public Affairs* 22 (2): 126-145.

Latour, Bruno. (2013). An Inquiry into Modes of Existence. Cambridge, MA: Harvard University Press."

Long, Stephen D. (2012). "Can (Analytic) Philosophers Tell Theologians the Truth? Richard Rotry and Methodological Nominalism." In Jacob L. Goodin & Brand Eliott Stone (eds.), *Rorty and the Religious: Christian Engagements with a Secular Philosopher*. Eugene, OR: Witts & Stock Publishers.

Patomaki, Heikki & Colin Wright. (2000). "After Postpositivism: The Promise of Critical Realism." *International Studies Quarterly* 44: 213-237.

Strydom, Piet. (2011). *Contemporary Critical Theory and Methodology*. London: Routledge.

Sri Aurobindo. 1962.Human Cycles. Pondicherry: Sri Aurobindo Ashram.

Sunder Rajan, R. (1998). *Beyond the Crises of European Sciences: New Beginnings*. Shimla: Indian Institute of Advanced Studies.

Tanesini, Alessandra. (2004). *Wittgenstein: A Feminist Approach*. Cambridge: Polity Press.

Vattimo, Gianni. (2011). *A Farewell to Truth*. New York: Columbia U. Press.

Notes

1 This is written in Bhagvad Gita. One can also read Paul Ricouer's *Oneself as Another* in a related way.

2 This resonates with Foucault's (2005) hermeneutics of the subject where to be a subject means to be critically reflective upon the models of individualization offered by the state.

3 These two may not be two separate birds; they may be two parts of the same bird—one part not only witnessing but meditating and the other eating which is a metaphor for engagement in action.

4 Strydom (2011) also draws our attention to foundational limitations of Bourdieu's approach to objectivity as he seems not to question dominant models and methods of science.

5 Vattimo (2011) writes: "I will use ontology in a sense I take from Heidegger for whom it denotes the thought of Being in both senses, subjective and objective, of the genitive. This is different from "most ontologists, who reduce ontology to a theory of objects. As for actuality, I use the term to refer to the common condition of our life at present." Vattimo (2011: 139-140) also links ontology of actuality to a quest for charity and solidarity:

> At the horizon line of the near future toward which we gaze, pragmatically assessing the utility of truth, there lies a more distant future that we can never really forget. Rorty alludes to this with the term solidarity, which I propose to read directly in the sense of charity, and

not just as the means of achieving consensus but as an end in itself. Christian dogma teaches that *Deus Caritas est*, charity is God himself. From a Hegelian viewpoint, we may take the horizon to be that absolute spirit which never allows itself to be entirely set aside but becomes the final horizon of history that legitimates all our near-term choices.

6 In his book, *Aesthetic Experience in Science Education*, Wickman tells us about practical epistemology in the following way:

> [..] Practical epistemology is not a description of how people should go about to find the right answers in life. Rather, it should be understood in a situated sense as a description of the actions usually used by people to deal with the events of life and to pursue their goals. [..] by calling it a practical epistemology , the intention is to stress that there are no cognitivist or deterministic assumptions made, and that the unit of analysis is not the individual mental capacities but the activities of individuals as participants in social practice (Wickman 2006: 52).
> Wickman also argues how practical epistemology has an aesthetic dimension as in the works of John Dewey and Leo Vygotsky.

7 Patomaki & Wright (2000) urge us to understand the link between epistemology and violence. Here what Alessandra Tanesini writes about Wittgenstein, feminism and epistemology shows us how feminist turn is still very much bound within the epistemic frame and it needs to be part of a transformative movement of ontological epistemology of participation: "In the *Tractatus* Wittgenstein does not characterize the notion of the subject in epistemic terms. The subject is not born out of the Cartesian search for certainty. Rather, it is the result of the need to transcend the contingent empirical world in order to create a place for meaning in one's lives. Recent feminist theorists, instead have often described the subject in epistemic terms" (Tanesini 2004: 55).

About linguistic turn, Stephen D. Long tells us that "[..] the methodological nominalism of the linguistic turn must be *exceeded*" (Long 2012: 34).

8 Elisabeth S. Fiorenza talks about wisdom emerging from dance of positions.

9 The vision and pathways of multi-*topial* hermeneutics builds upon the idea of *diatopical* hermeneutics proposed by Raimundo Panikkar. Building upon the seminal work of Raimundo Panikkar, Boaventuara de Sousa Santos elaborates *diatopical* hermeneutics thus: "The aim of *diatopical* hermeneutics is to maximize the awareness of the reciprocal incompleteness of cultures by engaging in a dialogue, as it were, with one foot in one culture and the other in another—hence its *diatopical* character. *Diatopical* hermeneutics is an exercise in reciprocity among cultures that consists in transforming the premises of argumentation in a given culture into intelligible and credible arguments in another" (2014: 92). Santos here talks about putting one's feet in cultures which resonates with my idea of footwork, footwork in landscapes of self, culture and society as part of creative research (cf. Giri 2012). Hermeneutics does not mean only reading of texts and cultures as texts but also foot-walking with texts and cultures as foot walks and foot works resonating with Heidegger calls a hermeneutics of *facticity* (cf. Mehta 2004). Santos talks about *diatopical* hermeneutics but this need not be confined to our feet only in two cultures; it needs to move beyond two cultures and embrace many cultures. Spiritual traditions also can help us realize that though we have physically two feet, we can realize that we have many feet. In the Vedas it is considered that Divine has million feet and similarly we can realize that humans also have million feet and with our million feet we can engage ourselves with not only creative foot work but also heart work (*Herzwerk* as it is called in German) in our acts of gathering of knowledge, self and the world. Supplementing Santos's *diatopical*

hermeneutics, we can cultivate *multi-topial* hermeneutics which is accompanied by a multi-valued logic of autonomy and interpenetration going beyond either-or logic. Art and aesthetics play an important role in both multi-topial hermeneutics and multi-valued logic as they help us to take gentle and careful artistic steps in difficult journeys across terrains and domains and making connections across fields usually constructed isolated and separate (see Giri, 2013).

24

Holistic Befriending of the Other in Buddhism

Noel Sheth, SJ
Prof (Emeritus), Jnana Deepa, Pune 411014

Abstract: Buddhist befriending is holistic: it befriends human beings, even enemies, and nature too. In Buddhism one befriends others, in all circumstances and without discrimination, whether they are friends or enemies, offenders and prisoners, the poor and the needy. It also includes other religions and cultures as well as nature. We find several examples in the Buddhist texts, in history and in the contemporary world. This befriending is done with an altruistic spirit, with forbearance, loving friendship and compassion. As in all religions, however, there are exceptions in the texts, in history and in the modern world. Still, overall, Buddhism has been more peace-loving and non-violent than several other religions. Buddhist and Christian befriending do resemble each other, e.g., both are opposed to malice and both go to the extent of loving one's enemy. Although there are similarities, there are also differences between Buddhism and Christianity with regard to the presuppositions, the cultivation, motivation and expression of befriending. While divergent world-views result in such differences, Buddhists, Christians and others need to hearken to the call of peace and altruistic love, to heal a broken world and build bridges of friendship and harmony with other human beings and with nature.

Keywords: Forbearance, Altruism, Enemies, Needy, Religions, Cultures, Nature

There are two forms of Buddhism, Hinayana and Mahayana. In Hinayana only one school is living, viz., Theravada, whose original texts are in the Pali language. In Mahayana there are many schools existing, and their original texts in India were in Sanskrit. Buddhist befriending is holistic: it befriends human beings, even enemies, and befriends nature too.

1. Befriending in the Buddhist Texts

A. *Befriending Other Human Beings*

a. Befriending Others in All Circumstances

In the Theravada scripture, the Buddha exhorts the disputatious monks of Kosambiya to live in mutual respect and harmony both in public and in private, asking them to be friendly in thought, word and deed, being united with one another in virtues as well as in their views.[1] A Theravada text declares that whoever bears enmity even to thieves who sever one's limbs, with a saw, does not carry out the teaching of the Buddha. Even in such a circumstance, one should not be harsh to the thieves or hate them, but rather one should be kind and compassionate and cultivate friendliness (*metta*) towards them as well as towards the whole world.[2] Mahayana texts exhort that one must forgive all types of offences (injury, insult, abuse, criticism), everywhere (in private and in public), at all times (past, present and future), in all circumstances (in sickness or health), in thought (not entertaining angry thoughts), word (not speaking harshly) and deed (not harming physically), without any exception (whether friend, enemy or indifferent person), and however wicked the offending person or however terrible the injury may be.[3]

In one of his previous lives as a Bodhisatta (in Sanskrit Bodhisattva),[4] Gotama (a Pali form corresponding to the Sanskrit Gautama) Buddha was born as Kundalakumara, who was later known as Khantivadi [Sanskrit Ksantivadin], i.e., "One who preached the doctrine of forbearance". Angry with Khantivadi, King Kalabu tested his forbearance, inflicting one agonizing torture after another. He first had him scourged all over his body, then had his hands and feet chopped off, and then his nose and ears cut off. Even though the king taunted him after every torment, Khantivadi never got angry, declaring himself to be a preacher and practitioner of forbearance. Finally, the king kicked him on his chest near the heart and walked off in a huff. The commander-in-chief requested Khantivadi to vent his wrath only on the king, but to spare the others and the kingdom. However, instead of taking revenge, Khantivadi uttered a blessing, "Long live the king!"[5]

We notice in such instances that the ideal is not even to feel anger or hatred even in the most trying circumstances. We could say that, strictly speaking, there is nothing to forgive, for there is no offence taken in the first place. The ideal seems to be a sort of stoic attitude of not being perturbed at all.

b. Befriending Others without Discrimination

I have elsewhere[6] shown how the Buddha endeavoured to reinterpret the caste system in terms of virtue and wisdom. Biologically, the human race is a single species: there is no distinction between the castes.[7]

The *Brahmanavagga* of the *Dhammapada* defines a Brahmin as one who has banished sin (*bahitapapo ti brahmano*).[8] The same *vagga* explains further that a person does not become a Brahmin through his family or birth, but by his virtuous life and deep knowledge. In the same vein, the *Vasalasutta* states that it is the wicked, ignorant and violent person who is an outcaste (*vasala*). It is not by birth (*jacca*) but by deeds (*kammuna*) that one becomes a Brahmin or an outcaste.[9] Thus the Buddha redefines caste in terms of ethical categories.

The Buddha's monastic Order (*sangha*) was open to all castes. There was no discrimination based on birth, occupation, social status or ritual purity. Women, however, were admitted by him only later – and that too, very reluctantly.

It may be remarked that the princely Buddha shows a preference for the Ksatriyas, for he maintains that they are superior to Brahmins, if one were to take lineage into consideration. He points out that a Ksatriya who has fallen into the deepest degradation is superior to a Brahmin who commits similar offences.[10] When the four castes are listed, the Ksatriyas are frequently mentioned before the Brahmins.[11] Is this a prejudice on the part of the Buddha, who was originally from the Ksatriya class, or of his disciples? Ultimately of course he does not put his trust in lineage. In the same *Ambatthasutta* where he makes the Ksatriya superior to the Brahmin, he makes it clear that it is the one who is perfect in wisdom and righteousness that is the best among deities and human beings.[12] In this context, it is unfortunate that the three *Nikayas*[13] among the monks in Sri Lanka are mostly based on caste differences.[14]

By stressing the equality of all castes and reinterpreting the caste system in ethical terms, the Buddha brought new hope and the experience of human dignity to the many Buddhist converts from the scheduled castes who, in their quest for psychological liberation from the shackles of casteism,[15] have followed Dr. Ambedkar[16] into the Buddhist fold.

We may mention in passing that, although there is no discrimination with respect to caste, sexist and other prejudices do survive in the Buddhist Scriptures in keeping with their times. Monks and nuns are superior to the laity, particularly in Theravada. Women are inferior to men; in the Order nuns are subordinate to the monks: e.g., a nun even of a hundred years standing must first salute a monk even if he is just ordained; she should never rebuke or abuse a monk; monks can admonish nuns, but not vice versa.[17] Still, it is worthy of note that the rights of the wife and of the employee (including wages, bonuses and leave) are emphasized.[18]

c. Befriending Enemies

In the Buddhist texts, one finds many reasons to motivate oneself to avoid resentment towards enemies. Buddhaghosa, a Theravada Buddhist, includes the following reasons in his *Visuddhimagga*: remembering the scriptural passages that exhort one to practise forbearance and avoid hatred, reflecting on the harmful effects of anger on oneself, developing compassion for one's enemies who will suffer in purgatories due to their succumbing to anger, recalling to mind the many examples of the Buddha, who in previous lives as a human adult or child and even as an animal did not entertain the slightest hatred towards his tormentors, reflecting that one's enemy may have been one's loving parents or brothers or sisters or sons or daughters in previous lives, realizing that the one with whom one is angry is not a substantial soul, but merely a series of momentary aggregates of various elements, and therefore one cannot make that person the target of one's anger.[19]

Similarly, Mahayana texts, too, try to motivate one to practise forgiveness. Firstly, one should follow the teaching and example of the Buddhas in forgiveness. The Buddhas will not forgive people unless they forgive others who offend them. Secondly, in reference to the person to be forgiven one may reflect in this manner: the present enemy may have been one's friend, relative, or teacher in a former birth. Since Mahayana Buddhism does not believe in a finite soul, strictly speaking, there is no perpetrator of injuries and insults, nor is any one injured or insulted.[20] All beings are evanescent and subject to pain and suffering, and so one should rather lighten their burden than be angry and unforgiving. The adversaries are conditioned by the results of their deeds (*karman*) in past lives, and are therefore not acting freely. Thirdly, one may also think with regard to oneself in the following vein: one is suffering insult and injury as a consequence of one's own evil deeds in previous existences; one's enemies are actually one's friends and beneficiaries for they preserve one from such worldly goods as wealth and fame, and give one the golden opportunity to practise forbearance, which leads to salvation. Fourthly, one should ponder over the ill effects of an angry and unforgiving attitude: it results in terrible punishments in various purgatories, and wipes out the merit one has gained through several lives. Hence, it is better to bear up with the comparatively negligible sufferings inflicted on one in this life than face terrible tortures in the future. Revenge always brings evil consequences on oneself. Being at peace with others results in great happiness to oneself. Often one is unforgiving because of pride, which needs to be replaced by the spirit of humble service. Finally, mercy and love urge us to forgive others.[21]

On occasion, the Buddha himself brings about reconciliation. In the Introduction to the *Kunalajataka*, it is reported that when the Koliya and Sakyan tribes were about to engage in a bloody battle over the right to the waters of the river Rohini, the Buddha persuaded them to desist from fighting by making them realize that there was no point in killing warriors of priceless value for the sake of some water that had comparatively little worth.[22] Not all, however, paid heed to the Buddha's mediations. He was unable to persuade the stubborn monk Tissa to ask forgiveness for not welcoming some visiting monks with respect and hospitality. Tissa was unforgiving because he was angry with those monks for having abused him for this fault of omission. In fact, in a previous life too he was not willing to ask pardon.[23]

d. Befriending Offenders and Prisoners

Unlike several Hindu texts that, in addition to expiation and reformatory punishment, also prescribe retributive and deterrent punishment, Theravada texts recommend punishment only after all other means of settling a dispute have been tried out, such as discussion, appeal to reason, repentance, etc., and even then, the punishment to be meted out is more on the milder and lighter side.[24] Theravada texts do not advocate capital punishment. So also, Mahayana texts are against capital punishment and amputation, and caution that, when punishment is to be administered, it should be with compassion.[25] Justice must be restorative, not retributive. It should also be clarified that, although justice in the near future is not always insisted upon, eventual justice will normally take place, for it is based on the law of *karman*; however, as in devotional Hinduism, divine beings in devotional Mahayana can forgive sins as well as wipe out, at least partially, the punishment due to sins.

e. Befriending Those in Need

Prompted by compassion, the Bodhisattvas give generously not only to relatives, friends and dependents, but also to all those who ask for help, to the poor, the pitiable, the beggars.[26] They give away not only external things like their house, spouses, children, etc., but they also part with their hands, feet, head, limbs, etc.; indeed, they sacrifice everything.[27] They even transfer their own merit to others for their welfare and wellbeing, both physical and spiritual, and even take upon themselves the sufferings of others.[28] They do all this and more at the appropriate time, with respect and the intention of promoting the welfare of all;[29] besides they do not expect anything in return.[30]

Both Theravada and Mahayana texts narrate hundreds of stories portraying the selfless and absolutely generous gifts of property, limb and life by men and women and even animals. Several texts, both in Theravada and in Mahayana, tell the story of the hare who, having no food, offers a guest his own flesh.[31] Similarly, both traditions narrate the story of King Sivi (Sanskrit Sibi) who became blind by donating his eyes.[32] The most famous story, again in both traditions, in this context of selfless and generous giving, is that of Vessantara (Sanskrit Visvantara) who, even after being banished by the king for his excessive generosity, gives away his horses and chariot, and even his children and wife.[33] A Sanskrit Hinayana text narrates the touching story of an extremely poor woman who gives away even the one piece of cloth that she was wearing.[34]

Mahayana texts emphasize compassion (*karuna*) towards others. I mention a couple of examples. After Vimalakirti accepted from Sudatta the pearl necklace, whose value was a hundred thousand (gold pieces), Vimalakirti divided it into two halves and gave one half to the poor of the town who were disdained by those who were present at the sacrifice offered by Sudatta earlier, and gave the other half to the Tathagata[35] Dusprasaha. Vimalakirti also declared that the donor who, without making any distinctions, impartially, and without expecting any recompense, donates gifts to the poor of the town, who are as worthy of the gifts as the Tathagata, performs the sacrifice completely.[36] Santideva exclaims, "May I relieve the sorrow of all beings, may I be the doctor and attendant of all who are ill, until disease does not arise. With rains of food and drink, may I destroy the agony of hunger and thirst. In the famine of the intermediary ages, may I be drink and food. May I be an imperishable storehouse for poor beings, and may I attend upon them with diverse means of subsistence. I sacrifice, without expectation, my own being, pleasures and auspicious things to accomplish the goal of all beings. Abandoning everything is Nirvana; if all has to be given up by me, it is best that it be given to beings. May I be a protector of the unprotected, the caravan leader for those on a journey, a boat, a bridge, a conduit for those who desire the further Shore. I would be a lamp for those seeking a lamp, a bed for those wishing to have a bed, a slave to those wanting a slave."[37]

In this context of compassion, we must particularly mention the most popular Bodhisattva Avalokitesvara or Padmapani, who is the very embodiment of compassion, and even goes to the worst purgatory and takes on the sufferings of the tormented beings there. Possibly, because of his great compassion, he became feminine in countries like China and Japan.

f. Befriending People of Other Religions

The Buddha declares that he did not preach the Buddhist religion (Sanskrit *Dharma*) in separate portions: one pertaining to the Disciples' Vehicle, another to the Vehicle of the Pratyeka-buddhas[38] and a third for the Mahayana. Whoever makes such distinctions is confused and rejects the true *Dharma* by describing it as divided.[39] Here no distinction is made between various Buddhist traditions.

In reference to other religions, the Buddha assures Nigrodha that, in wanting to teach the Buddhist religion (Pali *Dhamma*), he does not wish to get disciples for himself by alienating people of other religions from their teachers, rules, ways of life and right doctrines or by confirming them in their wrong views; all he intends is to help them get rid of things that cause corruption, suffering and rebirth.[40] At another time, the Buddha tells Dhammika that the one who reviles sages of other traditions who are self-composed and free from passion obtains great demerit (*apunna*).[41] It should be noted, however, that in the very next verse he adds that the one who reviles the Buddha's disciple who is accomplished in views (*ditthi-sampanna*), attains even greater demerit.

B. *Befriending Nature*

Gotama Buddha died of blood dysentery after eating a dish called *sukara-maddava* (soft pork).[42] Scholars have different opinions as to whether this *sukara* was pork or a vegetarian dish made from such items as a sprout or a mushroom, etc. However, the earliest Pali commentaries identify it as pork.[43] In the *Amagandhasutta* it is pointed out that destruction of life, cutting, binding, injustice, harshness, anger, envy, slander, injury, cruelty, disrespect, greed, hostility, etc. have the foul odour of rotting meat, but not so the eating of meat.[44] When Buddhist monks went on their begging rounds, they were expected to accept whatever was put into their begging bowls. Early Buddhists were therefore not strict vegetarians.[45] Nevertheless, in time Theravadins became increasingly vegetarian. A monk had to avoid eating animals that were seen or heard by him, or suspected to have been deliberately killed for him.[46] Theravada Buddhists should not be butchers, hunters and fisher folk, and should avoid any job that entails cruelty such as being an executioner or jailer. If they take up such occupations, they are tormentors of others.[47] Buddhism also reacted against the sacrificial killing of animals.[48]

Coming now to Mahayana, the eighth chapter of the *Saddharmalankavatarasutra* is wholly dedicated to making people turn away from meat-eating. Although a good part of the chapter is in reference to Bodhisattvas, it is clearly meant for all the Buddha's disciples (*sisya*). In contrast to the earlier exceptions made by Theravada texts, this *sutra* categorically states that it is not true that meat is permissible when it is not killed or caused to be killed by oneself and not deliberately prepared for oneself by another. It further asserts that, even though exceptions have been made here and there in canonical texts (*desanapatha*, lit. directive or instructional texts), in this *sutra* flesh is unconditionally forbidden for all, in whatever form, manner or place.[49] In most of the chapter it puts forward many reasons for avoiding non-vegetarian food. For example, given the fact that transmigration has been going on for a very long time, there cannot be any animal or bird who at one time or another has not been one's own mother or father or some other relative. How then can one bring oneself to eat a living being that is of the same nature as oneself? Flesh, which is born of semen, blood, etc., pollutes one's purity; it brings demerit, leads to rebirth as a carnivorous animal and in various demonic forms; it prevents knowledge, and is an obstacle to salvation (*moksa*). ~~nirvana)~~. Out of compassion we should refrain from consuming meat, for when an animal sees a meat-eater it is frightened for its life. Flesh has a foul smell even when burned, and spoils one's good name among noble (*arya*) people, whose food is vegetarian; meat-eating invites censure against Buddhism.[50] Looking upon all beings as our very own (child), we should refrain from devouring their flesh. Non-vegetarians suffer from disturbed sleep, terrible dreams and ill health. The consumption of meat successively results in pride, erroneous imagination, passion, delusion of the mind, and lack of liberation.

Buddhist texts are also against the unnecessary destruction of vegetative life. A monk should abstain from destroying the growth of seeds and vegetables.[51] The destruction of plant-life by monks is a *pacittiya* ("expiation")[52] type of offence, which requires confession.[53] Monks were of course permitted to eat vegetables, to use twigs to brush their teeth or to use herbal medicines.[54] The basic idea is to avoid unnecessary violence even to plant life and to develop sensitivity to the whole of nature. In fact, it is a *pacittiya* fault even to dig the earth or cause it to be dug:[55] this is in order to avoid doing violence to the living organisms and seeds in the earth.

2. Befriending in Buddhist History

A. *Asoka and Honen Befriending Enemies*

In the 13th Rock Edict, the Emperor Asoka publicly expresses his remorse and confesses how the carnage at Kalinga caused him great anguish. He also declares that he pardons, as far as it is possible, all those who have wronged him. He makes peace with the people living in the forests. He wishes all beings to be free from injury and to enjoy gentleness or joyousness.[56] He even took care to omit the 13th Edict from the texts carved on the rocks in Kalinga, lest even his words of repentance would serve as a spark to re-ignite adverse emotions in the Kalingas by reviving the memory of his fateful attack on their country.[57]

The father of Honen, the leader of the Japanese Jodo-shu school, was fatally wounded by a gang of robbers who attacked their home. On his deathbed, his father exhorted his son never to take revenge but rather to pray for the salvation of his father as well as of the attackers.[58]

B. *Befriending Other Cultures*

Already in India Buddhism assumed different forms, even though one kind may have been considered heretical by another. More importantly, when Buddhism spread to other countries in Asia, it took pains to inculturate itself into the different cultures it encountered, evolving into a wide variety of forms with differing beliefs and practices.

Perhaps there is no other world religion that has inculturated itself so much as Buddhism. Already from early times, Mahayana made efforts at translating its Scriptures into different languages. Sri Lankan Buddhists developed the practice of chanting the *Pirith* (chanting of *suttas* for the sake of protection), and participating in the Kandy Perahera, in which statutes of Hindu deities of four temples are carried in procession along with the reliquary of the Buddha's tooth. In Burma and Thailand, Buddhists venerate spirits called Nats and Phis respectively, and in both countries, it is the custom for every male to spend some time living the life of a monk. Chinese Buddhism integrated Taoist mythology, and emphasized nature mysticism and faith. Techniques of *wen-ta* (question and answer) and *kung-an* ("riddles") were developed to help achieve liberation (*tun-wu*). In Japan the Tendai school, which synthesized Mahayana and Theravada, reinterpreted ordination as a sacrament. The Jodo schools of Honen and Shinran emphasized faith much more than the corresponding Chinese Ching-t'u school. Zen integrated secular arts like archery and sword-fencing. It went further than China in developing still more the use of "riddles" (*koan*) and in cultivating a greater closeness to nature, manifested, for instance, in bamboo and rock gardens. Although initially Buddhism criticized the religions of Tibet as primitive and barbarous, it soon developed a uniquely Tibetan genre. It adopted the use of prayer-wheels, prayer-flags and prayer-walls, as well as trances and masked dances. Faith in the lama (*blama*) or *guru* was of the utmost importance. Also characteristic of Tibetan Buddhism is the belief in incarnation lamas. For example, the Dalai Lama is the indirect descent of the *Bodhisattva* Avalokitesvara and the Panchen Lama is the indirect descent of the Buddha Amitabha.

Thus Buddhism did not confine itself to one culture. Its openness, universal outlook and respect for pluralism enabled it to inculturate itself deeply in different cultures. It should be noted that in spite of the two main divisions of Buddhism acculturating themselves to different cultures, each still preserves a certain basic unity. The various Mahayana schools, which have incarnated themselves much more than Theravada, display a wide divergence in practices, rituals, meditational techniques, etc.; however, they differ but little in their philosophical or theological understanding of reality. In this way, each branch of Buddhism is able to maintain a unique unity in diversity.

C. *Befriending Nature*

In his 5th Pillar Edict King Asoka exempted several animals from slaughter, e.g., parrots, geese, swans, bats, boneless fish, etc., and certain animals when they were pregnant. He also prohibited the killing of fish and certain animals on particular auspicious days.[59] In his 1st Rock Edict he forbade the sacrifice of all animals in his palace. Formerly very many living beings were killed daily for his table; but he decreed that only three would be slain: two peacocks and one deer, and the latter would not be killed invariably. In fact, he said, even these would not be slaughtered in the future.[60]

In Theravada there developed the practice of setting up sanctuaries for birds and animals as well as tanks for fish, where they could move about freely without being hunted or caught. This was called *abhaya-dana* (the gift of fearlessness).[61]

Similar to the case of Theravada, the custom, and even ceremony, of freeing living creatures arose in Mahayana too. It consisted in purchasing birds, animals and fish that had been captured, and setting them free in their own habitats. In China and Japan, too, different kings prohibited the eating of meat and advocated non-violence towards animals, birds and fish.[62] It should be noted, however, that some Mahayana schools are non-vegetarian, while Theravada is vegetarian.

3. Contemporary Examples of Befriending

A. *Befriending Other Human Beings*

I shall first give some instances of modern Theravada Buddhists and then move on to present-day Mahayana Buddhists.

a. Ariyaratne of Sri Lanka

Dr. Ahangamage Tudor Ariyaratne of Sri Lanka started his Sarvodaya (Uplift or Awakening of All) Sramadana (Donation of Labour) Movement in Sri Lanka between 1956 and 1958,[63] and nurtured it for many years. Basing himself on traditional Theravada principles and also reinterpreting some of them to give them a social thrust, he set up volunteer work camps for social upliftment. Ariyaratne's Sarvodaya catered to ten fundamental needs of society: a pure and attractive environment, sufficient supply of pure water, basic requirements of clothing, an adequate diet, simple residential facilities, basic health services, communication infrastructure, fuel and other energy needs, a comprehensive education for daily living, and cultural and spiritual development.[64] In every village Sarvodaya tried to set up six groups: pre-school toddlers, schoolchildren, mothers, youth, farmers, and the elderly. Each of these groups is conscientized and helped to participate, in varying degrees, in a holistic and all-round development of the village.[65]

Although Ariyaratne is Sinhalese, he extended his hand of friendship and collaboration to the Tamil Hindus in Sri Lanka. His Sarvodaya played an important role as peace builder in the severe ethnic conflicts of Sri Lanka. It analysed the causes of the conflicts, worked out comprehensive programmes to resolve the problems in a humane manner, encouraged Sinhalese and Tamilians to work together as volunteers in each other's villages, organized peace meditations, peace camps, peace pilgrimages and marches, and peace meetings and conferences; initiated ways and means for the return and rehabilitation of refugees; and, for both the militants and the armed forces, to lay down their arms and return to civilian life, through techniques of inner transformation.[66] Although Sarvodaya was a Buddhist movement, it was open to others: Tamilians (many of whom were Hindus) too played important leadership roles in Sarvodaya peace initiatives. Tamilians who collaborated with Sarvodaya looked upon it not so much as a Sinhalese Buddhist organization, but a Sri Lankan association. In 1994 Ariyaratne met leaders of the LTTE, in an attempt to bring about reconciliation and peace.[67]

b. Uttarananda of Sri Lanka

The Sri Lankan monk H. Uttarananda, who was a member of the now defunct Humanist Bhikkhus'[68]Association (*Manava-hitavadi Bhikkhu Sangamaya*), proposed a Buddhist-Humanist view of the national ethnic problem in Sri Lanka. Following the typical Buddhist "middle path", he wanted to avoid the two extremes of a Sinhala Buddhist State and a free Eelam State. He acknowledged the inhuman atrocities perpetrated on Tamils in 1983 and thereafter by racist fanatics and governments, and was able to sympathetically understand the exasperated violent reactions of Tamils whose pent up rage boiled over due to the prolonged racist attitudes of successive governments. He called for reconciliation and strengthening of racial unity and peace.[69]

c. The Four Mahanayakes or Patriarchs of Sri Lanka

In a Press Conference in Tokyo on 3rd June 2002, the four Mahanayakes or "Patriarchs" of the Theravada Buddhist Order of Sri Lanka publicly released a Press Statement, which declared that the Order was for peace and development in Sri Lanka and solicited the support of the Japanese people in the peace process and in confidence-building measures which would benefit all three communities affected by the war, viz., the Sinhalese, the Tamils and the Muslims.[70] The Sri Lankan newspaper *The Island* reported that the Mahanayake of Asgiriya conferred his blessings on both the UNP Government of Ranil Wickremansinghe as well as the LTTE in their efforts to restore peace through peace talks held in Thailand.[71]

d. Sulak Sivaraksa of Thailand

Sulak Sivaraksa of Thailand is, on the one hand, rooted in the Buddhist Scripture. On the other hand, he frequently reinterprets traditional texts and doctrines to give them an explicit social and developmental orientation.

Sivaraksa founded a number of social welfare organizations or voluntary Non-Governmental Organizations (NGOs), in which people work with dedication for the uplift of the poor, both in the villages and the cities. Inspired by spiritual principles, they reach out to those in need – exploited men, women and children – and help them, through non-violent means, to regain their human dignity and stand on their own feet. They also pay attention to ecology and the environment: they work for integral and sustainable development.[72]

What is particularly notable is that Sivaraksa also engages in interreligious dialogue and cooperative interreligious social action for development. He started the Thai Interreligious Commission for Development. He also participated in the World Conference on Religion and Peace in Melbourne. He collaborated with a number of Catholic and Protestant development organizations in different parts of the world. He mentions several dialogue meetings with Christians, where all were equal, challenging one another in friendship, and working together for social uplift. Over many years, he was able to build bonds of friendship with individual Buddhists of other traditions, as well as with Christians, Jews, Muslims and Hindus in different parts of the world.[73]

e. The Late Maha Ghosananda of Thailand

In war-torn Cambodia, the late Maha Ghosananda of Thailand, five-time Nobel Peace Prize nominee, led nine *Dhammayietras* [Khmer or Cambodian for the Sanskrit *Dharmayatras*] or Pilgrimages of Truth to promote peace between rival Cambodian groups. Often opponents met and walked together in the spirit of reconciliation. In his first *Dhammayietra*, he preached repeatedly, "The suffering of Cambodia has been deep. From this suffering comes Great Compassion. Great Compassion makes a peaceful heart. A peaceful heart makes a peaceful person. A peaceful person makes a peaceful family. A peaceful family makes a peaceful community. A peaceful community makes a peaceful nation. A peaceful nation makes a peaceful world".[74] When, returning from his monastery in Thailand, he paid his first visit to the Sakeo Cambodian refugee camp, he distributed copies of the *Mettasutta*, a Buddhist Theravada scriptural text on loving kindness or friendship, and exhorted the refugees to forgive their persecutors.[75] A leader of the Khmer Rouge[76] requested Maha Ghosananda to visit Thailand and build a Buddhist temple on the border of Cambodia, and the latter readily agreed. Many were scandalized that he was helping an "enemy". However, he pointed out that love did not discriminate between good or bad; in fact, it was those who were deviants who needed loving kindness all the more because, often enough, virtue vanished from them because they did not experience the warmth of empathy from others. Quoting Mahatma Gandhi, he said that reconciliation consisted in destroying enmity, not enemies; loving kindness removed ignorance from adversaries as well as from us: we all needed to be freed.[77]

f. Aung San Suu Kyi of Myanmar

Nobel Laureate, Aung San Suu Kyi of Myanmar was at a public rally at the Shwedagon Pagoda in 1998. She appealed to the people to let bygones be bygones, to manifest their innate ability to forgive, not to abandon their traditional love for the armed forces and to resort to peaceful means of walking hand in hand with the authorities to build a united Burma.[78] When she was freed in 1995, after six years of house arrest by the military, and that, too, in spite of a landslide victory of her party, she expressed appreciation for the conciliatory tenor of the announcement of release by her captors, and highlighted the need for dialogue rather than confrontation for the restoration of peace. She declared that she did not harbour any bitterness against anyone for the treatment she received during those six long years.[79]

g. *The Dalai Lama of Tibet*

Let me now turn to Mahayana examples. Relying on Mahayana principles, the Dalai Lama, who was awarded the Nobel Peace Prize, has been advocating social responsibility and concern for nature. He has always embraced the policy of peaceful resistance to the Chinese, who occupied Tibet in 1950. He refers to the Chinese as his brothers and sisters and is motivated by tolerance, compassion and love. While wanting autonomy, he admits the fact that Tibet would continue to be linked with China.[80] In his Nobel Peace Prize Lecture, in speaking of the atrocities committed by the Chinese against Tibetans and their country and culture, he said that he did not speak with a heart filled with hatred or anger against the Chinese for, he added, they too were human beings striving for happiness and were entitled to compassion.

Elsewhere he also points out that enemies are valuable because they help us to advance in spiritual qualities such as forbearance and mental fortitude. He admits that, had he stayed in Lhasa, he might have been isolated and conservative. Hence, he is indebted to the Chinese since his exile helped broaden his perspectives. He felt very sad that Tibetans were infuriated against the Chinese and took part in burning Chinese vehicles.[81] His purpose in narrating the trials and tribulations of the Tibetan people was not out of vindictiveness or hostility towards the Chinese, but in order to inform the public. He also felt that many well-meaning Chinese were simply not aware of what was going on in Tibet.[82]

The Dalai Lama admits, however, that when people exploit the sincerity of a person, it may be necessary to retort. However, although on the surface level an apt reaction is resorted to, there should be an underlying spirit of forbearance, compassion and tolerance, without bearing any ill feelings.[83] Our real enemies are not outside us but inside us, e.g., arrogance, wrath and envy, and we have to wage a war against these internal foes.[84] World peace cannot be achieved without realizing that we are all sisters and brothers, and without cultivating kindness and compassion. However, this is not possible without inner transformation.[85]

h. Thich Nhat Hahn of Vietnam

The Vietnamese monk Thich Nhat Hanh did not bear any hatred towards the Catholic Diem regime that persecuted him, nor to the Viet Cong or the U.S. soldiers who attacked Vietnam. He could find excuses for the atrocities perpetrated by U.S. soldiers in Vietnam, attributing these to their hard life in the swamps and jungles infested by mosquitoes and other insects, and to their being in constant danger of death. Although initially angry, he did not blame a sea-pirate who had raped a twelve-year old girl, thinking that if he had had the same historical, economic and educational background as that pirate he would probably have behaved in the same way. This attitude of Thich Nhat Hanh is based on the Buddhist doctrine of Dependent or Conditioned Co-production (*pratitya-samutpada*; Pali *patticca-saumuppada*), according to which no being or event arises without a conditioning factor: this (resulting) being or event is because that (preceding) being or event is; this (resulting) being or event is not because that (preceding) being or event is not.[86] It thus helps the Buddhist to pay attention to attenuating circumstances, and hence be more understanding and forgiving.

B. *Befriending Nature*

A number of Theravada monks in Thailand are giving leadership in befriending nature. Phrakhru Manas Natheepitak, the abbot of Wat Bodharma, is said to be the first who came up with the novel idea of a ceremony that he called Tree Ordination, in which trees are wrapped in the saffron robes of Theravada monks. Many other monks follow this practice. When people see the saffron robes wrapped around the trees, they refrain from felling the trees. Similarly, another monk, Phrakhru Pitak Nanthakun, in addition to a more elaborate Tree Ordination ceremony, also instituted a ritual for sanctifying the river Nan, an important river in Thailand. This ceremony is modelled on a traditional rite for lengthening the life span of human beings and domestic animals. He, and other monks after him, have conducted this ceremony on different occasions and have reserved certain parts of the river as safe havens for fish so that fish can multiply without human interference.[87]

The Mahayana Buddhist country of Bhutan has a law that 60% of its land would be covered forever with forests. The King and Queen of Bhutan announced the birth of their first child on 5th February 2016. On 6th March 2016 the entire nation celebrated the prince's birth by planting 108000 saplings.[88] In June 2015, a team of 100 volunteers planted 49672 saplings in one hour, setting a Guinness record.[89]

4. Befriending Others with Friendship and Compassion

Buddhists approach all forms of befriending, of humans as well as nature, in the spirit of friendship (Pali *metta*; Sanskrit *maitri*) and compassion (*karuna*). They are two of the four Buddhist virtues called *Brahma-viharas* (Sublime States or Abidings); the third *Brahma-vihara* is joy (*mudita*) and the fourth is equanimity (Pali *upekkha*; Sanskrit *upeksa*). While Theravada gives more importance to friendship, Mahayana emphasizes compassion more. All the four Sublime States are to be cultivated or developed through meditation.

In Theravada friendship essentially consists in the wish that all beings may be happy. Just as a mother would protect her only child at the risk of her own life, even so one should cultivate unlimited love towards all beings.[90] In Mahayana friendship is a love that consists in the hope, prayer, keen desire for, and joy at, the happiness of others, without passion and the seeking of reward. It is of three kinds depending on whether it is directed towards living beings, phenomena (*dharma*) or no particular object.[91] Hence, both in Theravada as well as in Mahayana, friendship is altruistic love, and therefore *metta* or *maitri* is also translated as loving kindness.

Compassion includes all altruistic aspects of love. Bodhisattvas feel compassion for living beings like a father for his dear and only son.[92] The wise love all beings more than themselves, or their spouses, children, friends and relatives.[93] Tormented by the sufferings of others, the compassionate ones do not look for their own happiness.[94] Bodhisattvas desire enlightenment first for all beings and not for themselves.[95] In some passages, we notice that the Bodhisattvas act for the benefit of others (*para*) as well as themselves (*atman*).[96] However, in some other passages, we find that the texts speak only of the good of others, and not love for oneself,[97] thus emphasizing altruism much more.

5. Exceptions

As in all religions, in Buddhism too, there is doubtless a gap between the ideal and the existential. Here are a few instances:

A. *In the Texts*

In the Theravada Scripture, the Buddha asserts that no Ajivaka[98] has ever brought suffering to an end [i.e., attained liberation]; nay, in the ninety-one aeons (*kappa*) that he remembers, he does not know of any Ajivaka who reached even the temporary heaven (*sagga*), except one – but he was a believer in *karman* [i.e., he was not an orthodox Ajivaka].[99]

In a Mahayana scriptural text, it is said that those who scorn, and do not have faith in a *sutra* like the *Saddharmapundarikasutra* are destined to fall into Avici (the lowest level of purgatory), and to suffer many other torments, diseases, ill-treatment, etc. In fact, even a whole aeon (*kalpa*) is not enough to enumerate such a person's countless ills.[100]

One of the chronicles of Sri Lanka, the *Mahavamsa*, often portrays the island's Tamilians as enemies of the Sinhalese. Even though he had conquered King Elara, King Dutthagamani was disconsolate for he realized that he had slaughtered millions in the battle. But some Arahants[101] consoled him by telling him that this action of his would not prevent him from attaining a temporary heaven. He had killed only one and a half human beings, i.e., those who had declared themselves to be Buddhists, fully or partially. The rest were unbelievers and immoral, not worth any more than mere animals. He would bring glory to Buddhism and so should not let his heart be troubled.[102]

B. *In History*

In Sri Lanka, a Theravada king seized a Mahayana monastery and burnt its scriptural texts.[103] In Burma King Anuruddha (Anawratha) of Punnagama (Pagan) attacked the kingdom of Sudhammapura (Thaton) in order to seize a copy of the Scriptures and the relics of the Buddha, which King Manohari (Manuha) had refused to send him when requested to do so.[104]

The Mahayana Tibetan Dge-lugs-pa (Gelugpa) school – the Dalai Lama belongs to this group – often persecuted other Buddhist schools, attacking and destroying their monasteries and books. Tibetan Buddhists fought many wars against each other.[105] In Japan the monk Nichiren (1222-1282), who founded the militant, nationalistic Mahayana school called Nichirenshu,[106] launched a vituperative attack on all other Buddhist schools, denouncing them as heretics and holding them responsible for the many natural calamities and political troubles of Japan: "Nembutsu is hell; the Zen are devils; Shingon is national ruin; and the Risshu are traitors to the country."[107] From the sixteenth century right up to the beginning of the twentieth century, the Buddhists rabidly persecuted Shamanism in Mongolia: images and other sacred objects were destroyed and shamans were burnt alive or forced to renounce their faith.[108] In the face of such facts, the assertion of Rahula Walpola,[109] viz., that Buddhism had never persecuted or caused bloodshed in converting others and propagating its faith, will have to be modified.

C. *In Modern Times*

In the ethnic conflicts in Sri Lanka between the Sinhalese and Tamilians, there were nation-wide riots and massacres; temples were destroyed and images were desecrated. It is reported that, even in the refugee camps for Tamilians, there are many atrocities against them. At present, Buddhist nationalist groups in Sri Lanka, of which the Bodu Bala Sena (Buddhist Power Army) or BBS and Sinhala Ravaya (Sinhalese Roar) are the most prominent, are leading a hate campaign against people of other religions and doing violence to them. In

Myanmar monks played a part in the terrible Buddhist-Muslim riots of 1938. In the Great Recital of the Pali Canon in Burma (Myanmar) in 1954, monks who were not Theravadins were considered as lay people and given lower seats among the laity.[110]

In more recent times the military junta in Myanmar displayed a violent attitude to Aung San Suu Kyi and perpetrated various atrocities on people, such as rape, torture and forced labour. At present, there is widespread persecution of Rohingya Muslims by Buddhists in Myanmar. In Cambodia, Pol Pot[111] and the Khmer Rouge committed extensive genocide.

Let us now mention a couple of examples from Mahayana. The Japanese imperialism and its atrocities, especially in the initial years of their colonial rule in Korea, are well known. Koreans were coerced to work in Japanese factories or drafted as soldiers and sent to the front. Thousands of Korean women were recruited as "comfort women", virtually as sexual slaves for Japanese soldiers. The Japanese attempted to force Korean Buddhism to merge with Japanese forms of Buddhism. They also advocated the practice of married monks. Later, within Korean Buddhism itself, there was a schism on the issue of married versus celibate monks. The conflict between these two rival groups of monks, which also included physical violence, has a long and chequered history in Korea.[112] In spite of the Dalai Lama's plea for non-violence, Tibetans, including monks, have been reacting violently against the Chinese regime.

Certainly, the peace-loving, gentle and broad-minded Buddha would not have approved of such fundamentalist, intolerant and belligerent actions on the part of his followers. Sincere Buddhists will deplore the many forms of Buddhist intolerance. However, Buddhism has shown itself more peace-loving than several other religions. The historian Toynbee wrote, "The three Judaic religions[113] have a record of intolerance, hatred, malice, uncharitableness and persecution that is black by comparison with Buddhism's record."[114] Still, Buddhism must once again hearken to the call of the Buddha for friendship, to forget narrowmindedness, go beyond bigotry, and embrace the other in selfless altruism.

6. Comparison with Christian Befriending

Buddhist and Christian befriending do resemble each other, e.g., both are opposed to malice and both go to the extent of loving one's enemy. However, there are many important differences, springing from their different world-views. Christians forgive others because otherwise God will not forgive them.[115] But Theravada Buddhism does not admit any Supreme Being; hence the motivation is not the same. In Theravada, charity begins at home: one loves or practises friendliness first towards oneself; only then can one extend friendliness towards others.

In Christianity, the person befriended has intrinsic worth: the person is a child of God and has an immortal soul. In Theravada, on the other hand, the one who is befriended is neither created by a God nor has a soul: each individual is just a series of momentary aggregates, subject to the law of *kamma* [Sanskrit *karman*] (results of past deeds), and therefore does not have intrinsic worth, but should still be befriended. In Mahayana the human being has even less worth, for the individual does not exist even for one moment; only the Adi (First) Buddha, one of the technical terms for the Supreme and Only Being, exists. Yet, paradoxically, the ideal is to unilaterally befriend others who do not really exist even for a moment, except on the level of ignorance and from the practical point of view. In a sense, according to the doctrine of dependent co-production, dependence exists – which, in modern times, is further interpreted even as interdependence or a sort of interrelatedness – but individuals do not exist. Moreover, the interrelatedness in the Mahayana world-view is on the ontological level; ultimately there is absolute identity. As a result, while in Christianity one concentrates on overcoming differences between alienated people, in Mahayana one transcends these differences. Hence in Mahayana one can more easily identify oneself even with the oppressor.

While the cultivation and expression of Christian friendship is, in some measure, spontaneous, personal, and generally emotional, Theravada befriending, even if it comes naturally in the case of those who have attained perfection in it, is developed through a systematic, calculated method and expressed in a more impersonal, detached and emotionally more sedate manner.

Christian befriending is based on the inter-personal, communitarian world-view. In Theravada on the other hand, one can only do good or harm to oneself, for each one is reaping the fruits of one's own past deeds (Pali *kamma* or Sanskrit *karman*). One can help another only indirectly by one's example, by trying not to provoke resentment and anger in others and by the tranquil, detached vibrations of friendship (*metta*) sent out in different directions. Disagreeing with an acrobat, his apprentice pointed out that they would perform their act successfully not by watching out for each other but by each one watching out for himself.[116]

In Christianity, it is often said that God will not forgive us unless we forgive others. In Mahayana, too, the Buddhas will not forgive people unless they forgive others. However, it should be noted that even here there are differences. For example, it is not the Buddhas and Bodhisattvas who are the highest, but it is the Adi Buddha that is the Supreme Being. The dealings of the Mahayana Buddhists, however, are with the former.

The Buddhist doctrine of reincarnation motivates one to forgive and be reconciled, but Christianity does not believe in rebirth. On the other hand, for Christianity the person has intrinsic worth, but this is not the case with

Buddhism. Hence the motivation for practising forgiveness and reconciliation is also different in the two traditions.

Unlike Christian befriending, Buddhist befriending is more universal, since it is extended also to nature and not just to human beings. However, possibly due to influence from Buddhism and other Eastern religions, and with a growing awareness of the environment in the West, modern Christianity is moving in the direction of befriending nature too and even making restitution by efforts to heal the earth and by recognizing the rights of animals and plants.

One of the practical differences between Christianity and Buddhism is that Buddhism prescribes meditational techniques to help one develop a befriending disposition: merely making a good resolution is not enough. Christianity, on the other hand, only exhorts people to befriend, forgive and be reconciled, but there are no methods or techniques that enable people to become more befriending and forgiving and more reconciled.

Thus, we see that, while there are similarities in befriending between Christianity and Buddhism, there are many distinctions arising from the divergent world-views not only of Christianity but also of Theravada and Mahayana. These differences are found not only with regard to the presuppositions, but also in reference to the motivation as well as the expression of befriending.

While granting that divergent world-views result in differences with regard to the nature, motivation and expression of befriending, Buddhists, Christians and others need to hearken to the call of peace and altruistic love, to heal a broken world and build bridges of friendship and harmony.

Notes

1 *Kosambiyasutta*, in *Majjhimanikaya*, pt I, 48, p. 393ff. Unless otherwise stated, all references to the Buddhist Sanskrit texts cited by me are to the Darbhanga ed., published by the Mithila Institute, Bihar. However, references to the *Dhammapada-atthakatha* and the *Jataka-atthakatha* are from the Dhammagiri edition published by the Vipassana Research Institute, Igatpuri, Maharashtra.

2 *Kakacupamasutta*, in *Majjhimanikaya*, pt I, 21.5.20, pp. 172-173.

3 See the texts cited in Har Dayal, *The Bodhisattva Doctrine in Buddhist Sanskrit Literature* (London: Kegan Paul, Trench, Trubner and Co., 1932), pp. 209-210.

4 In Theravada, the term Bodhisatta (Pali form of the word) generally refers to Gotama Buddha in a previous life before he became enlightened. In Mahayana Bodhisattvas (Sanskrit form of the term) are special beings who delay their salvation for the sake of helping others, take on the sufferings of others, transfer their merits to them and give them grace: see *ACPI [Association of Christian Philosophers of India] Encyclopedia of Philosophy*, 2010, s.v. "Bodhisattva", by Noel Sheth, S.J., vol. I, pp. 183-187.

5 *Khantivadijatakavannana*, in *Jataka-atthakatha*, 4.2.3, No. 313, vol. 72, pp. 34-37. A Sanskrit version is found in the *Ksantijataka* in the *Jatakamala*, 28, pp. 189ff. Unless otherwise stated, all references to the Buddhist Sanskrit texts are from the Bauddha-Samskrta-Granthavali edition, published by the Mithila Institute of Post-graduate Studies and Research in Sanskrit Learning, Darbhanga, Bihar.

6 Noel Sheth, "The Buddha's Attitude to Caste", *Negations* 4 (October-December, 1982): 23-26.

7 *Assalayanasutta*, in *Majjhimanikaya*, pt II, 43, pp. 403-413; and *Vasetthasutta*, in *Majjhimanikaya*, pt II, 48, pp. 462-468.

8 *Dhammapada*, v. 388, in *Khuddakanikaya*, pt I, p. 54.

9 *Vasalasutta* of *Suttanipata*, 1.7, in *Khuddakanikaya*, pt I, pp. 287-290.

10 *Ambatthasutta*, in *Dighanikaya*, pt I, 3.6, pp. 84-86.

11 On Ksatriya claims to superiority, see G. S. Ghurye, *Caste and Class in India* (Bombay: The Popular Book Depot, 1950), pp. 71-72.

12 *Dighanikaya*, pt I, 3.6, p. 86.

13 These are monastic lineages or fraternities.

14 Anthony Fernando, "Contemporary Buddhism in Sri Lanka (Ceylon)" in Dumoulin and Maraldo, eds., *Buddhism in the Modern World* (New York: MacMillan and Co., 1976), p. 66.

15 Adele M. Fiske, "Caste among the Buddhists", in Harjinder Singh, ed., *Caste among Non-Hindus in India* (New Delhi: National Publishing House, 1977), pp. 102-103.

16 See his "Caste in India", and "Annihilation of Caste", in Dr. Babasaheb Ambedkar, *Writings and Speeches*, vol. 1 (Bombay: The Education Dept., Government of Maharashtra, 1979), pp. 5-96.

17 *Gotamisutta*, in *Anguttaranikaya*, pt III, 8.6.1, pp. 370-371.

18 *Singalasutta*, in *Dighanikaya*, pt III, 8.5.28 and 30, pp. 146-147.

19 *Visuddhimagga*, 9.15-38; see Nyanamoli, *The Path of Purification* (*Visuddhimagga*), 2nd ed. (Colombo: A. Semage, 1964), pp. 324-332.

20 It is interesting to note the contrary case in the Hindu *Bhagavadgita* (2.19), where Krishna urges Arjuna to fight against the Kauravas since the soul – which constitutes the essence of a person and is inactive – is neither a slayer nor is slain.

21 See the texts cited in Dayal, *Bodhisattva Doctrine*, pp. 210-212.

22 *Kunalajatakavannana*, in *Jataka-atthakatha*, 5.21.4, No. 536, vol. 74, pp. 408-410.

23 *Tissatheravatthu*, in *Dhammapada-atthakatha*, 1.3, pt I, vol.50, pp. 25-29; see Burlingame, *Buddhist Legends*, pt I, pp. 166-170.

24 Unto Tahtinen, *Ahimsa*: *Nonviolence in Indian Tradition* (London: Rider and Co., 1976), pp. 102-103.

25 *Encyclopedia of Buddhism*, ed. G. P. Malalasekera and others, s.v. "*Ahimsa*", by Hirakawa, vol. 1, p. 291.

26 *Jatakamala*, 31, vv. 63 and 65, pp. 227-228; 3, p. 16, lines 16-17.

27 *Siksasamuccaya*, 1.4, p. 16, lines 2-5.

28 *Bodhicaryavatara*, with the *Panjika* Commentary, 10, pp. 283-287

29 *Jatakamala*, 25, v. 29, p. 173.

30 *Mahayanasutralankara*, 19, v. 28, p. 158; *Siksasamuccaya*, 7.14, p. 81, lines 16-17. Note that, in addition to this high selfless ideal, some texts do mention other less lofty motives, such as fame, merit, rebirth in a better state, etc.

31 *Jataka-atthakatha*, 4.2.6, No. 316, vol. 72, pp. 44-47; *Jatakamala*, 6, pp. 30-35.

32 *Jataka-atthakatha*, 15.3, No. 499, vol. 73, pp. 359-370; *Avadanasataka*, 34, pp. 83-85; *Jatakamala* 2, pp. 7-15.

33 *Jataka-atthakatha*, 22.10, No. 547, vol. 76, pp. 227-381; *Jatakamala*, 9, pp. 55-69; *Bodhisattvavadanakalpalata*, 23, pp. 172-175.

34 *Avadanasataka*, 55, p. 140.

35 An epithet of any Buddha, but commonly used as an epithet of Gautama Buddha. The word is generally interpreted as "one who has thus (*tatha*) either gone (*gata*) or come (*agata*)".

36 L'Enseignement de Vimalakirti (*Vimalakirtinirdesa*), tr. and annotated by Etienne Lamotte, Bibliotheque du Museon, vol. 51 (Louvain: Publications Universitaires, 1962), pp. 216-217.

37 Santideva, *Bodhicaryavatara*, ed. by Vidhushekhara Bhattacharya, Bibliotheca Indica: A Collection of Oriental Works, Work 280, Issue 1580 (Calcutta: The Asiatic Society, 1960), III, vv. 6-11, 17-18, pp. 31-34.

38 In Theravada (Pali *Pacceka-buddha*), they attain liberation by their own effort but do not teach others; in Mahayana (Sanskrit *Pratyeka-buddha*) they do not teach others in the normal way, but do so through thought-transference. However, both in Theravada as well as in Mahayana, they are inferior to Buddhas and, in Mahayana, where the ideal is to become a Bodhisattva, they are also inferior to Bodhisattvas who, unlike Pratyeka-Buddhas, delay their own salvation for the sake of helping others to attain salvation.

39 *Siksasamuccaya*, 4.7, p. 56.

40 *Dighanikaya*, pt III, 2.8.27, p. 44.

41 *Dhammikasutta*, in *Anguttaranikaya*, pt III, 6.5.16, p.84.

42 *Mahaparinibbanasutta*, in *Dighanikaya* pt II, 3.19.62, p. 98.

43 Edward J. Thomas, *The Life of the Buddha as Legend and History* (London: Kegan Paul, Trench, Trubner and Co., 1927), p. 149, n. 3.

44 *Amagandhasutta*, in *Suttanipata*, 2.2.22-28, pp. 305-306.

45 This does not mean that they were not sensitive to animal life.

46 *Jivakasutta*, in *Majjhimanikaya*, pt II, 5.1.2, p. 39.

47 *Kandarakasutta*, in *Majjhimanikaya*, pt II. 1.4.8, p. 8.

48 *Brahmanadhammikasutta*, in *Suttanipata*, 2.7.88-93, pp. 313-314.

49 *Mamsabhaksanaparivartah*, in *Saddharmalankavatarasutra*, 8, p. 103, lines 10-11, 24-26; see also vv. 12 and 19, p. 105. The reference to earlier canonical texts that did make exceptions to pure vegetarianism indicates that Buddhism did permit meat-eating in former times.

50 The somewhat defensive attitude of the text in the face of actual criticism against Buddhists consuming meat seems to indicate that the text's pure vegetarianism is proposed as a reaction to this criticism: see Daisetz Teitaro Suzuki, tr., *The Lankavatara Sutra* (London: Routledge and Kegan Paul, 1932; reprinted 1956), p. 211, n. 1.

51 *Culahatthipadopamasutta*, in *Majjhimanikaya*, pt I, 27.2.8, p. 230.

52 Really speaking, there is no expiation required, but only confession: see I. B. Horner, trans. *The Book of the Discipline*, vol. 2, Sacred Books of the Buddhists vol.20 (London: Pali Text Society, 1957), p. 3, n. 4.

53 *Pacittiya*, no.11, pp. 54-56.

54 See Horner, tr., *The Book of the Discipline*, p. 229, n. 4.

55 *Pacittiya*, no. 10, pp. 52-54.

56 Radhagovinda Basak, ed., *Asokan Inscriptions* (Calcutta: Progressive Publishers, 1959), pp. 71-72.

57 Romila Thapar, cited by Rajmohan Gandhi, *Revenge and Reconciliation: Understanding South Asian History* (New Delhi: Penguin Books, 1999), p. 52.

58 Masaharu Anesaki, *History of Japanese Religion: With Special Reference to the Social and Moral Life of the Nation* (London: Kegan Paul, Trench, 1930; reprint ed., Rutland, Vermont and Tokyo, Japan: Charles E. Tuttle, 1963), pp. 171-172.

59 Basak, *Asokan Inscriptions*, p. 103.

60 Basak, *Asokan Inscriptions*, p. 4.

61 *Encyclopedia of Buddhism*, ed. G. P. Malalasekera and others, s.v. "*Abhaya-dana*," by Shuyu Kanaoka, vol. 1, pp. 20-21.

62 *Encyclopedia of Buddhism*, ed. Malalasekera, and others, s.v. "*Ahimsa*", by Akira Hirakawa, vol. 1, pp. 291-292.

63 A.T. Ariyaratne, *Collected Works*, ed. by Nandasena Ratnapala (vols. 1-3, 6-7), B. A. Tennyson Perera (vol. 4) and Jehan Perera (vol. 5), 2nd ed., 7 vols. (Ratmalana, Sri Lanka: Sarvodaya Vishva Lekha, 1999), vol. 1, p. 43.

64 Ariyaratne, *Collected Works*, vol. 2, pp. 115-116.

65 Ariyaratne, *Collected Works*, vol. 4, pp. 43-49.

66 Ariyaratne, *Collected Works*, vol. 4, pp. 94-100, 103-104.

67 George D. Bond, "A. T. Ariyaratne and the Sarvodaya Shramadana Movement in Sri Lanka", in *Engaged Buddhism: Buddhist Liberation Movements in Asia*, ed. by Christopher S. Queen and Sallie B. King (Albany: State University of New York Press, 1996), pp. 136-137.

68 *Bhikkhu* literally means a mendicant and refers to a Buddhist monk: the initial practice of begging for food is now generally defunct, except in a couple of countries like Thailand, Myanmar and Cambodia.

69 H. Uttarananda, "Sihala Buddhist Monks and the Rights of the Tamils", *Dialogue* n.s. 18:1-3 (January-December 1991): 6-9, 12-13.

70 From the text of the Press Release, sent to me by the Japanese Committee of the World Conference on Religion and Peace.

71 *The Island*, 5th November 2002, p. 1.

72 Donald K. Swearer, "Sulak Sivaraksa's Buddhist Vision for Renewing Society", in *Engaged Buddhism: Buddhist Liberation Movements in Asia,* ed. by Christopher S. Queen and Sallie B. King (Albany: State University of New York Press, 1996), pp. 200-208.

73 Sulak Sivaraksa, *Loyalty Demands Dissent: Autobiography of an Engaged Buddhist*, with a Foreword by the Dalai Lama (Berkeley, California: Parallax Press, 1998), pp. 155-164.

74 "Letter from Cambodia" [a newsletter], March 2002, p. 1.

75 "Editors' Introduction", in Maha Ghosananda, *Step by Step: Meditations on Wisdom and Compassion*, ed. by Jane Sharada Mahoney and Philip Edmonds, with a Foreword by Dith Pran and a Preface by Jack Kornfield (Berkeley, California: Parallax Press, 1992), pp. 17-18.

76 The name of the communist group in Cambodia that carried out a massive genocide under the leadership of Pol Pot.

77 Maha Ghosananda, *Step by Step*, pp. 62, 68-69.

78 Aung San Suu Kyi, *Freedom from Fear and Other Writings*, ed. with an Introduction by Michael Aris, with a Foreword to the first ed. by Vaclav Havel and a Foreword to the second ed. by Desmond Tutu, 2nd rev. ed. (London: Penguin Books, 1995), pp. 195-196.

79 Aung San Suu Kyi, *Freedom from Fear*, pp. 360-361.

80 Gandhi, *Revenge and Reconciliation*, p. 400.

81 Dalai Lama, *The Dalai Lama: A Policy of Kindness: An Anthology of Writings by and about the Dalai Lama*, comp. and ed. by Sidney Piburn, with a Foreword by Claiborne Pell, Ithaca (NY: Snow Lion Publications, 1990), pp. 16, 105-106. 133.

82 Dalai Lama, *Freedom in Exile: The Autobiography of the Dalai Lama* (London: Hodder and Stoughton, 1990; New Delhi: Rupa Paperback, 1991; 12th impression, 1994), p. 261.

83 Dalai Lama, *H. H. the Dalai Lama: The Bodhgaya Interviews*, ed. by Jose Ignacio Cabezon (Ithaca, N.Y.: Snow Lion Publications, 1988), p. 32.

84 Dalai Lama, *A Policy of Kindness*, p. 95.

85 Dalai Lama, *Bodhgaya Interviews*, p. 47.

86 Donald Nichols, "A Buddhist Contribution to Peace Spirituality", *Dialogue* n.s. 12:1-3 (January-December 1985): 2-3.

87 Pipob Udomitttipong, "Thailand's Ecology Monks", in *Dharma Rain: Sources of Buddhist Environmentalism*, ed. by Stephanie Kaza and Kenneth Kraft (Boston: Shambhala, 2000), pp. 193-194, 196-197.

88 108 is a sacred number in some Indian religions, including Buddhism.

89 "Bhutan Celebrates Newborn Prince by Planting 108,000 Trees", report filed on 11th March 2016 by Vishal Arora in *The Diplomat* [Asia-Pacific online newspaper]: http://thediplomat.com/2016/03/bhutan-celebrates-newborn-prince-by-planting-108000-trees/, accessed on 22nd March 2016.

90 *Suttanipata*, 1.8, v. 149, in *Khuddakanikaya*, pt I, pp. 290-291.This simile occurs in Mahayana texts too: e.g., the love (*prema*) of all beings as if they were one's only child (*Saddharmalankavatarasutra*, 8, p. 100, line 6).

91 *Siksasmuccaya*, 12.20, p. 117, lines 9-13.

92 *Saddharmapundarikasutra*, 5.44, p. 92, line 24.

93 *Mahayanasutralankara*, 19, v. 5, p, 154.

94 *Jatakamala*, 8, p. 43, line 1.

95 *Siksasamuccaya*, 7.14, p. 81, lines 4-5.

96 *Mahayanasutralankara*, 16, p.103, line 8.

97 *Mahayanasutralankara*, 3, v. 12; *Bodhicaryavatara*, with the *Panjika* Commentary of Prajnakaramati, 8. v. 173, p. 165.

98 A follower of another religion that existed in the Buddha's and Mahavira's time.

99 *Tevijjavacchasutta*, in *Majjhimanikaya*, pt II, 21.2, pp. 174-175.

100 *Saddharmapundarikasutra,* 3.113-135, pp. 66-68.

101 Those who have attained liberation while living.

102 *Mahavamsa*, 25; see Wilhelm Geiger, tr., *The Mahavamsa: The Great Chronicle of Ceylon* (London: Pali Text Society, 1912): pp. 177-178, lines 103-111.

103 *Nikayasamgraha*, cited by Phra Khantipalo, *Tolerance: A Study from Buddhist Sources* (London: Rider and Co., 1964), p. 105.

104 *The History of the Buddha's Religion (Sasanavamsa)*, tr. by B.C. Law, *Sacred Books of the Buddhists*, vol. 17 (London: Luzac and Co., Ltd., 1952), pp. 69-79.

105 R. A. Stein, *Tibetan Civilization*, tr. J. E. Stapleton Driver (Stanford: Stanford University Press, 1972), pp. 69 and 81.

106 *The Encyclopedia of Religion*, s.v. "Nicherenshu" by Murano Senchu.

107 E. Conze, *A Short History of Buddhism* (Bombay: Chetana Ltd.), p. 99, cited by Khantipalo, *Tolerance,* p. 111. See also Ryusaku Tsunoda and others, comps., *Sources of Japanese Tradition*, 2 vols. (New York: Columbia University Press, 1958; paperback ed. 1964; vol.1 reprinted 1967), vol. I, pp. 217-218.

108 *The Encyclopedia of Religion*, ed. by Mircea Eliade, s.v. "Mongol Religions", by Walther Heissig, vol. 10, pp. 55-56.

109 *What the Buddha Taught*, with a Foreword by Paul Demieville, rev. ed. (New York: Grove Press, 1974), p.5.

110 Khantipalo, *Tolerance*, p. 107.

111 He stayed in a Buddhist monastery for six years, two of which were spent as a monk. Later, however, he joined the Cambodian Communist Party.

112 Robert E. Buswell, *The Zen Monastic Experience: Buddhist Practice in Contemporary Korea* (Princeton: Princeton University Press, 1992), pp. 24-32.

113 He is referring to the three Semitic or Abrahamic religions, Judaism, Christianity and Islam.

114 Arnold Toynbee, *Change and Habit: The Challenge of Our Time* (London: Oxford University Press, 1966), p. 167.

115 See the Gospel according to Matthew, 6.12; 18.21-35.

116 *Sedakasutta*, in *Samyuttanikaya*, 47.19, pt 5, pp. 144-145.

25

Mysticism: A Way for Christian Muslim Befriending

Midhun J Francis, SJ
Henry Martyn Institute, 6-3-128/1, Shivrampally, Hyderabad, India

Abstract: The sematic religions have many common elements to look into for the dialogue. The Mystical experience of the Sufism (Islam) and mysticism in Christian East one of the elements, where we can come together in dialogue. Both these religions have a spiritual experience in mysticism, where they understand the 'oneness' of God and expression of this 'oneness' is seen in the life of the believer as following the commandments. This experience is not merely an academic, instead it is an intimate and transforming encounter with God, where both experience compassionate and merciful creator. This enables theme to do the service because, they have come across the God as loving creator to whole humanity.

Keywords: Dialogue, Mysticism, Oneness, Love, Service

Introduction

Sufism and Mystical experience of the Christian East can be a common ground for Christian, Muslim Dialogue, because there are common elements in both traditions. The mystical experiences of each tradition enable Christians and Muslims to understand each other as children of God. The mystical experience of the early Christian communities and the Sufi mystical experience of brotherhood is one of the paths, which can promote a deep and lasting collaboration between Christians and Muslims. This is because the mystical experiences of the persons of both traditions have several common traits. According to McIntosh we often use the term 'mysticism', though this is really something of an academic invention; earlier eras referred to the most intimate and transforming encounter with God as 'contemplation' (McIntosh, 1998: 11). If we analyse the goal of every mystic, we realize that it is God. In this essay, I would like to explore some of the possibilities of Christian, Muslim dialogue on the basis of the mystical experience of both religions, which enables 'interfaith dialogue in the present world'.

1. Early Islam in the Eastern Christian World

"The Middle East and North Africa are the cradle(s) of not only Christianity but also of two other great religions, Judaism and Islam. Despite a mutual origin, pressure is building up on the Christians in this region" (Riemenschneider, 2011: 6). Since its inception Islam has had a great contact with Christianity. 'Muslim-Christian communication is as old as Islam (Saab, 1964: 43). During the time of the Islamic birth in the Arabian Peninsula and spreading in the eastern provinces of Byzantium, there were lot of conflicts between the Byzantines and the local Christian communities, which had created so many conflicts and wars (Thomas et al., 2006: 1), which, in fact an easy access to the new religion to spread. Indeed, all "The Arab conquests of the Byzantine eastern provinces and the consequent establishment of Muslim dominance foreshadowed the end of the long tradition of Hellenism in western Asia" (Grypeou et al., 2006: 1). But, one can see both negative and positive the relationship between Christianity and Islam. Though the religions had also cordial in many places since its inception. John of Damascus is an example of the cordial relationship with the Caliph as his secretary followed by his father and grandfather (Thomas, 2005: 11), but he considers Islam as the sum of all heresies.

William Dalrymple, a Scottish historian, made two important observations on Christian Muslim relationship while traveling throughout the Middle East several years ago. First, he observed that while visiting ancient cells of monks near the Monastery of Mar Saba in the Israeli-Occupied West Bank, every cell had a prayer niche almost identical to the mihrab, which is a basic feature of all mosques today (Sharp, 2012: 11). He concluded that, ". . . the prayer niche must be another of those features of the early Christian world which has been lost to modern Western Christianity, yet which is still preserved in Islam" (Sharp, 2012: 11). "Dalrymple's second observation attests to a truth that Orthodox Christians and Muslims have known instinctively for centuries—that they originally came from one civilization and share the same ancestry" (Sharp, 2012: 12). Though they had a deep relationship with each other. The Islamic tradition as it is developing gradually puts more and more emphasis on the "Arab" nature of Muhammad and Islam. It is true that in the beginning, there is an appeal to commonality—not of ancestry so much as of salvation-history. However, as time goes on, it becomes important for Muslim tradition to distance itself from any dependency on the pre-existing Christian and Jewish "civilizations," and to trace its ancestry to Abraham back through the line of Ishmael and Hagar.

1.1. Early Islamic Growth in the Middle East

The presence of Christians in the Arab Peninsula had influenced Islam in its creation of Islamic theology. "The confrontation of Christianity with the early theological and political development of Islam addresses broader questions of intercultural relations and reciprocities and their impact on the formation of religious systems and identities" (Thomas et al., 2006: 4). Early Islam had direct contact with Syriac Christians (Thomas et al., 2006: 4), which separated at the Council of Ephesus in 431 AD (Angold, 2006: 511), as part of the Nestorian heresies and emphases that radical distinctions between the two natures of Jesus Christ, Jacobite Christians (Angold, 2006: 511), which separated at the council of Chalcedon in 451 AD (Angold, 2006: 511), and there were also Arab Christians who had a direct communion with Byzantium church. "Arabic and Syriac Christianity contributed to the emergence and rapid spread of Islam, and especially the specific Christian elements in the cult and faith that were formative upon Islam and became part of its tradition" (Thomas et al., 2006: 4). So, the relationship between the churches in Roman empire as well as Persian empire had influenced theological development of Islamic formation.

The early Muslims also had contacts with Maronite Christians and Alexandrian Christians. Ibn Jubayr, an Arab geographer and poet says, "It is strange how the Christians round Mount Lebanon, when they see any Muslim hermits, bring them food and treat them kindly, saying that these men are dedicated to Great and Glorious God and that they should therefore share with them" (Saab, 1964: 44) Syria is another place where Islam encountered Christianity. The Christianity in Syria was the product Nestorian heresy (Some Christians in Syria would have held a Nestorian position, but Syrian Christianity was not produced by Nestorianism), who separated at the Council of Ephesus from the main church. They were called the Assyrian Church of East. 'Coming to the development of religious systems within the 'Syriac Society,' Toynbee says that the Babylonian challenge produced two religious' movements: Judaism with its later development, Christianity, and Zoroastrianism (Siddiqi, 1964: 118). Ethiopia is another country Islam had connection from the beginning. "Ethiopia became a Christian state in about 300 A.D. Muslims and Christians have been living side by side in the region since the time when the Prophet Mohammad sent some of his followers there for sanctuary in 615 (Shetler & Yehualashet, 2013: 319). The relationship between these two religions was both cordial as well as conflict type.

1.2. Early Islam with Christianity and Idol Worshippers

In the fourth century, many Arab tribes joined Christianity following the teaching of the Church of the East (Thomas, 2007: 2). The prophetic revelation was given in two places called Mecca and Medina for 23 years. In Mecca, Muhammad had to encounter with Arab paganism where he was emphasizing on morality, but in Medina the situation was different there, he comes across, Judaism and Christianity. “Communication between Christianity and Islam began with the revelation of the Qur'an. As it was revealed to Muhammad in the seventh century in a peninsula, which was partly Christian, communication between Christianity and Islam became an integral part of the Quran” (Saab, 1964: 43). Prophet Muhamad had a very close relationship with Christianity, which was friendliness most of the times, because Muhamad was comfortable with the idea of monotheism which opposite to idol worshippers of the tribes in the Arabian Peninsula. “The Quran describes the Christians as the closest community to Islam” (Saab, 1964: 43) in many times. There were also times Quran critics the Christian theology such as Trinity, which goes against monotheism, Muhammad believes.

1.3. Trinity: Unity of God

“Twice the Quran criticises those who confess the Trinity. Sura 5: 72–73 calls on Christians to give up adding gods to the One True God” (Beaumont, 2012: 111). ‘They have certainly disbelieved who say, "Allah is the Messiah, the son of Mary" while the Messiah has said, "O Children of Israel, worship Allah, my Lord and your Lord. Indeed, he who associates others with Allah - Allah has forbidden him Paradise, and his refuge is the Fire. And there are not for the wrongdoers any helpers.” (Q 5:72) The second passage in which the Trinity is challenged is sūra 4:171. People of the Book, do not exaggerate in your religion. Only speak the truth about God. Christ Jesus, son of Mary, was the messenger of God, and His word which He cast on Mary, and a spirit from Him. Believe in God and His messengers and do not say “Trinity”; give it up for your own good. Surely God is One God (Beaumont, 2012: 111). These early attitudes of Islam made it very difficult for Christians to encounter Muslims because the revelation which they have received in the Incarnation (Word became Flesh) mystery is the truth to them.

Christians believed that Jesus is the Incarnated Logos (Jn 1;14) “For Christians direct or supernatural revelation came only to the Jewish people and found its fulfilment in Christ in his person and his gospel” (Knowles, 2011: 319). They also believed that the fullness of revelation in Jesus Christ; ‘in the past God spoke to our ancestors through the prophets at many times and in various ways, but in these last days he has spoken to us by his Son, whom he appointed heir of all things, and through whom also he made the universe. (Heb 1:1-2) They would need to defend their belief in God as one essence (*ousia*) in three persons (*hypostases*) which was shared by all denominations of the church in the Middle Eastern territories under Muslim rule. They may have been divided over their understanding of the union of the divine and human in Christ, but they were united in their faith in the Triune God. In a dialogue with the Caliph al-Mahdı- and Timothy I, Patriarch of the East Syrian (Nestorian) Church said, "That Christians believe in 'three *hypostases* (*aqānīm*) . . .The Father, the Son and the Holy Spirit, which are together one God, one nature, and one essence (*jawhar*)" (Beaumont, 2005: 115). It is the fundamental mystery of Christianity. Timothy explained to the caliph, "Just as the Caliph is one person in his mind and spirit, and these cannot be separated from him, so it is with God and his Word and Spirit" (Beaumont, 2005: 115). He believed that Jesus taught this great mystery clearly in the gospel and we can experience this mystery by studying created things.

"Gregory the Theologian claimed that Abraham received a vision of God, not in his role as deity, but as a man. Augustine of Hippo affirmed Abraham's understanding of the Unity of the Trinity: while greeting the three strangers, Abraham confessed to one God in three hypostases" (Strezova, 2014: 176-177). John of Damascus defended Trinity in Damascus, perhaps already at the monastery of Mar Saba near Jerusalem. John reports that Muslims accuse Christians of associating Christ with God in an unacceptable way because Christians say that "Christ is the Son of God and God. John suggests that Christians should quote the Muslim belief that 'Christ is the Word and Spirit of God' and say 'if the Word is in God it is obvious that he is God as well" (Beaumont, 2005: 113).

Abū Qurra (+830), Abū Rā'ita (+835) and Ammār al-Bas.rī (+860) who all attempted to defend and explain the Trinity in Arabic for a Muslim audience that was increasingly involved in debate with Christian intellectuals (Beaumont, 2005: 116). Abū Qurra says, "Christians do not believe in three gods when they say that the Father is God, the Son is God, and the Holy Spirit is God; and that the Father, the Son and the Holy Spirit are one God even though each of them is complete in himself" (Beaumont, 2005: 117). He is very sure that those who negate the Christian teaching object to the Trinity because their reason is confused by the Christian claims that the Father, the Son and the Holy Spirit are three hypostases (*aqānīm*) in one God (*ilah wāhid*), and that each of the hypostases is perfect God in himself (Beaumont, 2005: 117). "But Abū Qurra recognizes that the analogy with three men must not lead to the supposition that the Father, Son and Holy Spirit are separated or differentiated, since they would then be three divine beings rather than one divine being (Beaumont, 2005: 117)." He has supplied *wajh/ wujūh* as a translation of the

Greek term *prosōpon* (person) which was a synonym for hypostasis in Greek (Beaumont, 2005: 117). So, he refers to the divine nature in various ways. The three persons (*wujūh*) share the same nonphysical nature (*latafa*). Therefore, each of the persons shares the same essence (*dhāt*). The three persons share the same oneness of divinity (*wāh.idiyya al-lāhūt*) (Beaumont, 2005: 117).

"The first pillar of Islam is essentially a foundational pillar, which forms the backdrop of all the other pillars of Islam. This pillar consists of two testimonies the utterance of which enters one into the fold of Islam. The first part of the testimony is *Ash-hadu alaa ilaaha ilallah* (to testify there is nothing worthy of worship except" (Mirza & Bakali, 2010: 53). The worship is only to Allah. There are no gods except God. "The central creed of Islam consists of the two testimonies of faith or *Shahddahs*, which state that: There is no god but God, Muhammad is the Messenger of God" ("Common Word between Us and You," 2008: 243). This testimony is an utterance of pure monotheism negating the belief in all other deities, other than God (Mirza & Bakali, 2010: 53), which was popular among the Arabian tribes. The prophet had come across two types of people in the Arabian Peninsula. In Mecca he had encountered with Arabian Paganism. They were idol worshippers. In Medina, he had to encounter with Judaism and Christianity, which also influenced him to affirm for the monotheism. He was totally against idol worshippers. "God is absolute and therefore devotion to him must be totally sincere" ("Common Word between Us and You," 2008: 245). The testimony of faith emphasizes: "There is no god but God. it reminds Muslims that their hearts, their individual souls and all the faculties and powers of their souls (or simply their entire hearts and souls) must be totally devoted and attached to God" ("Common Word between Us and You," 2008: 248). It is the total submission to God. The word *Islam* means submission. The Trinitarian God of Christianity is the sources of unity in the church. This unity of God enables the Christian to engage in dialogue with Islam who profess the same God (Lumen Gentium 16, Nostra Aetate 3). Being a committed Muslim one must able to submit oneself fully God because it is "God who has created all human beings equal in rights, duties and dignity, and who has called them to live together as brothers and sisters, to fill the earth and make known the values of goodness, love and peace" (Francis & Al-Tayyib, 2019). The ultimate aim is to encounter the creator, who created the whole human beings.

1.4. The Quran and Early Christianity

"The Quran is the most important book in the Islamic lands, comparable to the Bible in the Western tradition. Transmitted orally, the text was soon committed to writing, and manuscripts - usually in the codex format - became the most common written work in circulation" (Blair, 2008: xx). Muslims believe that God reveals the word through the Angel Gabriel to Prophet Muhamad, who was illiterate. "That Muhammad was no theologian emerges on every page of the Koran. He was a preacher and a leader, political and military as well as religious"(Knowles, 2011: 318). It is the Arabic version that is considered by Muslims to be the true Quran, the direct word of Allah. No translation is considered to be the Quran or Word of Allah as such, and none has the same status as the original Quran. "The Quran, on the other hand, often appears to consider the Christians as a schismatic Jewish sect. They are included most of the time in what it says People of the Scriptures (*Ahl al-Kitâb*), judged mainly in judged mainly in the light of the Jews. Sometimes, however, Christians are presented in opposition to the Jews"(Ellul, 2007: 361).

In Christianity, the belief is that The Word became flesh and made his dwelling among us (Jn 1:14) in Jesus Christ, through the virgin Mary (Lk 1:27). It is the word, who was with God and he was God himself. (Jn 1:1-14) It is the pure word of God which enables creation. After Islamic rule had been established in the Middle East, the Christians found that the Muslims claim that the Quran is the only pure, all other scriptures are corrupt. (Beaumont, 2005: 195). "The earliest recorded Christian reading of the Qur'an comes from the writing of John of Damascus (d.c.750) who spent his career as a secretary to the Caliph in Damascus" (Beaumont, 2005: 195). John had three issues with Quranic understanding in Christian perspectives. They are: 'The Quran contains material unworthy of divine revelation (Beaumont, 2005: 195), 'the Quran shows Muhammad to be less than Muslims claim he is, (Beaumont, 2005: 197), 'the Quran sometimes supports Christian beliefs (Beaumont, 2005: 198).

1.5. Jesus in Quran

Jesus is considered as a word of Allah in Quran, 'The Messiah, Jesus, the son of Mary, was but a messenger of Allah and His word which He directed to Mary and a soul from Him.' (Quran 4;171) and Quran also approves the virgin birth of Jesus. She said, "How can I have a boy while no man has touched me and I have not been unchaste?" He said, "Thus [it will be]; your Lord says, 'It is easy for Me, and We will make him a sign to the people and a mercy from Us. And it is a matter [already] decreed.' " (Quran 19;20-21). Jesus was also considered as a servant, 'Jesus was not but a servant upon whom We bestowed favour, and We made him an example for the Children of Israel.' (43;59). But the Quran disagrees that Jesus is not created. 'She said, "My Lord, how will I have a child when no man has touched me?" [The angel] said, "Such is Allah; He creates what He wills. When He decrees a matter, He only says to it, 'Be,' and it is.' (Quran 3;47) the claim of John of Damascus is that "the Arian monk had given Muhammad mixed information about Christianity and this is echoed in the message of Muhammad. Support for Christian teaching can be found in the statement" (Beaumont, 2005: 198). Though John had a very prominent post in as secretary to caliph "John goes on to mock the teachings in the Quran about Christ, particularly that he was not crucified but only 'his shadow', and that he denied before God that he was his son, and continues to criticise Muhammad's unrestrained sexual appetite and what he regards as perverse teachings in various parts of the Quran" (Thomas, 2005: 11). "John thought Islam a false religion, based originally upon an encounter between Muhammad and a heretical Christian monk, from whom he gained some knowledge of the Bible. Thus, Islam can be dismissed as a Christian heresy since it has no integrity in itself, and whatever truthfulness or good it contained derived from the proper source of true teaching in the Bible" (Thomas, 2005: 11). Early Islam had a very deep relationship with Christianity which we have seen in the relationship on religious matters and political matters.

2. Eastern Mysticism and Sufism

"An ascetic and mystical element that was implicitly present in Islam since its very inception became explicit during the first Islamic centuries (the seventh and eighth centuries C.E.)" (Knysh, 2010: 1). Unlike Christian mysticism, the Islamic mysticism has not begun because of any persecution. One can say it has received an inspiration from Christian mysticism, which was popular in the Eastern and Western churches in the seventh and eighth centuries C.E. "This period witnessed the appearance of the first Muslim devotees and "moral athletes," who formed primitive ascetic communities in the central and eastern lands of Islam, primarily in Mesopotamia, Syria and Eastern Iran"(Knysh, 2010: 1). Many people started following the early mystics as part of being away from the secular sphere and luxuries of the world. "As an outward sign of this pietistic withdrawal, some of them adopted a distinct dress code, which often featured a rough woollen robe." (Knysh, 2010: 7). These mystics were known as Sufi saints in Islam. The word Sufism is a Latinised word which comes from the Arabic word *suf* which means wool (Knysh, 2010: 5). "By the end of the eighth century C.E., in the central lands of Islam the nick-name *suffiyya* ("wool-people" or "wool-wearers") became a self-designation of those given to ascetic life and mystical contemplation" (Knysh, 2010: 7). Sufism became a prevalent characteristic of the Muslim social order in the later Middle Ages (12 – 6th Centuries CE).

2.1. Communion as the Community

The mystics in the early Islamic traditions were called "moral athletes" (Knysh, 2010: 7) and they formed as *"tariquas"* or "brotherhood" (Knysh, 2010: 5). Muslim mystics often trace this term to the root *Safà* with the general meaning of "purity;" to the phrase *ahl al-suffa* ("the People of the Bench"), that is, the pious and indigent companions of the Prophet who lived in his mosque" (Knysh, 2010: 7); in other words, we may tend to interpret that these mystics lived in a mosque under a head. The Constitution of the Society of Jesus describes the brotherhood as 'union of hearts.' The 'union of hearts' is an expression of sincere communication between persons, which we see in the Acts of the Apostles in the Council of Jerusalem. Peter, as the head of the Apostles, and Paul as the head of the Church of Antioch, discussed and came to a decision on the controversy regarding the law of circumcision. "Certain people came down from Judea to Antioch and were teaching the believers: "Unless you are circumcised, according to the custom taught by Moses, you cannot be saved." This brought Paul and Barnabas into sharp dispute and debate with them. So, Paul and Barnabas were appointed, along with some other believers, to go up to Jerusalem to see the apostles and elders about this question." (Acts 15:1-2) "The early Christians considered that the Christian spirituality could not be experienced outside the community, which involved a multiplicity and variety of spiritual charisms" (Zizioulas, 1989: 27) because the Spirit was regarded as "communion" (Zizioulas, 1989: 27). They were living together and expecting the second coming of Christ as one body of Christ. The community life was an essential element among the early Christians. This type of community life was not just a living together under the same roof but it was a life of 'union of hearts. It was a life of communion among the members. This communion helped them to forget the self and thus enabled them to love one another.

2.2. Self-Renunciation

It was discovered that there were many people who lived in search of a pure life as ascetics in the Arab-Byzantine region (Knysh, 2010: 6). "The acts of penitence and self-renunciation, which their practitioners justified by references to certain Quranic verses and the Prophet's utterances, may be seen as a reaction against Islam's newly acquired wealth that often led many faithful to abandon the frugal and heroic ways of self-denial associated with the original Muslim community in Medina" (Knysh, 2010: 2). It was evident from the correspondences of the early Christian hermits in the church. When the church had acquired freedom in the Roman Empire, many of the clerics enjoyed political status too. They had forgotten the real value of Christ's teaching on self-renunciation, from which "arose a movement that in a variety of ways expressed a rejection of the conventional worldly values (Jean, 1989: 89).

Sufis also realized that many of these Umayyad and their officials were not following the spirit of the Holy Quran, which said, "Whatever you are given in this life is nothing but a temporary provision of this life and its glitter; what God has is better and more lasting. Will you not then understand?" (Quran 28:60). "They argued that the truly God-fearing person should try to save himself by withdrawing from the overbearing world and its sinful and unjust ways. "In an attempt to achieve this goal, the mystic had to contend not only with the corruptive trappings of the world, but also with his own base self (*nafs*), which Sufis see as the seat of egoistic evil lusts and passions impeding their progress towards God." (Knysh, 2010: 10). These ways of life are so much similar to the life adopted by the Christian ways of life in the deserts. Many of these people had very good contacts with the Christians of the Eastern countries like Syria and Constantinople. "This robe set them apart from people wearing more expensive silk or cotton. Wittingly or not, the early Muslim *religiosi* thereby came to resemble Christian monks and ascetics, who also donned coarse woollen clothes as a symbol of penitence and contempt for worldly luxuries" (Knysh, 2010: 7).

"Sufi movement developed a strict code of behaviour which encouraged repentance, abstinence from worldly delights, frugal living and voluntary poverty" (Knysh, 2010: 9), as we see among the early Christian hermits. "During the first century of Abbsid rule, renunciation was a widespread form of piety in Muslim communities. Renunciants (*zahid*) and pietists (*abid, andnasik*) of this period were not organised into a single homogeneous movement but came in different colours and stripes" (Karamustafa, 2007: 1). Self-renunciation is an important act of getting into the mystical life. The incarnation mystery of the Christian spirituality is a basis for the renunciation because being God, Jesus emptied himself and not considered himself equal to God (Phil 2:7). instead, he renounced everything and entered into the world of human race. The person who has renounced himself has to enter into this stage where he tries to understand this mystery. Every mystic has to go through this experience in his life.

2.3. Purification

A person who desires to renounce everything in the world has to be purified. In each religion, there is a process called purification in different ways. "Mystics in every religious tradition have tended to describe the different steps on the way that leads toward God by the image of the Path. The Christian tripartite division of the *via purgativa*, the *via contemplativa*, and the *via illuminativa* is, to some extent, the same as the Islamic definition of *shari'a*, *tariqa*, and *haqiqa*" (Schimmel, 2011: 98). Naturally these paths are narrow and difficult to go through. In other words, these difficulties experienced by the person can be called the process of purification. The early mystics in the church left the cities in order to purify themselves. They were also doing the works of charity in the form of discourses and giving advices to the common people. The personal purification is very important in the mystical life. "Most of early Muslim ascetics emphasized personal purity, moral uprightness, fear of God and strict compliance with the letter of the Divine Law, there were those who carried their search of God's pleasure a bit further" (Knysh, 2010: 8). In Sufism, "the ascetics, on the other hand, were allowed to practice self-imposed strictures which they deemed as preparation for the imminent Final Reckoning" (Knysh, 2010: 9). This purification process will make one to experience the ultimate or the absolute.

2.4. Union with the Absolute

The union of hearts among the mystics enables them to be one with the Heart of the Absolute. Mysticism is an experience of a Devotee "Seeing One's Own Face in the Face of God" (Nelstrop & Podmore, 2016: 1). It will enable the person to "ascend beyond cataphatic knowledge of God towards divine union, the divine idea became its entitlement and reality" (Nelstrop & Podmore, 2016: 1) This is one of the concepts called 'Deification' in Eastern Christianity and 'Becoming Another Christ' in Western Christianity. This personal experience can make these devotees from the two traditions of Sufis and Christian faith can engage in interfaith commitment in life." Whatever be the Sufi approach to renunciation and to the question of how far to detach themselves from mainstream social life, some prominent renunciants and the renunciant communities that formed around them began to direct their energies increasingly to the cultivation of the inner life. This inward turn manifested itself especially in new discourses on spiritual states, stages of spiritual development, closeness to God, and love; it also led to a clear emphasis on 'knowledge of the interior' (*ilmal-batin*) acquired through ardent examination and training of the human soul" (Karamustafa, 2007: 2). The human soul forgets himself or herself and become one with the absolute. In the early church we come across the mystics forgetting themselves out of love towards the other. St. Ignatius of Antioch's martyrdom story reminds us that even in suffering the name of Jesus was inscribed in his heart. "There is nothing left to distract the lover from God— the spiritual eye sees nothing but Him when the eye of the body is closed. He is enough for the loving soul: "O my Lord, whatever share of this world Thou dost bestow on me, bestow it on Thine enemies, and whatever share of the next world Thou doest give me, give it to Thy friends — Thou art enough for me" (Schimmel, 2011: 40). As the mystic feels that he is close to the heart of the absolute because he gets the awareness that his/her image and likeness (Gen 1:26) are the same as the creator. "The true knowledge of God was to be obtained by obedience to the uttermost" (Knysh, 2010: 36). The lost image and likeness has to regain through obedience.

2.5. Service and Love

"*Al-mu'min mir'at al-mu'min*, the faithful is the mirror of the faithful" — that is a Prophetic tradition that the Sufis considered an excellent maxim for social intercourse" (Schimmel, 2011: 228). Sufi saint is the one who experiences the union of heart with the absolute and live in the world. He has the moral responsibility of looking after the other as the greatest commandment Christ gave to the rich man, "Love the Lord your God with all your heart and with all your soul and with all your mind." This is the first and greatest commandment. And the second is like it: 'Love your neighbour as yourself. All the Law and the Prophets hang on these two commandments." (Mt 22:36-40). The practical application of this maxim can be clearly seen in the Sufi history and leads to the one of the movement's most nice aspects, namely, to the fraternal love, which originally came to exist among the Sufis of one community.

The parable of Good Samaritan is an example of a Christian commitment to the other which is emphasized much in Sufism. "Even Antony the Hermit recognized his total ignorance of divine mysteries and of the scriptures, and whose supreme value was love towards his neighbour" (Jean, 1989: 93). Service to humanity has always been one of the first phases in the preliminary steps of the path, but throughout his life it remains the true Sufi obligation (Schimmel, 2011: 228). For, "whoever excuses himself from the service of his brethren, God will give him a humiliation from which he cannot be rescued." (Schimmel, 2011: 229). In Sufism the service to the other is considered as divine encounter. They were commonly referred to as *nussàk* (devout [men]), *zuhhàd* (world renouncers or ascetics), *ubbàd* (worshipers)—terms that roughly correspond to the Latin concept of *viri religiosi* (Knysh, 2010: 6). These religious men are not called to be under a roof for pious practice alone; instead, they have to go out into the world in order to do their work. "More than just fulfilling their religious duties, they paid close attention to the underlying motives of their actions and sought to impregnate them with a deeper spiritual meaning. This goal was achieved through a meticulous contemplation on the Qur'ànic revelation, a thorough imitation of the Prophet's piety, introspection as well as voluntary poverty and self-mortification." (Knysh, 2010: 6). Love of God and love of neighbour are essential practices in Christianity. Christians cannot isolate themselves from service to others.

"The Sufis distinguish three organs of spiritual communication: the heart (*qalb*), which knows God; the spirit (*ruh*), which loves Him; and the inmost ground of the soul (*sirr*), which contemplates Him" (Nicholson, 2007: 49). Christian mystics also invite the people of God into contemplation where the communication of the devotee to God is enable through heart and mind. Experiencing God is an innermost happiness of a mystics which can be seen in the both traditions. "Mystics of every race and creed have described the progress of the spiritual life as a journey or a pilgrimage" (Nicholson, 2007: 21). One can see this progress of spiritual journey in both these great traditions.

3. Towards Interfaith

The Pontifical Council for Interreligious Dialogue (PCID) aims at "the promotion of interreligious dialogue in accordance with the spirit of the Second Vatican Council, in particular the declaration "Nostra Aetate". The

PCID wants to have a good relationship among Christians and Muslims. "It promotes mutual understanding, respect and collaboration between Catholics and the followers of others religious traditions" ("The Pontifical Council for Interreligious Dialogue," n.d.). There are two things very important in our interfaith dialogue. They are heart to heart relationship and participating in mutual Experiences.

3.1. Heart to Heart Relationship

"Too often the past missionary activity of Catholicism has been neither metanoia to new consciousness, new life and orientation, nor a life of grace and being graced, but a forced and imposed proselytism which Jesus himself rejected participating in mutual experience" (Cenkner, 1997: 130). Vatican Council II opened a new horizon for dialogue. In other words, one can say it was a heart-to-heart relationship because the Council encourages the Catholics to enter into dialogue with an open heart.

> One document of Vatican Council II, *Ad Gentes* 9, acknowledged truth and grace in other religions in both the people and the traditions themselves. Other documents, *Lumen Gentium* 17 and *Gaudium et Spes* 11, spoke of the spirit of God filling the universe, even in the rituals and cultures of other faiths. Yet another, *Nostra Aetate* 2, called Catholics explicitly to interreligious dialogue and cooperation. (Cenkner, 1997: 132).

Pope Francis in his address to inter religious meeting in Abu Dhabi emphasized that one cannot understand God, the creator, without understanding human beings. Every human life is sacred. Everyone is important in the eyes of God. ("Apostolic Journey to the United Arab Emirates: Interreligious Meeting at the Founder's Memorial (Abu Dhabi, 4 February 2019) | Francis," 2019). God cannot be partial to anyone in particular because he created everyone in his image and likeness. The one who received the image from God can easily identify the other as the image of God. There will be mutual understanding from the Heart. Once a mystic identified this reality of God and the other, which will enable him to go ahead with relationship with the other.

But in reality, there is a lot of violence perpetrated between Christians and Islam. There are attacks in Syria. The migration into the European continent is another difficulties the western Christianity faces. The PCID gives a certain solution on such violence. Its message to Muslims for the end of Ramadam (18 May 2018) says:

> To prevent and overcome these negative consequences, it is important that we Christians and Muslims recall the religious and moral values that we share, while acknowledging our differences. By recognizing what we hold in common and by showing respect for our legitimate differences, we can more firmly establish a solid foundation for peaceful relations, moving

> from competition and confrontation to an effective cooperation for the common good. This particularly assist those most in need, and allows us to offer a credible witness to the Almighty's love for the whole of humanity. ("Message to Muslims for the End of Ramadam," The Holy See 2018).

Muslims and Christians frequently can meet in formal and informal ways as neighbours and friends. They can participate in festivals. They can organize inter faith prayers, even though Muslims and Christians worship separately in the mosques and churches, they join together. They can collaborate in social works. Coexistence does not mean giving up distinctive identities. Every religion has a distinct identity which will enable to appreciate the other. The document Human Fraternity speaks on dialogue as Dialogue, understanding and the widespread promotion of a culture of tolerance, acceptance of others and of living together peacefully would contribute significantly to reducing many economic, social, political and environmental problems that weigh so heavily on a large part of humanity; Dialogue among believers means coming together in the vast space of spiritual, human and shared social values and, from here, transmitting the highest moral virtues that religions aim for. It also means avoiding unproductive discussions; The protection of places of worship – synagogues, churches and mosques – is a duty guaranteed by religions, human values, laws and international agreements. Every attempt to attack places of worship or threaten them by violent assaults, bombings or destruction, is a deviation from the teachings of religions as well as a clear violation of international law (Francis & Al-Tayyib, 2019).

This kind of dialogue is possible if one really has faith in God. The document affirms that, everyone was created by same God. "In the name of God who has created all human beings equal in rights, duties and dignity, and who has called them to live together as brothers and sisters, to fill the earth and make known the values of goodness, love and peace" (Francis & Al-Tayyib, 2019). Being the children of same God, we brother and sisters. We are called to be the keepers of the other. The document says, "In the name of innocent human life that God has forbidden to kill, affirming that whoever kills a person is like one who kills the whole of humanity, and that whoever saves a person is like one who saves the whole of humanity" (Francis & Al-Tayyib, 2019).

Participating in Mutual Experiences

One has to enter into the space of the other in order to have religious experience of other. This religious experience will enable one to understand who he is. Entering into the space of other is a difficult task. The one who enters may not be accepted by the other. The incarnation spiritualty gives a hope for the Christians to enter into the space of other. Jesus entered into the human space in order to be part of humanity in every sense. "A major challenge is creating spaces and means for "rubbing shoulders with diverse people in an increasingly pluralistic world. "Not only is there a call to "rub shoulders" with diverse peoples, but the call is to love our neighbours—our religious neighbours—in ways that push relational boundaries. Miroslav Volf argues that living with the "other" in peace is "an expression of our God given humanity" (King, 2016: 203). Human beings are created as social beings. There is a communication between all of them. The isolated human being cannot live a proper life. It is same with the isolated religion. No religion can live as an isolated entity. Every religion has a connection with other religion(s). The mutual sharing of religious experience of mysticism will enrich the other. This will enable to flourish and nurture the identity of the other and enable to go forward in a peaceful life and well-being. "Interfaith dialogue has emerged as a major means for interacting with peoples of different faiths that work toward achieving such goals." (King, 2016: 204). *Nostra Aetate* is an invitation to Christians to enter into this dialogue of experiences.

> The Church regards with esteem also the Moslems. They adore the one God, living and subsisting in Himself; merciful and all- powerful, the Creator of heaven and earth, who has spoken to men; they take pains to submit wholeheartedly to even His inscrutable decrees, just as Abraham, with whom the faith of Islam takes pleasure in linking itself, submitted to God. Though they do not acknowledge Jesus as God, they revere Him as a prophet. They also honor Mary, His virgin Mother; at times they even call on her with devotion. In addition, they await the day of judgment when God will render their deserts to all those who have been raised up from the dead. Finally, they value the moral life and worship God especially through prayer, almsgiving and fasting (Nostra Aetate 3).

"Since in the course of centuries not a few quarrels and hostilities have arisen between Christians and Moslems, this sacred synod urges all to forget the past and to work sincerely for mutual understanding and to preserve as well as to promote together for the benefit of all mankind social justice and moral welfare, as well as peace and freedom" (King, 2016: 204).

The courage of otherness is the heart of dialogue, which is based on sincerity of intentions. Dialogue is indeed compromised by pretence, which increases distance and suspicion: we cannot proclaim fraternity and then act in the opposite way. "The man who lies to himself and listens to his own lie comes to such a pass that he cannot distinguish the truth within him, or around him, and so loses all respect for himself and for others" (King, 2016: 204). The mutual sharing of experience can come from inter religious prayer. Faith in God is as essential element in the interfaith dialogue. Faith leads a believer to see in the other a brother or sister to be supported and loved. The document signed by His Holiness Pope Francis and the Grand Imam of Al-

Azhar Ahmad Al-Tayyeb on 'Human Fraternity' goes like this, "Through faith in God, who has created the universe, creatures and all human beings (equal on account of his mercy), believers are called to express this human fraternity by safeguarding creation and the entire universe and supporting all persons, especially the poorest and those most in need" (Francis & Al-Tayyib, 2019). *Lumen Gentium* 16 says: "But the plan of salvation also includes those who acknowledge the Creator, in the first place amongst are Muslims; these profess to hold the faith of Abraham and together with us they adore the one merciful God who will judge humanity on the last day" (Lumen Gentium 16). Reconciliation, a form of cooperation, requires some collective action Presuming an essential harmony of underlying interests between both faith communities, proponents of interreligious collective action for reconciliation seek to awaken similarly minded activists from different religious background (Francis & Al-Tayyib, 2019).

The common word between Christians and Muslims sates,

> The future of the world depends on peace between Muslims and Christians. The basis for this peace and understanding already exists. It is part of the very foundational principles of both faiths: love of the One God, and love of the neighbor. These principles are found over and over again in the sacred texts of Islam and Christianity. The Unity of God, the necessity of love for Him, and the necessity of love of the neighbor is thus the common ground between Islam and Christianity (Malik, 2013: 204).

The love commandment is given important in the statement. This is only possible through mutual participation and sharing. "ACW calls for future relations between Muslims and Christians to be predicated on acknowledging the primacy of the two commandments of love. These ethically salient affirmations suggest increased commitment to human equality and dignity and collaboration for the common" ("Common Word between Us and You," 2008: 458).

Conclusion

The eastern Christians in the early Muslims' kingdoms experienced freedom in many occasions. We have good examples as John of Damascus as the secretary to the caliph and Patriarch Timothy I had a very personal theological debate with the Caliph Al-Mahdı. There were also Arabic Christian theologians like Abū Qurra, Abū Rā'ita and Ammār al-Basrī who defend the unity of God in Arabic terms in order to create peaceful relationship in the Middle East countries. Dialogue is the place where we can find a common ground in order to work together. The focus must be given to more in common grounds of similarities rather than disputes. Jesus is considered as a word of God and a prophet. The oneness of God will enable one to understand the Islamic and Christian mysticism as a common ground for dialogue.

There is a lot of misunderstanding and conflict among peoples of differing faiths in the twenty-first century, very particularly among Muslims and Christians. These misunderstandings and conflicts challenged not only religious sphere but also academic level, which moved peacebuilding and interfaith dialogue to the top of academic agendas. The basic need of the human being is love; in other words, every human being wants to live in harmony and peace. Most of the time, the means one takes to acquire peace and harmony is violence and conflicts. People believe that, if one destroys one's enemy, one can live in harmony. But it is impossible. The quest for living at peace with one another made theologians and missiologists to explore a theological ground, with a view to creating understanding and encouraging human encounters that foster respect and dignity for all peoples. "Peacebuilding is considered a relational approach to increase dialogue, mutual understanding, and trust between two conflicting groups. In praxis, peacebuilding reframes contexts of violence as opportunities to improve upon broken relationships and increase awareness of areas of commonalities and mutual interests" (Malik, 2013: 204). The mysticism invites the common people to engage in interfaith dialogue of life and experiences. Mysticism in both traditions emphasize on the oneness of God, who is compassionate and merciful. Mystics make their hearts awaken and experience the oneness of God within their hearts. The contemplation enables one to enter into this level of mystical experience. Love is the fundamental law among the mystics; love of one self, love of God and love of neighbour. The one who has experienced love cannot hate anyone, that is the challenge of mysticism; and it leads to service.

References

Angold, M. (2006). *The Cambridge History of Christianity: Volume 5, Eastern Christianity*. Cambridge University Press.

Apostolic Journey to the United Arab Emirates: Interreligious Meeting at the Founder's Memorial (Abu Dhabi, 4 February 2019) | Francis. (2019, February 4). Vatican. Retrieved February 13, 2019, from https://w2.vatican.va/content/francesco/en/speeches/2019/february/documents/papa-francesco_20190204_emiratiarabi-incontrointerreligioso.html

Beaumont, M. (2012). Speaking of the Triune God: Christian Defence of the Trinity in the Early Islamic Period. *Transformation: An International Journal of Holistic Mission Studies*, *29*(2), 111-127.

Beaumont, M. I. (2005). Early Christian Interpretation of the Qur'an. *Transformation: An International Journal of Holistic Mission Studies*, *22*(4), 195-203.

Blair, S. S. (2008). Transcribing God's Word: Qur'an Codices in Context. *Journal of Qur'anic Studies*, *10*(1), 72-97.

Cenkner, W. (1997). Mission and/or Dialogue: A Roman Catholic Perspective. *Buddhist-Christian Studies*, *17*, 130-139.

A Common Word between Us and You. (2008, Summer). *Islamic Studies*, 243-260.

Document on "Human fraternity for world peace and living together" signed by his holiness pope Francis and the grand imam of al-azhar Ahamad al-tayyib (Abu Dhabi, 4 February 2019) | Francis. (2019, February 4). Vatican. https://w2.vatican.va/content/francesco/en/travels/2019/outside/documents/papa-francesco_20190204_documento-fratellanza-umana.html

Ellul, J. (2007). The Issue of Muslim-Christian Dialogue "Nostra Aetate" Revisited". *Angelicum*, *84*(2), 361-381.

Francis, & Al-Tayyib, A. (2019, February 4). *Document on "Human Fraternity for World Peace and Living Together" Signed by His Holiness Pope Francis and the Grand Imam of (Abu Dhabi, 4 February 2019)*. Vatican. Retrieved March 4, 2019, from https://w2.vatican.va/content/francesco/en/travels/2019/outside/documents/papa-francesco_20190204_documento-fratellanza-umana.html

Jean, G. (1989). Monasticism and Asceticism. In B. Mcginn (Ed.), *Christian Spirituality*. SCM Press LTD.

Karamustafa, A. T. (2007). *Sufism: The Formative Period*. Edinburgh University Press.

King, R. R. (2016). Music, Peacebuilding, and Interfaith Dialogue: Transformative Bridges in Muslim–Christian Relations. *International Bulletin of Mission Research*, *40*(3), 202-217.

Knowles, M. (2011). The Galatian Test: Is Islam an Abrahamic Religion? *New Blackfriars*, *92*(1039), 318-321.

Knysh, A. (2010). *Islamic Mysticism: A Short History*. BRILL.

Lumen Gentium. (2005). In *Vatican Council II: The conciliar and post conciliar documents* (A. Flannery, Trans.). Liturgical Press.

Malik, A. (2013, September). Reconciliation between Muslims and Christians: Collective Action, Norm Entrepreneurship, and "a Common Word between Us". *The Journal of Religious Ethics*, *41*(3), 457-473.

McIntosh, M. A. (1998). *Mystical theology: The integrity of spirituality and theology*. Blackwell Publishing.

Messaggio Del Pontificio Consiglio Per Il Dialogo Interreligioso Ai Musulmani Per Il Mese Del Ramadan E 'Id Al-Fitr 1439 H. / 2018 A.D. (2018, May 18). vatican.va. Retrieved February 9, 2019, from https://press.vatican.va/content/salastampa/it/bollettino/pubblico/2018/05/18/0367/00791.html#ingle

Mirza, K., & Bakali, N. (2010). *The Islam: The Fundamentals Every Teacher Should Know, in Teaching against Islamophobia*. Peter Lang AG.

Nelstrop, L., & Podmore, S. D. (2016). *Christian Mysticism and Incarnational Theology: Between Transcendence and Immanence*. Routledge.

Nicholson, R. A. (2007). *The Mystics of Islam*. World Wisdom.

Nostra Aetate. (2005). In *Vatican Council II: The conciliar and post conciliar documents* (A. Flannery, Trans.). Liturgical Press.

Riemenschneider, M. (2011). *The Situation of Christians in the Middle East and North Africa* (6-32). Konrad Adenauer Stiftung.

Saab, H. (1964, Winter). Communication between Christianity and Islām. *Middle East Journal*, *19*(1), 41-62.

Schimmel, A. (2011). *Mystical Dimensions of Islam*. University of North Carolina Press.

Sharp, A. (2012). *Orthodox Christians and Islam in the Postmodern Age*. BRILL.

Shetler, J., & Yehualashet, D. (2013, July). Building Peaceful Relations between Muslims and Christians: What We Can Learn from Ethiopia? *The Mennonite Quarterly Review*, *87*(3), 317-334.

Siddiqi, M. (1964, September). Syriac Society' as the Progenitor of Islam. *Islamic Studies*, *1*(3), 117-127.

Strezova, A. (2014). *Hesychasm and Art: The Appearance of New Iconographic Trends in Byzantine and Slavic Lands in the 14th and 15th Centuries*. ANU Press.

The Pontifical Council for Interreligious Dialogue. (n.d.). Vatican. Retrieved February 9, 2019, from https://www.vatican.va/roman_curia/pontifical_councils/interelg/documents/rc_pc_interelg_pro_20051996_en.html

Thomas, D. (2005). Changing Attitudes of Arab Christians towards Islam. *Transformation: An International Journal of Holistic Mission Studies*, *22*(1), 10-19.

Thomas, D. (2007). Arab Christianity. In K. Parry (Ed.), *The Blackwell Companion to Eastern Christianity* (pp. 1-22). Blackwell.

Thomas, D. R., Swanson, M., & Grypeou, E. (2006). *The Encounter of Eastern Christianity With Early Islam*. BRILL.

Zizioulas, J. D. (1989). The Early Christian Community. In B. Mcginn (Ed.), *Christian Spirituality*. SCM Press LTD.

26

Befriending the Other: Vatican II and the New Orientations

Kurien Kunnumpuram, SJ
President and Professor (Emeritus), Faculty of Theology, Jnana Deep, Pune

Abstract: in this paper the author wants to show that Vatican II has brought about radical changes in the Church's attitude to other Christian Churches, other religions and the modern world. These changes and innovations can be clearly seen if we keep in mind the totally different attitude which prevailed in the Church before the Council. Remarkably, the Council has taken several steps to befriend the non-Catholic Christians and their Churches, the non-Christians and their religions and the modern world. It is up to the Catholic faithful now to imbibe the spirit of this great Council and establish cordial relations with non-Catholic Christians, the followers of other faiths and the modern world.

Keywords: Vatican II, The Church's Openness to Other Religions, Befriending the Other Churches, Befriending the World

In this paper I shall contend that Vatican II has brought about radical changes in the Church's attitude to other Christian Churches, other religions and the modern world. These changes can be clearly seen if we keep in mind the totally different attitude which prevailed in the Church before the Council.

The situation of the Church during the last four hundred years (before Vatican II) was largely due to the impact of the Council of Trent. After pointing out that this Council had succeeded in stemming the tide of the Reformation that threatened to destroy Catholicism and in starting a process of Church renewal, Giuseppe Alberigo observes:

> But the price paid for this successful orientation cannot be overlooked; it can be summed up as a drastic isolation of Roman Christianity, now cut off and insulated from any interaction with the other Christian traditions of East and West, condemned to an attitude of defensiveness toward the modern world and, finally, surrounded by a *cordon sanitaire* to prevent contamination from alien cultures. Never in the history of Christianity had the *massa damnata* been made to include so much and so many; never had Christianity so extended and exacerbated its own estrangement from the fortunes of the human race (Alberigo, 1987: 13-14).

The Council of Trent had an enormous impact on the Church for about four centuries. During this period the Church's isolation from the other Christian Churches grew. The struggle with the Protestant Reformation and the opposition to modern culture led to the development of "the 'closed' ecclesiology of the post-tridentine period in which the Church is a fortified castle, jealous of its purity and bristling with condemnations" (Alberigo, 1987: 13-14). There was a strong resistance to all attempts break out of this fortress mentality and open up lines of communication with various cultures or to build bridges between the Church and the common human condition. The French Revolution and Vatican I only aggravated the situation. "Ecclesiocentrism thus reached levels that were new in relation to the entire Christian tradition" (Alberigo, 1987: 15).

Looking back on the Council and carefully examining its documents one can clearly see that its basic thrust was the Church's recovery of the integral Christian tradition and the establishment of cordial relations with the other Christian Churches, the diverse religions and cultures of humanity and the modern world.

1. Befriending the Other Churches

From Anathema to Acceptances

From the beginning of Christianity divisions began to take place in the Church. These divisions led to the emergence of different Churches. By the middle of the 5th century all the churches other than the Greco-Roman Church were shut out of the Catholic Church. In the 11th century the Greek Church got separated from the Roman Church. In the 16th century the Roman Church itself was split. As a result of the Reformation several Churches came into existence – Lutheran Churches, Reformed Churches of Calvin, Zwingli and so on.

The reasons for division in the Church were many and varied. First of all, there were theological reasons. Sometimes doctrinal differences paved the way for the emergence of new churches. Disciplinary matters too caused division.

But there is reason to believe that social and cultural factors also caused division in the Church. This was quite evident in the separation between the Greek Church and the Roman Church. Diversity of culture may have played a role in Luther's revolt against Rome – the Germanic culture against the Latin culture. As Christopher Dawson has observed: "Most of the great schisms and heresies in the history of the Christian church have their roots in social and national antipathies, and if this had been clearly recognized by the theologians the history of Christianity would have been a very different one" (Dawson, 2002: 32). Joseph Neuner calls attention to another factor: "Luther's revolt is not primarily a theological challenge of traditional doctrines but a revolution against the domination of the Christian people through the clergy in a spirit totally alien to Jesus Christ" (Neuner, 1983: 13).

The way the Catholic Church reacted to the members of these Churches were also alien to the spirit of Jesus Christ. They were condemned quite harshly.[1] In the Church there developed a feeling of animosity towards the members of these Churches. They were anathema to the authorities of the Catholic Church.

Befriending Non-Catholics

All this changed with Vatican II. The Council sought to befriend non-Catholic Christians and their churches. It admitted that the divisions in the Church were caused both by the Catholics as well as non-Catholic Christians and hence "both sides were to blame" (UR 3). In unmistakable terms Vatican II declared:

> However one cannot impute the sin of separation to those who at present are born into these Communities and are instilled therein with Christ's faith. The Catholic Church accepts them with respect and affection as brothers and sisters. For men and women who believe in Christ and have been properly baptized are brought into a certain, though imperfect, communion with the Catholic Church. Undoubtedly the differences that exist in varying degrees between them and the Catholic Church – whether in doctrine and sometimes in discipline, or concerning the structure of the Church – do indeed create many and sometimes serious obstacles to full ecclesiastical communion. These the ecumenical movement is striving to overcome. Nevertheless, all those justified by faith through baptism are incorporated into Christ. They therefore have a right to be honoured by the title of Christian and are properly regarded as brothers and sisters in the Lord by the sons and daughters of the Catholic Church (UR 3).

In this text two statements are quite significant: (1) The Catholic Church accepts the members of these Churches with respect and affection; (2) They are properly regarded as brothers and sisters by the children of the Catholic Church.

This was the first step in the process of befriending non-Catholic Christians. The second step was to recognize the non-Catholic Christian communities as Churches. In an earlier draft of the Dogmatic Constitution on the Church there was a statement which totally identified the Church of Christ with the Roman Catholic Church." The Church of Christ is the Roman Catholic Church" (LG 8). This was based on the teaching of Pope Pius XII that the Church of Christ, the Roman Catholic Church and the Mystical Body of Christ are one and the same thing (Neuner & Dupuis, 2008: 847, 858). The Council changed this statement to: "The Church of Christ subsists in the Roman Catholic" (LG 8). It then observed that "many elements of sanctification and of truth can be found outside of her visible structure" (LG 8). Whatever be the exact meaning of this changed formulation, it does imply that the Catholic Church does not exhaust the ecclesial possibilities of the Church of Christ. These ecclesial possibilities are realized in the other Churches. Hence the Council calls them Christian Churches (LG 15, UR 3).[2]

These Christian Churches have many elements in common with the Catholic Church: Sacred Scripture, faith in the Triune God and Jesus Christ the Saviour. They celebrate baptism and some of the other sacraments. Many of them have the episcopate and venerate the Blessed Virgin Mary.

The Council took a third step when it declared that these Churches have significance in the mystery of salvation. The Spirit of Christ uses them as means of salvation for their members (UR 3).

In its effort to befriend the other Churches, the Council took two more steps. While speaking about dialogue within and without the Church, Vatican II states: "Our hearts embrace also those brothers and communities not yet living with us in full communion" (GS 92). The Council also expresses its desire to collaborate with the members of the other Churches:

> Cooperation among all Christians vividly expresses that bond which already unites them, and it sets in clearer relief the features of Christ the Servant. Such cooperation, which has already begun in many countries, should be ever increasingly developed, particularly in regions where a social and technical evolution is taking place. It should contribute to a just appreciation of the dignity of the human person, the promotion of the blessings of peace, the application of gospel principles to social life, and the advancement of the arts and sciences in a Christian spirit (UR 12).

Such collaboration is to be extended to the fight against social evils like poverty and illiteracy. The Council goes on to add: "Through such cooperation, all believers in Christ are able to learn easily how they can understand each other better and esteem each other more, and how the road to the unity of Christian may be made smooth" (UR 12).

2. Befriending the Other Religions

Old Understanding of Religions

For centuries most Christians believed that Christianity was the only true religion since it alone was divinely instituted. Perhaps the best known exponent of this view was Dr. Henrik Kraemer of Netherlands, who, in 1938, published a book titled: *The Christian Message in a Non-Christian World* (Kraemer, 1938). "The main thesis of my book", he wrote in the Foreword, "is that the Christian Revelation is ... absolutely *sui generis* (Kraemer, 1938: ix). Following Barth and Kierkegaard, Kraemer maintained that there is an 'absolute qualitative difference' between the Gospel of Christ and all other religions. "When Christianity as a total religious system approaches the non-Christian religions as total religious systems, there is only difference and antithesis" (Kraemer, 1938: 131-132 & 115-120). Hence it is not possible to compare Christianity with any other religion. "There is no point of contact: ... there are no bridges from human religious consciousness to Christ" (Kraemer, 1938: 131-132). Moreover non-Christian religions are, according to this view, quite incapable of leading human beings to a true knowledge of God or of salvation.

And among Catholics a Church-centred ecclesiology held sway for a long period of time. According to this theology the Church was the only God-appointed means of salvation. There was no salvation outside the Church (Neuner & Dupuis, 2008: 810). The Church possessed the fullness of truth and can teach it infallibly. She was the only authoritative interpreter of the natural Law. By and large the Church's attitude to the other religions was quite negative. It was unthinkable that these religions might be ways of salvation for their followers. In 1867 Pius IX rejected as errors the following:

> Everyone is free to embrace and profess the religion which by the light of reason he judges to be true. Men can find the way to eternal salvation and attain eternal salvation by the practice of any religion whatever (Neuner & Dupuis, 2008: 810).

No wonder, then, that Catholic missionaries were not interested in dialogue and collaboration with the followers of other religions. Speaking of them E. C. Dewick has remarked:

> They went out with love for non-Christians in their hearts, but not with any thought of appreciating the non-Christian religions. Their purpose was simply to rescue souls from the clutches of heathenism in this world and from the fires of hell in the next. They went to give, and not to receive; to save, not to cooperate (Dewick, 1953: 116).

In all fairness it must be admitted that there were some Catholic thinkers like Cardinal Nicholas of Cusa who adopted a positive approach to the non-

Christian religions. But they were not representative of the position generally held by Catholics.

Positive Understanding of Religions

It is in Vatican II that an Ecumenical Council for the first time dealt with the non-Christian religions. While discussing the schema on the Church the Council Fathers requested that non-Christians be treated not globally but according to the religious groups to which they belonged. Hence *Lumen Gentium* deals with the Jews, the Muslims, those who believe in God and then the non-believers (LG 16). *Nostra Aetate* speaks of Hinduism, Buddhism, Islam and Judaism (NA). And Vatican II vindicates religious freedom not only for Christians but also for the followers of other religions (DH 4). Thus recognition is accorded to the world religions.

This is the first step in the Council's effort to befriend the other religions.

The second step is the expression of genuine appreciation of the positive values to be found in these religions – truth and goodness, grace and holiness (LG 16; NA 2; OT 16). Vatican II believes that God is the source of these values. According to the Dogmatic Constitution on the Church, "whatever goodness or truth is found among them is looked upon by the Church … as given by Him who enlightens all men and women that they may finally have life" (LG 16). Here the text refers to John 1:9 which says that the Word was the true light which enlightens everyone. John is here speaking of the eternal Word and not the incarnate Word. The Decree on the Missionary Activity of the Church regards whatever truth and grace are to be found among the nations "as a secret presence of God" (AG 9).

Hence for the Council these religions are not pure human creations. God is at work in their origin and growth.

This leads to the third step. Vatican II exhorts the children of the Church:

> Prudently and lovingly, through dialogue and collaboration with the followers of other religions, and in witness of Christian faith and life, acknowledge, preserve, and promote the spiritual and moral goods found among these men, as well as the values in their society and culture (NA 3).

The Council looks upon dialogue as a means to arrive at truth through love and as a spiritual pursuit:

> We also turn our thoughts to all who acknowledge God and who preserve in their traditions precious elements of religion and humanity. We want frank conversation to compel us all to receive the inspirations of the Spirit faithfully and to measure up to them energetically.
>
> For our part, the desire for such dialogue which can lead to truth through love alone, excludes no one, though an appropriate measure of prudence must undoubtedly be exercised (GS 92).

The Council also encourages collaboration among the followers of different religions:

> Since God the Father is the origin and purpose of all men and women, we are all called to be brothers and sisters. Therefore, if we have been summoned to the same destiny, which is both human and divine, we can and we should work together without violence and deceit in order to build up the world in genuine peace (GS 92).

Thus Vatican II looks upon the followers of other religions as partners in our common quest for justice and peace in the world.

3. Befriending the Modern World

Moving Away from the Middle Ages

Right from the beginning the Church's attitude to the world was ambiguous (Neuner, 1981: 449). On the one hand it looked upon the world as an object of God's love, since God created it and continued to care for it. On the other hand it regarded the world as hostile to God, since it had closed itself against God in its sinful self-sufficiency. Both John and Paul, among the New Testament writers, gave expression to this ambiguity (McKenzie, 1994: 942-944). During the centuries of Roman persecution the Church adopted a very negative attitude to the world. It thought of itself as a community of believers surrounded by a wicked world (Neuner, 1981: 448). Baptism was the moment of decision when a person renounced the spirit of the world and embraced the spirit of Christ (Schillebeeckx, 1981: 56). The Didache has preserved a text which shows thatthe Eucharistic celebration concluded with the words: "Let grace come, let this world pass away (Kleist, 1988: 109).

The Church of the Middle ages was somewhat ambivalent in its approach to the world. It fostered a spirituality based on a contempt of the world. As Alfons Auer had pointed out:

> The basic attitude of the Middle Ages was one-sidedly that of flight from the world. The monastic ascetical ideal prevailed also in the world; medieval Christianity was predominantly shaped by monks. Its ideal of life had a fascinating effect also upon laymen; one thought he could serve God best and most uncompromisingly when he bade farewell to the world (Auer, 1965: 6).

There was on the other hand an effort made to subjugate the world to the Church or even to absorb it. To quote Auer once again,

> In the greatness of the Middle Ages its very limitations become all the more apparent. No other age was able to achieve to the same degree a blending of the terrestrial and heavenly kingdom into a single universal order in which the temporal realms were directly ordered to the spiritual

> reality of the Church, and even – in order to maintain this order – directly or at least indirectly subjugated to ecclesiastical regulation. This unitary order necessarily resulted in a situation in which temporal matters were not adequately considered with respect to their inherent value nor sufficiently seen as fashioned according to their own laws. In the long run, the sacred order of the Middle Ages amounted to the same thing as Monophysitism (Auer, 1965: 8-9).

In a way the modern phenomenon of secularization is a reaction to this tendency on the part of the Church to absorb the world and not to respect it in its otherness. Gradually human beings, human society and its institutions, the arts and the sciences, work and professions began to assert their autonomy with respect to the Church and to affirm their intrinsic value. However, the Church reacted to this process quite negatively. As Avery Dulles observes,

> The papal encyclicals from Gregory XVI (1831-46) to Pius XII (1939-59) continually deplore modern errors. *The Syllabus of Errors*, published by Pius IX in 1864, comes to a climax with Error No. 80: "The Roman pontiff can and should reconcile himself with, and adjust to progress, liberalism, and recent civilization." In 1907 the Church condemned Modernism, a movement that had begun as an effort by Catholics to bring the Church abreast of the times. Much later, just as World War II was breaking out, Pius XII issued his first encyclical, Darkness over the Earth (*Summi Pontificatus*, Oct. 20, 19039), reflecting remnants of this antimodernist mentality (Dulles, 1974: 31).

Positive Attitude to the World

Pope John XXIII had quite a different attitude. In his Apostolic Constitution convoking Vatican II he emphatically declared: "Distrustful souls see only darkness burdening the face of the earth. We, instead, like to reaffirm all our confidence in our Saviour, who has not left the world he redeemed" (John XIII, 1991: 704). And in his opening address to the first session he made it clear that he was not one of those who "in these modern times... can see nothing but prevarication and ruin" (John XVIII, 1061: 712). Pope John's positive attitude to the modern world has had a great impact on *Gaudium et Spes*. That is probably why it has turned out to be one of the most inspiring documents of the Council.

Right at the beginning the Pastoral Constitution explains how it understands the modern world:

> Therefore, the Council focuses its attention on the world of men,the whole human family along with the sum of those realities in the midst of which that family lives. It gazes upon that world which is the theatre of man's history, and carries the marks of his energies, his tragedies, and his triumphs; that world which the Christian sees as created and sustained by

> its Maker's love, fallen indeed into the bondage of sin, yet emancipated now by Christ (GS 2).

There are three important elements in the Council's understanding of the modern world. This world is a world of human beings together with the subhuman creation in the midst of which they live. It is the scene of their history and bears the mark of their labour and their struggle, their successes and their failures. Though this world fell into sin it has been liberated by Christ. This is a very positive way of looking at the world. It is interesting to note that Vatican II regards the difficulties brought about by the rapid changes taking place in the world as a 'crisis of growth' (GS 4).

All this constitutes the first step in the Council's befriending of the modern world.

The second step is that Vatican II has adopted a positive attitude to the process of secularization. In unmistakable terms it declares:

> If by the autonomy of earthly affairs we mean that created things and societies themselves enjoy their own laws and values which must be gradually deciphered, put to use, and regulated by men, then it is entirely right to demand that autonomy. Such is not merely required by modern man, but harmonizes also with the will of the Creator. For by the very circumstance of their having been created, all things are endowed with their own stability, truth, goodness, proper laws, and order. Man must respect these as he isolates them by the appropriate methods of the individual sciences or arts (GS 36).

Such a view leads to the recognition of the freedom and legitimacy of the arts and the sciences. As *Gaudium et Spes* puts it,

> The Church is not against the use by human arts and sciences of their own principles and methods in their respective fields; therefore it acknowledges this lawful freedom and affirms the legitimate autonomy of culture and especially of the sciences (GS 59).

The third step that the Council has taken in befriending the modern world is this: It expresses its appreciation of the developments in the world:

> The Council, therefore, looks with great respect upon all the true, good, and just elements found in the very wide variety of institutions which the human race has established for itself and constantly continues to establish (GS 42).

Vatican II goes on to add:

> The Church further recognizes that worthy elements are found in today's social movements, especially an evolution toward unity, a process of wholesome socialization and of association in civic and economic realms. For the promotion of unity belongs to the innermost nature of the Church,

> since she is, "by her relationship with Christ, both a sacramental sign and an instrument of intimate union with God, and of the unity of all humankind" (GS 42).

A fourth step is the manifestation of the Council's eagerness to dialogue with the modern world. It believes that "this Council can provide no more eloquent proof of its solidarity with the entire human family with which it is bound up, as well as its respect and love for that family, than by engaging with it in conversation about these various problems" (GS 3).

In this context I would like to quote a pertinent observation made by Avery Dulles:

> The Pastoral Constitution, in particular, sought to bring the Church into dialogue with the world on a basis of mutual respect and reciprocal give-and-take… The Council sees the Church as involved with the world in the tremendous social and cultural transformations of our times, and affirms the Church's solidarity with 'the joys and the hopes, the griefs and the anxieties of the men and women of this age'. Renouncing any attitude of haughty superiority, the Council expresses 'great respect' for "all the true, good and just elements found in the very wide variety of institutions which the human race has established for itself and constantly continues to establish". The Church here professes its readiness to put its talents and resources to work in order to contribute to secular goals such as peace, freedom, justice and human dignity (Dulles, 1971: 11).

What is perhaps most significant in the Pastoral Constitution is that it conceives the role of the Church in the modern world as that of a servant. Inspired by no earthly ambition, the Church wishes only to carry forward the work of Christ who came not to be served but to serve (GS 3). Hence "Christians cannot yearn for anything more ardently than to serve the men and women of the modern world ever more generously and effectively" (GS 93). The document spells out concretely the kind of service that the Church can render to human persons, human communities and human activity in the world (GS 40-43).

Yet another step in the Council's befriending of the modern world is this: It gratefully acknowledges the benefits the Church has received from the world. Vatican II has stated:

> Thanks to the experience of past ages, the progress of the sciences, and the treasures hidden in the various forms of human culture, the nature of man himself is more clearly revealed and new roads to truth are opened. These benefits profit the Church, too (GS 44).

The Council goes on to add:

> Since the Church has a visible and social structure as a sign of her unity in Christ, she can and ought to be enriched by the development of human social life. The reason is not that the constitution given her by Christ is defective, but so that she may understand it more penetratingly, express it better, and adjust it more successfully to our times (GS 44).

Conclusion

To conclude: The Second Vatican Council has taken several steps to befriend the non-Catholic Christians and their Churches, the non-Christians and their religions and the modern world. It is up to the Catholic faithful now to imbibe the spirit of this great Council and establish cordial relations with non-Catholic Christians, the followers of other faiths and the modern world.

References

Abbot, W. R. (1966). *Documents of Vatican II*, New York: America Press, 1966.

AG: Ad Gentes, the SecondVatican Council's Decree on Missionary Activity, in Abbot, 1966.

Alberigo G. (1987). "The Christian Situation after Vatican II" in G. Alberigo and others (eds.) *The Reception of Vatican II*, Washington, D.C.: The Catholic University of America Press, 1987, pp. 13-14.

Dawson, C. (2002). *Dynamics of World History*, Wilmington: ISI books, 2002.

Dewick, E. C. (1953). *The Christian Attitude to Other Religions*, London: Cambridge.

DH: Dignitatis Humanae Vatican II, Declaration on Religious Freedom, in Abbot, 1966.

Dulles, A. (1971)."The Church in Communication" in *Catholic Mind,* 69.

Dulles, A. (1974). *Models of the Church*, Garden City.

GS: Gaudium et spes: Vatican II, Pastoral Constitution on the Church in the Modern World, in Abbot, 1966.

John XXIII, Pope Apostolic Constitution "*Humanae Solutis*" dated December 25, 1961, convoking the Council. Abbot, 1966.

John XXIII, Pope. (Dec 25, 1961). Apostolic Constitution "*Humanae Solutis*" dated December 25, 1961, convoking the Council.

Kleist, J. A. (1988). *The Didache*. New York, N.Y: Newman Press.

Kraemer, H. (1938). *The Christian Message in a Non-Christian World*, London: 1938.

LG: Lumen Gentium. Vatican II, Dogmatic Constitution on the Church, in Abbot, 1966.

McKenzie, J. L. (1994). *Dictionary of the Bible*. London: Geoffrey Chapman.

NA: Nostra Aetate. Vatican II, Declaration on the Church's Relationship to Non-Christian Religions.

Neuner, J. (1981). "The Role and Responsibility of the Laity in the struggle for a New Society" in D. S. Amalorpavadass, (ed.), *The Indian Church in the Struggle for a New Society*, Bangalore: NBCLC.

Neuner, J. (1983). "Exploring Global Dimensions of Jesuit Priestly Apostolate", in *Ignis Studies* 2 (1983) p. 13.

Neuner, J. and J. Dupuis. (2008). *The Christian faith in the doctrinal documents of the Catholic Church*. Bangalore: Theological Publ. in India.

OT: Optatam Totius, the Decree on Priestly Formation, in Abbot, 1966

Schillebeeckx, E. (1981). *Ministry: A Case for Change*, London: SCM Press.

UR: Unitatis Redintegratio. Vatican II, Decree on Ecumenism, in Abbot, 1966.

Notes

1 Speaking of the members of the other churches the authorities of the Catholic Church use expressions like "perverse opinions and errors", "extraordinary boldness", "arrogant claim" etc. See Neuner and Dupuis. 2008: 816.

2 It may be acknowledged that the Documents of Vatican II does not use inclusive language.

27

Befriending of Science-Religion: The Pursuit of Fulfilment and Happiness According to Sri Aurobindo

Kamladevi Kunkolienker
P.E.S' R.S.N. College of Arts and Science, Farmagudi Ponda, Goa.

Abstract: This paper tries to understand the need for befriending of so called the opposites, science and religion. In the beginning an effort is made to show how man had put together scientific spirit and spirituality to live a comfortable and happy life. Next, we see how development in science and technology prompted change s in our well-established values. That gave rise to certain values which estranged the relationship between the two. But it is the west which most feels the estrangement between the two. The East has been generally, inclusive and holistic in its approach, at least, Indian tradition is concerned. The purpose of befriending is explained, from human progress point of view and leading to happiness, which is our ultimate goal.

Keywords: Science-religion dialogue, Befriending science and religion, Spirituality and culture, Happiness and fulfilment.

"Science investigates, religion interprets. Science gives man knowledge, which is power; religion gives man wisdom, which is control. Science deals mainly with facts; religion deals mainly with values. The two are not rivals." -Martin Luther King Jr.

Man, indeed is different from all other creatures, that is, his fellow-species on earth, as we observe ourselves from different aspects, As Sri Aurobindo writes in the *Life Divine* (Aurobindo, 2013). Inspired by Aurobindo, I attempt to understand the need for befriending of "so-called opposites," science and religion. In the beginning an effort is made to show how man had put together scientific spirit and spirituality to live a comfortable and happy life. Next, we see how development in science and technology prompted change s in our well-established values. That gave rise to certain values which estranged the relationship between the two. But it is the west which most feels the estrangement between the two. The East has been generally, inclusive and holistic in its approach, at least, Indian tradition is concerned. The purpose of befriending is explained, from the point of view of human progress and leading to fullness and happiness, which is our ultimate goal of our lives. A life that encompasses it physical and spiritual dimensions.

Embracing the Physical and Spiritual

"The animal is satisfied with a modicum of necessity; the gods are content with their splendours'. But man cannot rest permanently until he reaches some highest good. He is the greatest of living beings because he is the most discontented, because he feels most the pressure of limitations" (Sethna & Baran, 1997: 31). It is also true that, the other species on earth live in the present moment, whereas man alone lives in three modes of time simultaneously, irrespective of the fact that he is conscious of it or not. Why is man what he is? Why is he created with this urge to know? Mankind is further marked by differences within itself_ depending on factors such as culture, religion, nationality, wealth, education, temperament, refinement and much more. To link the past with the present and the present with the future is propelled by the basic quest to know and realize oneself. There was a time when this basic quest in man, which may be termed his inner quest, because response to this only could come through an exploration of his consciousness, went hand in hand with his external explorations of his environment, Nature, in search of better living conditions. In the Indian tradition we find the example of rishis or sages, who were an explorer of inner mysteries of life and an architect of life in its social context, capable of leading a seeker along the spiritual path and guiding a king through his pragmatic political crisis. Also he could author an esoteric hymn and be a poet of splendours of life. For these sages, life was a field of experience embracing both the physical world and the spirit.

As we look at the West, we observe that, in the beginning the story was not very different from the East. However, with the advent of philosophy, the knowledge at a certain phase of human development resulted in the formation of two different paths: the path of the spirit and the path of the mundane world. The first meant a total preoccupation with the spirit ignoring the worldly affairs and the second meant a total absorption with the matter, the worldly affairs at the cost of the spirit. It was post-renaissance period during which science developed to such an extent that, it claimed to explain the origin of the universe and man without any recourse to god. Religion, of course, has existed for much longer. However, there is the thesis, according to which science and technology, on the one hand, and religion, on the other, are inversely related. Recent resurgences of religion and religious belief in many parts of the world, however, cast considerable doubt on this thesis.

Western and Indian Civilizations

Advancements in science and technology prompted or brought about tremendous changes in values. The relation between these two great cultural forces has been multi faceted. As mentioned earlier that humanity has many angles and therefore it is mandatory to know all possible aspects of it. There is possibility of science befriending religion, because the two are not exclusive. When both of them are taken as independent of each other, equally powerful, and when they are looked at from extremes, they have always harmed humanity and played havoc with society. Be it consumerism as a by- product of materialism or technology that is misused for selfish gains. Sri Aurobindo foresaw the negative impact of materialism, science and technology on our value system, and rather at the global level, as early as 1916 which he terms as 'mindless consumerism' which is the dominant characteristic of our Age. He observes that, human aspiration for happiness, which is a part and parcel of spiituality, was turned into "success" as a value. In the following quote he brings out the 'economic' and 'physical' barbarism endorsed by modern science:

> [Modern science] has encouraged more or less indirectly by its attitude to life and its discoveries another kind of barbarism, – for it can be called by no other name, – that of the industrial, the commercial, the economic age which is now progressing to its culmination and its close. This economic barbarism is essentially that of the vital man who mistakes the vital being for the self and accepts its satisfaction as the first aim of life .... Just as the physical barbarian makes the excellence of the body and the development of the physical force, health and prowess his standard and aim, so the vitalistic or economic barbarian makes the satisfaction of wants and desires and the accumulation of possessions his standard and aim. His ideal man is not the cultured or noble or thoughtful or moral or religious, but the successful man. To arrive, to succeed, to produce, to accumulate, to possess is his existence. ... life devoid of beauty and nobility, religion vulgarized or coldly formalized, politics and government turned into a trade and profession, enjoyment itself made a business, this is commercialism (Sethna & Baran, 1997: 53-54).

The ripple effect of this barbarism which he predicted on education, religion, politics, is something which we are witnessing today. Aurobindo comments with reference to the concept of civilization and religion from the viewpoint of a common man, " His idea of civilization is comfort, his idea of morals social respectability, his idea of politics the encouragement of industry, the opening of markets, exploitation and trade following the flag, his idea of religion at best a pletistic formalism or the satisfaction of certain vitalistic emotions" (Sethna & Baran, 1997: 54). The advancement in science made people value education for its utility, to make a man fit for success in competitive world and socialized industrial existence; value science for the useful inventions and knowledge so that he can live a comfortable life. In other words, the great capitalists and the organizers of industry are the supermen of this commercial age.

Like Aurobindo, Rabindranath Tagore also was not willing to accept the western concept of progress. He remarks: "With what is called material progress, property has become intensely individualistic, the method of gaining it has become a matter of science and not of social ethics. It breaks social bonds; it drains the life sap of the community. Its unscrupulous plays havoc all over the world, generating forces that can coax or coerce peoples to deeds of injustice and wholesome horror" (Indrani & Shashinungla, 1975: 58). It is not that Tagore did not have respect for science, rather he advocated limited use of science confined to man's welfare and not for plundering nature. According to him, science is truth and it gives us freedom in the realm of matter. Although he welcomed western science, yet he wanted science projects to be guided by moral ideas. For Tagore, a world of science minus moral norms is a world of violence and aggression, 'fit for the world of tigers'" (Indrani & Shashinungla, 1975: 58).

The fast development and ascent to modern civilization during last two centuries was possible because of the exponential growth of knowledge. As far as technology is concerned, there are fascinating prospects for the future. However, the development of a highly technological society does not free us from ethical and moral demands. Science cannot divorce itself from issues which take humanity beyond science itself. The mere technological advancements of which we boast and are proud of, should also take pain to have some insights about functioning of life in general and of nature in particular. Relativity may sometimes be used as the right way to understand reality. Relativity theory seems to be a theory of nature which has explained not only contemporary empirical data but is also suggestive of what ought to be in future. Some of the issues which affect humanity at present and to which science has not provided any satisfactory solution because alone it cannot, include the political, economic, religious and psychological problems of our age. Science cannot overcome racial divisions and religious extremism, it cannot create a world which is at peace. Issues like this are very much connected with culture itself. The loss of decency of humanity is at the heart of the crisis that calls for a discussion of value. What is it that is to be accepted as a value is inseparable from culture, that is created by man.

Culture is a very complex phenomenon. We find that, in the beginning, at the visible level what matters us are the artefacts, constructed social environment, overt behaviour. At the next level, culture is manifested as values, where actions and events are assigned meaning according to what ought to be. Next, these values which are consistently useful are transformed into assumptions, rather unspoken and they constitute deepest level of culture. Our intrinsic nature influences culture. The abovementioned issues are not necessarily the problems that modem science can address, since they are the problems of the heart, of the mind, of attitude and a way of life; as such they fall outside the scope of science as per the view of the scientists.

Religion too, has failed to understand man in totality. In the garb of religious rituals, the poor, the powerless are harassed. When religion that is practiced and preached is not realistic, it becomes an escape from reality. Humanity suffers from evil and it becomes 'ugly'. The culture and values are 'corrupted ' by social evils. Hence, science along with other complementary factors can play a very constructive role in correcting religion, transforming it and making it anew. Rather, culture and religion are entangled with values, which deal with all possible aspects of human life. There may be hierarchy of values in particular cultures of the world, as we find one in our own culture. The western world valued the material approach more than the spiritual or looking within, while Indians and the other eastern cultures valued the spiritual aspect more than the material. This is one of the most prominent factor for the technological advance in the Western world. However, it is undeniable that the impact such technology has made on our culture and values, has been negative, showing a kind of dissonance with already established values. The traditional values, which supported Indian civilization for thousands of years, need to be strengthened and perpetuated, as they can build a bridge between the past and the future of our country and between India and rest of the world.

Need for Befriending of Science and Spirituality

There is increasing proximity of both, science and religion, towards explaining and understanding certain basic or foundational issues like_ the nature of reality, origin of the Universe, human behaviour, evolution, moral behaviour and so on. This proximity either may lead to contempt or friendship. The path of contempt or conflict leads to self-limitation, whereas the path of friendship may open up new ways with positive attitude to understand these issues with a new paradigm.

The pressure felt due to the present challenges faced by the society, whether urban, rural, semi-urban or cosmopolitan on the one hand and the aspirations and the prospects of our future society on the other, calls for a friendship or a supportive attitude between science and spirituality. For instance, the challenge that we face of population explosion, creating healthy societies free from pain and suffering, threats from natural calamities where thousands of people lose their lives, and most important of all is living by the principles of ethics and morality, demand urgent solutions, which the lopsided development of science or spirituality cannot provide. Humanity is forced to look forward for such solutions in the coming together of these two great powers.

According to these great minds like_ M. Gandhi, Vinoba Bhave, Tagore, Sri Aurobindo, the most important thing is religiosity than religion. Religiosity being universal, will free man from institutions, churches, temples, sections and personal Gods. The static religion with, at least some of its age-old rituals and values are a hurdle in path of new paradigm. We do recognize beyond doubt the findings of science as attractive and useful, but the world does not belong to impersonal science, as it tries to capture the world as it is without the intervention of imagination. We are wrong in adopting scientific findings when we give science an Omniscient and Omnipotent status. As R. Tagore points out that, the world belongs to 'personality ', and human personality is such that it creates new relationships with the world. He accepts dynamism in every sphere of the universe, which constantly rearranges the meaning of things and which is displayed in his creations. The 'truth' lies not in the mass of materials, but in their universal relatedness, which only the human mind is able to understand. He observes further that it is possible for human personality to comprehend and transcend the details of the facts, knowledge, feeling, wish and will, as well as the individual's memory, hope, love, activities and all his belongings. This transcendence takes place through a unity, and this sublimation is a product of love. The realization of the existence of the 'other' makes the "I" realize his extension. Tagore says, " I become more in my union with others..." (Indrani & Shashinungla, 1975: 91).

Philosophers, cognitive scientist and social scientists agree that friendship is an essential ingredient of human happiness. Aristotle classified friendship into three distinct categories: of pleasure, of utility and of virtue. The first one brings direct pleasure while the second, is one where a tangible benefit either economic or political, is possible. According to Aristotle, the highest kind of friendship is that of virtue, which brings happiness. He believed that friends hold a mirror up to each other and through that mirror they can see each other in ways that would not otherwise be accessible to them. It is this reciprocal mirroring that helps them improve themselves. In the similar fashion, in the new paradigm also of religion and science befriending each other, we expect that it will work together for global happiness. The solution to the global issues facing mankind requires an ethical transformation, which lies in the area of human relationships. In the light of interconnectedness and interdependence, that is observed in nature, and proved by quantum science, we should aim at the oneness of religion. The oneness of religion asserts that, individuals must seek education and knowledge that is greater than themselves. We find that the posture of social and behavioural sciences to study the interactions between individuals is a right one. Our greatest joys as well as problems involve human relationships, and successful human relationships involve love and happiness.

Science and spirituality, both the parties involved in this relationship will contribute to the relationship in order to enrich it, since they share a complementary relationship. Care should be taken to see that this relationship does not fall into customary practice or dead habit. It should be dynamic and flexible enough to assimilate the innovative ideas with a positive attitude. This should bring about not only the material and social construction, but also new values catering to our inner life.

The need for befriending of science and spirituality is felt more by the Western world, which believes in sophisticated technology more than the Eastern culture. Sri Aurobindo in his book on 'Foundations of Indian Culture' writes about how a culture or civilization can be evaluated: "A true happiness in this world is the right terrestrial aim of man, and true happiness lies in the finding and the maintenance of a natural harmony of spirit, mind and body. A culture is to be valued to the extent to which it has discovered the right key of this harmony and organized its expressive motives and movements" (Aurobindo, 1997: 56).

The eastern religion – what may be considered the deeper and more significant elements – are not only compatible with science but enrich its findings. The best evidence of this is science's response to the religions of the East over the course of the last 200 years. As the French Nobel laureate Romain Rolland said early in the 20th century, "Religious faith in the case of the Hindus has never been allowed to run counter to scientific laws." The same can be said for Buddhism, which derives from the same Vedic roots.

Also, most of the Hindu gurus, Yoga masters, Buddhist monks and other Asian teachers who came to the West framed their traditions in a science-friendly way. Emphasizing the experiential dimension of spirituality, with its demonstrable influence on individual lives, they presented their teachings as a science of consciousness with a theoretical component and a set of practical applications for applying and testing those theories. Most of the teachers were educated in both their own traditions and the Western canon; they respected science, had actively studied it, and dialogued with Western scientists, many of whom were inspired to study Eastern concepts for both personal and professional reasons.

The cooperation between science and spirituality is most noted today in the field of medicine. There is a growing body of research which suggests that, spirituality does play a role in health matters. The researchers observe that, the religious faith not only promotes overall good health, but also helps in recovery of serious illness. Certainly, science and religion have contributed towards our understanding of this universe in multiple ways, and whatever they have accomplished is truly impressive. In order that there should be an overall integral development of humanity, perhaps the time has come for science and religion to acknowledge each other's power and influence, join forces and work together in mutual respect to help solve the world's problems. This process should bring about the change in the attitude towards values, as there should be consistency and harmony in the values themselves that we take as foundational in this journey. The goal of all this is the pursuit of happiness of mankind, which is included in spirituality itself.

Conclusion

Science and religion are not negations of each other, rather they are two great forces which have shaped humanity and its culture for thousands of years. It depends upon how our scientists and theologians interpret the working of these forces for common man, that will bring about change in our attitude towards values. The ultimate goal of humanity is happiness and well-being of all, which includes both, our material progress as well as moral development, which is a part and parcel of our quest for spirituality itself.

References

Aurobindo, Sri. (2013). The Life Divine. New York: E.P. Dutton.

Aurobindo, Sri. (1997). Renaissance in India and Other Essays on Indian Culture. Pondicherry: Sri Aurobindo Ashram Trust.

Indrani, Sanyal and Shashinungla (eds). (1975). Ethics and Culture: Some Indian Reflections. Kolkata: Jadavpur University, and Descent Books, New Delhi.

Sethna K.D. and Nirod Baran (eds). (1997). Quoted in "Riddle that is Man," Sri Aurobindo and the New Age: Essays in memory of Kishore Gandhi. Pondicherry: Sri Aurobindo International Centre of Education.

28

"Be Human to Nature": A Call from the World of Sciences

S. Stephen Jayard

Professor, Philosophy of Science and Cosmology, Jnana Deepa, Pune

Abstract: This article deals with the clarion call from the contemporary sciences to "befriend" nature; they also remind us that **every *human being* needs to move towards *being human***. The call and the reminder become serious and urgent, more than ever before, as the damages done to the earth and the environment increasingly become more severe and alarming and some of the damages are even irrevocable. Let us analyze the issue from three specific angles, in which contemporary sciences invite every human being to move towards being human: the fact of **mystery**, the need for **meaning in life** and the demand for **wisdom**. The author expects science to collaborate with other disciplines to enrich humanity. It is high time that we realized, as Philip Clayton declares, "... science alone will never provide the answer" (Clayton, 2006: xvi). To look for meaning of life merely in scientific endeavors will be like looking for the right thing in a wrong place, or the wrong thing in a right place... but in both the cases, we will be the losers! ***Why should we, as rational beings, who are able to develop sciences, be the losers after all?***

Keywords: Science-religion dialogue, Wisdom, Mystery, Meaning in life

Human beings of the ultramodern society are invited by the contemporary sciences to befriend nature. As the technologies develop in a very rapid manner, the life-styles change drastically, the value systems undergo a lot of changes, the ways how humans look at nature and the environment also change a lot. The changes in the outlook towards nature are unfortunately detrimental to it, and that, in turn, affects not only humans but also all living creatures and the whole of the environment. This article, given this scenario, deals with the clarion call from the contemporary sciences to "befriend" nature; they also remind us that **every *human being* needs to move towards *being human***. The call and the reminder become serious and urgent, more than ever before, as the damages done to the earth and the environment increasingly become more severe and alarming and some of the damages are even irrevocable. Let us analyze the issue from three specific angles, in which contemporary sciences invite every human being to move towards being human: the fact of **MYSTERY**, the need for **MEANING IN LIFE** and the demand for **WISDOM**.

Interconnectedness in Nature

There is a very burning need to befriend the earth and the environment. When I say that we need to befriend nature, I don't mean at all that nature is always hostile to us, nor that we are strangers to it. In fact, we all are very much part of nature. The inter-connectedness between us and nature is so much that, it is said, about fifty minerals, salts and chemical elements, like iron, carbon, oxygen, calcium, potassium, magnesium, iodine etc., that are in our bodies are also abundantly found in nature, in plants, animals, insects and even in the distant stars, millions and billions of light years away. As we are very much part of nature, the mother earth, for instance, does not reject us when we are buried after we die, nor the atmosphere rejects the smoke that comes out when our bodies are burnt.

All these chemicals and minerals have to be in our body at right quantities and ratio. It is astounding to realize that all these minerals and chemicals are lifeless in themselves but are very essential for us to have life! For instance, the presence of iron in our body – we all know that iron is very necessary for blood production. Nearly 70 % of the body's iron is available in the red blood cells (hemoglobin) and in muscle cells (myoglobin). This hemoglobin does the job of transferring oxygen in the blood from the lungs to the tissues. The presence of the required amount of iron in our body is very important. The deficiency of iron (anemia) causes several bad effects in us like, unusual tiredness (fatigue), paleness, shortness of breath, headaches and dizziness, heart palpitations, dry/damaged hair and skin, swelling and soreness of tongue and mouth, restless leg syndrome (i.e., a strong urge to move the legs when at rest), brittle/spoon-shaped nails, craving for some types of food, feeling anxious, cold hands and feet, more frequent infections and so on. Similarly, the need and the importance of phosphorus in our body is indeed very significant – it builds strong teeth, it is responsible in controlling the mechanism of how our body stores and uses energy up, it helps in reducing muscle pain after exercises, it is important for the process of filtering out waste in our kidneys, it helps to grow, maintain, and repair tissues and cells all over the body, it is helpful in producing DNA and RNA, the genetic building blocks of life. If the amount of phosphorus in our body is less than the required amount it causes bone diseases such as rickets (in children) and osteomalacia (in adults). If there is an improper balance of phosphorus and calcium it may lead to cause osteoporosis.

We are, thus, very much part of nature and nature is part of us. We cannot but be friends to nature. Of course, sometimes when we are struck by natural disasters like earthquakes, floods or tsunamis, we tend to think that nature works out against our survival and well-being. But in many of such cases it can be traced out that nature, in its efforts to maintain its own fine balance, just reacts to our actions; so these natural disasters can be seen just reactions of nature to our actions, which are very often highly detrimental to nature. For instance, at present (May 2020) the whole world is greatly challenged by the invisible (and invincible as of now!) enemy of Covid19. More than 200 countries in the world face the brunt of this alarming threat by this virus; more than 200, 000 have unfortunately lost their lives and more than three million have been affected by this virus; our deep sympathy to those suffering in one way or the other; heartfelt condolences to those who have lost their dean and near ones; sincere prayers that those who died may find the Eternal Rest and hearty appreciation to those who work day and night to cure the affected, to curb the spread of the disease and to find out the vaccine. On the other hand, nature seems to be breathing with ease these days, with less pollution in the air and water; the Mount Everest easily visible from Punjab, a few hundreds of kilometers away, which was not so earlier, due to heavy pollution in the air; the river Yamuna is cleaner; about one million square KM of hole in the Ozone layer has healed itself. All these remind us that we need to rethink about life-styles and priorities in life. In fact, when we take care of the environment we actually take care of ourselves indirectly!

Needless to say that nature sustains all sorts of lives on the earth – microbes, insects, plants and animals, including humans. It is sheer arrogance (or ignorance!) on our part to think that we, as human beings, have special rights over the natural environment compared to other creatures. The earth has been, and continues to be, a comfortable home and a safe haven for millions and millions types of creatures. Every creature has a right for safe its living on this planet earth. The tendency to demand that humans have more rights over the natural environment is known as "speciesism" – this idea was first introduced by the English philosopher Richard Ryder (1970s) and later developed by the Australian philosopher Peter Singer. Speciesism is basically a type of discrimination based on species membership; it tries to treat members of one species as morally more significant than members of other species, even when their interests are equivalent. Going along this, humans justify that they have greater moral rights than non-human animals. This kind of attitude finds nothing wrong in killing and using other animals for humans' well-being.[1] Of course there is a strong inter-dependence among all the creatures; one is eaten by others to survive; the food of one creature becomes the death of another one. So it goes without saying that for our survival we obviously need to depend on plants and animals. All living beings, other than humans, moved by their instincts, are quite sober, natural and considerate in using the natural resources ***ONLY*** for their survival and sustenance. For instance, an elephant does not generally destroy sugarcane plants or banana trees, unless it goes berserk! When it eats leaves, it eats as much as it can and leaves the other leaves untouched. We don't find greediness among the animal kingdom and they take from nature just what they need for their survival. Some 'intelligent' creatures may store for future, but not for several generations to come, which only humans can do. They don't eat for luxury, nor for pleasure, nor for taste nor for styles; unfortunately we, who claim to be the most rational and intelligent beings in the universe are doing all these three; still worse, by deliberately doing all these we spoil our health and the fine balanced fabrics of nature.

No other ling being is **seen to damage and destroy the earth** and the environment as human beings have recklessly done, and are still doing; the damages are unfortunately on the increase! It is high time that we realized that rivers, oceans, forests, birds, animals, insects, microbes and so on can live without us; in fact they can even live better without us, but we can never live without them. Einstein seems to have said: *If bees disappeared off the face of the earth, man would only have four years left to live."*[2] It is quite shocking; we and the whole eco-system depend on these little creatures, because the honey-bees contribute to the growth and maintenance of the plants and trees in nature by the process of pollination in the plants; if we are so fundamentally dependent on other species, and we cannot just think of surviving without them, how on earth can we justify that humans are better and more important species on the earth?

Human Being vs Being Human!

Being born as a human being is something that has happened to us, we have not chosen or worked for that;[3] but 'being human' is a choice that demands a radical change in our attitudes and actions. Biologically and genetically we are, no doubt, human beings, but to be emotionally, psychologically and morally human is our choice; for instance, I can choose to be an immoral person in my words, actions and attitudes. Human beings have to positively act to become human (and humane) in their dealings with one another and nature. When human beings thus become 'human' they automatically become wise, humble, considerate and friendly. They become aware of their own finitude and their dependency upon one another and nature for their very continued existence. How to be human towards nature? It is by befriending nature and the environment.

Science with all its recent researches, discoveries and inventions, seem to teach us that it is not enough that we are human beings, but we need to learn how to be human (and humane). We need to learn from science how to be human. Being human involves, among many other, being humble to learn, being considerate to live and let live, and above all, to be responsible in protecting nature and the environment, because, as the most rational beings of all the known creatures in the universe, we have the utmost duty and we are morally bound to save the earth for our future generations.

The modern philosophy of science makes us realize that that science cannot be value-neutral but value-bound. Value-based science is the need of the hour, as the value-neutral science can easily lead us to self-destruction. Contemporary sciences force us to revisit our very concept of science; it demands us to be wise, not otherwise.

I like to approach the call of contemporary science to 'be human' from three specific angles: the roles played by ***Mystery, Meaning*** and ***Wisdom*** in contemporary science.

The Fact of MYSTERY

Contemporary science questions the classical understanding of 'reality'. The new discoveries and observations, both in the macro and the micro worlds, challenge the dogmas of scientism and they "radically alter the status of knowledge and the place of the knowing subject" (Magnin, 2006: 140). ***The mysterious nature of matter:*** Heisenberg's principle of uncertainty and Bohr's principle of complementarity suggest that the actual nature of reality escapes our complete understanding, because, "The elementary particle is neither a wave nor a corpuscle but a 'thing' that combines the two images" (Magnin, 2006: 146). Therefore, at that level, matter ceases to be 'material' and "Matter has lost its substance" (Thuan, 2006: 181). ***The Mystery of the 'Fine-tuning':*** The study of biotic coincidences and the anthropic principles seems to suggest that the universe has been very meticulously fine-tuned to be ready to receive conscious human beings; being convinced of this Freeman Dyson asserts that "the universe knew we were coming" (Dyson, 1979: 250) and Paul Davies declares that "We are truly meant to be here" (Davies, 1992: 232). Fine-tuning in the universe, though may not be a proof, but a strong indicator for an intelligent design behind the universe; for instance, the initial density of the universe had to be meticulously fixed to an accuracy of 10-60 and this precision is like an archer hitting a one-centimeter-square target placed fifteen billion light-years away (Thuan, 2006: 184). Several scientists-turned theologians, like John Polkinghorne, Arthur Peacock, Ilya Prigogine etc. also find something more to the evolution process than mere chance. They have gone beyond reductionism and are open to mystical and metaphysical overtones in their approach to reality. Even great minds, like Einstein, are also convinced that such fine-tuning in the universe cannot be the outcome of a mere chance.

If one argues that all these fine-tunings are just fixed by laws of physics, then the question arises: "Where do the laws of physics come from? And why *those* laws rather than some other set?" (Davies, 2006: 31). Therefore, the mystery still remains! Such a realization of mystery in nature makes the investigation of the universe meaningful and thereby gives meaning to for our existence.

The Need for MEANING IN LIFE

One of the fundamental ways to define humans is to see them as 'seekers of meaning'. As Victor Frankl[4] shows, the search for 'meaning in life' becomes more fundamental to life than food, shelter and clothing; for, even if one has enough food, shelter and clothing, one cannot still manage to live, if one does not have meaning in life. Philip Clayton[5] shows that the meaning-quest is related to the very nature of human being and sciences alone will not be sufficient to comprehend human nature, and therefore, the quest for meaning cannot be satisfactorily fulfilled by science alone, though science may contribute something in the process of meaning-seeking.

Though humans are biologically very much a part of creation and share a lot with other creatures, yet they seem to be far different from all of them, in terms of reason, will power, ability to imagine, the exercise of control over natural passion and above all the ability to go beyond the immediate environment.[6] However, we cannot easily define life, nor its meaning or purpose, ***because the "questioner" and the "questioned" are one and the same here***. Modern neuroscience may succeed in mapping the areas of the brain to find out what happens when one is filled with love or hatred, fear or tranquility; Psychology may come up with convincing theories about the good effects of love and the bad effects due to its absence. ***But science cannot exactly define what love is, and since it is this love that makes one find meaning in life, science can comprehend neither love nor meaning***.

The Demand for WISDOM

As science proceeds we realize that we lose our grip over reality. The classical notions of certainty, causality, absolute measurability and stability are significantly challenged today. We are forced to get reconciled with arbitrary nature of the initial conditions, irreducibility, uncertainty, and unpredictability. By this "we are reminded of the contingence and finite nature of man" (Magnin, 2006: 142). Such realization of our finitude makes us wise and humble. We are cautioned not to meddle with the wisdom of nature that has been there for about fourteen billion years.

If we lose the sense of mystery, if we are not able to find meaning in our existence, and if we don't become wise enough not to ignore the place of values in science, we will have to face the doom of humanity. As Francis Bacon wished science must take us back to the glorious state of pre-fallen state. It should make us wise, not otherwise; unless we are smart and humble enough to learn from nature, nature will teach us some certain things in a hard way. Science is like a sword, having sharp ends on both sides and unless we are careful, we may end up using science as a tool of desolation and it would be like chopping-off the very branch of the tree upon which we are sitting. In fact, Claude Levi Strauss cautions us that "the world began without the human being, and will end without him" (Levi-Strauss, 1955).

Conclusion

A revised understanding of science, that is, science with the human face, will surely enrich humanity. Enriching humanity would mean, among many other things, making humans more sensible to mysteries, enabling them to find more meaning in their existence and wiser. Though humans have enormous cognitive power, yet they are cosmically very insignificant in the vast dark universe, known and unknown. As Blasé Pascal has it, "Man is only a reed, more frail than nature, but he is a thinking reed. It does not need the whole universe to wipe him out; a breath, a drop of water, is enough to kill him..." But still humans are more powerful and noble than the universe, because, "he knows that he dies and knows the advantage the universe has over him" (Pascal, 1976: 231 & 145), whereas the universe that kills him does not, cannot know anything.

With due admiration and respect to science, we dearly expect science to collaborate with other disciplines to enrich humanity. It is high time that we realized, as Philip Clayton declares, "… science alone will never provide the answer" (Clayton, 2006: xvi). To look for meaning of life merely in scientific endeavors will be like looking for the right thing in a wrong place, or the wrong thing in a right place… but in both the cases, we will be the losers! ***Why should we, as rational beings, who are able to develop sciences, be the losers after all?***

Reference

Clayton, Philip, (2006). "Foreword", in Staune. (2006)

Davies, Paul, (2006). "Glimpsing the Mind of God", in Staune, Jean.

Davies, Paul. (1992). *The Mind of God.* NY: Simon & Schuster.

Dyson, Freeman. (1979). *Disturbing the Universe.* NY: Harper & Row.

Levi-Strauss, Claude. (1955). *Tristes Tropiques* Paris: Librarie Plon.

Magnin, Thierry. (2006). "Moral Philosophy – A Space for Dialogue between Science and Theology", in *Science and the Search for Meaning – Perspectives from International Scientists*, Jean Staune (ed.), PA, USA: Templeton Foundation Press.

Pascal, Blasé. (1976). *Pensees*, ed. Philippe Sellier. Paris: Mercure de France.

Staune, Jean. (2006). *Science and the Search for Meaning: Perspectives from International Scientists*, PA, USA: Templeton Foundation Press.

Thuan, Trinh Xuan (2006)."Science and Buddhism", in *Science and the Search for Meaning – Perspectives from International Scientists*, in Staune. (2006)

Notes

1 However, from the religious perspectives one may argue that humans are the climax of all creations and they have been created in the image and likeness of God. One may quote the book of Genesis in the Bible that God allowed humans to subdue the whole earth and to have dominion over it; but the scripture scholars seek to interpret that powerful dominion as responsible stewardship, which invites humans to be co-creators with God, in preserving and enriching nature. Genesis 2:15 says, "Then the LORD God took the man and put him into the garden of Eden to cultivate it and keep it"; this makes it clear that human beings must be responsible to take care of it, not to dominate and destroy it for selfish purposes. Be that as it may, but from the nature's point of view, humans are one among the millions and millions of creatures in the world, though they are the only self-conscious beings.

2 See: https://www.vice.com/en_in/article/d7ezaq/what-would-happen-if-all-the-bees-died-tomorrow. Accessed on 4 May, 2020

3 Of course, from religious and faith perspectives one may say that God has a great plan from eternity that I am born and he knows even before I am formed in the womb of my mother. But still one might argue that I did not actually make any choice to be born!

4 For details see: http://www.inquiriesjournal.com/articles/660/viktor-frankls-logotherapy-the-search-for-purpose-and-meaning. Accessed on 4 May, 2020.

5 See: https://www.yumpu.com/en/document/view/19108279/science-and-the-search-for-meaning-philip-clayton. Accessed on 4 May, 2020.

6 In spite of all these special and unique features, in terms of sharing the earth's resources we cannot easily justify that we have more rights than the other creatures, as we discussed above.

29

Science and Theology: Befriending Each Other Epistemically

Augustine Pamplany
Little Flower Institute of Philosophy and Religion, Aluva- 683101, Kerala

Abstract: The author wants to indicate the need for dialogue between science and religion for the sake of human wellbeing. Science and theology have ever been the two most powerful and influential enterprises of humans determining the properties of their very being and defining the destiny of the humanity at large. The dictums and contours of the world of their meaning have been extensively processed by science and theology. The apparent dissonance between them, as was vivid in the past and even today, leaves one amused as to their meaning-making task besides raising several serious fundamental questions. Given the interwoven and overarching framework of their enquiry, what justification is there for the discordant note that they strike with each other? The tension between the religious experience and the quest for an absolute and certain knowledge, does it betray a fundamental dichotomy in the very structure of our rationality or our failure to reconcile the seemingly opposing elements of our knowledge-process? The belief in the fundamental unity of human rationality and the concern of science and theology with fundamental questions refuse to admit a fundamental dichotomy at their conceptual domains. There can be no tension between truth and truth. Once we discover the unitary conceptual grounds and frameworks of interaction, we will be able to identify the real problem in the apparent discordance between science and theology. The author argues that the assimilation and integration between science and religion becomes an imperative for the humanity as well. He agrees with Whitehead that "When we consider what religion is for mankind, and what science is, it is no exaggeration to say that the future course of history depends upon the decision of this generation as to the relations between them"

Keywords: Science-religion dialogue, Epistemological crisis, Revelation revisited, Science as hermeneutics, Common quest

Science and theology have ever been the two most powerful and influential enterprises of humans determining the properties of their very being and defining the destiny of the humanity at large. [1] The dictums and contours of the world of their meaning have been extensively processed by science and theology. The apparent dissonance between them, as was vivid in the past and even today, leaves one amused as to their meaning-making task besides raising several serious fundamental questions. Given the interwoven and overarching framework of their enquiry, what justification is there for the discordant note that they strike with each other? The tension between the religious experience and the quest for an absolute and certain knowledge, does it betray a fundamental dichotomy in the very structure of our rationality or our failure to reconcile the seemingly opposing elements of our knowledge-process? The belief in the fundamental unity of human rationality and the concern of science and theology with fundamental questions refuse to admit a fundamental dichotomy at their conceptual domains. There can be no tension between truth and truth. Once we discover the unitary conceptual grounds and frameworks of interaction, we will be able to identify the real problem in the apparent discordance between science and theology. Once the problems are identified we learn to ask the right questions on issues of dissonance.

Revelation Revisited

Traditionally theology has been defined as "the faith seeking understanding." The data of this enterprise come from revelation and tradition. The revelation that has taken place in history is encoded in the Scripture. Personal experience of God and its expressions in various forms constitute the norm of truth and authority to which believers respond in faith. The language of revelation, so fundamental to religious epistemology is a profound proclamation before the humanly constructed epistemological modalities testifying to the non-rational and supernatural horizons of truth, over and above the rational and natural domains. Revelation comprehended in its proper sense will be a holistic activity subsuming and subserving all other modes of knowing. For this, the hermeneutical matrix and the interpretative tools of revelation must be as holistic and as dynamic as the content of any authentic revelation. The process of understanding the "historical" revelation will be an ongoing hermeneutical enterprise so as to encounter the trans-historical aspects of the divine mysteries.

Nevertheless, the apologetic writings relying heavily on rational and historical evidences for the legitimization of revelation have tended to enclose it into quite parochial frameworks of reason, history, etc. The categories of revelation have been conceived of as products than processes. When the language of revelation is conceived as complete in itself, a beleaguered recourse to faith alone becomes the only way to comprehend them. This realist approach towards revelation with its consequent faith reductionism have forced the compartmentalization of itself as yet another mode of knowing, often in tension with other modes, perpetuating a radical dichotomy at the heart of the activity of knowledge. Truth has been considered as an object to be preserved in custody. The extreme reliance on faith and static outlook towards truth seem to have alienated the revelatory truth from cognitive and natural credibility. The final outcome was a systematically produced disillusionment in at least some of the hearers of revelation.

The claims of the supremacy of authority was evident in the statement of Pope Pius XII: "Investigations in science may go forward as long as all are prepared to submit to the judgment of the Church...." (Pius XII, 1990: 181). The claims of the supremacy of revealed knowledge on supernatural grounds is very vulnerable to critical assault, because the parochial understanding of theology of the supernatural as well as natural rules out the critical analysis of the fundamental assumptions of its own categories. An adequate knowledge of the material, physical, and biological aspects of the object of description ever escaped the attention of dogmatic formulations. Hence at the basis of theological knowledge was a set of static categories.

This is not to overlook the hermeneutical or mystical consciousness of theology. Despite the awareness of the historical and cultural dependence of the theological statements, a serious consideration of the material and the organic matrix and the laws and principles governing it which permeate every animate and inanimate being still eludes theology. The Scripture had underscored the role of the created realities in unraveling the mystery of the creator. "They shall not hurt or destroy in my entire holy mountain; for the earth shall be full of the knowledge of the LORD as the waters cover the sea" (Is.11:9 RSV). "Ever since the creation of the world, the invisible existence of God and his everlasting power have been clearly seen by the minds understanding of created things" (Rm.1:20). In the fourth century St. Augustine had called nature the prime Word of God. However it is doubtful whether these verses have obtained sufficient attention in Christian thinking more than their rhetorical and aesthetic values, except for a few mystical traditions.

In the modern times, the serious challenge to the taken-for-granted assumptions of the theological fundamentals comes from physics and philosophy. Although history and historical categories are fundamental to Christian theology, except for the cultural and social dimensions, the more fundamental nuances of being historical like space, time, etc., seem to have eluded Christian theology. The ever progressive understanding of the scientific fundamentals like space, time, mater, energy, etc., can revise the often static and deterministic nature of such concepts in theology. And as we discover the full nuances of the very fundamentals of theology many of the supernatural might turn out to be quite natural or some of the "natural laws" might be proved to be only "human laws."

A thousand years ago, Western philosophy had raised the splendid question: what is a thing? The epistemological crisis that still haunts the Western philosophy has shown that asking "what is a thing" is also to ask "what does it mean `to be'?" (Isham, 1993: 81-82). As the foundations of science and philosophy are shaken by the epistemological "revolutions" of the times, a credible theological proposition that does not submit itself to such serious and fundamental epistemological scrutiny will not be able to withstand the test of the times. Unless the natural and inward dynamisms of revelation are explored with critical acumen, revealed set of truths, the very starting point of theology itself would be proved to be a secondary reality. Such an introspective operation would reassert revealed knowledge itself as not that non-cognitive or non-objective as we have made it of. This will be the great epistemological awakening into the unity of knowledge dispelling the stubbornly persistent illusion of the dichotomy between reason and faith.

There are schools of thought which still uphold the supremacy of religious premises on a discordant note. "Religious thought is concerned with language and with the riddle of life, and has no need to defer to highly specialized and marginalized forms of technical expertise (like science)" (Cuppitt, 1990: 4). "Yet it is not clear if viewing God `within' nature (as implied by the scientific worldview) is any better than seeing him `outside' of nature..." (Langsfeld, 1997: 111). These statements only betray the intellectual addiction to the traditional dualistic epistemology. It is slightly surprising that St. Augustine had a challenging response to such thinking in the fourth century itself:

> It often happens that even a non-Christian knows a thing or two about the earth, the sky, the various elements of the world, about the movement and revolution of the stars and even their size and distance.... How are they going to believe our books concerning... the kingdom of heaven when they think they are filled with fallacious writing about things which they know from experience or sure calculation? There is no telling how much harm these rash and presumptuous people bring upon their more prudent brethren when begin to be caught and argued down by those who are not bound by the authority of our Scriptures, and when they then try to defend their flippant, rash, and obviously erroneous statements by quoting a shower of words from those same Sacred Scriptures, even citing from memory those passages which they think will support their case (Cited in Macior, 1997: 30-31).

It is an optimistic fact that the Church has come to this realization, as evident in the words of Pope John Paul II: "It (Theology) must be in vital interchange today with science.... Theology will have to call on the findings of science to one degree or another as it pursues its primary concerns for the human person,.... Can we not hope that the sciences of today,... may invigorate and inform those parts of the theological enterprise that bear on the relation of nature, humanity and God?" (Cited in Russell, 1990: M11, M12).

Another imperative for the intersection of science and theology is generated by culture. The praxis of modern culture, including its life-styles, values, metaphors, language, myths, etc., have been generated and dominated by science. The scientific culture is universal because, as Peacocke has rightly judged, "today one of the universal languages of humanity cutting across all cultural boundaries is that of science" (Peacocke, 1989: 11). The meaningful articulation of the theological truth in a scientific age necessitates an integration of the reliable scientific insights into theology. "We need to apply our reason to our sources - the Bible, the tradition.... The contemporary person needs to hear the word that is eternally uttered by the creator to his creation in a language that he or she can understand and respond to" (Peacocke, 1989: 11). Thus science can enable theology for a praxis based cross-cultural theology. The moral values and standards advocated by theology without scientific plausibility will be theologically arbitrary and socially unappealing.

Science as Hermeneutical

As regards science, the necessary corollary of the awareness of the unity of knowledge is openness for constructive dialogue with theology. The methodic and epistemic challenges in the self understanding of science, as discussed earlier, have dispelled the unjustified claims associated with physical and mathematical realism. Physicist Despagnat's classic distinction between "the meaningful" and "the scientifically meaningful" as suggested by the terms themselves provide a solid analogy to the demarcation between the finite horizons of meaning possessed by science and the infinite horizons transcending it. Given that the megalomaniac claims of the scientific theories of the past are untenable and also given the new metamorphic and evolutionary understanding of them, science itself is to be viewed as a dynamic hermeneutic enterprise. More than a custodian of truth, it is a candidate for reality always open to modification and correction from the data, more accurate concepts and models.

An extrinsic dynamism that can enhance the scientific picture of reality is recognition of the relation of its truth with the religious truths. "A scientific community that ignores the relation of its truth and its life to law, to morals, and to fundamental religious symbols... only makes itself and its culture vulnerable to ideological capitulations. Ignorance of the religious in both its demonic and its creative forms can be even more fatal for a scientific culture than ignorance of new scientific and technological developments" (Gilkey, 1986: 68).

It is necessary that those scientifically trained thinkers venturing on the coupling of the scientific discoveries with theology have the preliminary knowledge of theology as well. One author's serious contention is that the number of individuals in the universe must be finite if God is to be able to exercise care for each (Ellis, 1988: 384-386). Another author's crucial anxiety is "can God escape the consummation of the world?" (Worthing, 1996: 159). Physicist Davies Paul thinks that the speculated presence of humans on other planets causes serious problems to the Christian doctrine of incarnation whereby Christ was born only on this earth (Davies, 1987: 11). Such theological anxieties only betray the unequipped and unreflective juxtaposition of science and theology.

There is much more a broadening of the scientific horizons necessary for a full length appropriation of the theological beauty into the sciences, although it may be presumptuous to imagine so much and science may not be science as such as understood today at such a level of knowledge. The scientific assumptions on uncertainty, indeterminacy, etc., are not to be viewed as a retreat to the human pursuit after truth, but as an awakening into the innumerable polyvalence of truth and reality. This is a momentum towards the replacement of the reductionist strategies with the holistic approaches. It is in completing the picture of truth that faith and theology come to the aid of science. Unlike the age-old theological intrusions into science through the God of the gaps, today the new scientific scenario is much conducive to a constructive accommodation of the rich theological metaphors. The God of the physicists, as some physicists would say, is the cosmic order. Science also has the profound insight into the inherent harmony of the entire creation. But, will science ever be able to call this order as a principle of love? Or, to identify this harmony as a supreme ultimate, say, the Father of Jesus Christ? The rich elusiveness of theology has many things at stake whereby it can play a vital role in complimenting, bettering, and even perfecting the picture of truth portrayed by the natural sciences. Vitalising the scientific reductionist caricatures and sweeping away the vacuum of the nihilist know-how-s of science are possible only with the collective elusiveness of the religious and theological themata.

Paul Davies must be right in saying that science offers us "a surer path to God than religion," a path that can lead to several hitherto unknown polyvalence of truth. This is not a path that neither begins fully in sciences nor that ends fully with sciences, but a path that passes through the sciences. It is a path extending down through the history of the intellectual curiosity of the humanity. The scientific colouring of this path is so tempting and fascinating that it rejuvenates and re-invigorates any passer-by on it.

The Common Quest

The unity of experience entails the fundamental unity of the expressions. The unity of experience invalidates an ontological dichotomy in reality. A true apprehension of the metaphysical unity of beings enables us to look beyond the conceptually constructed dichotomies of expressions to the unifying thread among them, while preserving the methodic and epistemic distinctiveness of the diverse modes of expressions. This hermeneutical dialectic has been reinforced by the philosophical openings provided by modern sciences. The more-than-scientific contents of the scientific questions today is an authentic assertion of the ontological unity of the scientific formulations and theological expressions. "Every great scientific synthesis stimulates efforts to view the whole of reality in its terms.... But the views of reality that originate in this way are not in themselves scientific..." (Greene, 1962: 132). This new epistemological awareness of the metaphysical One in the many can very much remedy the conceptual polarizations and discontinuities of the theological knowledge. In transcending such polarizations we learn that there is more to revelation than we have so far "seen" or "heard." God's intervention in history is not an occasional or irregular activity, but the God who governs history is in a way the history itself. The mountains and plains where He has appeared and spoken give us the very vision and voice of God Himself. Metaphorically speaking, creation cannot be "finished" in just six days or the number of the patriarchs cannot be restricted to three.

The scientific analysis of the world discloses to us the metaphysical fabric of the unified milieu of mystery, experience and expression with its "de-materialization" of matter and "mystification" of the world and thereby the re-enchantment of the whole of reality. This tempting metaphysical fabric of natural knowledge in a way conceives of the entire cosmos as a metaphor in congruity with the metaphorical insinuations of the revealed knowledge. It enables us to articulate meaningfully the summit points of Christian revelation like the Holy Trinity, the Incarnation, the humans as the image of God, eschatology, etc. Our faith affirmations, confessional formulae, ethical exhortations, etc., would acquire broader implications and deeper applications in this endeavor.

As the deceptively held epistemological dichotomy between science and theology gets dispelled, we realize the pseudo nature of their conflict. "Never mind whether religion and science were really in conflict; they were increasingly *thought* to be in conflict." Once the pseudo nature of the problem is identified there emerge the domains of substantive and constructive interaction between science and theology. If God is the all-encompassing reality, the biological, chemical and physical languages also will be evocative of a deeper experience of God. The theological claim of the divine unity of creation necessarily entails a coherent and unified conception of reality. As this totalistic view of reality begins to be mutually implicated and structurally shared by science and theology, both would transcend their finite horizons into the overarching horizons of truth and reality. Tremendous will be the implications of this fusion for the perennial issues of the human pursuit after truth, viz. God, world, and human. That sets the agenda for the rest of our inquiry. The assimilation and integration of it becomes an imperative for the humanity as well. As Whitehead has remarked: "When we consider what religion is for mankind, and what science is, it is no exaggeration to say that the future course of history depends upon the decision of this generation as to the relations between them" (Whitehead. 1981: 111).

Reference

Augustine, St. (1997). *De Genesi ad Litteram,* 1:19. Cited in Macior, Lazarus Walter. (1997). "Critical Scientific Concepts in the Creation/Evolution Controversy," in *Creation and Evolution Evolution - Proceedings of the ITEST Workshop*, October, 1997. Missouri: ITEST Faith/Science Press.

Cuppitt, Donn. (1990). *Creation Out of Nothing*. Philadelphia: Trinity Press.

Davies, Paul. (1987). *God and the New Physics.* Harmondsworth: Penguin Books.

Ellis, G. F. R. (988). "Theology of the Anthropic Principle," in Russell, *Physics, Philosophy and Theology – A Common Quest for Understanding*. Vatican City: Vatican Observatory.

Gilkey, Langdon. (1983). "The Creationist Issue: A Theologian's View," in Tracy and Lash (eds.), *Cosmology and Theology.* New York: Seabury.

Greene, John C. (1961). *Darwin and the Modern Worldview.* Baton Rouge: Louisiana State University Press.

Isham, C. J. (1993). "Quantum Theories of the Creation of the Universe," in Russell, *Quantum Cosmology and the Laws of Nature.*Vatican: Vatican Observatory Publications.

John Paul II, Pope. (1990). Message on the Occasion of Newton Tricentennial in 1987, in Robert John Russell, et.al. (eds.), *John Paul II on Science and Religion - Reflections on the New View from Rome.* Vatican City: Vatican Observatory Publications.

Langsfeld, Paul (1997). "Creation and Evolution," in *Creation and Evolution - Proceedings of the ITEST Workshop*, October, 1997. Missouri: ITEST Faith/Science Press.

Macior, Lazarus Walter. (1997). "Critical Scientific Concepts in the Creation/Evolution Controversy," in *Creation and Evolution Evolution - Proceedings of the ITEST Workshop*, October, 1997. Missouri: ITEST Faith/Science Press.

Pamplany, Augustine. (2005). *Theological Mysteries in Scientific Perspective.* Bangalore: Asian Trading Corporation.

Peacocke, Arthur. (1989). "The Challenge of Theology to Science and the Church," in John M. Mangum, (ed.), *The New Faith-Science Debate - Probing Cosmology, Technology and Theology.* Minneapolis: Fortress Press.

Pius XII, "*Humani Generis*," (199)). in Claude Carlen (ed.), *The Papal Encyclicals 1939-1958.* Pierian Press.

Russell, Robert John et.al. (eds.) (1990). *John Paul II on Science and Religion - Reflections on the New View from Rome.* Vatican City: Vatican Observatory Publications.

Whitehead, Alfred North. (1967). *Science and the Modern World* (New York: Free Press.

Worthing, Mark William (1996). *God, Creation and Contemporary Physics.* Minneapolis: Fortress Press.

30

Collapse of Quantum Wave Function and Its Interpretations: Befriending Consciousness According to Quantum Mechanics

Gregory Mathew Malayil CMI
Faculty of Philosophy, Dharmaram Vidya Kshetram, Bengaluru

Abstract: Collapse of wave function is a paradox in quantum mechanics and the attempts to sort it out don't seem to be comprehensive. The concern of any branch of science is *what is observed or measured.* As science cannot give any meaning within its own frame, interpretations are much relevant. Since any science is a reductionistic approach, this impediment is quite natural. In this paper a few interpretations to the measurement problem associated with collapse of wave function are analysed. Implicitly or explicitly all the interpretations have a concern to consciousness, which actually lies outside the frame of the present quantum mechanics. I would like to comment that even interpretations which don't make any reference to consciousness, are 'consciously' trying to avoid the meeting with consciousness. A re-thinking on the way which we perceive collapse of wave function and filtering out unwanted or wrong assumptions would enable us to propose a better solution to the measurement problem.

Keywords: Collapse of wave function, Measurement problem, Consciousness

Introduction

Quantum mechanics is the best available tool to deal with the quantum world or the atomic world where the kinetics of particles cannot be comprehended with classical mechanics. However, quantum mechanics does not replace classical mechanics the way the Sun-centered solar system replaced the earlier view with Earth as the cosmic center.[1] Rather, quantum mechanics, encompasses classical mechanics as a special case. In general, classical mechanics is an extremely good approximation for the behavior of macroscopic objects or objects that are much larger than atoms. If we go to the deeper levels of any natural phenomena, say, physical, chemical, biological, or cosmological, we meet with quantum mechanics.[2] One of the novel features of quantum mechanics is its notion of physical state which is described by the wave function. In classical mechanics the physical state of a system of particles and fields at any instant 't' is described by specifying its positions and momentum at 't' of the particles and the values of the fields. The term *collapse of the wave function* describes the change from a system with many possible quantum states (eigen states) to only one of those possible states randomly. Although, in general, the collapse is thought to be caused by a measurement or observation, collapses can occur whenever quantum systems interact with each other, or even spontaneously.

This paper is an attempt to critically examine the concept of collapse of wave function and its various interpretations. Though the focus of each of the interpretations for collapse is different, one way or another consciousness is a common concern. However, since consciousness is not a physical entity, present physics cannot accommodate it within its frame. A re-thinking on the interpretations is an important objective of this work. Out of the several interpretations concerned, only six popular as well as unique with typical features, are analysed here.

1. Features of Wave Function

The concept of the wave function introduced by Schrodinger to describe the wave-like behavior of microscopic particles is the most fundamental one in quantum mechanics. All particles in this universe are described by wave function. Schrodinger's real physical waves were replaced by the probability interpretation of Born[3]. According to Born's interpretation, which is considered as the standard one today, the wave function represents a probability amplitude, and the square of its absolute value provides the probability density for a particle to be measured in certain locations.

Quantum mechanics has always been in search of interpretations for its mathematical formulations as well as experimental observations. An interpretation accounts what a world would be like in which the theory is true.[4]

As quantum mechanics is expected to be a theory of everything physical, an account reconciling quantum mechanics with our common sense conception of the macroscopic phenomena including measurement is necessary. An interpretation of a theory might involve modifications either to the theory or to our common sense conceptions in order to achieve these goals.[5]

2. Measurement Problem

It is evident that the laws governing the quantum world differ from those governing our everyday classical world. For example, quantum particles can exist in two or more states or locations simultaneously, where such a multiple coexisting superposition of alternatives would be described mathematically by a quantum wave function.[6] The measurement problem in the context is the question of why we don't see such superpositions in the consciously perceived macroscopic world where we see objects and particles as material, and in specific locations and states.[7]

As we have already seen in the introduction, any quantum mechanical system exists as eigen states and any measurement makes the system to jump into one of the eigen states of the quantity being measured. Since we do not know what measurement is in quantum mechanics, we cannot construct a model of it with linear operators acting on eigen states.[8] To put it more precise, the measurement problem is the conflict between two procedures in quantum mechanics, namely (i) continuous evolution of eigen states and (ii) the discontinuous jump to an eigen state when an observation or measurement takes place. The measurement operation alone will not be able to collapse the resulting state into an eigenstate, with our understanding of measurement. The measurement apparatus itself is composed of quantum particles and hence the measurement leading to collapse of wave function is a paradox and hence known as measurement problem.

3. Measurement Problem: Interpretations

The measurement problem has been a serious concern at least from 1920's. The solutions proposed appear either absurd in some way, or as incorporating something outside quantum mechanics for which we have no explanation. Also, there is no experiment to discriminate between the different proposals and all of them remain in the realm of metaphysics or philosophical speculations. We have already seen above that the experimentally testable aspects of quantum mechanics lead us to conclusions that are quite absurd but nonetheless correct. A few proposed solutions to the measurement problem include John von Neumann's theory, the Copenhagen Interpretation (CI), Bohmian Mechanics (BM), the many-worlds hypothesis, decoherence and the ORCH-OR theory.[9]

3.1. John von Neumann's Interpretation

John von Neumann argued that quantum theory makes physics' encounter with consciousness inevitable with an example of an atom simultaneously in two boxes.[10] With setting a Geiger counter, Von Neumann inferred that no physical system obeying the laws of physics could collapse a superpostion state wave function to yield a particular result. However, when we look at the Geiger counter, we will always see a particular result, not a superposition. Von Neumann concluded that only a conscious observer doing something that is not encompassed by physics can collapse a wave function. From the perspective of the present physics the problem with this approach in my opinion, is the role of a 'conscious observer'.

3.2. Copenhagen Interpretation

The Copenhagen Interpretation (CI) was developed at Bohr's institute in Copenhagen with Niels Bohr as its principal architect. The CI considers two realms: the macroscopic-classical realm and the microscopic-quantum realm. Our measuring instruments are in the classical realm and their function can be explained with classical mechanics.11 The kinetics of the microscopic-quantum realm of atoms and sub-atomic particles are best explained by Schrödinger equation in quantum mechanics. According to the CI, we never deal directly with the quantum objects of the microscopic realm and hence need not worry about their physical reality, or their lack of it. Observation creates the physical reality of the microscopic world, but the observer can, for all practical purposes, be considered to be the macroscopic measuring device, a Geiger counter, for example.[12] Since the difference in scale between atoms and Geiger counters is so vast, it's okay to treat the microscopic and macroscopic realms separately.[13]

The CI asks us to accept quantum mechanics pragmatically. When physicists want to avoid dealing with philosophy, they tacitly accept the CI.[14] To deal with microscopic objects, the performance of laboratory apparatus is the only available means and these macroscopic apparatus do not present any paradox and need not be considered in superposition states. However, we talk of microscopic objects, visualize them, and calculate with models of them as if they are real objects. But if confronted with any paradox, we retreat to the CI that microscopic objects are just theories.[15] Bohr and others gave the CI broad philosophical underpinnings. CI provides a logical basis for physicists to get on with the practical aspects of physics without concerning themselves with the deeper meanings.[16]

3.3. Bohmian Interpretation

Bohmian Mechanics (BM) is based on philosophical concepts such as causality, determinism, language, perception etc and certain hidden variables of quantum mechanics.17 Quantum mechanical wave function in the CI is purely a mathematical quantity which describes probability amplitude and thus helps to predict the probability of the outcome of measurement. In Bohmian interpretation, the wave function gets a real physical meaning as a kind of pilot wave, which guides the particle on a trajectory that is fixed deterministically with given initial conditions. Hence, if the position and momentum of a particle at a certain instant are known, its movement for all future times can be predicted. In BM an ontological separation is held between the observing and the observed systems without any influence of the observing system on the system of interest. It does not mean that the observing and the observed systems are not in interaction. The measurement process is separable from the theoretical mechanism and it does not affect the physical meaning. The Bohmian results are reproducible and consciousness or the decision of the human observer has no role to play in the measurement process as in the classical mechanics.[18]

BM involves neither collapse of wave function nor any sudden termination of wave function as in CI or splitting of worlds as in the many worlds interpretation. The Bohmian interpretation describes a physically real, completely deterministic world. Quantum randomness appears only because we cannot know the precise initial position and velocity of each particle.

3.4. Decoherence and Consistent Histories

Decoherence refers to a well-studied process in which the wave function of a microscopic object interacts with the macroscopic environment to produce the result the CI describes as collapse. Decoherence explains the mechanism of suppression of superposition to give classical like probabilities and the interaction of systems with the environment.19 The phase relation or difference between the components is responsible for the interference. The phase relations are just distributed over a large system through spontaneous interaction with the environment leading to suppression of interference in environmental decoherence. The environment will couple to the system and hence suppress interference between a preferred set of states while the system itself gets entangled with the environment. Under further interaction with those states among which interference is suppressed get least entangled with the environment.20 Though decoherence approach solves the measurement problem for practical purposes, it does not provide a complete solution.

'Consistent histories' can be seen as an extension of the decoherence idea. This interpretation is boldly presented in order to apply quantum theory to the entire universe, from beginning to end. No observers were around in the early universe, and no external observers exist at any time; the universe includes everything. Since one can't deal with the infinite complexity of the universe, one treats only with certain aspects and averages over the rest.[21]

Since these are characteristic features of classical systems, classical reality has emerged from the quantum substrate. Decoherence therefore explains why we do not see quantum super-positions in our everyday world.

3.5. Many-Worlds Hypothesis

According to the *Many Worlds Hypothesis* which was proposed by Everette,[22] there is no collapse of the wave function. Rather, each possible outcome of a measurement actually exists, but in different 'worlds'. Performing a measurement causes reality to split into multiple branches or worlds, and multiple replicas of the observer then exist, one for each world.23 Though this approach is truly bizarre, it does not obviously violate any laws of quantum mechanics, and claims not to require anything other than linear quantum mechanics to describe everything, including the observer. Quite a large number of distinguished physicists accept this many-worlds interpretation. However, it remains a mathematical speculation and no opening exists to prove it, as the different worlds are mutually exclusive.

3.6. ORCH-OR Theory

The ORCH-OR theory proposed by Penrose and Hameroff is based on the concept of quantum gravity and ideas from mathematical logic and neuronal biology.[24] Following William James' concept of 'stream of consciousness'[25] and the theory of 'perceptual moment' of Stroud,[26] Roger Penrose interprets the discrete 'moments' as the results of a process called Orchestrated Objective Reduction (ORCH OR) where the fundamental mechanism is the collapse of quantum mechanical wave function.[27]

According to Penrose consciousness is generated as discrete moments. Penrose proposes a physical process beyond the present quantum theory that rapidly collapses macroscopic superpositions to actualities. In general, it causes 'and' to become 'or'. This process collapses, or 'reduces,' the wave function objectively, for everybody, without an observer.[28] Penrose argued that consciousness emerging in a non-computable process occurs in brain for which collapse of quantum mechanical wave function is the possible physical basis. The theory of objective reduction was proposed as Penrose himself was not happy with the random nature of the process of collapse. He suggested that each quantum superposition has its own piece of space-time curvature, and when these become separated by more than one Planck length, they become unstable and collapse. According to him, objective reduction represents neither randomness nor algorithmic processing, but instead a non-computable influence in space-time geometry from which mathematical understanding and, by later extension, consciousness derived. Joining with Penrose, Stuart Hameroff suggested that the objective reduction takes place in microtubules which are composed of tubulin protein dimer subunits.[29] Furthermore, he proposed that electron condensates in one neuron could extend to many others via gap junctions between neurons[30] and, thus, forms a macroscopic quantum feature across an extended area.

Collapse of the wave function of this extended condensate results in conscious experience, according to Penrose and Hameroff.[31] Though the foundation of this theory seems questionable, there is an insight into a possible future as well as a break-through for science, especially for Physics. The three bases of the Penrose-Hameroff theory — non-computability, the involvement of quantum gravity, and the role of tubulins — are each controversial.[32]

Conclusion

Copenhagen interpretation does not accept the existence of a reality independent of the observer and nothing has a reality until observed. 'Many world hypothesis' escapes from the complications of collapse of wave function by introducing splitting of an eigen state into many worlds. Bohmian mechanics while rejecting the collapse as presented by Copenhagen interpretation, asserts the emergence of classical probabilities and does not rule out the role of consciousness. Von Hoffman interprets collapse as a consequence of a conscious observation. Roger Penrose infers that human consciousness is an outcome of collapse of wave function taking place in neural structures of the brain. If consciousness is a 'physical' phenomena, then it would be a quantum mechanical phenomena. Though neurology explains consciousness in its own way, it is certain that neuro-physiological states and events involve chemical and electrical phenomena, a complete understanding of which involves quantum theory. Copenhagen interpretation seems an attempt to avoid the presence of consciousness in quantum mechanics. In any interpretation, starting with quantum mechanics, directly or indirectly we encounter consciousness.

Interpretations are always central to understanding and establishing any scientific theory. In this paper a few significant interpretations in quantum mechanics have been critically analysed. All these apparently diverse perspectives on quantum reality have certain common grounds. The crux of all the interpretations is the measurement problem or collapse. Though the interpretations appear totally different, once we remove unwanted assumptions, if any, and recognizing the special context of the existing assumptions, the interpretations will be more or less the same. The fact that consciousness is directly or indirectly implied in most of the interpretations, provides scope for further study and research. No science in itself provides any meaning. Science just tells us what will happen or predicts what will be observed. Science can not reveal no real world beyond what is observed. Here lies the relevance of philosophical interpretation which would open new portals for science.

Notes

1 Bruce Rosemblum and Fred Kuttner, *Quantum Enigma: Physics Encounters Consciousness* (Oxford: Oxford University Press, 2006), 51.

2 Rosemblum and Kuttner, *Quantum Enigma,* 51.

3 Rosemblum and Kuttner, *Quantum Enigma,* 76.

4 Barey Loewer, "Consciousness and Quantum Theory: Strange Bedfellows," in *Consciousness: New Philosophical Perspectives*, ed .Quentin Smith, 507-524 (New York: Oxford University Press, 2003).

5 Loewer,"Consciousness and Quantum Theory," 510.

6 Hameroff and Penrose, "Consciousness in the Universe: A Review of the 'ORCH- OR' Theory," *Physics of Life Reviews*, 11 (2014): 49.

7 Penrose, "Consciousness in the Universe," 49.

8 David A.B Miller, *Quantum Mechanics for Scientists and Engineers* (Cambridge: Cambridge University Press, 2008), 451.

9 Miller, *Quantum Mechanics for Scientists and Engineers*, 458.

10 Bruce Rosemblum and Fred Kuttner, *Quantum Enigma: Physics Encounters Consciousness* (Oxford: Oxford University Press, 2006), 180; See: von J Neumann, *Mathematical Foundations of Quantum Mechanics* (Princeton: Princeton University Press, 1955); German original: *Die Mathematischen Grundlagen der Quantenmechanik* (Berlin: Springer, 1932).

11 Rosemblum and Kuttner, *Quantum Enigma,* 100

12 Rosemblum and Kuttner, *Quantum Enigma,* 156

13 Rosemblum and Kuttner, *Quantum Enigma,* 100.

14 Rosemblum and Kuttner, *Quantum Enigma,* 110.

15 Rosemblum and Kuttner, *Quantum Enigma,* 110.

16 Rosemblum and Kuttner, *Quantum Enigma,* 111.

17 David Bohm, "A suggested Interpretation of Quantum Theory in Terms of "Hidden" Variables", I and II. *Physical Reiew.* 85 (1952): 166-193.

18 Mathew Chandrankunel, *Philosophy of Quantum Mechanics; Quantum Holism to Cosmic Holism: The Physics and Metaphysics of Bohm* (New Delhi: Global Vision Publishing House, 2008), 197.

19 W.H Aurek, Decoherence, Einselection and the Quantum Origins of the Clasical," *Review of Modern Physics*, 75 (2003): 715.

20 J.P. Paz and W.H. Zurek, "Environment-Induced Decoherence and the Transition from Classical to Quantum," in *Coherent Atomic Matter Waves*, Les Houches Session LXXXII. ed. R. Kaiser, C. Westbrook and F. Davids, 533 (New York: Springer-Verlag, 2001).

21 Rosemblum and Kuttner, *Quantum Enigma,* 159.

22 Hugh Everett, III, "Relative State" Formulation of Quantum Mechanics," *Reviews of Modern Physics*, 29 (1957): 454-62.

23 Rosemblum and Kuttner, *Quantum Enigma,* 159.

24 Stuart Hameroff and Roger Penrose. "Conscious Events as Orchestrated Space–Time Selections." *Journal of Consciousness Studies* 3,1 (1996): 36–53.

25 William James, *Principles of Psychology* (New York: Henry Holt and Co., 1913), 708.

26 J. M Stroud, "The Fine Structure of Psychological Time," in *Information Theory in Psychology*, ed. Quastler H (Newyork: Free Press, 1956), 174-205.

27 Hameroff and Penrose, "Consciousness in the Universe," 41.

28 Rosemblum and Kuttner, *Quantum Enigma,* 190.

29 Rosemblum and Kuttner, *Quantum Enigma,* 190.

30 Roger Penrose, *Shadows of the Mind: An Approach to the Missing Science of Consciousness* (Oxford: Oxford University Press, 1994), 352-354.

31 [22]Hameroff and Penrose, "Consciousness in the Universe," 42.

32 Rosemblum and Kuttner, *Quantum Enigma,* 190.

31

Mirror Neurons: Neurological Appraisal of the Other as Other

Roy J. J. Pereira, SJ
Charles & Mary Heider Chair, School of Medicine, Creighton University, USA

Abstract: This study on mirror neurons shows that they dissolve the barrier between self and others. Inspired by this notion, the aughor argues that the philosophy of vasudhaiva kutumbakam,meaning "the world is one family," would underlie all our strivings to bring about the befriending of the other for the common good of all.

Keywords: Mirron neurons, Befriending the Other, Insula, Amygdala.

Today in many countries around the world, there are opposing groups debating, hurting, fighting and even killing one another on a number of issues where they don't see 'eye to eye.' In India, the merits of demonetization, the Uniform Civil Code, the beef ban and the freedom for minorities to practice their own religion have people fighting against each other. In the United States, it is the issue of free sale of guns or not, vouchers or affordable health care, charter schools or public schools? In some other countries, it is the allowing of marriage for all peoples irrespective of their orientation that has polarized people. In Europe, it is the question of how many refugees do we allow in? Do we intervene in Syria or let them fight it out till the end? In all these debates, each group sticks to its own viewpoint without even listening to the other. How do we get people to see the other's point of view? How do we create a climate of dialogue? How can be bring people to sit around the table and look for the best possible option?

Zooming in more specifically to the theme of "Befriending the other' we do realize that many societies around the globe are becoming more multicultural, multiethnic, and multiracial. In any metropolitan city we are constantly meeting people who are so different from us. In most cases, we learn to get on and the diversity adds to the richness of the city and ultimately the country. This is very much different from a village situation where for the most part people are similar to each other. Even in those places where the caste system separated groups, the rites and rituals of daily living were so set in stone that one didn't have to "learn on the go." In an atmosphere which is multicultural, multiethnic and multiracial, can 'mirror neurons' teach us something? Can an understanding of our neurological systems and more specifically the ones relating to empathy play a role in helping people live together in harmony?

You are sitting at the dining table and you reach forward to grab a cup of tea just poured out for you. As soon as you touch the cup you realize it is far hotter than you imagined and an "ouch" escapes your lips. In your brain a certain pathway has lit up. You leave the room to hold your hand under cold running water and after five minutes you enter the room and at that very moment you see your friend reach out for a cup of tea offered to her and she also yells "ouch" on touching the cup. The very same pathway in your brain lights up (assuming that you were being observed under an imaging device). The ability to feel with others, to emphasize with others is due to a set of neurons that are now being called "mirror neurons." The pathway in the brain that lit up when I yelled "ouch" is the very same pathway that lit up when I saw my friend touch the cup and yell "ouch." Figure 1 below shows the areas of the brain that light up when one executes the action of reaching for the cup and also when one just observes the action of reaching.

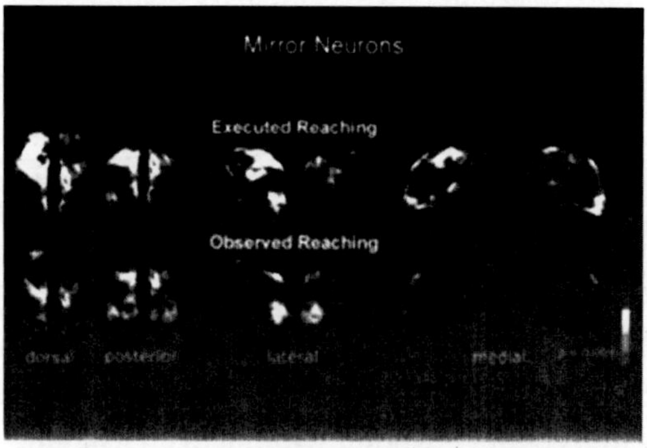

Mirror neurons are a type of brain cells that fire when one does a particular action and also when one observes someone else do the same action. Susan Perry writing for *Brain Facts* elaborates:

> Before the discovery of mirror neurons, scientists generally believed that our brains use logical thought processes to interpret and predict other people's actions. Now, however, many have come to believe that we understand others not by thinking, but by feeling. For mirror neurons appear to let us "simulate" not just other people's actions, but the intentions and emotions behind those actions. When you see someone smile, for example, your mirror neurons for smiling fire up, too, creating a sensation in your own mind of the feeling associated with smiling. You don't have to think about what the other person intends by smiling. You experience the meaning immediately and effortlessly.

Right at the start we would like to state that even though we are using the term 'mirror neurons' it must be understood that this does not preclude other parts of the brain from being involved. In fact, it would probably be more accurate to speak of 'shared neural networks' involved in empathy. There is evidence that additional networks that are used in social cognition can be recruited during empathy, depending on the circumstances and the data available from the environment. Further, Bernhardt and Singer (2012: 2) point out that

> On the basis of their structural and functional patterns of connectivity, and their involvement in other functional processes at the interface of sensory, affective, and cognitive domains, regions such as AI and dACC/aMCC may generally contribute to the generation of subjective experiences and adaptive responses to actual and predicted states in the self and others. These general processes may then subsume empathy as a special case.

There is also more than one factor that modulates or counteracts empathy. This could be environment, culture, the desire for revenge or when one's own safety is at stake. And of course there could be the case where mirror neurons and the likes are lacking in certain persons and since humans are by their very nature social beings this could create problems. The most classic case is autistic children. They are unable to empathize with or understand others. Social and interpersonal skills is a marker of the extreme sociality of our species that those who don't much care for other people are at best labelled something unflattering like 'hermit', and at worst diagnosed with a disorder like 'psychopathy' or 'autism'. Successfully navigating our highly social environment requires a brain that is superbly evolved to process this type of complex and subtle information and to orchestrate appropriate responses (Dunbar, 1998). Figure 2 below points out parts of the brain affected by autism.

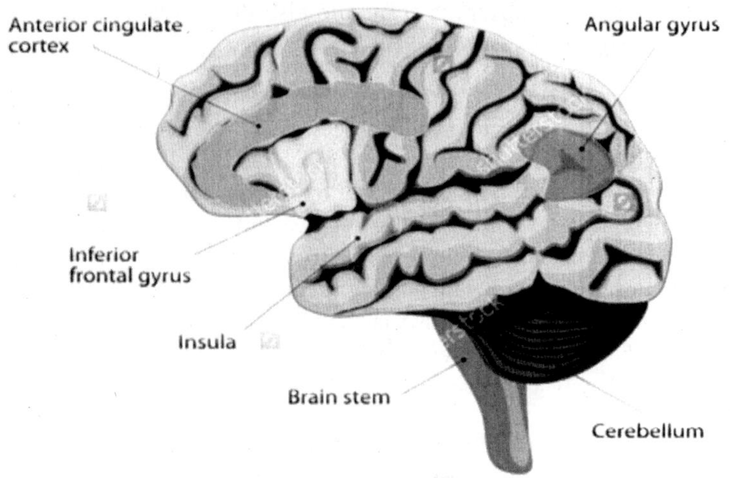

We will see later on in this article that when a person feels empathy many of these very same parts light up in a scan.

Figure 3 points out broader areas of the brain affected by autism.

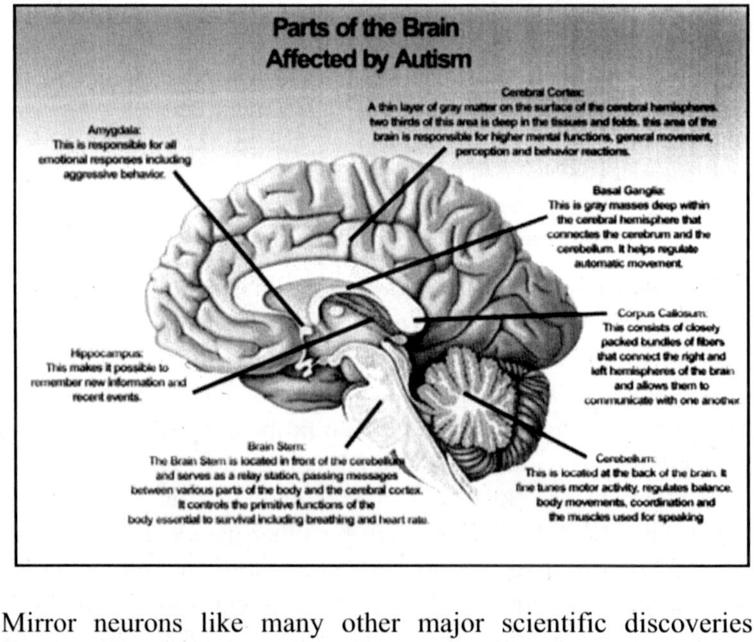

Mirror neurons like many other major scientific discoveries were discovered serendipitously. In the year 1995, Giacomo Rizzolatti and his group of scientists were observing the activities of neurons in brains of the Macaque monkey as they performed certain movements. "One day a researcher inadvertently mimicked the monkey's movement while it was watching, and found that the neural activity in the monkey's brain that sparked up in response to the sight was identical to the activity that occurred when the monkey made the action itself" (Carter, 2009: 11).

This discovery of mirror neurons is one of the most significant discoveries of neuroscience in our times. They were first found in the motor-planning area but later it was found that in humans it also existed in those neuronal areas of the brain that deal with sensations, emotions and probably intentions. Their function is to allow a person to know or predict what someone else is feeling and probably what action s/he is going to take. We use this all the time when driving. It is also thought to be the basis of mimicry, empathy and gives pointers to a theory of the mind. Since we are speaking of intention it is obvious that these neurons would be connected to the frontal lobe. In humans, they are found in the primary motor cortex, the lower part of the premotor cortex and part of Broca's area. They are also found in the parietal lobe (inferior parietal lobe) which deals with sensations. Let us look at these four broad areas of movement, sensations, emotions and intentions.

Movement: Mirror neurons are activated when one moves but also when one is observing movement. In a similar manner, mirror neurons are activated when contemplates an action of movement and one sees someone doing that actual movement. In short, when one sees someone doing an action, in our brain we do the same action. But for this to take place, 'seeing' the action must vibrate with a sequence of actions which the brain has done before or learnt previously. Let us say that someone is feeding his mouth with a handful of popcorn. In this case, neuronal activity will be detected in the premotor cortex and that section of the primary motor cortex which deals with the hand and mouth movement as well as in the parietal cortex. If someone is watching him then that person's brain will show neuronal activity only in the premotor cortex and the primary motor cortex but not in the parietal cortex.

Sensations: It appears that mirror neurons are found in the somatosensory cortex of the brain responsible for our sense of touch. I use the word 'appears' because there are only limited studies from which we get our current data. In one particular study,

> Subjects' brains were scanned, first while their leg was brushed, and then while they watched a video of someone else's leg being touched. Activity in their brains revealed that some parts of the somatosensory areas are activated only by direct touch and others are activated by the sight of another being touched. A third group of neurons, however, are activated both by direct touch and by seeing others being touched. (Carter, 2009: 120)

In this particular study, this third group of neurons were limited to the left hemisphere. In other experiments they were found in both hemispheres.

Emotions: Earlier, we had described how touching a hot cup of tea lighted up certain areas of the brain and those same areas were lit up when your friend touched the hot cup of tea. This happens in the amygdala which is the seat of emotions. When someone smiles at us our immediate reaction is to return the smile. That smile triggers signals that begin our own smiling process. Thus, facial expressions have a dual role. They signal to us someone's intention and the state of mind of that person. But they also perform the task of creating empathy between people. "Expressions are initially processed unconsciously by the amygdala, which monitors incoming data for emotional content. It responds by generating the emotion that has been observed. A fearful expression, for example, produces amygdala activation that triggers fear in the observer. Soon after the amygdala activation the expression registers in the face-recognition area situated in the fusiform gyrus" (Carter, 2009: 137) It is observed that less of the amygdala is activated when there is a neutral expression. The face recognition area is diagonally below the amygdala and the pathway from the amygdala to the face-recognition area is not so much activated as the brain is not taking in as much information as when the face is expressive.

Intentions: While it is easy to understand how mirror neurons relate to sensations and emotions what is truly fascinating is how mirror neurons can pick up the difference in intention. Suppose I see my friend pick up a stone to throw at an attacking dog and the same friend picks up a stone and aims it in my direction I am able to pick up the difference in intention even though the action is the same. So the action of picking up the stone in both cases would light up the same area in my motor cortex but the brain is able to recognize the difference in intention in both contexts. Thus, our brain besides giving us a clue as to how the body of the other person is acting also gives us a hint of their intention of acting in a particular way. This allows us to figure out what a person is thinking and predict how they are going to act without having to do some immense calculations. We now know how we are still alive inspite of driving through mad traffic behaviours.

Having seen four major areas wherein mirror neurons and other parts of the brain have an influence and the different ways they functions let us move into the topic per se, the neurological appraisal of the other as other. It is a common cliché to say that the human person is a social animal. Due to this fact, we are constantly navigating our social space to relate to the other whether they be family, friends, neighbours or strangers. This has necessitated the development of complicated neural circuits which allow for relationships to be formed, for cooperation to take place between individuals and groups, for being able to predict what the other is going to do because we also recognize that the other has a mind of its own.

The frontal cortex is that part of the neocortex that envelopes the frontal lobe. It is responsible for many of the capacities that make us human, consciousness, self-reflexive thinking, emotion, concept development and organization, abstract reasoning and so on. This area of the brain is the most recent in terms of our evolutionary history. Further the neocortex is much larger in humans and this could be attributed to the fact that our ancestors lived in community and there were constant interactions between the tribe and later on the village. "Social living creates challenges such as moderating one's own behaviour in order to accommodate others, competing subtly for reproductive rights and predicting how others will behave, all of which require neocortical activity" (Carter, 2009: 136)

Given the demands of social interaction it is evident that large areas of our brain would be involved in navigating this social playground. We would need to develop a sense of 'self' and a sense of how this 'self' interacts with the 'self' belonging to another human being whom we refer to as the 'other'. How do we relate to the 'other' when the 'other' belongs to our in-group and when the 'other' belongs to an out-group? How do we celebrate with acceptance and recognition? How do we deal with maybe being ignored in a social set up or worse still being rejected by the 'other'? What happens when this is one person and when it is from a whole group of people? Let us now zoom into the various parts of the brain involved in all these questions. Revisiting Figure 2 may help for visual clarity.

Insula: is an oval region found in each hemisphere of the cerebral cortex, lateral to the lentiform nucleus and situated within the sylvian fissure. It is involved in sensation, emotion, and autonomic function. For our purposes, what is important is that it is thought to be the locus of the following three phenomena, namely, the experience of the 'self', having a sense of the confines of the 'self' and the distinction between the 'self' and the 'other'. Self-reflection takes place here. Most scientists today believe that rational thought cannot be separated from emotions and their impact on the body. The insula detects body states induced by emotions and this helps in bringing these emotional experiences to consciousness.

Amygdala: is an almond-shaped mass of gray matter located deep within the brain's medial temporal lobe and is known to be the 'seat of emotion' when it occurs in us as well as when it occurs in the 'other.' For our particular purposes, it is important to remember that the amygdala though not the fear centre of the brain as is commonly believed is responsible for detecting and responding to threats and only contributes to feelings of fear indirectly. When the amygdala detects a threat situation it results in the secretion of neurotransmitters throughout the brain (norepinephrine, acetylcholine, dopamine, serotonin) and hormones (adrenalin and cortisol) through the body.

Temperoparietal junction: is the part of the brain where the parietal and temporal lobes meet at the back of the Sylvian fissure. In addition to the frontal lobes which are the classical areas for our ability to process others' mental states such as beliefs, intentions and desires, the left temporoparietal junction (TPJ) has also been found necessary for reasoning about the belief of others (Samson et. al., 2004) Ethical and moral judgments are made with information from this area. A sense of where the body is in space and its relation to other objects is also obtained from the TPJ.

Motor cortex: is divided into three regions, the primary motor cortex (M1), the pre-motor area (PMA), and the supplementary motor area (SMA). These are located in the rear portion of the frontal lobe, just below the central sulcus. It describes regions of the cerebral cortex which are involved in planning, control, and execution of voluntary motor processes. The performance of physical actions confirms our sense of self.

Fusiform gyrus: is a convolution extending lengthwise over the inferior aspect of both the temporal lobe and the occipital lobe in Brodmann area 37. It is demarcated medially by the collateral sulcus and laterally by the inferior temporal sulcus. While it also has the function to process colour information and word recognition, for our purposes it is important because it deals with face and body recognition and more broadly in-group identification. It analyses faces for emotional signals.

Anterior Cingulate Cortex (ACC): is the frontal part of the cingulate cortex, that resembles a "collar" from around the corpus callosum. It includes both the ventral and dorsal areas of the cingulate cortex, and plays a role in a wide variety of autonomic functions, such as regulating blood pressure and heart rate, as well as rational cognitive functions, such as reward anticipation, decision-making, empathy and emotion. It selects action correcting intentions according to the social context. It registers rejection.

Prefrontal cortex(PFC): is the cerebral cortex which covers the front part of the frontal lobe. It is responsible for planning, decision making, personality expression and gives us the ability to control our emotions in an external forum. It orchestrates our thoughts and actions in accordance with our internal belief systems. Much of the prefrontal cortex, especially the medial PFC helps us to judge appropriate behaviour when we are in a social setting.

Both the ACC and the medial PFC are connected with rejection. Social rejection causes the same type of activity in the ACC as physical pain. The ventral PFC then interacts with the ACC to reduce the pain of social rejection.

While talking of mirror neurons and neural networks which point to empathy in the brain, it is important to point out the work of Prinz (1984, 2005) which suggested a link between action and perception through common coding schemes. This helped to inspire the work of Preston and de Waal (2002) which resulted in their seminal article suggesting that "the observation and imagination of others in a given emotional state automatically activates a corresponding representation in the observer, along with its associated autonomic and somatic responses" (Bernhardt & Singer, 2012: 3).

Further when mirror neurons were discovered in monkey premotor and parietal cortices activated during execution and observation of actions it gave a neural basis for shared representations in the domain of action understanding (Gallese et al. 2004, Keysers and Gazzola 2007, Rizzolatti et al. 2001).

Subsequent studies based predominantly on fMRI, have investigated empathic brain responses for a variety of states including pain (Morrison et al. 2004, Singer et al. 2004), disgust (Benuzzi et al. 2008, Jabbi et al. 2007), anxiety (Prehn-Kristensen et al. 2009), anger (de Greek et al. 2012), sadness (Harrison et al. 2006), neutral touch (Blakemore et al. 2005, Ebisch et al. 2008, Keysers et al. 2004), pleasant affect (Jabbi et al. 2007), reward (Mobbs et al. 2009), and higher order emotions such as social exclusion (Masten et al. 2011) and embarrassment (Krach et al. 2011). All of these studies refer to empathy when the emotion involved in pain. But there are other studies as with regards to empathy from other emotions and sensations.

All these other studies further confirmed the important role of AI and ACC/MCC in the process of empathy. Wicker and his group used disgusting smells and found that subregions of AI and ACC fired neurons during the time when the odours were inhaled and also when looking at pictures of disgust on people who inhaled the same odours (Wicker et al. 2003). A couple of years later another group followed up on this experiement and came to the same conclusion. Jabbi and team found that the AI was activated during both the observation and the imagination of disgust in others as well as when the subjects tasted the bitter liquids themselves (Jabbi et al. 2008). Referencing the work of Jabbi's team, Bernhardt and Singer make the following comment, "Similar to the findings in the domain of pain, common AI activations were accompanied by differential coactivation across thee various conditions. Indeed, while AI activation showed increased functional connectivity only with IFG regions during the observation of disgust, the direct experience and imagination of disgust were related to more extended network coactivations " (Bernhardt & Singer, 2012: 8).

But it is not only the case that negative emotions trigger the 'mirror-neuroning' phenomena. It was found that positive states activated the insular and adjacent frontal-opercular regions. Again Jabbi and team found that as when perceiving disgusted facial expression, even when subjects observed pleasant facial expression in others activity in the AI region was observed (Jabbi et al. 2007). Another study that looked at compassion and admiration found activity in the AI, dACC, and hypothalamus. A fascinating find by Immordino-Yang was that the onset of AI responses took place more quickly when the subjects were observing physical pain as compared to when they were observing social pain or admiration for positive attributes (Immordino-Yang et al. 2009). A meta-analysis study summarized empathic responses across various domains. Most of the studies by Fan and his group (2011) were those of pain but "AI and ACC activation could also be confirmed when subjects observed fear, happiness, disgust or anxiety in others" (Bernhardt & Singer, 2012: 8).

While in most of the studies done so far AI and ACC/MCC featured prominently this does not hold true universally. It was found that observation studies of neutral touch showed activations in somatosensory cortices, but not in limbic structures (Blakemore et al. 2005, Ebisch et al. 2008, Keysers et al. 2004). Mobbs and group (2009) recorded subjects who observed socially desirable others being rewarded. They found that there were activations in the ventral striatum which is normally a reward center. Bernhardt and Singer (8) surmise, "The perceived similarity between the target and observer correlated with increased activity in ventral ACC, possibly mediating an effect of self-relevance in vicarious reward."

We explained the mirror neuron system earlier and how our brains are quick to pick up what is going on in the 'other' through movement, through facial expression, to subtle signs. It allows for us to mirror the actions of others. It is interesting to note that this phenomenon is is quite powerful such that if 'B' does not mirror the action of 'A' it makes A doubt its own action that could cause a faltering in the action. This is termed as the 'interference effect.' It is the effect that is caused when one' s mirroring goes haywire or when one does not get a response to one's mirroring of the other. It is interesting to note that this happens only in the case of the 'other' being a human being. It is not produced when a robot does not mirror an action even when the action may be similar to that of a human.

Thus, the first task in our quest for "befriending the other" would be to mirror the behaviour that one is seeking to see around. As Mahatma Gandhi said, "be the change that you want to see." If I want others to listen to me, I need to listen to others. This would seem to be pretty obvious but the fact that it is not happening may necessitate bringing the point in through the doors of science.

A second point arises from our mention of autistic patients earlier on. They do not comprehend the feelings and emotions that the other is going through. In the same way, we may have experienced people who "give a damn" for the other. While in most cases the neurological appraisal of the other as other takes place naturally in some cases it may have to be legislated. Laws have to be enacted to ensure that the rights of all are taken care of. Take for example, a person coming from a culture where women are understood to be second class citizens. It is a given for that particular society. If such a person moves to a country where culturally women have an equal place in society then the person moving there will have to be re-educated with regards to the place of women in that society. It is only through such a process of acclimatization that the person will be able to then look upon a woman as an equal other. Thus, the second task that helps is that of appropriate legislation.

From this develops a third point. We can see that the environment will also have a role to play in "forming" the mirror neurons of a person in order to enable that person and his or her future generations to be able to see things differently in respect to the role of women. We would need to understand deeper the working of mirror neurons and see how this can be placed into our education system so that children grow up understanding and empathizing with those different from themselves. Thus, the third task of in the quest of 'befriending the other' is the process of education.

Knowing that nurture does play a role then how much of a role does nature have to play in mirror neurons? This fourth point, the role of nature can be seen in the form of a ladder. The genetic make-up of a person will determine his neuronal and synaptic biophysics, which will in turn determine cell types. Cell types in turn will determine connectivity leading to neural data and reduced descriptions which will ultimately lead to behavior. The research in this area is very much in its nascent stage considering that the discovery of mirror neurons itself is very recent. The task here would be to see at which point in the ladder can one make interventions.

The mirror neurons, it would seem, dissolve the barrier between self and others. Dissolving the "self vs. other" barrier is the basis of many ethical systems, especially eastern philosophical and mystical traditions. This research implies that mirror neurons can be used to provide rational rather than religious grounds for ethics (although we must be careful not to commit the is/ought fallacy). And with this fifth task we conclude with the eternal hope that no matter how many differences and divisions there are, no matter how many wars and battles are being currently fought, our efforts to create a peaceful and just world will not be in vain. That the philosophy of *vasudhaiva kutumbakam,* meaning "the world is one family," would underlie all our strivings to bring about the befriending of the other.

References

Bernhardt BC, Singer T. 2012. The Neural Basis of Empathy. *Annu. Rev. Neurosci.* 35:1-23

Benuzzi F, Lui F, Duzzi D, Nichelli PF, Porro CA. 2008. Does it look painful or disgusting? Ask your parietal and cingulate cortex. *J. Neurosci.* 28:923–31

Blakemore SJ, Bristow D, Bird G, Frith C, Ward J. 2005. Somatosensory activations during the observation of touch and a case of vision-touch synaesthesia. *Brain* 128:1571–83

Carter R, Aldridge S, Page M, Parker S. 2009. *The Human Brain Book.*

de Greck M, Wang G, Yang X, Wang X, Northoff G, Han S. 2012. Neural substrates underlying intentional empathy. *Soc. Cogn. Affect. Neurosci.* doi10.1093/scan/nsq093. In press

Dunbar RIM. 1998. The social brain hypothesis. *Evolutionary Anthropology: Issues, News, and Reviews* 6:178-190.

Ebisch SJ, Perrucci MG, Ferretti A, DelGratta C, Romani GL, Gallese V. 2008. The sense of touch: embodied simulation in a visuotactile mirroring mechanism for observed animate or inanimate touch. *J. Cogn. Neurosci.* 20:1611–23

Fan Y, Duncan NW, de Greck M, Northoff G. 2011. Is there a core neural network in empathy? An fMRI based quantitative meta-analysis. *Neurosci. Biobehav. Rev.* 35:903–11

Gallese V, Keysers C, Rizzolatti G. 2004. A unifying view of the basis of social cognition. *Trends Cogn. Sci.*8:396–403

Harrison, NA, Singer T, Rotshtein P, Dolan RJ, Critchley HD. 2006. Pupillary contagion: central mechanisms engaged in sadness processing. *Soc. Cogn. Affect. Neurosci.* 1:517

Immordino-Yang MH, McColl A, Damasio H, Damasio A. 2009. Neural correlates of admiration and compassion. *Proc. Natl. Acad. Sci. USA* 106:8021–26

Jabbi M, Bastiaansen J, Keysers C. 2008. A common anterior insula representation of disgust observation, experience and imagination shows divergent functional connectivity pathways. *PLoS One* 3:e 2939

Jabbi M, Swart M, Keysers C. 2007. Empathy for positive and negative emotions in the gustatory cortex. *Neuroimage* 34:1744–53

Keysers C, Gazzola V. 2007. Integrating simulation and theory of mind: from self to social cognition. *Trends Cogn. Sci.* 11:194–96

Keysers C, Wicker B, Gazzola V, Anton JL, Fogassi L, Gallese V. 2004. A touching sight: SII/PV activation during the observation and experience of touch. *Neuron* 42:335–46

Krach S, Cohrs JC, de Echeverria Loebell NC, Kircher T, Sommer J, et al. 2011. Your flaws are my pain: linking empathy to vicarious embarrassment. *PLoS One* 6:e18675

Masten CL, Morelli SA, Eisenberger NI. 2011. An fMRI investigation of empathy for 'social pain' and subsequent prosocial behaviour. *Neuroimage* 55:381–88

Mobbs D, Yu R, Meyer M, Passamonti L, Seymour B, et al. 2009. A key role for similarity in vicarious reward. *Science* 324:900

Morrison I, Lloyd D, di Pellegrino G, Roberts N. 2004. Vicarious responses to pain in anterior cingulate cortex: Is empathy a multisensory issue? *Cogn. Affect. Behav. Neurosci.* 4:270–78

Perry S. 2008. Mirror Neurons http://www.brainfacts.org/BrainBasics/Neuroanatomy/Articles/2008/Mirror-Neurons

Prehn-Kristensen A, Wiesner C, Bergmann TO, Wolff S, Jansen O, et al. 2009. Induction of empathy by the smell of anxiety. *PLoS One* 4:e5987

Preston SD, de Waal FB. 2002. Empathy: its ultimate and proximate bases. *Behav. Brain Sci.* 25:1–20; discussion-71

Prinz W. 1984. Modes of linkages between perception and actions. In *Cognition and Motor Processes*, ed. W Prinz, AF Sanders, pp. 185–93. Berlin: Springer

Prinz W. 2005. Experimental approaches to action. In *Agency and Self-Awareness*, ed. J Roessler, N Eilan, pp. 165–87. New York: Oxford Univ. Press

Rizzolatti G, Fogassi L, Gallese V. 2001. Neurophysiological mechanisms underlying the understanding and imitation of action. *Nat. Rev. Neurosci.* 2:661–70

Samson D, Apperly IA, Chiavarino C, Humphreys GW. 2004. Left temporoparietal junction is necessary for representing someone's belief. *Nature Neuroscience* 7, 499 – 500

Singer T, Seymour B, O'Doherty J, Kaube H, Dolan RJ, Frith CD. 2004. Empathy for pain involves the affective but not sensory components of pain. *Science* 303:1157–6

Wicker B, Keysers C, Plailly J, Royet JP, Gallese V, Rizzolatti G. 2003. Both of us disgusted in my insula: the common neural basis of seeing and feeling disgust. *Neuron* 40:655– 64

32

Befriending the Other: Highlights of the Conference

George Cordeiro SJ
Research Scholar, Jnana-Deepa, Pune 41104

Extraordinary, excellent and exquisite were the words on the lips of the participants during the inauguration function of the diamond jubilee celebration of the Jnana Deepa, presided over by the chief guest His Excellency, Archbishop Salvatore Pennacchio, Apostolic Nuncio to India and Nepal. The other eminent guests were His Eminence, Cardinal Oswald Gracias, His Grace Bishop Peter Machado, His Grace Bishop Valerian D'Souza, Rev. Dr. George Pattery SJ, the vice chancellor of JD, Rev. Fr. Elmo Dias, Rector of the Kandy Seminary, Rev. Dr. Selva Rathinam SJ, the President of JD, and finally, the Rector of the Papal Seminary, Rev Fr. Jose Thayil SJ. The President of JD, Fr. Selva Rathinam SJ, welcomed the guests of honor with great warmth, cheer and amicability which instantly emitted the message of befriending the other followed by His Excellency Archbishop Salvatore Pennacchio, elucidating the theme of befriending the other in the context of South Asia. Summarizing the Asian context is presently filled with friendly and unfriendly climate. In such a climate the mission of the church is to be Christ like in our situation by loving our enemies and including the excluded. Befriending the other can bring about peace and unity in the world. He suggested three methods that could speed up the process of befriending, viz., dialogue, inculturation, and finally, caring and sharing. The mind and the heart of the church vibrates with such a theme today.

The other guests spoke from their heart creating a congenial atmosphere for not only to understand the concept of befriending as an intellectual exercise but also to feel the pulse of befriending running in the participants as they heard the JD anthem being sung by the choir in 12 languages and with the release of the newly published books. The student's council prepared a short video on the miles covered by the Papal Athanaeum and JD till the present day highlighting the key points. It refreshed the memories of the alma mater and the present generation.

The international seminar on all four days began with the solemn Eucharistic celebration in the Papal Seminary Chapel. On the first day the main celebrant was His Excellency Archbishop Salvatore Pennacchio; the second day, Rt. Rev. Bishop George Pallipparambil SDB, who led the congregation to gain a taste of Syro-Malabar Rite and thirdly, on the third day, Rev. Fr. Cyril Anand OIC, filled us with the grace of enjoying a Syro-Malankara rite mass and finally, Rt. Rev. Bishop Thomas Dabre, celebrated the thanksgiving Eucharist on the last day.

In the Plenary session of the first day, His Eminence Oswald Cardinal Gracias, Rev Fr. Dr. George Pattery SJ, and Rev. Dr. Elmo Dias, invigorated the minds of all the participants with the understanding of the concept of "befriending the other." The situation that is prevalent in our society and the world around has given rise to such a concept in order that we may unite all our understanding, evidence-based knowledge and our total energies and focus them, univocally and relentlessly towards the eradication of all the blocks that curtail befriending the other. Here as expressed by the eminent speakers, "others" would essentially include all people who inhabit the earth, God and the environment which sustains us. The emphasis was on assessing, understanding the dilemma and moving towards the mission of befriending the other.

Followed by the plenary session was the chain of twelve parallel sessions in four halls. The papers were presented by national and international resource persons. Chae Young Kim, Arjen Tete, and Charles Davies, underscored the need for a paradigm creating a congenial atmosphere for an authentic encounter of the other through the framework of Bernard Lonergam; followed by the need to care for the environment by committing ourselves towards protecting the water resources of the planet and finally, gaining inner freedom and insight in dealing ethically with the other and creating an atmosphere of safety and dialogue, so that all can live in peace on the same planet.

The second parallel session was as impressive as the first one, the leading philosopher of science, Fr. Job Kozhamthadam, led the participants to understand a creatively active and actively befriending universe and the ways and means to enhance such an encounter among the humans. Cosmology was followed by quantum physics wherein Gregory Mathew Malayil, made the group reflect upon the converging points of quantum interpretations and consciousness and the whole universe internally moving towards the other. Science today is only opening up the eyes of the humans to create network of relationships that could enhance the joy, peace, and happiness of befriending the other. Such a thought was placed before the participants by Kamaladevi R. Kunkolienker.

The third parallel session was on the verge of opening the consciousness of the participants to experience the nature and all her manifestations. M. Arif and Rehana Arif passionately presented an a practical pattern of thought through which one could practically become part of the nature and feel within one's self the vibes of nature. Such a process was furthered by Thomaskutty Mathew who described the thought of Pope Francis as appeared in Laudato Si, wherein, the conscious and effortful pathways are being earmarked for the encounter and befriending of the other. Going forward in the same direction Kurien Kunnumpuram enlightened the sessions with the outlines of the Vatican II and the new orientations for the Church of today.

The fourth parallel session focused on the otherness in a much more detailed manner. Victor Ferrao elucidated the multilayered, easily identifiable and repetitive markers of sameness and differentiation leading to the true encounter of the micro and macro world of the other. Our world is a web of cultures, spiritualities, and differently styled and abled people, which needs to be integrated into our world without diluting the boundaries and the differences but by creating enriching network of relationships. Such thought was analytically presented by Kuruvilla Pandikattu. Further, Teresia Tarimo, sailed the participants to people of Africa wherein pre-Christian and pre-personal values which were used as tools to befriending the other in their cultural contexts.

JD PG block was vibrating not only with ideas, thoughts, and sharing of the experiences about the topics dealt with but also with a congenial and amicable atmosphere to befriend the other who were on the vicinity. There was also the inauguration of the Asian/Indian Association for Religious Studies to promote scientific research in the line of befriending the other religions.

The animated and activated minds looked rested well on the next day for the second plenary and other parallel sessions of the day. It was the Bishops' Day. The four dignitaries of the Church spoke vociferously during the plenary session and brought to the fore the core message of the person and mission of Jesus. Jesus was a man for others. Jesus Christ is the Savior of mankind and He established the Church to spread the message of befriending God, humans and the environment. The mission of the Church was to live in a committed manner and die for the other in its quest to "befriend the other." It was a foundational message which was to be analyzed and crystalized in the four parallel sessions.

In the fifth parallel session Isaac Pandinjarekuttu elucidated the intellectual challenges to Christianity from within and without. Church has faced many challenges since her inception and now she needs to march forward with courage, faith, hope and love and articulate afresh the message of Christ. Moving forwards Jacob Parapally placed in front of the participants many challenges that are mushrooming in other cultures which can be a fertile ground to discover Christ within those cultures. Befriending and being with other requires both the parties to respect, accept and acknowledge subjectivity, objectivity and more so, "transpositional subjectiveobjectivity," stated, Ananta Kumar Giri. He unraveled the deeper levels of intersubjective encountering process. Finally, Konrad Noronha, suggested that "the other," is often diluted in the multicultural and diverse world, wherein, people are somehow go unrecognized for who they are and remain at the margins of the society as anawim. Including the excluded seems to the call on which befriending needs to be worked upon.

In the sixth parallel session, Peter Knox elicited a model arising from South Africa to befriend the other, the environment, who sustains us all through. The socio-economic and politico-environmental crisis gave rise to the movement with which UDF seemed to have befriended the other with great success. Joseph D'Mello re-voiced the message of Pope Francis in considering the treasure of the Church lies in people not in things, and therefore, in the poor. Though the context of the world seems to affirm the negation of the poor yet, the Church is vociferously inviting us to befriend the poor in whom lies our treasure.

In the seventh parallel session, George Kudilil, based on the experiences of St. Paul, went ahead in enriching the participants with an inclusive and opportunistic attitude Paul had cultivated and nurtured to befriend the other. Paul's main aim was to unite all in Christ. Keith D'souza took forward the theme of the inclusivity not only towards the other but to oneself. He emphasized that we as humans need to grow and blossom into what God has created us to be and it is only then, that we will befriend others and take them along the way. Suresh Pathare furthered the scientific and philosophical conversation to the practical ways of befriending while working in the field of social work.

The parallel session eight was earmarked with the philosophical and neurobiological reflection on the ability and inherent capacities a human has been endowed with for the mission of "befriending the others." Being Human as stated by Stephan Jayard takes us deeper into the mystery, meaning and wisdom that lies buried in every human person. Binoy Pichalakkattu furthered the mystery part of the human person and invited those who wanted to befriend the other to move towards the scientifically and amicably embrace the fuzziness of the other. Roy Pereira suggested that neuroscience has gone far enough to scientifically prove that our brain is hardwired for the other and therefore it has inherent mirroring capacities and thus the very existence of mirror neurons in the brain dilutes the hardbound inter-subjective-cultural boundaries. Thus, the task of befriending the other is biological and natural given.

The movements of the intellectual discussions were leading the group to come to a concise point of practically befriending the other in their own situations. Here is where Pradeep Sequiera enlightened the participants with practical attitudes, approaches and skills to be used in the process of befriending the other. Lorenzo Fernando led the group to understand the socioeconomic and political dynamics prevalent in India and how they actively block the befriending of the other. He suggested theological and pastoral perspectives to ease the way in befriending the other in India. The world news of today is flushed with the plights of the migrants all over. So, Paul Raj, enlightened the participants in understanding migrants have existed since the beginning. Scriptures bear witness to the fact of migration. Now, Church though, being migrant, needs to recognize and shower its love and care for the migrants.

In the tenth parallel session the resources persons moved in different directions to include various world views on befriending. Mohan Doss, elaborated upon Jesus' way of befriending. His thoughts, attitudes, and ways of reaching out to the other led people to encounter the Living God in Him. Such encounters transformed people. Eugenia Thomas, re-affirmed the above and went ahead in illuminating the participants that separation based on nationality, ethnicity, religion, caste and class creates anguish and pain and becomes a block to befriending. A worldwide cry to rise above all these seems evident in all the events that we witness in the world. Finally, P. T. Joseph, dwelt upon the wide use of social media though brings people together yet, has a devastating effect on humans when such media is being misused and abused.

The second last session witnessed a growing expansion of consciousness in the understanding of the concept of befriending the other. Noel Sheth through his scholarly and scientific approach to Buddhism and Sanskrit, gave the participants of glimpse of the core structure of Buddhism. He explained that the nonviolence and moving in compassion to the other formed the basic configuration of a Buddhist mind. John Peter Vallabadoss came in at this point and re-emphasized the siddha understanding of non-duality between all that exists. Such non-duality and communion is the foreground for befriending the other in the India situation. From both the above paradigms arose the next wherein A Pushparajan compared and illustrated from the lives of Gandhi and Ambedkar, the methods and pathways of respectfully befriending the other.

In the final parallel session, Joseph Mattam, redirected the energies of the participants towards understanding power of reconciliation. Reconciliation with the other was the main mission of the Church and so it can be used powerfully and effectively to befriend the other. To tie up the loose ends in the avenues of understanding the Indian tradition and faith, Stephen Thadam, placed in front of the participants a parallel course adopted by Buddhism and Sankara in befriending the other in the Eastern context. Explorations on befriending the other were coming to an end and at this juncture, Francis Gonsalves, introduced the Trinitarian and trialogicial dimension to befriend the other. It was on such a high note that all the session ended and participants waited expectantly to the next and the last plenary session to wind up the process of exploration and understanding of the concept of befriending the other in a scientific and scholarly way.

In the plenary session, Fr. Selva Rathinam, concluded that God created humans and reached out to them constantly. He befriended them all through. The scriptures are a story of God's continuous befriending of the humans. Such a process culminates in Jesus who "became flesh and dwelt among us," and reconciled us with God forever. He lived, died and resurrected and handed over the mission of befriending the other to his followers. We are his followers and therefore endowed with a mission to befriend the other all through our lives.

33

Epilogue: Befriending the Other for Our Collective Survival

Kuruvilla Pandikattu, SJ
Dean, Faculty of Philosophy, JD, Pune 411014

We live in a world divided or fragmented through diverse ethnic, cultural, political and religious identities. Identity is essential for human development and flourishing. Diverse identities are part of our social nature. But when the identity become too exclusivist and at the cost of the other, then it becomes problematic. When we cultivate one's parochial identity at the expense of the other, it becomes dangerous. When one's identity threatens the other, it gives rise to violence and hatred.

Unfortunately, we are confronted today with such clash of identities or civilizations. Some of our leaders make use of identity politics and division to grab power or to entertain their selfish desires. We live in a world divided by politics, religion, language and cultures.

Such a divided and fragmented world is just not sustainable. We will perish if we keep on overstressing our own narrow boundaries. The very survival of humanity depends on how we deal with each other. A parochial and narrow-minded stress on one's own identity at the cost of the other creates fear, hatred and violence.

It is in this context that we have organized the conference eon "Befriending the Other." After recognizing the strengths of our own identity, we need to reach out to the other, who is different from us. The other is not a threat to our own identity. The other enriches and enables our own identity. If so, we can truly befriend the other, with their own distinctive identities and history.

The articles in this volume are written mostly from the perspective of Indian Christians. Some articles are also from African perspectives. Rooted in the Christian faith and grounded in the Indian traditions, the authors attempt at analyzing who the "Other" is how we can live together with the other, respectfully and reverentially.

Even when the other harms us or inflict violence on us, we need to affirm the other's dignity and love them. Precisely then we need to be inspired by Jesus who said, "But I tell you, love your enemies, bless those who curse you, do good to those who hate you, and pray for those who mistreat you and persecute you" (Mt. 5:44). We are also inspired by the Father of the Nation, who reminded us that "An eye for an eye only makes the whole world blind."

So, we hope that this volume will help us to understand our own self-identity and enhance this identity critically and creatively by interacting with others, with their own differences and identities, in a mutually enriching and synergetic manner. It is our hope that this volume will help us Indian Christians to understand and deepen our own identity, by embracing the identities of other. The other is not a threat. The other does not evoke fear or angst. So, the other is never the Hell. But the other makes us what we are! The other enables and empowers us.

In this process, we are guided by the Indian thinker, who sang: "Where the world has not been broken up into fragments by narrow domestic walls." We also own to Martin Luther King, Jr. who affirmed: "We must learn to live together as brothers or perish together as fools."

Thus recognising, affirming and befriending the other as other is indeed need for our collective survival. We need to remember and act in such a way that the other makes things possible for us. Our identity is strengthened and fostered by the other!

Our Contributors

Cordeiro, George SJ is a Jesuit of Bombay Province with specialized training in psychology and neuro science. He is a professional counsellor and author of numerous articles. Currently he is pursuing his PhD research at Jnana-Deepa. He is also the moderator of Philosophy students at Papal Seminary.

D'Sa, Francis X. SJ is a Jesuit belonging to Poona Province. He is Professor Emeritus, Jnana-Deepa, Pune. Director, Institute for the Study of Religion, Pune. Guestprofessor: Innsbruck, Fribourg, Salzburg, Frankfurt, Freiburg and Tübingen Universities. Lectured extensively in the German speaking countries. Publications in English and German. Series of Sanskrit Concordances. Latest book: Regenbogen der Offenbarung. Five years of endowment professorship at Würzburg University. Involved in social projects empowering women, esp. rural & tribal women. Doctor h.c. from the Frankfurt University, Germany (2007) and Universität Tübingen, Germany (2016).

D'Souza, Valerian is Bishop Emeritus of Poona. He was appointed the Bishop of Poona on July 9, 1977 by Pope Paul VI and has served the Diocese of Poona for 32 years. Commonly called the "Singing Bishop," his weekly sermons in Facebook has become a hit especially among the youths. At the age of 87, he passed away on 25 February 2020 at Pune.

Dabre, Thomas: Born on October 23, 1945, in Vasai, Rt Rev Bishop Thomas Dabre was ordained a priest on October 31, 1971, by Cardinal Simon Pimenta. Later he served as a professor at Jnana Deepa, Pune and in 1982 went to study Christology and Trinity at Berkeley University in Chicago (USA) and Toronto (Canada). Dabre obtained his Doctoral Thesis on the topic "the God experience of Sant Tukaram — a study in religious symbolism" in 1979. Saint John Paul II first appointed him as Auxiliary Bishop of Bombay in 1990 and then in 1998, as the first Bishop of the newly built diocese of Vasai. In 2009, Dabre was canonically appointed as the Bishop of the Diocese of Poona by Pope Emeritus Benedict XVI.

D'Souza, Keith is Rector, St. Xavier's College, Mumbai and President, Association of Christian Philosophers of India (ACPI). He was Philosophy at St. Pius College, Mumbai and continues to teach philosophy. His PhD is on Paul Ricoeur. Email: keith@jesuits.net. ORCID: 0000-00020-3967-3013.

Ferrao, Victor is Dean of Philosophy, Patriarchal Seminary, Rachol, Goa. He did his doctorate from Jnana Deepa on science and religion dialogue. He has written six academic books and publishes regular articles on politics, science and religion. Email: victorferrao@yahoo.co.uk. ORCID: 0000-0002-5008-8114.

Giri, Ananta Kumar is Professor, Madras Institute of Development Studies 79, II Main Road, Gandhinagar, Adyar, Chennai 600020. Ph.D in Anthropology from The Johns Hopkins University in October 1994 on the ecumenical movement in the U.S. called Habitat for Humanity. Thesis is "Margins of Shacks: The Vision and Practice of Habitat for Humanity." M.A. in Anthropology from The Johns Hopkins University, Baltimore, U.S.A. in 1989 with concentration on: Anthropology of Post industrial Societies, Ethnographic Perspectives on American Culture and Comparative Social Movements. M.A. in Sociology from Delhi School of Economics, University of Delhi, India with a Gold Medal (1986). He has authored numerous books, articles and organised national and international academic seminars. Email: aumkrishna@gmail.com ORCID: 0000-0002-7090-0923.

Gonsalves, Francis SJ: Prof Gonsalves is a Jesuit of the Gujarat Province and Dean, Faculty of Philosophy, Jnana-Deepa. He has a Licentiate in Theology from the Gregorian University, Rome, and a Doctorate from the University of Madras, Chennai. He was former Principal and Professor at the Vidyajyoti College of Theology, Delhi, having lectured at other faculties in India, USA, Italy, South Korea and Latin America, too. Since June 2015 he has been on the Faculty of Jnana Deepa, Pune. He has authored five books and edited six others, besides publishing extensively on theology, spirituality and social-justice issues in India and abroad. He regularly writes in The Asian Age and The Deccan Chronicle national dailies, contributing a fortnightly 'Mystic Mantra' column since 2010. While being critical of globalisation, he believes that thinkers have a special role to spread the 'joy of the gospel' through their writings, today.

Gracias, Oswald: His Excellency Oswald Cardinal Gracias is an Indian Cardinal of the Roman Catholic Church. He was appointed Archbishop of Bombay by Pope Benedict XVI on 14 October 2006 and was raised to the cardinalate in 2007. In 2008, he became Vice-President of the Conference of Catholic Bishops of India; and in 2010, he was elected President. He is also the President of the Federation of Asian Bishops' Conferences. On 13 April

2013, he was appointed to the eight-member Council of Cardinals, informally the Council of Cardinal Advisers, established by Pope Francis to help with governing the Catholic Church and reforming its central administration.

Jayard, S. Stephen is a residential faculty, Jnana Deepa, Pune. Having received his doctorate from Central University, Hyderabad, he has been teaching philosophy of science and cosmology. Author of 7 books and visiting faculty at various national and international universities, he is well sought after guide and mentor for scholars. Email: sjayard@jdv.edu.in. ORCID: 0000-0003-3021-8775.

Kim, Chae Young is currently the Professor of Religious Studies at Sogang University and the President of Korean Association for Religious Studies. His degrees are from Seoul National University in Korea (1986, M.A.), Madras Christian College, University of Madras in India (1988, M.A.), and University of Ottawa in Canada (1992 Ph.D.). He is also serving as an editorial board member in international journal, Religion, and as an internatiional advisory board member in British Journal of Religious Education. His fields of research and teaching are Theory of Religion and Methodology of Religious Studies, Philosophy of Religion, Psychology of Religion, Religious Education, and Thanatology in relation to the thought of Bernard Lonergan. He has published books and articles on Philosophy of Religion, Religious Education, and Korean Christianity. He is also the translator of William James's The Varieties of Religious Experience and Ernest Becker's The Denial of Death into Korean. Email: chaekim@sogang.ac.kr. ORCID: 0000-0002-9258-7499.

Knox, Peter: He is a South African Jesuit from Johannesburg. He trained as an industrial chemist, before entering the Society in 1983. After novitiate and philosophy in England, he returned to work in Soweto for two years, before doing theolgy in Natal, South Africa. He completed a doctorate in systematic and historical theology in St Paul University, Ottawa, Canada. He was one of the founding fathers of the Jesuit Institute in South Africa, before moving to Nairobi, Kenya, where he teaches systematic and environmental theology at Hekima Jesuit School of Theology. He is currently acting principal of that College.

Kozhamthadam, Job: He is a Jesuit belonging to the Province of Delhi. His Doctorate is in History and Philosophy of Science from The University of Maryland, USA, in 1986. Professor in Philosophy of Science, Cosmology, Hume, Science and Religion and Basic Science from 1986 to the present at Jnana Deepa, Pune. He has served JD as Dean and President. He is also the Founder-Director of Indian Institute of Sciene and Religion. His book "The Discovery of Kepler's Laws: The Interaction of Science, Philosophy and

Religion" is named Outstanding Academic Book of the Year 1994 by Choice Magazine.

Kunkolienker, Kamaladevi, Associate Professor, Dept. of Philosophy, .E.S' R.S.N. College of Arts and Science, Farmagudi Ponda, Goa, has teaching experience of 32 years She has been awarded "Sahitya and Bhasha Seva Puraskar 2014" by "Goa Konkani Academy" for book written in Konkani language (Academic Research Work) titled "Samsarik Tattvagijnana: Itihas ani Valakh." Presented several research papers at international and national level conferences including "World Congress for Philosophy" at Boston - USA, Seoul - South Korea, Athens - Greece. Awarded a certificate of "Honourable Mention" of achievements and contribution to Science Religion Dialogue in India for the last ten years, awarded by JD Center for Science Religion Studies, Pune. Appointed as subject expert in Philosophy to frame and review syllabus of Courses in Philosophy Discipline at IGNOU. Email: kaamakhya_k@rediffmail.com ORCID: 0000-0003-0641-5410.

Kunnumpuram, Kurien SJ (1931-2018) is the founder, *Jnanadeepa: Pune Journal of Religious Studies* and faculty of Jnana Deepa, Pune for more than 40 years, serving as Dean and Rector. He is a pioneer of Vatican II in India. We remember his contribution to the Indian Church and Jnanadeepa. He passed away on October 23, 2018.

M. Arif: Dr. M. Arif is a Retd. Associate Professor in Zoology, now a Visiting Faculty at the Pemraj Sarda College, Ahmednagar. He has 30 Yrs of U.G & P.G teaching experience. He has co-authored 8 books pertinent to Zoology syllabus of Savitri Bai Phule Pune University. He has 16 Research papers in peer reviewed journals and 2 Research projects to his credit. He specializes in Entomology (Study of Insects), cultivated skills & Expertise in Beekeeping and Environment Management.

Mattam, Joseph SJ: He is an Indian Jesuit and an emeritus professor of theology, was the founder and first director of the Gujarat Regional Theologate at Ahmedabad, and later of the Gujarat Vidya Deep, the Regional Seminary, also at Ahmedabad and later at Vadodara. He lectures in many theologates, seminaries and formation centres for the Religious in India and abroad, especially Africa and Bangladesh. He directs retreats and seminars for the Religious Sisters, Brothers, Priests and Bishops. He is a member of various national and international associations like IAMS, EATWOT, ITA, etc and was the president for a period of FOIM (Fellowship of Indian Missiologists, an ecumenical association), and author of: The Land of the Trinity, Religious Life within a Christian Vision of Reality, Celebration of Life: Rediscovering the Sacraments, and Weaving Solidarity, Reflections on Mission Today, and has edited nine books of the FOIM series and two of the Indian Theological

Association, and many articles in theological and missiological Journals in India, Africa, France and the US.

Midhun, J. Francis SJ is a Jesuit priest of Kerala province. He has MA in Philosophy and Licentiate in systematic Theology from JD, Pune. He is doing Arabic and Islamic studies in Henry Martyn Institute, Hyderabad. He is also working in the Christian-Muslim relationship for the South Asian Assitancy of Jesuits. ORCD: 0000-0002-9691-0951.

Noronha, Konrad J., BHMS, PhD., NCC, LCPC is the Director and Coordinator of the Center for Pastoral Management at Jnana Deepa, Pune, India. He has a Masters in mental health counseling from Loyola University, Maryland and a Doctorate in Counselor Education and Supervision from Loyola University, Maryland. He is a nationally certified counselor (NCC) and a licensed clinical professional counselor (LCPC) in the United States of America. He is a licensed homoeopathic physician (BHMS) in India. He has done extensive clinical work at sites that include the Johns Hopkins Bayview medical center, Baltimore, Maryland; the counseling center at Stella Maris, Timonium; Maryland; Mercy medical center, Baltimore, Maryland; Loyola University, Maryland, and in India. Email: konrad.noronha@jdv.edu.in ORCID: 0000-0002-8391-9762.

Padinjarekuttu, Isaac is Professor of Church History and Dean at Oriens Theological College, Shillong, Meghalaya. He obtained his Doctorate in Theology from the Philosophisch-Theologische Hochschule Sankt Georgen, Frankfurt am Main, Germany in 1993. From 1994 to 2006 he taught Church History at Jnana-Deepa, Pontifical Institute of Philosophy and Theology, Pune, where he was also the Dean of the Faculty of Theology. He has written or edited seven books and published more than hundred articles on Church History and related subjects.

Palliparambil, George SDB: Born in Thodupuzha, Kerala on 15th May 1954, Bishop Palliparambil joined the Salesian seminary in Shillong and graduated in Philosophy from Sonada, Darjeeling. He has his MA in Utkal, Orissa, Ph D from Pacific Western University, USA. He was appointed Bishop on 7th December 2005 and was ordained as first bishop of Miao, Arunachal Pradesh, on 26th February 2006.

Pamplany, Augustine CST is the Director of the Institute of Science and Religion, Aluva. He was one of the founder-publishers of Omega: Indian Journal of Science and Journal. He has completed his MPh in JD and has served both as Dean and Rector of Little Flower Seminary, Aluva. He has published numerous articles and books, especially in the field of Science and Religion. Email: apamplany@gmail.com. ORCID: 0000-0002-5142-8774.

Pandikattu, Kuruvilla is Dean, Faculty of Philosophy and editor, Jnanadeepa. He has written/edited 60 books and authored 175 articles. www.kuru.in Email: kuru@jdv.edu.in. ORCID: 0000-0001-9815-3707.

Parappally, Jacob: Prof Parappally MSFS holds a doctorate in Theology from the University of Freiburg, Germany and awarded Professorship by Vatican in 2000. He taught systematic theology at Jnana-Deepa (JD) Pune where he served as the dean of the Faculty of Theology. He is visiting professor at the University of Freiburg and many theological faculties in India. He was the rector of Tejas Vidya Peetha, Institute of Mission-Oriented and Contextual Theology, Bangalore. From 2005-2011 he was the President of the Indian Theological Association and the author of many books including Emerging Trends in Indian Christology. He translated the book Jesus of Nazareth (Vol II) by Pope Benedict XVI from German to Malayalam.

Pennacchio, Salvatore: His Grace Pennachio is an Archbishop and diplomat of the Holy See. On 8 May 2010, Pope Benedict XVI appointed him Apostolic Nuncio to India and from 13 November 2010 to Nepal. On 6 August 2016, Pope Francis appointed him Apostolic Nuncio to Poland.

PT Joseph: Dr Joseph is a Jesuit belonging to Jamshedpur Province, He has his Ph.D. in Electrical and Computer Engineering, Marquette University, USA, 1992 and M.B.A. St. Joseph's University, Philadelphia, USA, 1987. He completed his M.Th. from JD, Pune, 1986. He was the Director, Xavier Institute of Management, Bhubaneswar, Odisha, 2002-2007. He has authored many outstanding books.

Pereira, Roy J. J. SJ Charles & Mary Heider Chair, School of Medicine, Creighton University, USA, was the Provost / Vice-Principal (Academics) and Head of the Department of Chemistry at St. Xavier's College (Autonomous), Mumbai. Teaching here since 1993, in 2012, he began an innovative programme in Neuroscience. He was awarded two research fellowships, spending the fall semester 2016 at Berkeley Campus of Santa Clara University and the spring semester 2017 at St. Louis University U.S.A. His research covers the effects of cell phones, internet usage and social media on the brain for which he was invited by Google Headquarters, Mountain View, CA in December 2016 to speak to their employees. His research also involves the understanding of the Mind-Body Link, the effect of meditation on health outcomes, the placebo effect, neuro feedback and ways of dealing with stress in our lives. In this connection he was invited by Harvard University in January 2017. He has been invited to speak on various topics in US, Canada, UK, Australia and New Zealand including doing a TEDx talk. Email: RoyPereira@creighton.edu.

Sheth, Noel SJ (1943-2017) was Professor of Indian and Asian Religions in the Department of Interreligious Studies at St. Xavier's College (Autonomous), Mumbai. Earlier he taught for 35 years at Jnana Deepa, Pune, where he was the President for several years. He was also Rector of Papal Seminary, Pune. He holds a doctorate in Sanskrit from Harvard University. His publications are on the exegesis of Sanskrit and Pali texts, on Indian-Asian religions and on comparative theology and philosophy. He has received many awards, is a member of various international learned societies and administrative bodies, and on the Board of Editors or Advisers of some international journals. He was an Adviser to the Jesuit General for interreligious dialogue.

Tarimo, Teresia: Rev Teresa is a Holy Spirit Sister. She pursued her Theological studies at Jordan University in Morogoro Tanzania, she worked at Rauya Theological Pastoral Centre as a Teacher. Then she got her Licentiate and Doctorate in Moral theology at the University of St. Thomas Aquinas in Rome (2014). Currently she teacher and Principal at Rauya Theological Pastoral Centre, Tanzania.

Tete, Arjen SJ, got his PhD from the Jesuit School of Theology, Santa Clara University and has been teaching systemtic theology at Jnana Deepa, Pune. He belongs to the Calcutta Province of the Society of Jesus. Currently he is the Conference Delegate for Formation of the Jesuit Assistance of South Asia. Email: arjensj@gmail.com.

Thomas, Eugenia: Sr Thomas was born in Moshi, Tanzania. She joined the Holy Spirit Sisters in 1975. After being a Representative General Superior from 2003 to 2007 she studied Philosophy and Theology in JD. Then she taught at the Theological Pastoral Institute Rauya. She was elected General Superior in 2008 and served till 2014.